EFFECTIVE STRATEGIC MANAGEMENT
Analysis and Action

Kenneth J. Hatten
Boston University

Mary Louise Hatten
Graduate School of Management
Simmons College

PRENTICE HALL, Englewood Cliffs, New Jersey 07632

Library of Congress Cataloging-in-Publication Data

HATTEN, KENNETH J.
Effective strategic management : analysis and action / Kenneth J. Hatten, Mary Louise Hatten,
p. cm.

Includes index.
ISBN 0-13-245200-6
1. Strategic planning. I. Hatten, Mary Louise. II. Title.
HD30.28.H383 1988
658.4'012—dc19 87-20589
CIP

Editorial/production supervision and
interior design: *Pamela Wilder*
Manufacturing buyer: *Ed O'Dougherty*

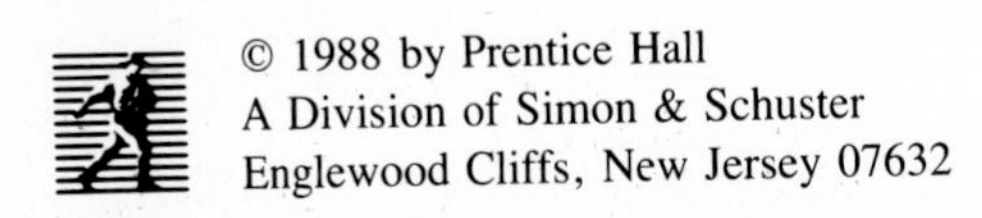

Printed in the United States of America
10 9 8 7 6 5 4 3

ISBN 0-13-245200-6 01

Prentice-Hall International (UK) Limited, *London*
Prentice-Hall of Australia Pty. Limited, *Sydney*
Prentice-Hall Canada Inc., *Toronto*
Prentice-Hall Hispanoamericana, S.A., *Mexico*
Prentice-Hall of India Private Limited, *New Delhi*
Prentice-Hall of Japan, Inc., *Tokyo*
Simon & Schuster Asia Pte. Ltd., *Singapore*
Editora Prentice-Hall do Brasil, Ltda., *Rio de Janeiro*

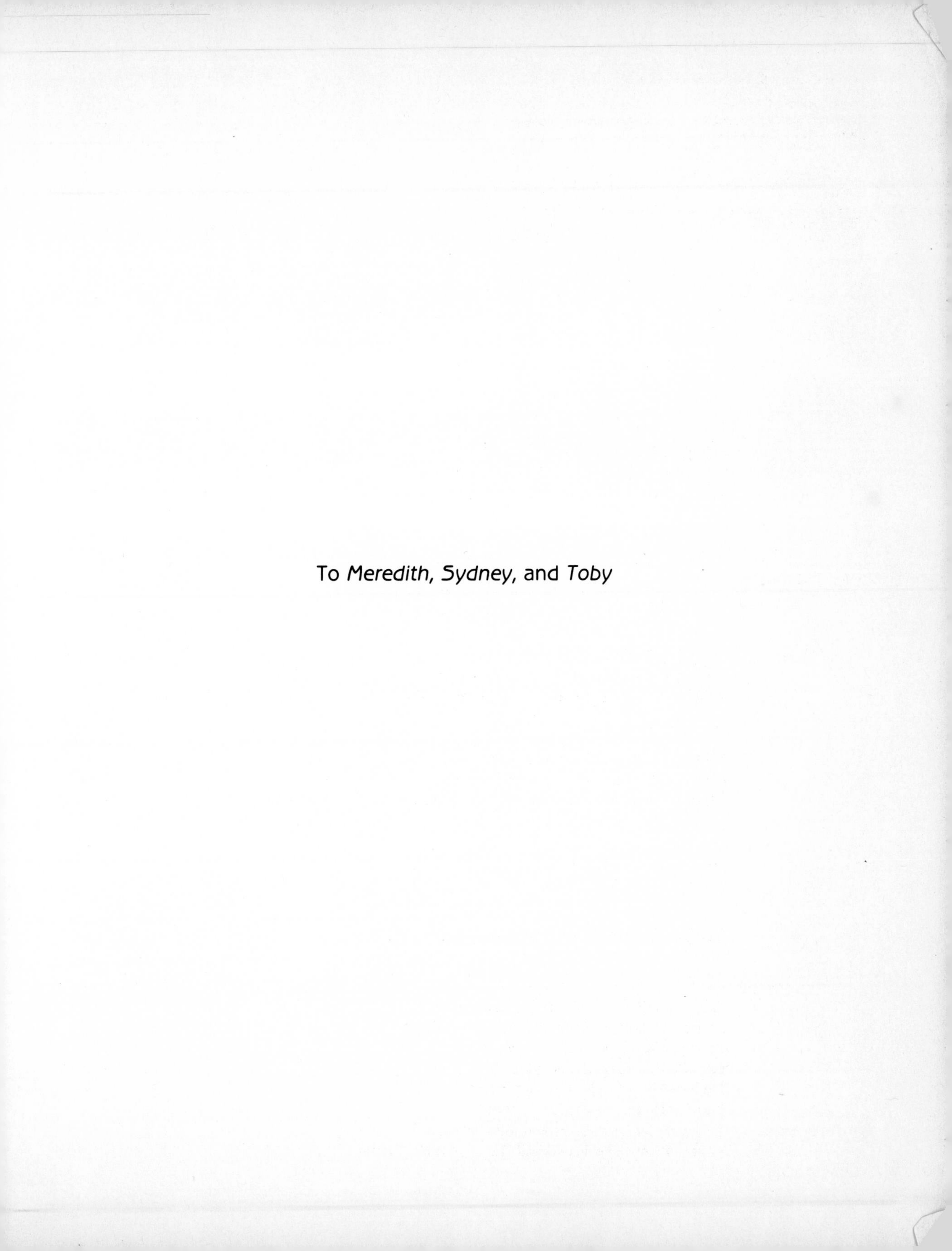

To *Meredith*, *Sydney*, and *Toby*

Contents

Preface

Organizations grow, decline, diversify, and expand from a continuing base of business in a changing world. The balance between continuity and change is delicate, founded on analysis and executed by action.

Analysis and action are the hallmarks of strategic management. Since effective strategic action stems from opportunities recognized in the analysis of the organization's strengths relative to its competition, both analysis and action are necessary for successful management.

Analysis and Action structures the strategic management area, adding our own conceptual frameworks to historic management thought and business practice. Strategy is the integrator, which focuses and coordinates corporate actions.

Our frameworks are designed to help you understand and apply the strategy paradigm to your problem, whether corporate or case situation. Our frameworks are tools for you to apply. You might think of them as sets of lenses: in different contexts, you will select different lenses to help you understand what a company is doing and why and to judge whether it should change. With experience, your selection of the appropriate lens will be more sure, and you can speed up the process. In other contexts, you may have to work through many frameworks before you have the confidence to act, or the confidence to change.

The French say, *Plus ça change, plus c'est la meme chose*—the more things change, the more they stay the same. So it is in strategic management practice and theory. The underlying questions remain: What are we doing? Why? Should we change? And, most important, how? In this book, the rich tradition of strategic management and relevant insights from wide-ranging disciplines, such as development psychology, organizational development, and industrial organization economics have been integrated. Thinkers from all these fields have contributed to the strategy area, sharpening insights for analysis and administration.

Our purpose here is to offer a selection of techniques as well as a source of reference for your future needs. The book synthesizes what we believe are the most frequently used primary sources for strategic thinking, and we have cited these sources extensively because we believe strategic literacy has value for all who must wrestle with the problems of corporate purpose and administration.

This book is comprehensive, beginning with strategy at the business level, because that is where most managers first grapple with the problems of strategy formulation and capability assessment. Our own firm is also where our knowledge base is largest, so we lead from our strength. Next, we turn to the external environment and explore competition and the values of the corporation stakeholders, each of which influences strategic choice.

Implementation is as important as analysis in strategic management. Hence, we emphasize the organizational factors important to success. Understanding the organization's history and culture lowers the organizational risks and costs of change and enhances the prospects of effective and efficient action, that is, doing the right things right.

Businesses are the building blocks of the corporation, just as functions are the building blocks of businesses. Thus, considerable space is devoted to corporate strategy and diversification as well as the role of strategic planning in institutionalizing strategic management within an organization. You will find that these chapters both synthesize facets of corporate strategy with which you are already familiar and add to your appreciation of the central role of resource allocations to strategic business units in corporate management.

Strategy is a simple concept. Its power lies in its simplicity, but learning to master that power requires practice and an ability to cope with complexity.

Indeed, strategic management could be defined as "management with your head screwed on." Effective strategic managers are confident about their actions and self-assured enough to change when new information warrants it; they have learned the importance of sensitivity to detail and have developed their own frameworks for structuring that detail efficiently.

The art of strategic management is founded in an ability to make sense of current events and to discern their meaning for the future. This book can alert you to issues that you may have overlooked in the heat of past battles, as well as areas where you can take a new approach to improve your effectiveness. Transparency masters are available from Prentice Hall to highlight the main points for each chapter.

The book is built upon our professional and personal backgrounds, and we want to acknowledge the many colleagues who have played critical roles in our professional development. Dan Schendel and Arnold Cooper of the Krannert Graduate School of Management at Purdue University intoduced us to strategic management; Andy Whinston at Purdue introduced us to the importance of rational decision making techniques. At Harvard, the former Dean, Lawrence Fouraker, and the current Dean, John McArthur, as well as Frank Aguilar, Norman Berg, Joe Bower, Neil Churchill, John Matthews, Bill Poorvu, Malcolm Salter, Howard Stevenson, Tom Raymond, Hugo Uyterhoeven, and also Mark Teagan and the late Jack Glover have influenced our lives in important and subtle ways. Dan Thomas, Ken Hatten's colleague at Harvard, who later taught at Stanford before founding his own consulting firm, was particularly helpful in the early developments of some of the frameworks used here. The late Bill Glueck of the University of Georgia shaped our application of these techniques to diverse organizational needs.

At Boston University, Deans Henry Morgan and John Russell as well as Ken Hatten's department chairmen, first, Fred Foulkes and later, Ted Murray, provided him with welcome professional assignments that gave us the opportunity to develop this book. Boston University colleagues Bob Dickie, Liam Fahey, John Mahon, Jim Post, and Jules Schwartz have each contributed insights to the refinement of the text. Special thanks are due to Tim Edlund for his careful and constructive comments on the text as well as to the people who reviewed the manuscript for Prentice Hall. At Boston College, Dean John

Neuhauser was remarkably supportive of Mary Louise Hatten's concurrent efforts as department chairman and author, and Walter Klein reacted to the social issues discussed in the text. Deans Margaret Hennig and Anne Jardim at Simmons College provided Mary Louise with a hospitable and encouraging environment in which to complete the manuscript. By influencing our thinking and writing, all these people, as well as our students in graduate, undergraduate, and executive classes at Boston University, Simmons, and Boston College, as well as Vanderbilt, Harvard, and Purdue have played a critical role in the development of the material.

Alison Reeves and Pam Wilder at Prentice Hall have particularly supported all aspects of this project, and we appreciate their help in coordinating their efforts with our own as we have all tried to do the right things right and on time.

Our families, of course, deserve special thanks—the returns from doing a book should never be calculated on an hourly basis. Our children, particularly, have been terrific as they've lived with a book in their home, even though they'd much prefer a cat!

We are grateful to everyone connected with this book, and we wish you success in using *Analysis and Action* effectively in your own organization.

Kenneth J. Hatten
Mary Louise Piccoli Hatten

chapter 1

What Is Strategy?

DEFINITIONS AND AN EXAMPLE

Strategic management is the process by which an organization formulates objectives and is managed to achieve them. Strategy is the means to an organization's ends; it is the way to achieve organizational objectives.

A strategy is a route to a destination; an objective is the destination. Picking a destination is the choice of an objective. Selecting a route represents a decision. Driving along it is the implementation of that decision. Of course, both decision and implementation are necessary if you are to reach your strategic objective.

Strategic management is an artful blending of insightful analysis and learning used by managers to create value from the skills and resources which they control. Let us use a brief example to see how management, with an appreciation of the resources it controls, attempts to find an opportunity to create value and sustain the growth of a company. In 1969, senior management at Philip Morris, a major US cigarette manufacturer, explained to its shareholders:

> Inevitably our [Philip Morris's] domestic cigarette business will level off as our market share increases and growth in consumption stabilizes around one to two percent per year. Our cash flow will increase dramatically at that time and we need growth businesses in which to invest this cash flow. . . . [However] it's hard to find another business that is as good as this one. . . . Beer probably comes closest to matching our skills with a market opportunity. (Philip Morris, Annual Report, 1970, p. 25)

In May, 1969, Philip Morris purchased 53 percent of Miller Brewing. Twelve months later Philip Morris increased its shareholding to 100 percent of Miller and shortly thereafter management said:

> We believe the long-range potential of Miller will be best served by increasing its share of the growing premium beer market rather than by emphasizing short-term profit goals. (Philip Morris, Annual Report, 1970, p. 25)

Strategies and objectives evolve as problems and opportunities are identified, resolved, and exploited. Philip Morris's strategy was to enter the brewing industry by acquisition. This decided, it first tried one route, Canadian Breweries. When a better opportunity, Miller, presented itself, the first was allowed to die and the second seized. Recognizing the inconsistency of its objectives with the interests of Miller's minority shareholder, the DeRance Foundation (which wanted dividends for the Miller family and the foundations which the family funded), Philip Morris took time to gain complete control and then defined its objectives for Miller: growth before short-term profit.

Miller's management developed a strategy which encompassed a program of massive advertising, product development, and capacity expansion. Miller's image was changed from the "Champagne of Bottled Beers" to "Miller Time" as the reward at the end of a day of hard work. The former champagne of beers was sold in a wider range of packages, bottles, and cans than ever before. Miller Lite, a low-calorie beer similar to those which the Rheingold and Meister Brau companies had introduced unsuccessfully as diet beers for women, was reformulated to taste like Coors and promoted to appeal to the heavier-drinking males. As sales rose, new, larger breweries were built to meet the growing demand.

Strategies and objectives exist and have relevance at all levels of management. At Miller, specific strategies and objectives at the product level were made to fit with higher-level strategies at the brewing business level. Miller's management, in turn, had to develop strategies and objectives which were consistent with Philip Morris's corporate strategies, objectives, and resources. While the overall thrust of Philip Morris's entry into the brewing business was determined at the top, much of the impetus for change at the product level came about because of the actions and insight of specific people, often middle managers.

Other companies' histories can also illustrate the link between objectives and strategy. When Coca Cola bought Taylor Wine, its objective was to own a nationally known vintner. Under Coke's aegis, Taylor's strategy shifted from producing New York State wines with heavy East Coast distribution to include producing nationally distributed California wines with a new brand name, Taylor California Cellars. Polaroid wanted to revolutionize instant photography and establish new patents to protect its business from competitors. To do so, it developed the new SX-70 camera and film and manufactured them itself rather than contract production to Timex and Kodak as it had done previously.

Interlocking objectives and strategies characterize the effective management of organizations; they bind, coordinate, and integrate the parts into a whole. Effective organizations are tied by means-ends chains into a purposeful whole (in our terminology, *means* refers to strategy, and *ends* are objectives). Indeed, a high-level manager's strategy to achieve corporate goals can itself provide objectives for lower-level managers. For example, Miller's top management could have seen the introduction of Lite beer as a strategy to boost Miller's market share growth, but it was the task of Lite's product managers to develop the product and the promotional strategy necessary for the success of Lite beer.

KEY STRATEGIC CONCEPTS

To design successful strategies, there are two key rules:

1 Do what you do well.
2 Pick competitors you can beat.

Distinctive competence is the term that describes the first rule: Work out what you are best at, what your special or unique capabilities are, and do those things (Selznick, 1957). Philip Morris saw its distinctive competence as marketing ability in the package goods industry; it has been a successful marketer of leading cigarette brands, including Marlboro and Merit. Polaroid's distinctive competence during the 1948–1976 reign of its founder, Edwin Land, was product research and development.

Competitive advantage comes from the selection of markets where you can excel and where your competence gives you an edge: Choose markets where you can beat your competitors or avoid them. Indeed, if there is no competitive advantage, there is no ability to earn a true economic profit (returns higher than the average returns in the industry). Philip Morris entered the brewing industry at a time when smaller regional brewers could not afford the investments in capacity and advertising required to match the operating and marketing efficiency of the nationals like Anheuser-Busch. Bic moved into the US ball-point pen market in the late 1950s against very small, no-name competitors when Scripto, which had been the major branded popularly-priced competitor, was showing signs of internal decay and when its corporate interests were moving beyond pens, Scripto's mainstay. In this situation, Scripto opened a strategic window for Bic's entry to the market (Abell, 1978).

Strategists and researchers have confirmed the importance of focusing on what you do well and choosing your competition so that you can succeed. Sun Tzu, a Chinese military strategist, wrote circa 500 BC:

> He who knows when he can fight and when he cannot will be victorious. . . . [Know] the enemy and know yourself and in one hundred battles you will never be in peril. (Sun Tzu, 1963, pp. 82,84)

Chester Barnard (1966), who distinguished managerial effectiveness from efficiency, stressed the need for focus and self-knowledge when he defined the strategic factors as the limiting factors which are crucial to success in a changing environment. More recently, Peter Drucker (1973) described effective management as doing the right things as opposed to doing things right, again stressing the need to focus on what matters and the factors that can make a difference. Selznick (1957) also believed that one of the critical roles of the chief executive officer was to understand what was different about his or her organization and to protect and develop the firm's distinctive competence. Andrews (1980) extended this idea, stating that the corporation must be organized and administered to implement a unique strategy which must be based on its distinctive competence.

GOOD MANAGERS CREATE VALUE

The job of the manager is ultimately to create value: to allow the firm to capture (more of) the returns from its productive activities. Strategy is the means used to create value, since management allocates resources to opportunities which contribute to the implementation of strategy and manages opportunities to achieve results which increase the value of the firm.

Opportunities where the competence of the firm can be leveraged with its other resources to give the firm a competitive advantage must be recognized. To identify these opportunities and to make them profitable, a manager must answer the following important questions:

1 What business are we in?
2 What business should we be in?
3 How can we get the resources and commitments we need to succeed?

On the surface, these questions are simple. But in fact they are very difficult to answer. Their simplicity gives them power, yet at the same time makes them hard to handle.

Managers, however, can only do their jobs and create value if they can answer these questions and use their answers as the foundation of a strategy which demands the purposeful commitment of resources—people and capital and all else that is needed to make an idea a valuable opportunity. For example, Dr. Edwin Land's ideas for instant photography themselves had a certain value, but he increased their value substantially by building the Polaroid Corporation to manufacture and sell the products developed from those ideas.

Commitment to a strategy and the conversion of that strategy into an operating plan has an inherent value for managers seeking to improve performance. ''It [a plan] suppresses or reduces hesitancy, false steps, unwarranted changes, of course, and helps to improve personnel. It is a precious managerial instrument,'' wrote Henri Fayol (1972), a very successful early twentieth-century French manager.

ANALYSIS AND ACTION ARE INTEGRAL TO STRATEGIC MANAGEMENT

Strategy is a means to the organization's objectives. But selection of the route is not enough; implementation is required to actually achieve objectives. Strategies must be formulated then implemented if they are to have results, and it is on results that organizations and managers are measured. *Analysis and action are essential.* Robert Adler, the President of the Bic Pen Corporation, said:

> What's important once a decision is made is to make sure that it comes out right. The decision is not so important; it's the outcome. A president must say to himself: "I will now make my decision successful."[1]

In successful organizations, a review of results achieved leads to more successful strategies. Analysis and action are linked over time and strategic management is, in a sense, learned. Argyris (1977) has termed this type of process ''double-loop learning,'' distinguishing it from ''single-loop learning'' which is restricted to attempts to correct specific errors. Double-loop learning, in contrast, requires thinking which questions fundamental premises and assumptions to determine how a company's resources can be put to better use.

Some authors have focused on the learned nature of strategic action, pointing out that the learning is slow and occurs one step at a time. Quinn (1980) used the term ''incrementalism,'' since future strategy is generally based on past experience and modifi-

[1]Bic Pen Corporation (A) HBS Case Services No's 374-305, 1974.

cations of past strategy. Ohmae (1982) sensibly pointed out, however, that although strategy may be learned and developed through an iterative process, creative insights founded in experience are the hallmarks of the outstanding strategist and of successful value creation.

The competition between General Motors and Ford in the 1920s illustrates the interplay of analysis and action, learning and insightful creativity. At a time when the favorite quotation of Henry Ford's observers was his dictum, "You can have it in any color as long as it's black," General Motors chose to provide "a car for every pocketbook." GM's strategy addressed the individual needs of its customers in a way Ford could not. Instead of competing head-on with Ford on a cost basis, Ford's strength, GM broadened its product line to offer more value to its customers through their choice of GM's Chevrolet, Pontiac, Buick, Oldsmobile and Cadillac automobiles. Ford saw its earnings decline substantially as the market changed. Only after GM had successfully taken the leadership position in the industry did Ford respond by broadening its product line to imitate GM.

Analysis and action, learning and creativity, are also evident in the early story of Timex. Joachim Lehmkuhl, Timex's founder, competed with the established Swiss watchmakers by offering a mass produced pin lever watch which everyone could afford, in a market where people were used to buying a watch as "the gift of a lifetime." Lehmkuhl wanted to sell Timex watches at low prices and low margins, but jewelers rebuffed him. Turning to drugstores as an alternative channel, Lehmkuhl added a one-year guarantee to affirm his watch's reliability. Timex's strategy eventually captured 50 percent of the US watch market. As Timex watches grew more popular, the company promoted watches as fashion goods in its efforts to continue to increase sales. Greater volume allowed Timex to lower its costs still further and enhance its already superior assembly skills.

In the recent past, Bic has fought Gillette with various degrees of success in a number of markets, including the ballpoint pen and the disposable lighter markets. In its most recent attack on Gillette, Bic has used all its experience and resources to develop and execute its strategy in the razor market. It attacked Gillette's enormous strength in razorblades with the single-unit disposable razor—certainly a creative and insightful attempt to unseat the Goliath of the world razor business.

STRATEGIES AND OBJECTIVES AT ALL MANAGEMENT LEVELS

Although the stories of strategic change in organization sometimes make strategy formulation and implementation sound like the prerogative of the chief executive officer (CEO) and board of directors, strategic analysis and action is spread throughout every organization. Strategy is, therefore, relevant to every manager, senior or junior, top-level and middle. Strategies are implemented by people at all levels in the organization, not just people at the top. The analytical inputs and creative insights required to define or formulate a strategy, as well as the actions needed to implement it, occur at every level in an organization. Strategic analysis encompasses the likely reactions of affected people to the proposed strategic actions as well as likely market responses. Managers at every level have different roles to play in the formulation and implementation of strategy.

Consequently, strategies and objectives must be designed to link the levels of the organization together so that efforts are focused and coordinated and the desired results are achieved. The hierarchy of strategies and objectives is, therefore, one of the underlying rationales for the administrative and organizational structure of the firm. For example, when there are corporate, divisional, product, and functional strategies and objectives, there should be a parallel organizational structure. All these organizational levels are linked by the ends-means chain, the hierarchy of objectives and strategies, and each level provides results and environmental data needed for management of the firm. The strategies at one managerial level define the objectives of the next lower level of management, with the firm's top-level objectives reflecting the goals of its major stakeholders.

WHY LEARN ABOUT STRATEGIC MANAGEMENT?

As a future manager, ability to understand your firm's strategy is an important skill for it will enable you to be a more effective manager of the resources for which you are responsible. As you use this book, you will develop experience in case discussions. On the job, the sooner you think and act like a manager, the faster you will be one—and an effective one.

Strategic management training helps you develop a sense of what an organization's critical problems and priorities are. If you recognize what your organization wants of you, you can make yourself more valuable in the organization. By producing results that matter, you can enhance your power to get things done. You need power to get results, and results beyond expectations enhance power. Salancik and Pfeffer (1977) wrote, "Power adheres to those who can cope with the critical problems of the organization."

The worth of strategic management, then, extends to personal career management. The skills you will develop in sizing up environments and organizations can help you make better personal career decisions. They will help you recognize the opportunities which really match your skills, interests, and needs.

PREVIEW

This text is structured to help you understand and use the concept of strategy. The strategic management process is outlined in Chapter 2 and the steps needed to formulate and design strategies for single-business firms are discussed in detail in Chapters 3 through 10. Implementation is discussed in Chapters 11 to 14. We examine the complexities of the multibusiness firm, the use of strategic management concepts in diversified corporations, and the global corporation in Chapters 15 through 19, and conclude with a discussion of leadership in Chapter 20.

The cases in this book have been selected to allow you to practice strategic analysis and to explore the merits of alternative actions in real managerial situations. You will meet strategists who are brilliant and those who are not, managers who are effective implementers and some who are not. You will see for yourself how the systematic approach of strategic management can improve the effectiveness and efficiency of many kinds of organizations.

Your reading and discussion of the case material will uncover personal factors, beliefs, and values which affect the workings of an organization and the choices it makes. The personal feelings of the firm's stakeholders have meaning and implications for the efficient functioning of an organization and affect the contributions they are willing to make (Barnard, 1966). Individuals are a major influence on organizational performance.

To sum up, strategic management requires analysis and action. An effective strategic manager adds value, marshalling resources and people to work effectively and efficiently in the environment of the firm and within its organization to achieve its objectives. To be a successful manager, you must develop strategic management skills. Take this opportunity to learn to think and act strategically.

chapter 2

The Strategic Management Process

INTRODUCTION TO THE MODEL

In this chapter, we introduce and outline the strategic management process. The framework will guide you through the book as you develop your own capacity to think and act strategically. Your understanding of this process will develop as you focus in turn on each of its stages in the following chapters.

The model presented here is shown in *Figure 2-1*. It is founded in the reality of good management practice, since it moves from the *present* strategy of the firm, supported by the resources and strengths generated in the *past*, to the design and implementation of a strategy which will carry the firm successfully into the *future*. It is an iterative process, that is, a process repeated over time, since the strategy in use must be evaluated from time to time to determine whether it is likely to succeed in the future.

The strategic management process is consistent with the best traditions of management. For example, Henri Fayol in 1916 described the administrative system he used at the French steel company, Comambault, as

> . . . concerned with each and every part of the undertaking. It shows the situation in the present, in the past, and in the probable future. The historical part . . . deals with the considerations that led to the formation of the enterprise, the changes that have taken place, and the results that have been achieved. The present situation is shown in full detail as to the resources and needs of the undertaking, looked at from every point of view. The probable future is arrived at by taking into account the past, present, and the prevailing circumstances, economic, political, and social. (Fayol, 1972, p. xi)

You will see it is related to our model. This was essentially the model upon which James McKinsey developed the analytical practices of McKinsey and Company, one of the most successful international management consulting firms (Wolf, 1978).[1]

[1]Gilmore (1970, 1971) used a model of the strategic management process which began like ours with the reality of current strategy and its subsequent evaluation. So did Henderson (1979).

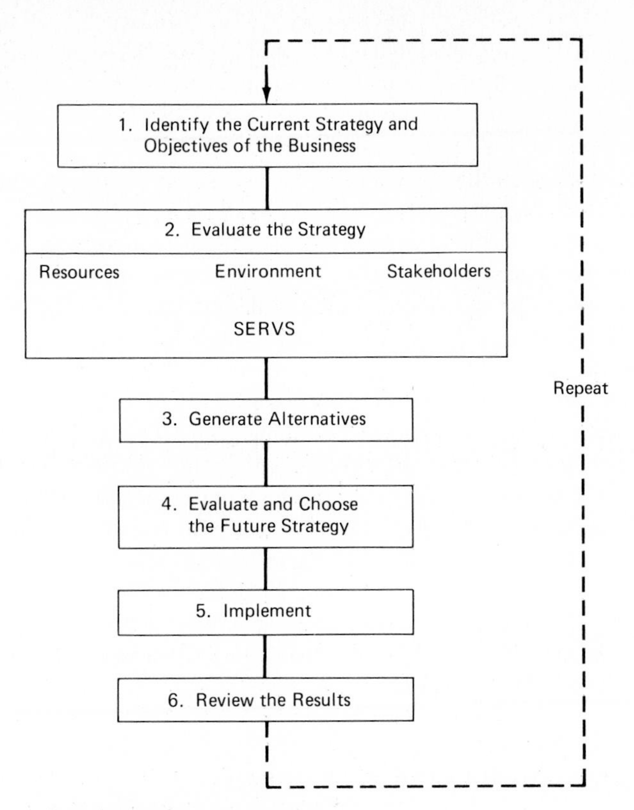

FIGURE 2-1 The Strategic Management Process

With this outline of the entire strategic management process, you will be able to move quickly into an active, participative role in case discussions. Of course, your performance in the various stages of the strategic management process will improve as you learn more and put your knowledge to work. The overview of the complete model is, therefore, a roadmap which you can use to develop your understanding of the cases you study. You can also use it to monitor your mastery of the strategic management process as you become more experienced with each step. Let us now outline each step of the process.

STEP 1: IDENTIFY THE CURRENT STRATEGY AND OBJECTIVES

To reach any destination, you need to know where you are, your starting point. Identification of the organization's current strategy and objectives gives you a starting point: the management approach currently being followed.

Current strategy need not be explicit, but it always exists. Current strategy is what the company is doing presently. Its objectives are what it is trying to do. Managers have to make decisions and get results in some way.[2] Even if they cannot articulate their strategy

[2]Even the product champions who have succeeded in bringing major innovations to market have controlled the risks they have faced by first demonstrating results and winning the allegiance of more powerful sponsors who can absorb early losses (Schoen, 1969).

precisely, it can be discovered in the pattern of actions, decisions, and commitments they have made in each of the functional areas and operations which comprise the business, or in each of the businesses which comprise the activities of the multibusiness corporation. Their objectives are similarly revealed by their results.

Since strategy in the context of a single business coordinates the functional areas, the functions represent the starting point for strategic analysis anchored in current reality. Awareness of the functional activities—for example, marketing, finance, production, human resources management—is the key to identifying the business strategy. At Miller Brewing (to use a single-business example), the marketing strategy was to reposition the Miller brand for broader appeal, extend the product line, and advertise extensively. The production strategy was to increase capacity and technical efficiency by building new, large-scale breweries. The financial strategy used resources from the parent, Philip Morris, to increase the fixed assets and working capital available to expand and operate Miller. The human resource strategy brought Philip Morris's cigarette managers with package goods marketing skills into the brewing company. All these strategies were linked together by their objective, the commitment to growth in the marketplace. Indeed, Miller's overall strategy could be characterized as sales growth to gain a dominant competitive position in the industry. Since objectives and strategies form an ends-means chain linking all levels of the corporation, it is logical that functional objectives carry information on the higher-level business strategy, and business strategy defines the objectives of the lower-level managers.

STEP 2: EVALUATE THE STRATEGY: RESOURCES, ENVIRONMENT, AND VALUES

Once identified, a strategy must be evaluated to determine whether it should be changed. Since strategies are designed to achieve objectives, they are evaluated by focusing on the results they have achieved or promise.

Strategies are evaluated by examining their present or expected results in the light of the firm's resources, its probable environment, and the interests of its stakeholders. Evaluation first requires a consideration of results against the resources available to support them. Are the resources applied against consistent objectives? Are the goals consistent, coordinated, and mutually supportive? Do the results to date represent a satisfactory return on the resources invested? Can the resources available yield the desired results in the future? Secondly, evaluation requires an analysis of the probable results of the strategy in the likely future environment of the firm. Will the strategy work in the future? Finally, it is important to determine whether the strategy's likely results will satisfy the interests of the organization's stakeholders, since their opposition may prevent the successful implementation of the strategy.

Evaluating strategies with respect to the *resources* available will reveal the firm's competences, strengths, and weaknesses. But there are no strengths or weaknesses in an absolute sense; they exist only in relation to the competition in the probable future environment (Stevenson, 1976). For example, Polaroid's strategy and resources appeared weaker after Kodak entered the instant photography market in 1976.

Probably one of the most serious errors which can be made in strategy evaluation is to ignore the *environment* in which the strategy will be implemented, behaving as if the strategy had a life of its own independent of the industry, the macroeconomy, and the social-political environment. Environmental assessment is a necessary component of strategy evaluation. The future environment must be forecast to estimate what the likely future results of a strategy will be.

The environment important to the firm's success is multifaceted. Obviously, the environment exists at the level of the industry—the competitive arena. But it also includes the macroeconomic environment which affects demand, prices, capital costs and returns within an industry. It further encompasses the social-political environment which can rapidly alter stakeholder power and objectives and thereby affect the viability of a particular strategy or objective.

The *values and objectives of the firm's stakeholders* must be understood to assess the strengths of commitment or resolve behind any strategy. Managers must become conscious of the interests, power, and objectives of their internal (e.g., employee) and external (e.g., outside stockholders, suppliers) stakeholders, because stakeholder groups can either support or block implementation of a particular strategy. We need to remember what Cyert and March (1963) wrote: ''Organizations do not have objectives; only people do.'' Action, and particularly unified action, is only possible when sufficient numbers of critical people can be induced to support the strategy—at reasonable cost.

People typically have to get something or expect future rewards before they give their support to a cause. Unless people support a strategy, its results are likely to be unsatisfactory (Bourgeois, 1980). Hence, in evaluating the strategy, it is important to determine who is getting what, and why. This is also a preliminary step to developing more effective and efficient action; strategic action will succeed only if the firm's stakeholders are managed. If people do not like the results they get, they are unlikely to act as they must for the strategy to achieve the objectives it was designed to realize. Dr. Edwin Land of Polaroid, for example, wanted to develop instant photography. He believed that instant photography was superior to conventional photography and he would not commit resources in the older field. Even though 35 mm. photography has become popular as a large segment of the photography market, Dr. Land's values and beliefs prevented Polaroid from taking timely advantage of this market, ignoring it until more than thirty-five years after the corporation was formed.

To summarize, an organization's resources, its environment, and its stakeholder objectives must all be considered in evaluating a strategy. The essence of good strategy is internal consistency and a good fit with the current and future environments. A good strategy will be one where the firm has the resources it needs to succeed; where the functional strategies and resources are internally consistent and support the business strategy; where environmental trends will increase its likelihood of success; and where the objectives of sufficient numbers of the firm's stakeholders are achieved in order to garner support and commitment.

A simple acronym may be helpful to you in developing a strategic perspective in your early case analyses: SERVS, which stands for current Strategy – Environment – Resources – Values – future Strategy. To formulate a new strategy, a firm's current strategy, environment, resource base, and stakeholders' values must all be balanced and integrated. A strategy for the future which integrates all of these factors and takes their interdependencies into account will ''serve'' the organization well. The ''S'' on the ends of SERVS should remind you that strategic management is an ongoing process, reassessing and modifying the organization's commitments and objectives when improved performance is possible and worth the effort.

STEP 3: GENERATE ALTERNATIVES

Of course, if there is nothing wrong with a firm's strategy, don't fix it. The status quo is always an option which deserves consideration, often because it has the lowest monetary and organizational costs since it is already in place. The status quo option can be used to highlight risks and rewards of other options if they are compared to the current course.

But what if the fit between the current strategy and the environment, resources, and values in the firm is not good, if the firm's resources, environment, and some of its stakeholders' objectives do not match its current strategy? Then there is a strategic problem. In many companies, the strategy evaluation process reveals problems which must be resolved and new opportunities whose potential should be assessed. A manager seeking to improve the organization's performance first must determine what problems and opportunities exist and then decide which are worth the effort and will contribute to the organization's future success. In this context, it is important to realize that every problem or threat is an opportunity to implement an improved strategy which may result ultimately in far greater success than the original strategy could promise.

Generation of alternatives is the step which requires shifts between analysis and synthesis, because it demands both types of thinking. One useful way to generate alternatives is to work out what is needed, through analysis of resources, environment, and stakeholder objectives, and then determine what actions will achieve the desired position.

Typically, your sense of problems within a business will come from a failure to meet objectives, from organizational strife, from inconsistencies you have identified, from a sense that your competence has been declining or that you are losing financial vigor. While these are all signs and symptoms of problems, it is important to address causes when you develop solutions. Your sense of opportunity will come from your successes, from the enthusiasm your organization has for a particular project, from your sense of an unserved market ignored by your competitors, and a realization that you have money to invest—that is, underused resources.

Concentrate your efforts on the critical issues and the most promising opportunities. Typically, 80 percent of the problems are in 20 percent of your operations and 20 percent of your initiatives will contribute 80 percent of your successes. Your planning and information system should be designed to separate the good from the bad.

When evaluation shows the firm would benefit from rethinking its strategy, what kinds of alternatives are sensible and attractive? Strategists rarely move directly to new and untested concepts; strategic change is rarely radical. It is generally evolutionary, exploiting the firm's resource base and momentum with trials and experiments, with "incremental" changes to the original (Quinn, 1980). Few managers will "bet a company" or a career on a completely unknown and untried course; the risk of failure and its costs are too high.

Another way to develop alternatives exploits "brainstorming," focused on ideal solutions instead of problems. This approach works best when there is a strong foundation of fact and experience on which to begin, and when traditional problem solving is unproductive (Emshoff, Mitroff, and Kilmann, 1978). It moves from the ideal to the possible, seeking ideas which contain the germ of a strategy that will work. Creativity without immediate evaluation and discarding of ideas is important if you use this approach, however, since nay-sayers at this stage only constrain the organization to traditional and limited views of itself and its options. Levitt's message in "Marketing Myopia" (1960), Ansoff's concept, "common thread" (1965), and Ohmae's *The Mind of the Strategist* (1982) all stress the value of creative or insightful thinking as a base for strategic change. Unbridled creativity is the essence of brainstorming, although criticism is useful later when the raw ideas are honed for use in the organization. Note, too, that the leap from idea to practical insight, invention and innovation is, to quote Thomas Edison, "95 percent perspiration and 5 percent inspiration."

STEP 4: EVALUATE ALTERNATIVES AND CHOOSE THE FUTURE STRATEGY

To evaluate alternative strategies, their results must be anticipated and again considered with respect to their fit with resource availability, the environment, stakeholder objectives, and current direction of the firm. New strategies require implementation, so the plan to make the proposed strategy work in the organization must be developed and evaluated in light of the organization's ability to marshall the necessary resources and garner internal organizational support. Thus, the proposed strategy's fit with the organization must be examined both analytically in the context of the competitive market, and for its ability to induce commitment and actions in the organization and thereby succeed.

STEP 5: IMPLEMENT

A decision alone does not solve a strategic problem. Action must follow analysis. It is at least as important to think about how something will be done, who will do it, and when, as it is to think about what is to be done, the strategy itself.

Implementation must fit the current and likely future organizational realities. It must be practical within the organization's culture and acceptable to the organization's stakeholders, particularly its internal stakeholders, since their support is critical to its implementation.

Thinking through the implementation process first is likely to alert a good strategic manager to contingencies which could weaken the strategy's effectiveness. Predetermined milestones, or bench marks, facilitate a "try and check" approach, allowing review of the strategy while it can still be modified. Limited commitments represent a practical approach to the problem of strategic innovation and the management of corporate and personal, or career, risk exposure.

STEP 6: REVIEW RESULTS

Effective managers limit commitment and use time to develop results which they use to justify greater resource commitments. Argyris (1977), Quinn (1980), and Braybrooke and Lindbloom (1970) all stress the use of milestones to facilitate learning about what works and what does not and thereby improve strategic performance on an ongoing basis. The availability of milestones and your ability to modify particular alternative strategies must be considered when you evaluate strategies.

Good managers make decisions while there is still time to choose among alternatives. They thus limit the risk associated with the new strategy and gain the freedom to experiment. This freedom and flexibility can be preserved over time if the results of the selected strategy can be monitored and the strategy modified when the results are not satisfactory.

SUMMARY

Strategy is the means used to achieve an organization's ends. Good strategic management requires marshalling the resources, accumulated by the organization during past and current operating cycles, to perform effectively in the likely future. It requires creative generation and rational evaluation of alternative strategies using information on the past and forecasts of the future, followed by reviews of results to ensure that the organization is performing as desired and maintaining a viable relationship with its environment and its stakeholders.

Strategic management is a learning process. Organizations and strategists can learn from their past and current results what works in the market and in their organization, and what does not. The objective of this learning is effectiveness. Indeed, strategic management is an ongoing organizational activity; it is always seeking a better match between an organization's strategy and its components, its resources, its environments, and its stakeholders' objectives.

Strategy must serve the organization while the organization serves the strategy. The concept is simple, yet its simplicity is both a source of frustration and a source of power. Effective strategies work, ineffective strategies do not. This is a very simple principle, much like the stockbrokers' rule, ''Buy low, sell high''—easy to understand but difficult to implement. Similarly, there are only eight notes in a musical scale, yet they can be arranged in an infinite number of ways. The rules are simple, but only practice leads to mastery. So it is in the field of strategic management: you must practice to master it.

chapter 3

Identifying the Strategy and Objectives of a Business

INTRODUCTION: THE SHORT CUT TO STRATEGY

Management must assess the current reality of its business before trying to move an organization in a new direction toward some future position. The first step of the strategic management process, then, requires identification of an organization's current strategy and objectives as a prelude to deciding whether changes are necessary. There is another important reason to learn how to identify strategy and objectives: understanding your competitors means understanding their strategy. This chapter shows you how to identify the strategy of a business using a technique we call Functional Analysis.

Identifying a strategy means discovering or isolating the critical and essential elements of what the firm does in the competitive marketplace. Suppose we met an organization's chief executive officer at a party and asked, "What does your company do?" The answer we would receive would probably be a summary of the firm's strategy. The response requires clarity, directness, and brevity, and it would highlight the special elements of that organization which distinguish it in the marketplace. For example, an entrepreneur in the shoe industry might say, "We make and distribute fashionable children's shoes using the latest available technology." Dr. Land of Polaroid might have answered, "We develop the technology of instant photography." Both answers express the focus of the firm and the CEO's perceptions of his or her own activities.

Indeed, "What does your company do?" can generate quite a conversation. The verbs used to respond to the question describe the key actions of the firm, its strategy. Subsequent discussion in response to an implicit question, "Why?"—as, for example, "We want to be the biggest in the industry," or, "Because man has always wanted an instant record of his activities"—reveal the objectives of the firm.

OBJECTIVES AND STRATEGY

Objectives are very important. They point towards desired future achievements rather than describe current activities, and so must be differentiated from strategies. Objectives are the ends of business strategies; strategies are the means used to achieve them.

Strategy identification encourages managers to reduce the activities of a business to its essentials, and so requires a view of the linkages between the business's various activities. Levitt (1960) advises managers to define their business in a few words and so get at the essential kernel of their activities. However, although abstractions like "railroads are in the transportation business," and "oil companies are in energy," may be provocative and useful in certain circumstances, they tend to be too generalized and brief for managers who need tangible products and plans to guide them. To satisfy this need, we can follow Andrews (1980) and advise managers to focus on their own organization's distinctive competence and to develop their future strategies from that base.

An ability to see things freshly by selectively exploiting abstractions or tangible product-based or resource-based approaches is important when you are developing and evaluating strategic alternatives. Applying established skills and using the resources you control is easier and less risky than tackling opportunities which require totally new skills and new resources. Levitt (1960) pointed out that "marketing myopia" (too narrow a view of the firm's activities) can blind managers to the opportunities on which they might build future markets. Nevertheless, research suggests that wandering too far afield is rarely profitable (Rumelt, 1974, 1982; Salter and Weinhold, 1978; Salter, 1979).

The job of adding value is simpler when you put your current skills and resources to work, using your distinctive competence to gain a competitive advantage. This means you must know your current strategy and understand both the opportunities it presents and the constraints it imposes on your future actions.

IDENTIFYING BUSINESS STRATEGY: FUNCTIONAL ANALYSIS

If organizations always clearly and explicitly stated their own strategies, identifying strategy would be easy for most people. But this happens infrequently and, besides, organizations drift; what they intend is not always realized (Mintzberg, 1978). Normally, we must discover the strategy in the practices of the organization, that is, by looking at what people do at the functional level. We call this Functional Analysis and it is summarized in *Figure 3-1*.

The first step in Functional Analysis is to develop a description of what the company is doing in each of its functions. We simply record what is done in each function—marketing, finance, operations, human resource management, for example. Next, we identify the objectives of each function and extend the analysis by tracing the relationships between subfunctional elements within functions and across functions. Awareness of the important elements within each functional area helps us gain insights into the firm's current strategy, its distinctive competence, and the sources of its competitive advantage.

Figure 3-2 is illustrative of the functions and subfunctional strategies which a manufacturer might consider. Service organizations use similar, if not exactly the same, activities to deliver their services. Let us briefly examine each function before discussing how functional actions reveal business strategy.

FIGURE 3-1 Strategy Identification via "Functional Analysis"

What Functions Matter: What Do You Do Now Function by Function?

Marketing	*Production*	*Finance*
Customer Segments	Plant Size & Production	Earnings
Product & Product Line	Process Development	Debt
Product Development	Cost Position	Liquidity
Prices	Technology	Credit
Promotional Mix	Flexibility	EPS
Distribution	Integration	Deployment
	Labor	Dividend

Note:
Consider what you do, *not* what you would like to do (or what would be better).
How long have you done it, and why? What are the functional objectives?
What interrelationships exist between the functions?
How did the strategy evolve over time?
What elements and interrelations are the key to success?
What explicit and implicit assumptions underlie the functional strategies?
Are they valid? Are they consistent function by funciton?
Where is power concentrated in the organization? How is it earned?
Is power where you want it to be? Which function is autonomous?
What are your competitive strengths? Your advantages?
What is your distinctive competence, the most critical of your strengths?
Where does top management spend its time; is it on the correct things?
Do the functional objectives add up to, that is, do they define a coherent and consistent business strategy?
What is the purpose of that strategy, its real objective (at a higher administrative level)?

Marketing Strategy

Marketing manages the relationships between a firm and its markets, the demand relationships for its products. To describe a firm's marketing strategy, we must begin by identifying the firm's market as well as take note of the firm's views of the served and potential markets for its products or services.

We recommend that you use the "4 P's" of marketing to describe the significant elements of marketing activities: *Product, Price, Promotion,* and *Place* (distribution) (McCarthy, 1960). By examining in turn what the organization is doing on each of the 4 P dimensions, its current marketing strategy will become clear.

Sometimes it is useful to categorize marketing strategy as "Push" or "Pull." *Push* means that the firm attempts to force its product through the distribution system with dealer discounts or promotions slanted toward the distributor, raising the distributor's margins, and so inducing the distributor to sell more of the product. Procter and Gamble, for example, may reduce its price to distributors by 20 percent for a two-week period and so push its Duncan Hines cake mixes through the system.

FIGURE 3-2 Functional Analysis

Marketing

Market:
Geographic scope and target segments
Unserved potential

Product:
Physical or tangible product
Supplementary service/benefits
Technology level
Extent of product line
Focus of development

Price:
Relative price level and range
Use of price changes

Promotion:
Use and role of sales force
Choice and use of media, discounts
Push or pull emphasis

Place (Distribution):
Number of channels
Channel role(s) services rendered
Margins allowed

Product Development

Production/Operations

Scope of Operations:
Extent of vertical integration
 Owned
 Contracted

Functions Performed:
Sourcing
Number, size, location of plants
Logistical spread
Value added
Product line

Type of Operations:
Process type
Flexibility/specialized
Breakeven volume
Operations leverage/contribution margin
Focus of plants
Capital/labor intensity

Development:
Process/product
Technology risk level
Engineering content

Operations Control:
Plant focus
Stability of line
Size and role of inventory
Control
 Operations/scheduling
 Quality
 Cost reduction practices
Labor
 Skill level
 Supervision needed
 Union status

Cost Position

Experience Level

Finance

Source of Funds:
Use of debt

Deployment of Funds:
Dividend payout percentage
Additions to fixed assets and working capital

Liquidity Position

Capital Structure

Earnings per Share Pattern:
Smoothed or varying

Growth:
Internal
Acquisition—
 Stock
 Cash

Administrative Strategy

Structure:
Type
Role of hierarchy
Span of control
Formal/informal structure

Systems:
Clarity of objectives
Performance measures
Performance appraisal
Resource allocation
Planning and control information

Human Resources:
Recruiting
Development
Compensation
Bonuses
Promotion
Job security

Culture:
Principles
Attitude to risk/reward
Fit

Pull strategies, in contrast, appeal to the product's final consumers with brand advertising, promotion, or "cents off" coupons, for example. Wisk laundry detergent's "ring around the collar" ads provide an example of Lever Brothers' use of a pull marketing strategy, with the corporate message focused on the final consumer. New products may greatly benefit from a pull strategy when distributors are reluctant to add to their line. A pull strategy might make consumers sufficiently aware of the new product to ask store managers for it; store managers may, in turn, demand it from their distributors.

Operations Strategy

Operations strategy refers to the elements of production, or supply, which are materials, labor and plant. Knowing how the product or service is sourced, produced, and delivered is essential, because control of a major source of raw material or a unique process may provide a cost, quality, or reliability advantage for the business. To identify the operations strategy, examine the operations tradeoffs management has made. For example, how specialized is the production process, and how close to capacity does the company operate its production facilities? Concerning capacity expansion, it is important to note what risks the firm takes. Does it "frontload" by building capacity ahead of sales, or "backload" by building sales and market share before committing to capacity additions? In the brewing industry in the 1970s, Schlitz followed a financially risky and expensive front-loading production strategy, betting that management could quickly develop new markets, while Miller backloaded and risked having some unsatisfied customers rather than inexorable fixed costs and lower returns.

Financial Strategy

Financial management must fund the organization's strategy while satisfying the needs of its financial stakeholders. The company's sources of funds and its use of those funds reveal its financial strategy. Operations, debt, and equity are the principal sources of funding for most organizations. Their proportions reveal who has what stake in the organization and where the potential sources of additional funds are.

Financial strategy gives insights into the firm's ability to change direction, its flexibility. Liquidity can be used to balance business and financial risk and give the firm staying power in bad times or an ability to take advantage of opportunity. A liquid position is often maintained by firms who differentiate their products with additional services, such as inventory or credit availability to customers and cooperative advertising with distributors.

A firm's deployment of its assets points to what management thinks about its future. Heavy commitment to fixed assets signals confidence in the stability of future demand, for example. Likewise, a firm's choice of growth strategy—internal development of markets or products, or acquisition, as well as its choice of acquisition terms (stock or cash)—tells of its expectations about its future, reveals the importance of personal control to management, and shows where the company sees future opportunity.

Administrative Strategy

Administrative strategy is concerned with the ways managers work through others to get things done. Managers do not do everything themselves. They design structures and systems, and choose people to manage the firm's resources and produce the results demanded by its strategy and objectives.

The administrative strategy defines how human needs are met, how roles are defined, and how the formal and informal interrelationships within the company are used to achieve business results. *Structure* is necessary to put experienced people in the right places—positions where their experience will add value and reduce risk. *Systems* are needed to measure results and provide information to key people so they can control the firm's operations and improve the allocation of the firm's resources. Results are the basis for reward. Plans and budgets specify results wanted. *People* must be recruited, trained, compensated, and selected for promotion. Management must allocate resources, give appropriate people authority over resources and hold them accountable for results.

Since people are a major resource (ironically, they never appear on the balance sheet, although a few figure in the annual report), human resource strategy is a major aspect of administrative strategy. Indeed, labor may be the only resource which has the potential to generate virtually limitless returns, since it is the only creative resource. Thus, a firm's strategy for handling its people—executives *and* workers both—plays an important role in its business strategy. Specifications of who works in what roles, and how they are chosen, retained, developed, and managed provides important information about the organization.

Managerial time spent on human resource problems is particularly revealing of the strategy followed by the firm. Senior management's time should be spent on people who count, those who can contribute most. In small organizations particularly, management time has a very high opportunity cost since it can be used profitably on many other tasks, and its use in one task precludes its use on another.

For example, the owner of a Midwestern food processing company has limited the time he spends on human resource management, illustrating a simple, understandable, but not necessarily effective human resource strategy. In his firm, over sixty members of the owner's extended family have managerial positions, so their retention depends on their continued good personal relationship with the owner rather than on performance. Retention in this firm is high while accountability is low. The owner spends the bulk of his time on the firm's critical customer relationships and has centralized all strategic decision making. With this strategy, he has done nothing to develop the management capabilities of his firm and has denied his family the opportunity to develop their own strategic management capabilities. He has thereby put his enterprise in long-term jeopardy, since it is unlikely that there will be effective leadership for a lengthy period when he ultimately leaves the company.

This discussion of the components of Functional Analysis points you towards the types of data you will need to collect and categorize to fully describe the functional strategies of the single business firm or business unit. Next, we turn to the important interrelationships between the functions which are critical to business success. Let us now comment briefly on the importance of the interconnections and interdependencies among the components of the strategy.

INTERRELATIONSHIPS AMONG FUNCTIONS: KEYS TO IDENTIFYING BUSINESS STRATEGY

We have noted that to understand strategy at any level in an organization, it is necessary to look down one level at the parts of the organization and catalog what is done and how the parts are interconnected. Indeed, business strategy coordinates the actions of the firm in the market and uses the functions to relate the firm to its environment. Interconnections and interrelationships among functions reveal the important elements of business strategy. In extending your functional analysis, therefore, look for the interrelationships which link the functions.

Among the most important connections are functional objectives. Each functional objective gives insights to the strategy of the business, because it is the higher-level business strategy which specifies the ends, or objectives, of lower-level functional management.

Identification of the functional interrelationships should also help you identify the firm's distinctive competence—the asset or skill upon which its competitive strength has been developed. The interrelationships will also let you develop your view of how that competence is leveraged with the firm's other resources to develop a competitive advantage. Recognizing the distinctive competence and competitive advantages of a business provides more insight into what the business does—its strategy. An illustration which demonstrates the use of Functional Analysis will help you understand these ideas.

STRATEGY AND ITS COMPONENTS: AN ILLUSTRATION

We will use Functional Analysis to identify the business strategy of the Dr. Pepper Company, a soft drink firm, during the 1970s. Since we are interested in a business, we examine its functions and collect data which describe what the company has been doing. This information has been tabulated for Dr. Pepper, function by function, in *Figure 3-3*. If you study this figure for a few minutes and reflect on what you may already know about Dr. Pepper, you will almost instinctively begin to make connections between the parts.

Functional Analysis uses these connections or interrelationships first to identify functional objectives, and then key elements of business strategy. What were the principal components of Dr. Pepper's strategy and the keys to its success? Try to specify the interconnections, so you can see what is central to its success and what is peripheral.

First, focus on identifying the objectives of the functions. Why does the company do what it does? What results would constitute success for the manager of each function?

At the bottom of *Figure 3-3,* we present our view of Dr. Pepper's functional objectives. Note that they are not single-word objectives in this case; they are what we believe Dr. Pepper's managers wanted, function by function:

1. Marketing: Stable controlled growth. Pull via trial; push via service and relationships with distributors.
2. Production/Operations: Volume sales with limited asset commitment.
3. Finance: Small-company atmosphere. Large dividend payout, liquidity, and tight control.
4. Administrative Strategy: Tight control and stable relationships with distributors cemented by service.

Also, note that Dr. Pepper's objectives, function by function, ''add up.'' They support one another. In fact, they reveal the company's strategy, because the firm is the level above the functions, and it is the firm's strategy which defines the objectives of the functions in the ends-means chain.

What was Dr. Pepper's strategy? Dr. Pepper was a tightly held family-dominated company whose marketing was characterized by consumer pull and distributor push. Its operations were piggybacked onto the operations of the strong franchises of its much larger soft drink rivals, Coke and Pepsi. Dr. Pepper marketed soft drinks by having the soft drink industry's distribution giants carry it to the market. And it was successful because Dr. Pepper is an incremental income opportunity which imposes low costs on its distributors' operations. Its growth was limited by opportunity in the marketplace, or demand, and controlled by its takeout—or, inversely, its willingness to invest.

Note at this point that we have an operational definition or description of Dr. Pepper's strategy which summarizes a very large amount of data. Note, too, that we have not troubled ourselves about what Dr. Pepper's managers said their objectives were. We have inferred the functional objectives for ourselves by looking at results.

Recognize that objectives can be inferred, like strategies, from the pattern of decisions and actions which a company makes and the results it produces. Later in our analysis, we will contrast stated and unstated objectives and seek the managerial and strategic significance of any differences we observe.

Now, we will extend the functional analysis to determine why the company made money during the 1970s and achieved the results it had—over forty years of dividends and market share growth. Consider the functions, one by one. What substrategies are most important? How are the substrategies interconnected? The more linkages there are, the better focused the functional strategy will be. What function is most important and how are the functions themselves linked? The more linkages there are between the functions (and between the parts of each function), the better focused the firm's total competitive effort will be. The more all of the parts support common objectives and each other, the more effective that focus is likely to be in creating a competitive advantage for the firm.

At Dr. Pepper, there were some powerful linkages. Dr. Pepper's uniqueness appears to be, as the company's advertising tells us, its ''original flavor.'' Dr. Pepper asked for and got a high price from its distributors because the flavor and promotion appeal to a ''want to be different'' market segment, ''the Peppers'' who really like and are loyal consumers of Dr. Pepper. The high price allowed high promotional expenditures which facilitated Dr. Pepper's distribution relationships with dominant cola bottlers.[1] Note that marketing and production functions were synergistic; both, in our view, sought volume by reinforcing the company's relationships with its distributors.

In addition, Dr. Pepper's production strategy—piggybacking on Coke or Pepsi distributors and, like Coke, principally supplying only concentrate—both minimized Pepper's fixed asset commitments and limited its rate of growth. These two outcomes lifted dividend potential and increased management's control, since the company had the ability to plow large amounts of money back into the business through promotion and franchisee services. Pepper's high returns were due to uniqueness, focus, and reinvest-

[1]Because the courts have ruled that Dr. Pepper is not a cola drink, cola distributors are permitted to sell Dr. Pepper without violating their exclusive flavor bottling agreements with Coke or Pepsi.

FIGURE 3-3 Functional Analysis: The Dr. Pepper Company

Marketing	Production/Operations	Finance	Administrative Strategy
Market: Principally the southwest US; covers rest but penetration still comparatively low. Customers "hooked." *Targets:* Regular: 8-18. Diet: women 18-49. *Product:* Concentrate, fountain syrup, and carbonated soft drink. Regular and sugar-free. Unique, fruit-flavored. 6-8 repeats after trial creates loyal customer. *Price:* Above competition to bottlers. Competitive at retail level. Rare price promotions. *Promotion:* Heavy (20% sales). Intense personal selling/service to bottler. Focused spending on strong markets. Uses coop programs on 2:1 basis to supplement bottler effort. Packaging/point-of-sale important. Advertising emphasis is local (60%). Fountain business pushed to build trial and volume. *Place:* Bottlers 59%; fountain 20%; canners 21%. Franchised bottlers are strong businesses, usually Coke or Pepsi franchises with territory under contract to Dr. Pepper.	*Plants:* 2 concentrate plants, Dallas and Birmingham, AL. Texas operation integrated forward as producer of own canned and bottled drinks. Serves largest markets as canner and bottler. *Product:* A secret formula or recipe mixing 23 fruit flavors. Sold as concentrate. Fountain syrup and carbonated drink, not a cola. *Quality:* "Must taste right." 4 checks on bottler annually. *Sourcing:* Sugar is major ingredient; fructose substitution possible in part. *Wholesale Operations:* Principally through strong bottlers of Coke and Pepsi. Usually the #1 distributor in territory. Since Pepper is not a cola, law and other agreements allow this arrangement. Company provides market planning, subsidizes fountain business development. Provides extra minor flavors for those who need them. Travel award incentive program. Maintains personal business relationship. Franchise department tries to limit taxes for franchisees.	*Source Funds:* Operations. Uses no debt financing. Stock tightly held. *Use Funds:* Limited fixed investment. Maintains high cash or liquidity position. Limited need for working capital. High dividend payout (60% earnings). Concentrate and fountain sales contribute most income to company. Company operates integrated plant in Texas, its most deeply penetrated and largest market. *Note:* In 1975, company was $138 million sales, $58 million assets; equity $150 million; income $12 million.	*Structure:* Simple functional structure, divided geographically in marketing area. 7 layers between CEO and bottler. 2 areas, 7 zones, 34 divisions. *People:* Experienced top management. Emphasis on marketing. Depth developing. Internal promotion favored. "Messianic belief in product." *Culture:* "Golden Rule: "Do unto others as you would have them do unto you." *Principles of Marketing:* • *perfect product* • *availability via strong distribution* • *sampling/trial* • *point of sale advertising* • *media advertising.* *"Pepper Family." Performance rewarded.*

Functional Objectives

Stable controlled growth. Pull via trial; push via service and relationships.	Volume sales with limited asset commitment.	Small-company atmosphere; large takeout, liquidity, and control.	Tight control and relationship with distributors through service.

ment in controlled growth, along with a genuine commitment to follow the Golden Rule in its business dealings: sharing the rewards of a coordinated business effort with its distributors. Note that those distributors who were more committed to Dr. Pepper got more resources spent in their markets and so reaped bigger rewards—as did Dr. Pepper.

To conclude this analysis, let us consider what the distinctive competence of Dr. Pepper was, and see if we can determine how that competence was applied in the market to earn the company a competitive advantage which yielded high returns. Dr. Pepper's unique asset is its "most original flavor," but, in our judgment, its distinctive competence was its marketing skills. These are the skills with which "Foots" Clements, Dr. Pepper's Chairman and CEO was most concerned. It was in marketing, too, that Clements enumerated his five principles, which are listed in *Figure 3-3* under Culture. Clements once commented:

> . . . there is one absolute and rigid criterion for every market. Every program for every market must be built around and with the complete utilization of the basic fundamentals—not just one—but all five. J.C. Penney once said they don't rewrite the Bible every Sunday; the same applies to these basic fundamentals.[2]

Dr. Pepper's management was most concerned with marketing, not operations. Essentially, they have delegated the operations function to the experts, the Coke and Pepsi bottlers.

Dr. Pepper's choice of operational strategy allowed them to avoid competition and turn their rivals' strengths to their own company's advantage. Pepper's competitive advantage stemmed from its ability to produce a large incremental profit for its distributors. By applying its own financial and marketing resources forcefully in those markets where it had market share and a strong active distributor, Dr. Pepper cemented its relationship with these same distributors and created a competitive advantage, a low cost position, for itself and them. Again, Dr. Pepper followed "Foots" Clements's personal philosophy—to practice the Golden Rule:

> I don't hesitate to profess my beliefs in God and in my business. He gave you whatever talents you have. You can't just take; you have to put something back.[3]

Indeed, one explanation of Dr. Pepper's poor performance in the early 1980s and subsequent leverage buyout by Forstman Little in 1984 was that it moved away from the Golden Rule. It sought a growth level by going national with Dr. Pepper and by purchasing Canada Dry, a strategy which diverted management attention and corporate resources from bottlers in the best Dr. Pepper sales areas.

STRATEGIC EVALUATION: THE NEED FOR CONSISTENCY

Of course, strategies once identified must be evaluated to determine whether they are serving the organization well. But there is one initial criterion that seems to characterize successful businesses: Their functions are balanced, coordinated, and ultimately focused

[2]Dr. Pepper Co. HBS, 377–146 p. 7.
[3]*Ibid.* p. 29.

on the same business objectives. Functional strategies must be internally consistent and seek the same ends. Indeed, if a particular function is allowed to dominate the organization, the organization may not be strong enough in its other areas to sustain itself if the conditions which presently suit the business strategy change. On the other hand, if the functions work at cross-purposes, resources will be wasted. Abraham Lincoln understood this when he said, "A house divided against itself cannot stand."

Robert Adler, the CEO of Bic, once gave a vivid example of the importance of balance when he likened his business to a car in which all four wheels (the functions) must be on the ground and pointing in the same direction before the car can move. Dominance by one function—the strategic equivalent of a car with a spinning wheel—can generate a source of power which may be inappropriate for the firm's current or future resources and environment. If the wheels are unbalanced and misaligned, tires and gas will both be wasted. So, in business, inconsistencies and misalignments waste resources.

PREVIEW

In this chapter, we have begun the strategic management process by sizing up the reality of the organization. Of course, being able to identify your own strategy means that you have developed the ability to be able to identify and, later, evaluate the strategies of others. It is the critical step in competitive analysis. Knowing your competitors and yourself is important.

In Chapter 4, we move to strategy evaluation. We go beyond internal consistency to test current strategy for its fit with current and future resources and with the environment, and for its ability to deliver performance deemed important by stakeholders—individuals whose views influence the organization's choices and whose support is important to effectively implement the organization's strategy.

chapter 4

The Strategy Evaluation Process

This chapter introduces strategy evaluation and provides an overview of the following, more detailed chapters on evaluation. The next three chapters deal with the data that managers need to collect and analyze to evaluate their strategy thoroughly. The fifth chapter of the set, Chapter 8, is concerned with the synthesis of the analysis and the summarization of the evaluative effort.

The purpose of this chapter is to alert you to the key concepts used by strategists as they evaluate their own and their competitors' strategies and to explain why evaluation warrants so much attention. If you keep the key concepts of strategy evaluation in mind as you read the following chapters, you will read them more purposefully and find them more valuable than if you use a less deliberate approach.

EVALUATION: AN OVERVIEW

A thorough identification of an organization's current strategy and objectives, its distinctive competence, and its perceived competitive advantage reveals important parts of the reality confronting management. But they are only parts. Moreover, since the thrust of strategic management is to move the organization successfully into the future, then the future environment, the resources available to get the firm there, and the people whose support is needed, must all be considered before the firm commits its resources.

Evaluating a strategy means evaluating its results—past, present and probable. Resources are the accumulated results of past actions. The results of the current operating cycle are the best indicators of what aspects of our current strategy are working in the present environment. Together, past and current results point out the current direction of the organization and reveal likely near-term futures.

Every organization reaches its future by moving from the past through the present to that future. Strategy is a bridge between past and future. Current strategy has a momentum which both constrains an organization's freedom to change and facilitates change if it is exploited. The future results of the current strategy must be anticipated, therefore, before management can prudently recommit to or change its strategy.

When we evaluate a strategy, we focus on results. Resources, future environment, and stakeholder interests are the factors that we have to consider when we look at the firm's current strategy and resources and try to determine what to do next.

Essentially, evaluation helps us to make sense of experience, to determine the meaning of our current results—what led to them, and what they are likely to be in the future. At this point, we can note that managers never *know* what will work. They can only judge what is likely to work best and act on their judgment. They can tell if they're right only after the event (Vickers, 1965).

Usually, managers cannot wait for perfect or complete information but must act in a state of uncertainty. They must be aware that mistakes, errors of judgment, and errors of commission will occur; inappropriate and mistaken actions will be taken. They are not expected to be prophets, merely forecasters. Accountability means that they are responsible for results—what actually happens. They are not expected to be always right—merely to make things work out properly.

With these factors in mind, what managers need first of all is a process that is comprehensive, so that they have an opportunity to review *all* the information that is available to enlighten their judgment. Second, they need a process which is structured to focus their judgment on what counts while protecting them from hastily drawn false conclusions. Finally, it should be possible to abbreviate or collapse the process so that managers facing a developing situation can quickly and effectively bring their experience to bear on the data available and act in their own and their company's best interests.

In the next chapters, we will evaluate a strategy sequentially by reviewing its results in the light of its resources, its environment, and its stakeholder interests. In each chapter, as we collect new data and review the strategy's results, we will reach the following conclusions which indicate key concepts in strategy evaluation:

1. In looking at our results in light of resources, we will identify the *strengths and weaknesses* of the firm and get a sense of what we can do.
2. In examining the environment and anticipating our future performance, we will identify *opportunities and threats* lying ahead and get a sense of what might be done.
3. In determining what our stakeholders' interests, power and objectives are and how they are changing, we will develop a sense of what is *wanted, or possible, or unthinkable,* what actions will serve our interests and others'.

Thus, evaluation means assessing the results produced by our past actions and gauging the likely future success of our current strategy to set the stage for the development of more appropriate and vital objectives and future strategies. Following the sequence—past,

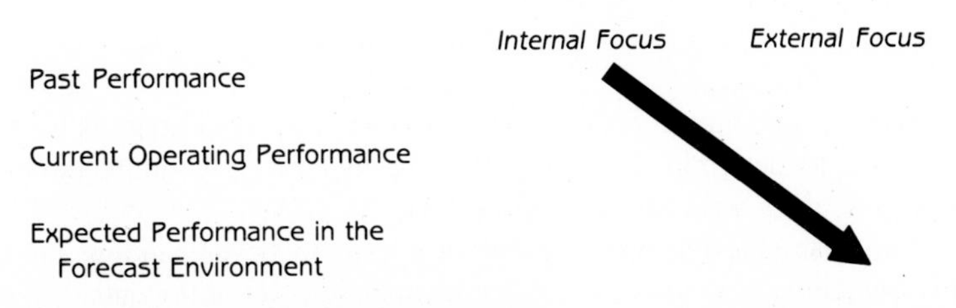

FIGURE 4-1 The Shifting Focus of Strategy Evaluation

present, and future—the strategist shifts the focus of his or her analysis from internal to external factors, as the line in *Figure 4-1* suggests.

Now, before we develop each chapter in detail, let us outline the rationale underlying Chapter 5's emphasis on resources, Chapter 6's focus on the environment, and Chapter 7's concentration on stakeholders. Once this is done, we will develop our synthesis and summarize strategy evaluation.

RESOURCES

Resources are the results of the firm's past strategies. They are the sources of strengths and weaknesses which will affect current and future performance. Resources which have a positive effect on performance are strengths; those which have a negative effect on performance we call weaknesses. For example, a strong brand name would be a positive resource for new product introduction, while poor relations with distributors would be a negative resource and would handicap a new product entry.

Resources can generally be identified with functions—marketing resources in the above example—or with businesses in a diversified enterprise. Since resources are the results of strategies, it is helpful to turn again to functional analysis. In this instance, however, we differentiate between strategies, which are the action verbs, and results, the nouns that are the output of strategies over sequential operating cycles. Of course, a successful past strategy will have produced the results desired and achieved the objectives set earlier. Large disparities, however, will exist between the objectives of unsuccessful strategies and the results they achieved.

Resources come from the past, but the focus of the strategy evaluation process is on the future. Resources link the past and the future; that is, they sit between the past and the future, because they are what the firm has available for its future competitive efforts. Resources are our basis for competing in the future.

Distinguishing those resources which are critical for future competitive success puts us in a position to improve the current strategy. The strategic factors, or keys to success, are the functional strategies which either exploit or result in critical resources. Indeed, one mark of a good manager is that he or she develops and protects the firm's most important resources since, as Chester Barnard (1966) wrote, "Critical resources limit or sustain a company's power and are 'strategic.'" Strategies which focus on critical resources will be successful. Losing strategies neglect what matters most and waste resources, thereby constraining future options and, ultimately, performance.

ENVIRONMENT

While it is important to determine whether the current strategy is working now, it is also important to determine how it will work in the likely future environment. How will today's strategy work in the likely future?

In assessing the environment, we have to be demanding but also realistic. The environment is the outside world; it encompasses everything outside the firm itself. Hence it is unlikely that we can be right about the future all the time and in every detail. Forecasts are needed to guide our actions and a logic is needed to guide our forecasting efforts.

The principle that we advocate is relevance. Focus just on what is most relevant to what you do and avoid aimless ''blue-sky'' speculations. This principle means that we emphasize what is most critical to the future success of the enterprise and the changes that appear likely, and then broaden our perspective selectively. Thus we first examine the industry of the firm, our suppliers, customers, and competitors, their power and their impact on our strategy. Next we focus on the macroeconomy and its likely impacts on our industry and our firm's strategy. We finally move to our stakeholders, those who constitute the most relevant social and political environment of the firm and who can seriously affect our ability to implement certain strategies.

Environmental assessment is *not* simply environmental extrapolation. We may expect a future like the past, but acting on this opinion requires judgment about the future. Casual extrapolation is an easy way to avoid thinking carefully about the future, that is, about the elements of the past likely to carry over into the future and those likely to be very different. Extrapolation is a common mistake in firms where success has come easily and critical strategic elements have never been carefully assessed. Thinking about the unthinkable and seeking new insights signify assessment rather than extrapolation.

By assessing the likely future—within the industry and competition, at the level of the macroeconomy, and in the larger social-political environment of the firm—we hope to be effective as well as efficiently exhaustive. Thinking through likely competitive reactions to your current strategy prevents many surprises. Understanding the impact of the business cycle and macroeconomic policies on your strategies prepares you to cope with macroeconomic change on a strategic level. Because the firm does not operate solely on an industrial or financial basis, it is better to assess the future social-political environment of the firm early. Early, there is time to prepare to meet it. Later, your actions or reactions are more tightly constrained and so may not be as effective.

Environmental assessment focuses attention on the results you are likely to achieve in the expected future. By first identifying the factors in the environment critical to your success, you can put research and time-consuming forecasting efforts where they are most warranted. You can determine where the strategy must be closely monitored to be sure the future is unfolding in a way consistent with the assumptions you have made about it, and the resources available, thus insuring the success of the strategy.

STAKEHOLDER OBJECTIVES

Organizations are people, not things. And people have a stake in organizational performance. Both internal and external stakeholders in an organization have values which influence their personal objectives, their views of the organization's results, and, ultimately, the objectives of the organization. To manage your stakeholders, it is important to distinguish your stakeholders' ''wish lists'' from those objectives they will actively support.

Stakeholder objectives which have been internalized by the organization may be discovered by asking, ''What is the organization trying to accomplish?'' The firm's objectives may be explicitly stated, or they may be unstated and implicit in the firm's priorities and past behavior. But whether explicit or implicit, recognition of stakeholder objectives is important in determining how a strategy will be implemented.

While maximizing profit is the economist's view of a firm's objective, actual objectives are not always or necessarily profit-dominated. For example, John K. Hanson, the founder and major shareholder of Winnebago, the Iowa-based recreational vehicle (RV) manufacturer, probably limited his firm's success by refusing to open plants throughout the country which might have cut transportation costs of the finished RV's and increased the firm's ability to hire professional managers. As a major stakeholder, however, one of his objectives may have been to maintain employment in his home town of Forest City, Iowa. In any event, Winnebagos were manufactured only in Forest City for many years. His actions as a manager certainly were consistent with his personal values. Understanding this key stakeholder is important in evaluating Winnebago.

In evaluating a strategy, it is important to note that a strategy which conflicts with major stakeholder objectives is likely to be very difficult to implement because it has no clear mandate to support it. On the other hand, strategies which appear to be supported by powerful stakeholders are unlikely to be blocked by less powerful individuals inside or outside the organization.

EVALUATION WITHIN THE STRATEGIC MANAGEMENT PROCESS

Evaluation involves analysis, then synthesis, and is a necessary prelude to strategic action. Considering resources in relation to the environment, improved strategies build on strengths and selectively repair weaknesses which are likely to impair future success. Good strategists take advantage of selective opportunities and work to avoid threats in the environment. Strategies can be implemented successfully only if they fulfill major stakeholder objectives and thereby win stakeholders' support and commitment. Of course, because stakeholder objectives will fit to varying degrees with the good of the firm, an element of strategic implementation is developing support for appropriate objectives and choosing which stakeholders to satisfy and which to disappoint.

To summarize, strategy must be made to serve the organization, moving it from the past, through the present, to the future. The important elements which management must synthesize and balance to develop a new strategy are (current) strategy, environment, resources, and values. In the following chapters, we discuss resources, the future environment, and stakeholders in greater depth. Only by increasing our understanding of these factors can we develop our ability to evaluate the current strategy of complex organizations (and competitors) and set the stage for strategic change and improved performance.

chapter 5

Resource Assessment

OVERVIEW

When we outlined the strategic management process, we said that strategy evaluation requires a consideration of both current and likely future results against the resources committed to the strategy. Do the results to date represent a satisfactory achievement given the resources committed? Can the resources available yield the future results required?

Answering these two questions is never easy. The first question, concerning "satisfactory achievement," points to opportunities to improve the performance of current operations. The second, involving "future results," tests the more venturesome entrepreneurial activities of the firm for feasibility—that is, consistency with the firm's capabilities. Answering the questions requires an integrative judgment encompassing results, resources, the future, and competition, as well as objectives and strategy.

Both strategy identification and resource assessment require an understanding of the firm's current situation. Using the current reality as an anchor for thinking about the future, the strategic management process moves from an organizational consensus about facts toward areas of uncertainty where different judgments can be reached by reasonable people. Thus, while strategy identification forces us to confront the reality of what we are doing, resource assessment forces us to review how well we are doing and the reality of what we have. Resources are what we have available for tomorrow's competition. You must know yourself to know what to look for in others; our objective in assessing resources is to identify our competitive strengths and weaknesses.

WHAT ARE STRATEGIC RESOURCES?

Strategic resources are the results of our past strategy. While strategies are verbs, resources are nouns. Strategies are actions, and resources are outcomes.

Resources range well beyond finance and the bottom line. Successful strategic action builds market relationships, arranges supply contracts, and constructs world-scale plants. It develops relationships with distribution channels, confidence in the capital markets, and human and technological capabilities within the firm, as well as earning a profit. Even though most strategic results are nonfinancial, they enhance the firm's market value because they contribute to future earnings growth. Although the board may allow some resources to flow out of the firm as dividends to shareholders, most of the results of successful action accrue to the company and are available for recommitment in subsequent operating cycles.

Resources are enhanced by success, debilitated and wasted by neglect and failure. Of course, when a current strategy is totally successful in achieving its objectives, plans are realized and the current resource inventory will be what was expected. Flaws in a strategy or in its execution will be exposed if the firm does not have resources where management expects or needs them, or if important resources are underutilized.

Having resources allows freedom of action. Having to pursue resources when you are under pressure is a trap which turns energies away from the pursuit of future opportunities. To use resources well, you must know what resources you have. Prudent strategists work within the constraints of their current resource base. In assessing the competitive value of an organization's resources, remember that different resources can have a positive or negative impact on the success of a particular strategy. Positive or negative implies that resources can be strategic assets or liabilities. Assets will generally be the result of past success, while liabilities stem from underachievement, dissipation, or failure.

Note that resources are not absolute quantities but are relative and have a time dimension. Assessing resources involves comparisons with the competition over time. It is the competitive value of resources at a particular time that determines whether they afford a firm advantage or disadvantage, whether the firm is strong or weak. In the real estate industry, for example, prudent people never commit to a project without an understanding of the revenue and cost streams of comparable projects. It should be the same in every business, since it is relative competitive strength in the future which will determine the success of our strategic actions.

In this chapter, we will discuss the various types of resources available to an organization by focusing on each function in turn. Resources exist in marketing, finance, production, and administrative functions, and it is substantially easier to inventory and examine them within those categories than in any other way. Since we identified a firm's business strategy by examining functional strategies, our functional approach to resource assessment exploits a parallel structure and facilitates integrative thinking.

MARKETING RESOURCES

Market power is a firm's ultimate marketing resource. Customers', distributors', and competitors' views of your firm in the marketplace underpin your organization's marketing resources. Their perceptions of your ability to use the 4 P's of marketing (product, price, promotion, and place) to manage your relationships with them affect the firm's market power.

In assessing current market reality, it is reasonable to begin with your customers—your chosen market. How many customers do you have? Who buys what? These may seem like simple questions, but many firms have been surprised by the answers. A frequently cited but astoundingly accurate rule of thumb is that, for most firms, 20 percent of the customers buy 80 percent of the goods. The strength of these relationships with the top 20 percent of the customers and the nature of the relationship—for example, the relative power and security of customers and supplier—provide information on the basic strength of the business situation.

Different definitions of markets can provide useful information on well-served and underserved (therefore potential) market segments. Majaro (1977) writes of a British pharmaceutical manufacturer which found that an allergy drug had different market shares:

> Stanton, a British ethical drug manufacturer, held 20% of a £5 million retail market for anti-asthma drugs. Trying to sharpen its strategic marketing practices, Stanton researched its markets and discovered that the drug had a 30% share of total prescriptions issued for anti-asthma drugs, although only 18% of doctors actually prescribed Stanton's drug. When asthma sufferers were contacted, 40% were found using Stanton's drug.

This example points to the information content and diagnostic potential of alternate market share definitions. Such information provides important market data to use as a resource in reformulating strategies to hit more effectively the segments that are most profitable to the firm.

In addition to knowing who your customers are, it is also important to know who actually makes purchase decisions. Supermarkets, for example, are finding that men are doing the family shopping more often than some advertisers assumed. The length, quality, and closeness of customer relationships and the quality and quantity of customer contact also give insights into the worth of a customer base as a marketing resource, as well as the costs of servicing certain customers. A positive market resource may be a loyal customer base needing little encouragement, while a fickle, very price-sensitive, or disappointed customer base is obviously a negative marketing resource.

The firm's *products* are a resource, as is the breadth or specialized depth of the product line. Breadth or depth is a positive resource if it contributes to profitability, negative if it contributes excessively to costs or if it has weak elements or gaps which limit sales. Keep in mind the 80 : 20 rule here, too—80 percent of the profits are likely to come from 20 percent of the products. Value to the firm and its customers is the telling product characteristic. It is important to examine each product line's reputation or perceived quality level to understand the roles of function, associated service levels, and socio-psychological benefits, both before and after the sale.

Indeed, the most important aspect of a product as a marketing resource is its perceived value, or the relationship between price and quality. The product's technology also may be important to the market's perception of quality. For example, for the producer of a high-technology product which has a sketchy in-service record, reputation may be a negative resource. This judgment may be softened, however, if the older technology is becoming prohibitively expensive or if the market is made up of early adopters tolerant of in-service difficulties.

Time makes a difference to the value of a product as a strategic resource. What is acceptable early in the product life cycle may be unacceptable later. At what stage of their life cycles are your products? Is demand building, stable, or declining? The product life cycle, shown in *Figure 5-1,* has been criticized because few products experience the

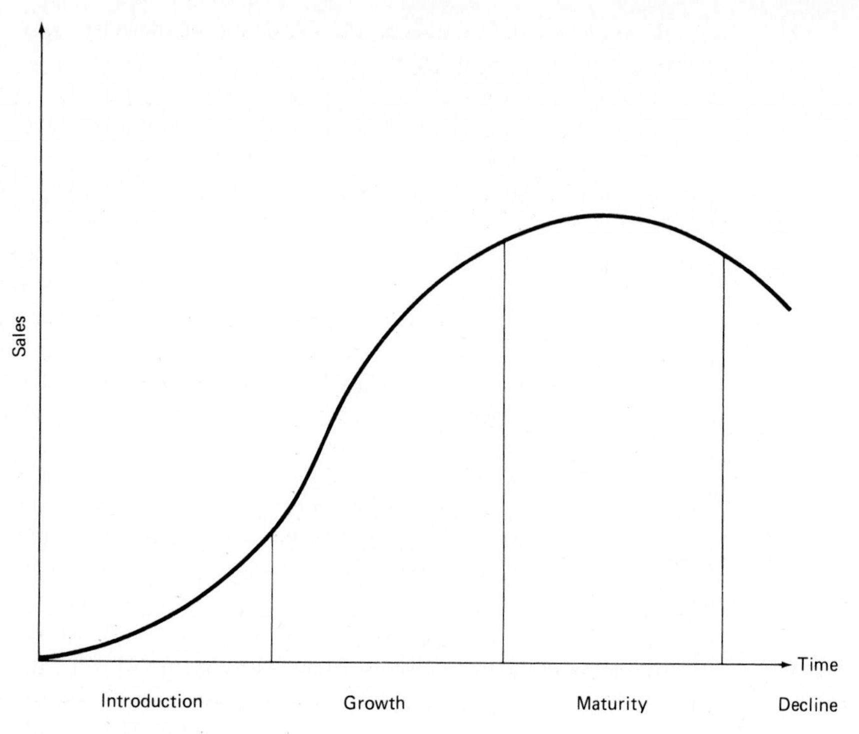

FIGURE 5-1 The Product Life Cycle

classic S-shaped growth pattern, beginning slowly with early adopters, speeding up as the product's reputation spreads, and leveling off as the market is saturated and the product matures. Nevertheless, the life cycle is a useful forward-looking tool for strategic managers and alerts managers to the forces which are likely to affect future sales and profits (Webster, 1979). We will refer to the product life cycle later in this chapter as we inventory the firm's resources in relation to the product's growth stage, and elsewhere in this book when we evaluate strategy and discuss strategic alternatives.

Price position and pricing power in the marketplace refer to another strategic area. Price elasticity of demand, (ϵ) (the absolute value of the percentage change in quantity divided by the percentage change in price), tells much about the firm's ability to charge high prices and gain revenue in the process. A product with an inelastic demand ($\epsilon < 1$) is one where volume responds very little to price increases, allowing the firm to raise total revenue by raising prices.

Firms often are reluctant to raise prices, but when they test their price elasticity, they are sometimes surprised to find the customer willing to pay a much higher price than they had expected. Indeed, this points to a situation where the firm has given away much of the value of its product over time. Successfully raising the product's price proves that it was more valuable to consumers than was originally thought, and the firm has not captured that value for itself by charging a higher price earlier. Relative elasticity, a firm's elasticity compared with others in its industry, summarizes a firm's ability to raise price, or its price leadership. The firm with the lowest elasticity in its industry is the one with the most price power in the marketplace.

Value added is another important characteristic of a product and is related to price. Value added refers to the value added in production, that is, the product's selling price minus its materials costs. A high value added and a high margin demonstrate that the firm's product is highly regarded by the market and that some price cutting may be a feasible strategic option. A high value added and a low margin point to a high capital- or labor-intense business with little market power, dependent on high turnover to earn a satisfactory return.

Price robustness, another marketing resource, is the firm's ability to hold its price in apparently unfavorable situations, such as drops in industry demand (for example, recession), or price cutting by competitors. A robust-priced product can withstand these crises because the customer believes it is still worth paying for. Price robustness is a sign of perceived value and possibly price leadership.

Pricing may also vary over the product life cycle, and management should evaluate its pricing pattern to see if it has enhanced profitability over the life cycle. Polaroid, for example, has used a "cream-skimming" pricing strategy for its instant cameras, setting h.gh prices in the product introduction phase followed by lower prices as the product line gains volume. Kodak, however, typically enters the market with moderate price. It did this with its instant camera product line, possibly believing that a moderate entry price would be more consistent with its mass market strategy. Each company's pricing strategy fit its corporate strategy—Polaroid was a camera company, while Kodak made its money on film and film processing.

Price splits value between the producer and the consumer, resulting in a particular profit-level for the producer and an overall product satisfaction for the consumer. High prices allow the producer to retain more value, while lower prices raise the product's value to the consumer. A wise manager will generally price to retain value of the product, realizing that drastic price reductions will always sell more units but may annihilate producer margins. And past producer margins can be a valuable resource to aid the manager in pursuing an expensive but pre-emptive long-term strategy against competitors.

Figure 5-2 illustrates this price/value concept by showing the producers' and consumers' surpluses for a particular product. Producers' surplus, BCP, refers to the gain over costs which efficient producers experience at the P price level. Consumers' surplus, ABP, refers to the satisfaction gained by consumers who would have been willing to pay more than P to get the product. A price P_1 below P would raise the consumers' surplus and lower the producers' surplus.

In discussing price resources, elasticity, robustness, and value, a useful summary question is: "Are you pricing to value or giving it away?" While lowering prices is often the only way that managers refer to price as a competitive variable, the ability to raise prices unscathed certainly demonstrates competitive power and can achieve a firm's profit objectives without more difficult cost controls. Indeed, having the image of a price cutter can sometimes sully the reputation of a quality product. Raising prices successfully, however, is the mark of a price leader with obvious market power.

Promotion, the third of marketing's 4 P's, is also a repository for marketing resources. What is the organization's media position? Does it do well with the most effective media? How has promotion enhanced the product's quality perception or name

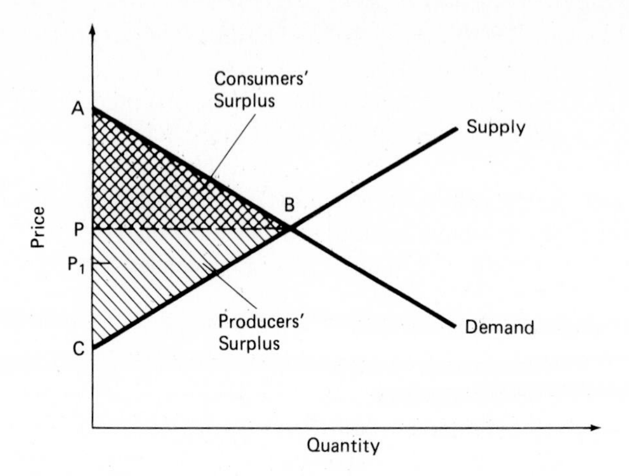

FIGURE 5-2 Producers' and Consumers' Surpluses

recognition? Can its brand, such as Bic or Timex or Kodak, successfully carry new and different products to the marketplace? Are its promotional efforts expected and ineffective, or do they generate interest and excitement? Is its sales force exceptional? Do its customer services cement relationships?

How well do the firm's promotional resources match the product's life cycle stage? Firms introducing products to the mass market early in the life cycle may need only limited promotional resources. A late entrant may need very substantial sums of money to promote its products and achieve a successful entrance. Bic, a $60-million company in 1973, spent amounts equivalent to 30 percent of its $10 million operating cash flow to introduce its disposable cigarette lighter into the US market against Gillette. Bic still had cash and securities of $10 million on hand to prime the promotional pump for subsequent new product introductions, since its strategy has been late entry in emerging markets and such a risky strategy demands high promotional expenditures and reserves should an entry attempt fail.

Firms with more mature products, with substantial brand recognition, may be able to spend differently and spend less on promotion than their competition. Anheuser-Busch, for example, time-pulses its advertising (that is, heavy advertising in a market, followed by no advertising, followed by intense advertising again) across the media to maximize promotional efficiency and limit expenditures (Ackoff and Emshoff, 1975). Coca-Cola is in a similar enviable position in the soft drink market.

Under the promotional heading, too, remember the sales force. Lincoln Electric's salesmen are all trained welders and so are expert sales engineers who can help their customers solve problems at the cutting edge of welding technology. Tasty Baking, manufacturers of the famous Philadelphia Tastykake, has a waiting list of qualified, experienced salesmen stretching out two years ahead of its needs, each one waiting for a call to start work—a remarkable resource, indeed.

To evaluate *place* as a marketing resource, we examine both position in the distribution chain and geographic market. Channel power, power in the distribution chain, is achieved by a firm when the rewards are heavy for little risk, and when the services rendered by the chosen channels are high—for example, the distributors hold title, carry inventory, or provide after-sales service.

In discussing a product's geographic market, we also consider the geographic barriers around our markets, or the barriers around others' markets—a firm could hold a geographic niche. If place is a positive market resource, geographic barriers around us will be high, and those around others very low. The Japanese computer manufacturers, for example, operate in a system where the barriers around them are high due to import restrictions; the barriers around US competitors are low, due to virtually free trade in electronics equipment in the US.

An assessment of market power is a convenient summary of a business's marketing resources. Market power encompasses power in the channel, the ability to raise price, and the ability to set a quality standard. It is important to identify the firm's source of power—the dimension on which it offers great value—and to consider whether it can be sustained.

PRODUCTION RESOURCES

In order to assess production resources, we must understand the production process. What is the technology and process used in production? Is it proprietary or otherwise unique to the firm? Is the product hand-produced or automated, job shop or continuous process? How does the firm relate to suppliers, by contract or integration? What kind of control or planning exists to avoid *ad hoc* coping responses to production snags? Do inventory policies smooth production, yet limit the risks of loss of business and obsolescence appropriately?

How well does the production process fit with the company's marketing strategy and the marketplace? Hayes and Wheelwright (1979) link what they call process life cycles with the product life cycle. They argue that different processes fit better with specific product structures and use *Figure 5-3* to illustrate their case. Note that there are some absolute mismatches, since the further the firm departs from the diagonal, the more complex it is to maintain a useful effective and efficient match between marketing and production. Generally, stable product lines will fit below the diagonal—with heavier investments in plant—while more diverse and changing product lines will fit above the diagonal.

Another indicator of the fit between marketing and production is focus (Skinner, 1974). Are manufacturing and marketing well-coordinated and mutually supportive? Are the plants focused on a limited number of objectives or many? Plants which have a limited number of objectives tend to have higher effectiveness and efficiency, that is, they can more readily and more cheaply achieve their objectives. Focus is a resource.

Costs of production are an indication of managerial flexibility and skill. How are fixed and variable costs balanced, relative to market, and what is the operating leverage? How is the bulk/value tradeoff managed, and do the logistics of transporting supplies and products make economic sense?

Costs of production also shift over time. Here, too, cost escalation or lack of control becomes obvious. How has the cost position changed? Are costs under control? Have cost cutting measures been used? How is quality controlled?

Learning and experience in production should enable unit costs to drop. A firm which has taken advantage of its production experience and opportunities to modify its operating technology should have a production resource or strength contributing to its overall profitability. Firms which have ignored the potential of experience will have high cost positions. We discuss experience in detail in Chapter 6.

Process technology plays an important role in many industries. Specialized, rather than flexible, technology may increase efficiency or quality, but the commitment carries with it strategic risk for the firm because it locks the firm into particular products or processes. The organization's current production technology may be a positive or negative

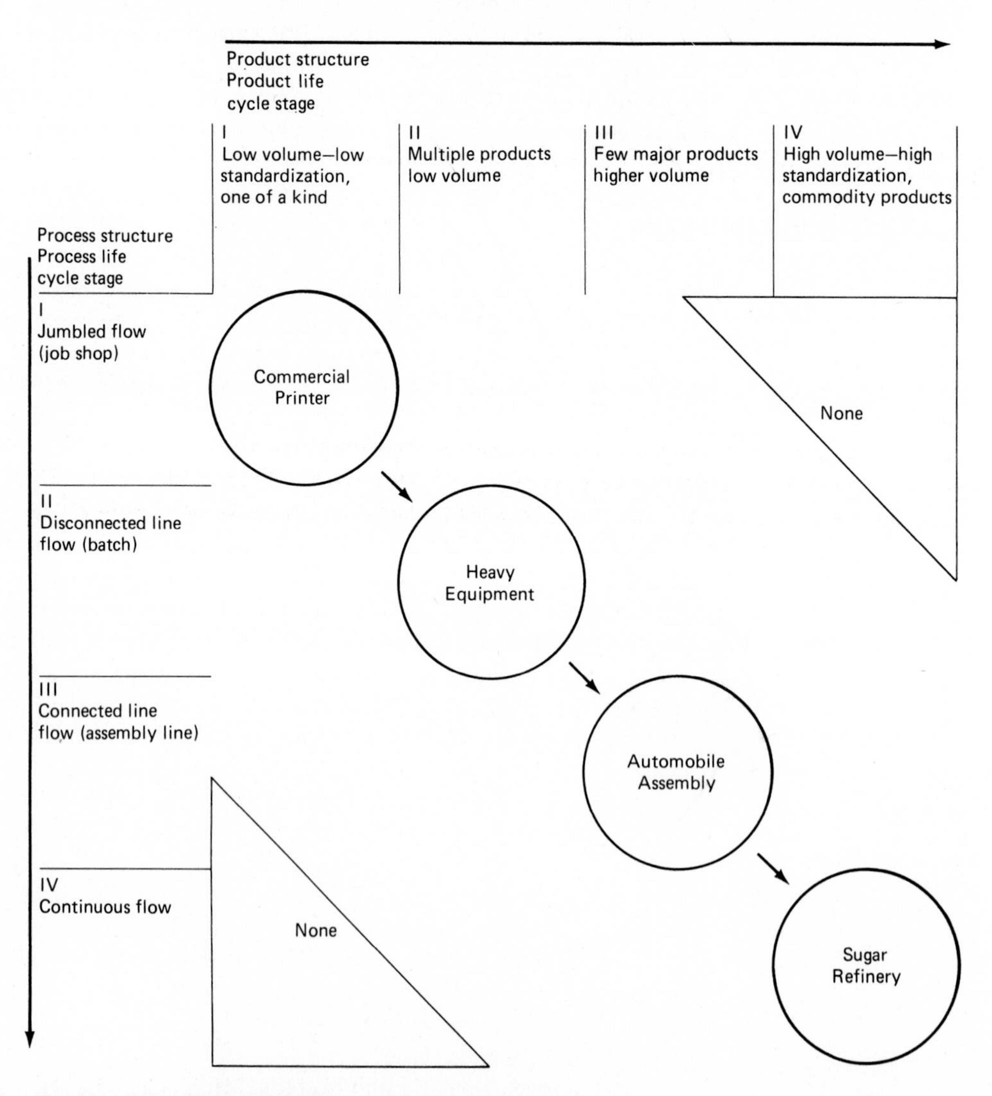

FIGURE 5-3 Matching Major Stages of Product and Process Life Cycles

Source: Robert Hayes and Steven Wheelwright, "Dynamics of Process-Product Life-Cycles," March 1979. Reprinted by permission of the *Harvard Business Review*.

resource; the same is true of its ability to learn a new technology. Most technologies require significant skill, labor and capital tradeoffs, and have certain efficient operating ranges with different breakeven volumes which may contribute to or hinder the success of particular strategies.

Research and development (R&D) skills are also a production resource. Product or process R&D, and expertise for basic or applied research may be among the resources of a firm. R&D capability can enhance a firm's competitive ability, or it can be a poorly managed and costly activity.

Utterback and Abernathy (1975) provide a useful model of process and product innovation which is relevant in our assessment of R&D skills. As *Figure 5-4* shows, the Utterback and Abernathy model hypothesizes a declining rate of production innovation concurrent with a rising and then falling track of process innovation, with innovation being stimulated by different corporate and market needs as the product matures. The key question for management is: Are the R&D resources appropriately deployed for the competition ahead? However, to answer this, we need to know just what resources are available now and how they are employed.

Finally, let us discuss capacity. While underutilized capacity is a problem, when conditions change slack capacity becomes a resource. What is critical is the match between sales and capacity, that is, between demand and supply. As a market grows, capacity in place may deter others from entering a market. In some businesses, the competition becomes so intense that overcapacity conditions prevail and marginal operators leave the industry. Nevertheless, slack capacity can be an expensive and fleeting asset, since competitors can build capacity themselves and reduce any market response advantage held by the firm with slack. Also, capacity and location are intimately linked: *where* it is may have a larger impact than *what* it is.

FINANCIAL RESOURCES

Financial resources reflect the numerical reality of a company, the numbers measuring its performance under the current strategy. Indeed, an increase in financial resources will generally confirm or suggest the existence of positive resources or strengths in other areas, while a decline in financial resources indicates problems.

An initial question to assess financial resources is obvious: Is the firm wealthy? A wealthy organization is one which has assets appropriate for its business needs as well as a cushion for likely contingencies. Such a cushion requires liquidity to cope with the unexpected. This liquidity can be in the form of idle working capital—for example, marketable securities, expected cash flow—or funding in reserve, such as unused credit lines or the owners' willingness to provide further backing. Heavy fixed assets also have a bearing on a firm's liquidity, since they often necessitate heavy fixed costs and leave the firm constrained in its other spending.

Assessing who owns the firm, who controls its financial destiny, is also important when you evaluate the firm's financial staying power, or, if you like, the quality of the firm's money. Trade creditors can be an important source of funding; their ability to give the firm flexible financing arrangements represents a resource area. Lenders to the firm are also important as *de facto* owners who represent resources of credit or constraint. Legal owners have the right to the residual value of the firm and are its final call for more

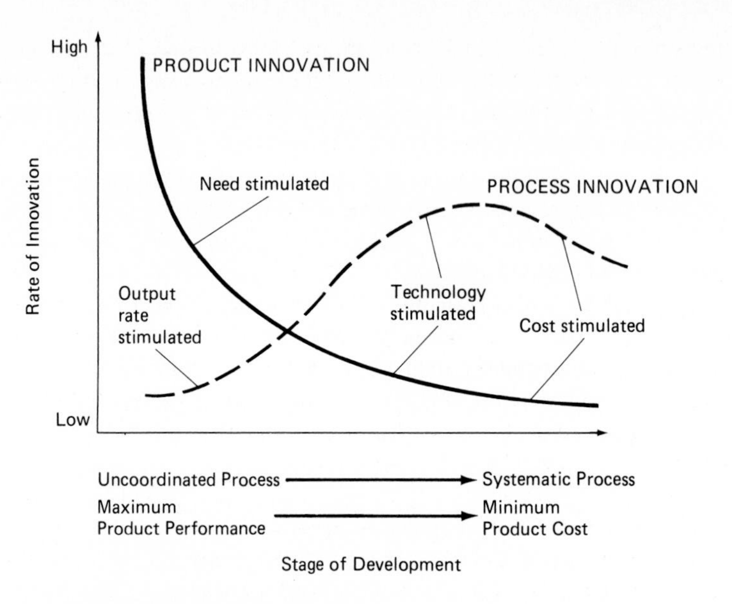

FIGURE 5-4 Innovation and Stage of Development

Source: Reprinted with permission from *OMEGA, the International Journal of Management Science*, vol. 3, Utterback and Abernathy, "A Dynamic Model of Process and Product Innovation," © 1975, Pergamon Press, Ltd.

capital; their present willingness and ability to commit more capital to the firm is a major resource.

Although this discussion of financial resources has thus far centered on balance-sheet issues, current income is a resource because profits enhance and losses deplete the firm's long-term financial base. A firm with a record of strong current income is likely to understand and increase its revenue sources and manage costs, including the impact of high or rising fixed costs. Current income flows represent an important financial resource; changes here are an alert to new strengths or flaws in a firm's current strategy. The DuPont formula links return on equity with sales margins, with asset turnover (a product of both current activity and balance-sheet resources), and with leverage, from the balance sheet, allowing us to analyze profitability.

How has the firm generated its profits? We will use the DuPont formula to analyze profitability:

$$\frac{\text{Profit}}{\text{Equity}} = \frac{\text{Profit}}{\text{Sales}} \times \frac{\text{Sales}}{\text{Assets}} \times \frac{\text{Assets}}{\text{Equity}}$$

Profitability analysis will point to changing competitive strengths as the margin shifts, to new efficiency as turnover rises, and to heightened leverage as debt use increases. A sense of past financial resource development will give important insights into how the firm currently makes its money and into the skills on which its profitability is founded.

A critical resource is cash flow. Whether from operations or financial transactions, the firm's cash flow links balance-sheet and income statements. If current operations can produce surplus funds, the firm's financial strength will be enhanced. If external sources are tapped, usually the firm suffers some loss of flexibility, although additional leverage may enhance profitability. What probably matters most is how the firm deploys its assets and, in particular, its cash flow. Are they invested in businesses and projects which enhance the firm's value, or are they wasted in low-return ventures, relics of the past, or spread so thinly that they have no competitive weight?

A firm whose product is at an early growth stage will be pumping cash from operations back into the company (and even taking on debt) to add to capacity and working capital, and to buy promotion necessary to stimulate future growth. A mature product, however, may allow asset redeployment. A mature volume product may be able to win financial concessions from suppliers and buyers who now depend on its high volumes as the mainstay of their own businesses. For example, they may be able to operate with large payables and small receivables, since they have power in their relationships with suppliers and customers.

Over the life cycles of its products, the firm's cash flow should shift from investment to return. Even in the smallest businesses, the successes of the past supply the seed corn of the future. Shareholders who eat too much in the form of dividends are a problem and will destroy the value of the firm if not restrained.

The value of the firm is the ultimate corporate resource. Stock market values reflect current earnings and financial strength and the market's perception of the future success which management is likely to enjoy. While stock market value does not always quickly result from good management, the job of the manager is to create value. Stock market value is a resource in acquisition or a defense against takeover; it should be enhanced by effective strategic management.

ADMINISTRATIVE AND HUMAN RESOURCES

Administrative and human resources consist of the people in an organization, their skills (by level and by function), and the way they are organized. These resources may be the most important of all because a firm's distinctive competence is frequently based on the skills of its people. Indeed, Stevenson (1976) found that higher-level managers, those who are most responsible for the long-term success of the organization, are more concerned with human resources than with any other functional resource.

The organization's strategic management capability and experience, too, rest in its human resources at both the managerial and administrative levels, and so strategic management ability must be assessed within a human resource audit. Employee and management stability and loyalty are important to firms which consciously attempt to develop their people-based distinctiveness. Appropriate compensation for performance also affects the quality of the firm's human resources.

The memory of critical experiences in a firm can seriously affect current operations, sustain its *esprit de corps,* and define a code for employee behavior. Such an *esprit de corps* may provide the basis for a future strategy and is a valuable resource. Timex's critical experiences include the collapse of its bomb fuse business after World War II and its rebuff by jewelry stores which refused to distribute its low-priced watches in the early

1950s. Timex turned to the drugstores and the emerging discount chains. Indeed, volume was exactly what Timex needed to enhance its manufacturing skills and enable it to lower its costs. These were the only channels available, but channels which better matched Timex's product and market, since the discounters and drugstores needed volume sales and only low-priced watches could sell in volume. Timex has moved very deliberately since that time. The company seems unfazed by the rapid rise of the electronic watch and has never been tempted too far from its manufacturing and assembly competence, although it may have been unable to finance early entry into electronics and was caught for a time with an obsolete watch technology.

Critical experience, however, may hinder a firm from taking appropriate action. It can become a negative resource, a source of weakness. Some firms which have survived recessions with judicious, controlled penny pinching find their managers become too conservative to reap the full benefits of the succeeding prosperity. The retailer Montgomery Ward is a notable example. Thirty years after the Great Depression, Ward maintained its liquidity as a reserve for the next depression, sacrificing its competitive position to its past experience. As Sears moved aggressively into the suburbs and malls of America, Montgomery Ward watched and waited with its cash for a "future" which never developed (in the way Ward expected). The result was prosperity and growth for Sears and years of decline and ultimately a takeover for Ward, ironically with its own cash (reserves) being used to pay for the purchase.

Personal values are an important element of human resources: What do the people in the organization want? Examples of employees with differing values include the professional interested in the job, the man or woman interested in "the company" and its role in the community, and the individual interested in the paycheck. An organization's value structure is a resource which can support or limit a firm's strategic success. For example, when times are tight, employees who believe in the organization may continue to work even for reduced or deferred pay; personal values may be a strong strategic resource.

Power is an important organizational resource. Because power can be used to grant authority over other resources, a person or group with power can shift the organization's priorities and strategies. Thus, it is important to note who has power and why, how power is used and shared. Who has autonomy? How does structure reflect power, and how does the administrative system enhance the organization's ability to focus resources where they are needed for strategic success? The question, "Who's in and who's out?" reveals where power resides. Remember the old adage, "If you're not in, you're out" (Jennings, 1980).

To summarize the human resource assessment, identify the firm's distinctive competence and the critical people by whom it has been built and maintained. For the modern strategic thinker, people are the ultimate source of value. People are the only resource which can determine the effective, creative use of human and nonhuman resources. Ohmae (1982) calls this creative factor insight; the right person will always defeat a machine because only people can create beyond experience.

RESOURCES: AN ILLUSTRATION

We will discuss resource assessment for Dr. Pepper, the firm whose strategy we identified in Chapter 4. *Figure 5-5* shows the resources of Dr. Pepper, arranged in a functional structure parallel to that used for strategy identification. Resources are the result of past functional strategies.

FIGURE 5-5 Resource Assessment—Dr. Pepper: Mid-1970s

Marketing	*Production*	*Finance*	*Human Resources*
Market: Primarily in the Southwest, but sold throughout US with some international sales, including Japan. In 1982, dropped from 3rd to 4th in national market share, behind Coke, Pepsi, and 7-Up. *Product:* Unique taste of 23 flavors, identified by some as similar to rootbeer, almonds and/or cherries. Also, sugar-free Dr. Pepper. Often available in fewer sizes than competitors. Mature product in Southwest, small market share in Northeast. *Price:* Often higher-priced than competitors. Inelastic and robust to loyal drinkers, less inelastic and robust in new markets. *Promotion:* Point-of-sale ads, in conjuction with ads and samplings through local bottlers. Some national promotion. *Place:* Primarily manufacturer of concentrate, some co-owned manufacturing and bottling plants. Strongest in Southwest, which has a growing population, although nationally distributed via strong local cola bottlers. Strong in traditional markets, recently growing but now slipping nationally.	Concentrate production requires few employees and simple equipment; low capital investment needed to increase capacity. High fixed cost stage of production and expensive transportation of soft drinks provided by strong, local cola bottlers. Canning and bottling require more employees, working capital and capital investment. Presold bulk palletized delivery (on pallets moveable by forklift) to large grocery chains saves money and provides better service than traditional route delivery. Large user of sugar, paying current commodity prices. High quality. *R&D:* Use of new containers, development of powdered Dr. Pepper for hot drinks. Powerful as low cost concentrate producer. Powerful in distribution chain, due to quality and taste.	History of growing profits; profits fell in 1982. Formerly heavy cash, but now increasing debt to acquire Canada Dry. Falling sales margin. Stock price: depressed from previous high. Uses financial strength of bottlers with its own. Quarterly dividends. Resources spent in acquisition and national distribution. Power as a concentrate producer.	Employees as believers in Dr. Pepper's uniqueness, quality, and position in industry and community, illustrating Golden Rule in business. Led by W. W. ("Foots") Clements as chairman. Recently hired president from Procter and Gamble replaced after less than 3 years, in Nov. 82, by R. Q. Armstrong, president of Canada Dry when Dr. Pepper acquired it (1982). Cadre of loyal employees, spreading "word" of Dr. Pepper to raise market penetration.

You will note after analyzing *Figure 5-5* that the resources for Dr. Pepper are generally strong in its Southwest markets, signifying that the past strategy in its traditional operating area has been successful. For a firm whose past strategies have earned mixed results, the resource assessment will show weaknesses as well as strengths. Weaknesses are areas of past strategic failure which may require additional effort if they leave the firm vulnerable to a competitor's strengths. Dr. Pepper's falling national market position, following an expensive bid for national market share, was a sign of growing weakness.

Dr. Pepper was a substantially weaker company earlier when bottlers were not willing to risk their franchise agreements with the major colas (which specified that they could bottle only one cola) in order to add another brown soft drink with a unique, possibly cola-like taste. This situation limited its bottlers to those who were weaker number three's in the local markets and who could not afford the advertising and sampling expenses required to win Dr. Pepper drinkers. Thus, until the court ruling that Dr. Pepper was not a cola,[1] Dr. Pepper was vulnerable against the richer, stronger cola manufacturers even when it sought to expand slowly outside its original Southwest markets.

Resource assessment gives you information about what Dr. Pepper is, to add to the strategy identification data on what it is doing. Current position as well as strategic thrust are important in assessing where Dr. Pepper is likely to go in the future. Current position also provides a base, questions, and priorities on which to begin an analysis of the likely relevant future environment in which Dr. Pepper will operate. And, although we have not yet discussed alternative strategies in detail, this strategy and resource analysis of Dr. Pepper provide a strong foundation for W. W. Clements's 1983 statement:

> We lose the effectiveness of our marketing money when we try to paint with too broad a brush. This doesn't mean we'll abandon the Northeast, but we'll certainly try to strengthen our position where we're already strong. (Clements, 1983)

RESOURCES AND THE FUTURE

A resource inventory is a foundation for assessing the competitive strengths and weaknesses of your organization. The full synthesis required to determine your relative competitive power will be made later when you understand your competitors' objectives, strategy, and resource bases, and have developed your own sense of the future.

In moving towards that identification of strategic strengths and weaknesses, some relevant empirical research can guide us. Be careful: relative competitive strength is what matters, yet often that is not where managers focus. Stevenson (1976) found that managers typically use different criteria to define strengths and weaknesses. Historical criteria, such as experience, intra-company comparison, and budget are used to judge strength; weaknesses are judged against normative criteria such as consultants' opinions, management's understanding of the business literature, rules of thumb, and opinion. He also found managerial position affecting interpretation of the importance of certain resources, with functional managers giving more weight to marketing and production issues and top

[1]In 1962, Pepsi-Cola sued Dr. Pepper for trademark infringement over the use of the word "pep" by Dr. Pepper. Pepsi won, but Dr. Pepper countersued and won a ruling, later supported by the Food and Drug Administration, that Dr. Pepper was a unique and separate flavor rather than a cola.

managers giving more weight to financial and human resources. But it is important to take an integrative and competitive view, no matter what your position.

Because the job of management is to create value, the ultimate test of management is that the cumulative impact of the resources in the current and future marketplace exceeds the sum of its parts. If management cannot create such a synergy, it cannot justify the costs of administering the parts of the organization to develop a united front in the marketplace. Since synergy or value creation can occur in a number of ways in the future, resources must be evaluated qualitatively, integratively, and competitively, focusing extra selective attention on those resources whose presence or absence is crucial for strategic success (Barnard, 1966).

PREVIEW

Resource assessment is, initially, a static analysis, to identify and inventory the current base, the foundation for future strategy. But resource evaluation takes place in the light of current and future needs. One of the reasons we introduced the product life cycle and mentioned the experience concept in this chapter is to give some attention to the likely future, even as we inventory our resources. Both models thrust us toward the future, have a competitive content and help us forecast what our future resource needs are likely to be. We discuss experience as a concept summarizing resource strength in Chapter 6. We move from a current resource base to the future as we explore the industry, competitive and social-political environment in Chapters 7, 8 and 9.

Resource identification links current strategy with past results, while resource evaluation requires a look at the likely future to fully assess resource strengths and weaknesses in light of future needs. Some guidelines will enhance the productivity of your analysis of the strengths and weaknesses of your firm in relation to the competition.

1 Be selective. Not all weaknesses are correctable or worth correcting, and there are some you must live with. Of course, all weaknesses inhibit our ability to fulfill purpose (Stevenson, 1976). Knowledge of what they are means that you can avoid putting strain on areas that cannot withstand it (Hussey, 1968).
2 Be sensitive to what is opinion and what is fact. Stevenson (1976) has found that managers are more willing to judge strengths against historical comparisons than against competitive factors. And managers rely on outsiders' opinions to highlight weaknesses rather than their own assessment of the competition.
3 Do not be absolute. Use your resource inventory to alert you to areas for competitive comparison rather than to what are absolute strengths or weaknesses.

Ultimately, one of the principles of competition is to focus strength against your rivals' weakness. This means you must exploit others' errors and weaknesses and guard your own. Sun Tzu wrote, circa 500 B.C., "Know the enemy and know yourself; in a hundred battles you will not be in peril" (Sun Tzu, 1963, p. 84). Experience, as we address it in Chapter 6, summarizes our knowledge of our own resources.

In Chapters 7 to 9, we move to an analysis of the future environment. Environmental assessment must be married to resource assessment to gain a full view of the world in which our strategy must work.

chapter 6

Experience, Price and Value: Summarizing Resources

INTRODUCTION

Experience, price and value collectively tell us a great deal about our most significant competitive resource, our relative strength in the market. Experience is the strategist's shorthand for the track of unit costs over time. Price is a measure of market power. With cost, it determines margin, revealing how much of the value created by a particular product or service offering is being captured as profit. Indeed, it is profit dollars that ultimately fund growth.

In this chapter, we will describe in detail the experience curve, its slow application in the strategic management area and its strategic implications. We will show how price and value are affected by strategies based on the experience curve.

LEARNING AND EXPERIENCE: A BRIEF HISTORY AND DEFINITION

In 1925, aeronautical engineers observed that the manufacturing labor content of airplanes fell as the total output accumulated. They attributed the decline to learning. People doing repetitive tasks, like building an airplane, learn to do it better and so save time on later units.

In the early 1960s, the Boston Consulting Group (BCG) staff observed similar price and cost patterns across a number of industries and across all costs. They called the phenomenon ''the experience curve'' and promoted its use in the strategic management arena through their 1968 publication, *Perspectives on Experience* and their professional work. Typically, total real unit costs decline at some ''characteristic rate'' each time accumulated production is doubled—from almost nothing to a rate as high as 60 percent each time accumulated production doubles (Ghemawat, 1985). In the electronics industry, for example, real costs typically decline by 30 percent as production is doubled.

By 1981, however, *Fortune* reported that the strategic importance of the experience curve had passed (Kiechel, 1981). It seemed business had begun to use the tool in an uninformed manner. Inexperienced managers had begun to misuse it, for example, applying it slavishly in inappropriate contexts. Nevertheless, it seems inappropriate to discard a powerful tool simply because it has been poorly understood and applied improperly.

Let us examine the experience curve in more depth so that it can be properly applied as an aid to strategic analysis. We can learn more about its strengths and limitations if we follow its history.

The Experience Curve

The experience curve, then, is simply a trace of real unit costs as volume accumulates. The usual formulation, shown in *Figure 6-1*, is:

$$C_x = a\, x^{-b}$$

where c_x = cost of x-th unit

a = cost of the first unit

b = a constant that depends on the learning rate.

Figure 6-2 illustrates this as a function linear in the log:

$$\log c_x = \log a - b \log x$$

while *Table 6-1* lists the values of the exponent b for various experience curves.

We can note here first that accounting practices within firms and across industries often complicate ''cost'' estimates and make comparability difficult. Secondly, we note that the cost of any multicomponent product is probably complicated by different cost

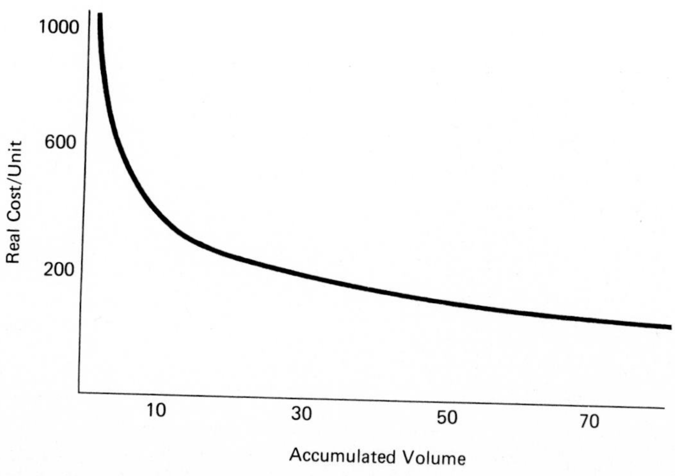

FIGURE 6-1 An 80 Percent Experience Curve: Linear Scale

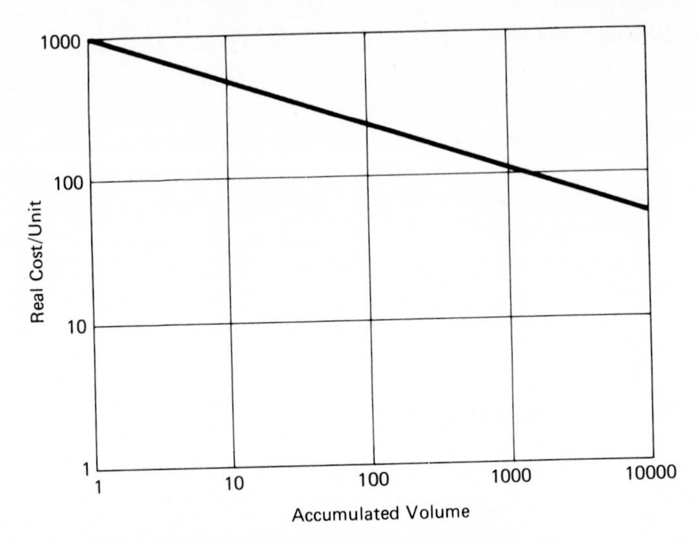

FIGURE 6-2 An 80 Percent Experience Curve: Logarithmic Scale

curves for those components (Hax and Majluf, 1984). Moreover, the cost of the first unit and accumulated experience at a particular time point is rarely known. BCG advised:

> Estimates of the cumulative unit volume obtained by the first year in the series were made by the Boston Consulting Group. The rule used was: previous experience about equals the amount added in doubling the annual unit rate. Thus, if 5 years are required to double the annual rate, the sum of production in the 5 years approximates the cumulative experience at the beginning of the 5 years. This rule is accurate in all cases in which a constant growth rate applies. It should be noted that the estimate on initial cumulative volume is significant on logarithmic scales only when long prior experience and slow sales growth apply. (1968, p. 69)

THE EVOLUTION OF THE EXPERIENCE CONCEPT

People have long recognized the value of experience, learning to do things well and more efficiently. For example, experienced tradesmen, like experienced managers, are more valued and more highly paid than others because they have met the test of experience. It is

TABLE 6-1 Value of Exponent for Various Experience Curves

Experience Curve	*b*
100%	0.000
90	.152
80	.322
70	.515
60	.738

not only mastery of repetitive tasks that characterizes such people but their ability to use what they know in new and difficult situations to define problems so they can be solved. In this way, experienced people extend their experience. Let us see how the notions of learning and experience entered the lexicon of the strategic manager.

Noting the advantages of automation in the Industrial Revolution, Chauncey Jerome, a pioneer clock manufacturer, wrote in 1860:

> The business of manufacture of them has become so systematized of late that it has brought the prices exceedingly low and it has long been the astonishment of the whole world that they could be made so cheap yet be good. (Abell and Hammond, 1979, p. 106)

Yet, despite the obvious need to explain this industrial productivity, little systematic study took place.

Indeed, it was not until 1925 that the commander of the Wright-Patterson air base observed ''learning'' and reported that the number of direct labor hours required to assemble a plane decreased as the number of aircraft assembled increased. Moreover, his observations were not made public until 1936 when T. P. Wright, then CEO of Curtis-Wright, Buffalo, New York, published ''Factors Affecting the Cost of Airplanes'' in the *Journal of Aeronautical Sciences* and suggested an exponential model of the learning phenomenon of the same form as the model cited above.

World War II provided many opportunities to observe learning, not only on planes but on Liberty Ships and other major and minor military equipment and munitions. Rapping (1965) reported that the cost index of Liberty Ships fell from 100 in December, 1941, to 45 by December, 1944—a 40 percent productivity gain made possible in part because of the new scale of shipbuilding needed to satisfy the war effort. New designs, the use of mass production techniques, initially inexperienced labor like ''Rosie the Riveter,'' and managers who were ignorant of shipbuilding, were all crucial elements of a naive start-up scenario followed by long and large production runs which ''exaggerated'' the learning effect over the cost declines normally observable in industry.

Nevertheless, the use of the ''aircraft learning curve'' was restricted to the defense and allied industries and their government customers. Upper management as well as business educators appeared not to see the relevance of the learning concept.

Only in 1954 was business generally given its first public view of learning by Frank J. Andress in the *Harvard Business Review*. Andress, who argued that the concept could be applied outside the aircraft industry, began with a description of the following incident:

> During World War II an executive of a home appliance manufacturing company chanced to cross paths with an executive of a large West Coast aircraft firm. The appliance executive mentioned that it had taken his company two years to determine the exact cost of the electric refrigerator which it manufactured.
>
> The aircraft executive pointed out that in many cases his company had been forced to determine costs on similar items in a matter of a few minutes, and said, "I'll bet you a steak dinner that I can predict the cost of your 200,000th refrigerator within 120% accuracy by using a learning curve based on aircraft production."
>
> The manufacturing executive accepted the bet. The only information he furnished was the weight of the refrigerator and the cost of the first unit produced.

During the next few minutes he watched while the aircraft executive worked with pencil, ruler, and log-log graph paper.

When he had completed plotting the curve, the aircraft executive stated: "Your 200,000th unit should cost you $162.50."

"Just drop the 50 cents," the appliance executive said. "It was actually $162.00."

Andress advised business that learning by repetition led to efficiency, that the scope and pace of cost improvement was regular and predictable, and he argued that the concept could be widely applied across industry. Indeed, in 1954, Andress anticipated the application of the learning curve to the nonmanufacturing operations of a business, and he argued that growing competition would make such a search for efficiency a necessity.

We must emphasize that Andress published this in 1954, twenty-nine years after the learning phenomenon was first measured. Note, too, that it was fourteen years later that the Boston Consulting Group published its treatise on experience, applying learning in just the way Andress had forecast. It had taken forty years for business to begin applying the lessons of experience, and according to *Fortune* only twelve years or so to misapply it and then begin to discard it (probably out of ignorance). The experience curve is a classic example of the difficulty of innovating in business.

Andress made other contributions which demonstrate the value to managers of thoroughly using research. Moreover, his contributions suggest that little progress has been made in developing greater universal knowledge of the experience phenomenon in the past thirty years, perhaps because users of the experience concept have ignored Andress's and others' cautions about the tool. Andress wrote, ''From the management viewpoint, there is a real problem in the constant need to be on guard against errors creeping into the data for the learning curve and distorting it,'' and he warned against errors which contemporary authors have also cited.

- He distinguished between productivity and learning because learning is repeated whenever a new model is introduced while productivity gains per se are sustainable.
- He pointed out that the slope of the curve could be expected to differ depending upon the labor content of the work—a higher labor content afforded greater opportunities for learning.
- He also advised that the slope of the curve (the rate of labor cost reduction) could be expected to change as output accumulated noting that ''subsequent factors entered the picture, and the curve became quite unpredictable.''
- He warned that the cost of proceeding down the learning curve had to be weighed against the benefits of a lower cost position and he attracted attention to the significance of the anticipated length of the production run in making that decision.
- He warned that it is the cost portion of value which is subject to learning and that changes in operating methods and labor costs (and even purchasing practices where sales prices are constrained by competition) all affect the short-term rate of cost decline.
- Finally, he cautioned that rate of production and capacity utilization affect labor costs.

In 1959, Conway and Schultz presented a paper on the ''Manufacturing Progress Function'' and noted that increased efficiency and cost reductions stemmed from other sources besides learning. They added considerably to our knowledge of the variability and difficulty of using learning curves and also introduced rate or production and total accumulated volume (as well as duration of production) as factors to be considered in managing costs. Tooling methods, design changes, quality incentives—all were held to contribute to cost declines.

Significantly, they noted a problem associated with the aggregated cost of many products, for example, airplanes. Airplanes are assembled from many products and components, some unique to one plane or model, others used in many. Thus the cost of an airplane is an aggregated cost, and they pointed out that the sum of a series of exponential functions is not another exponential function unless the bases are identical. They stated their conviction that, for various types of operations, the powers or characteristics of learning curves differed—"hence the attainment of a convex shape rather than a linear shape would follow their addition" (p. 44).

It is worth noting the full range of their conclusions and advice on the use of learning curves:

- First cost is difficult to estimate *de novo*. Most engineering estimates are better made for a "stable" level of production, say the one-hundredth or two-hundredth, or one-thousandth or two-thousandth unit, depending on the expected production run, and the earlier curve estimated based on expected slopes. Typically, early points are overemphasized when plotting log-log lines.
- Model fit is not stable; for example, if redesign occurs or if rework is eliminated, a new model may be necessary.
- Wide ranges of slopes occur.
- Once a control or quantitative objective is imposed on an organization, there are strong forces created to make the performance fit the objective; thus use of an experience curve as a control mechanism will affect the data.
- Effort is needed to get cost down, and central to marshalling that effort is expectation. Progress does not occur unless it is expected *and* rewarded.

Conway and Schultz concluded:

> There are significant differences in patterns of progress for different industries, firms, and products and type of work. There is no such thing as a fundamental law of progress such as the 80% learning curve used in the aircraft industry. *No particular slope is universal, and probably there is not even a common model.* (p. 53, emphasis added)

WHAT MAKES COSTS GO DOWN?

Alchian (1959) and Hirschleifer (1962) were among the first economists to attempt to reconcile the classic U-shaped cost curve of static economic analysis (where unit costs fall and then rise) with the dynamics of the experience curve and its seemingly endless unit cost decline. Hirschleifer noted the paradox: Although economic theory teaches that at equilibrium in a competitive market marginal cost must be rising (since it becomes increasingly costly to raise output to meet successive increments of demand with stable technology and input prices—the law of diminishing returns), managers feel that additional units are *not* increasingly costly to produce, except under extreme and exceptional conditions.

Alchian moved towards a resolution of this inconsistency between theory and practice by proposing that cost is a function of *rate* of output and scheduled *volume* of output. Economics heretofore had largely focused on total volume per period and ignored accumulated volume. Nevertheless, expected volume additions and total historical volume are both cues to management's assessment of the strength of demand over time. Thus, Alchian and Hirschleifer brought Conway's and Schultz's notions of accumulated volume into the economists' purview—rate of growth, duration, and cumulative expected production all became relevant. Engineers and managers, of course, have dealt with these distinctions in many different circumstances over the years. Power station design, for example, requires a long-term commitment to both peak and base loads, and utility regulation necessitates an assumption about the life of a project and the total demand for the services it can provide.

Accumulated volume and volume growth are crucial issues in management decision making. An assessment of total demand and the rate of demand growth over the life of a production facility is necessary before committing to an initial cost position, and these same factors determine whether there will be opportunities for cost reduction. The duration of high demand affords opportunities for both learning and technological progress in both product and process design. Total expected production will influence the primary choice of process and scale—in accounting terms, the commitment of fixed capital and a commitment to a particular mix of variable costs.

Faddish goods, such as hula hoops, require subcontracted production rather than commitments to high fixed costs. By comparison, Coleco's phenomenal and relatively long-lasting success with its Cabbage Patch dolls warranted plant commitments, while its inability to supply the huge market it found was a result of its initial decision to subcontract production.

PRICE AND EXPERIENCE

In 1968, the Boston Consulting Group published its *Perspectives on Experience* and hypothesized:

> Prices follow the same patterns as cost, if the relationships between competitors is stable. If they don't, the relationship between competitors becomes increasingly unstable.
>
> If cost is a function of accumulated experience, then profit is a function of sustained market share, which therefore has an intrinsic and calculable value. (1968, p. 19)

The importance of these two hypotheses in practice is considerable. They suggest that management should consider attempts to reduce its costs so that it can cut prices and capture market share. Cutting costs thus gives the firm an opportunity to develop a defensible and increasing competitive advantage.

These general propositions and their obvious implications were intended as a platform for company-specific research by BCG on particular consulting engagements. Nevertheless, they led many companies to foolhardy cost and price reduction programs without benefit of counsel and with no consideration of the long-run implications of their growing capital investments and price cutting decisions in their particular industry circumstances. Paradoxically, these companies were ignoring the accumulated experience of many industries and, indeed, the experience we have just reported—the experience which had accumulated over time in the application of learning curves in industry. The Boston Consulting Group warned its readers of just these dangers—but apparently its cautions went unnoticed as many companies jumped on the ''cost cutting'' bandwagon and began what ultimately became destructive and profitless fights for market share (Fruhan, 1972; Chevalier, 1974).

LEARNING VERSUS EXPERIENCE

The major difference between the aircraft industry's 80 percent learning curve and the Boston Consulting Group's experience curve was BCG's emphasis on price and total costs, rather than manufacturing costs, and its emphasis on the competitive value of high market share. BCG's empirical support for its propositions was restricted to price-based experience curves, which presented a remarkably consistent set of patterns ranging across a wide variety of industries, including electronics, petrochemicals, and primary metals. The evidence supported their case that prices declined by constant percentages with each doubling of total units produced. But the critical part of their argument was that, if prices declined (according to a predictable pattern), sellers' costs had to decline quickly enough to stay below prices and preserve margins. And, they argued, if costs declined more quickly than price, the margins would grow, signalling competitors of an opportunity worth investigating. More competition, and more capacity, would put new pressure on prices to bring them back in line with the consistent cost decline pattern, as *Figure 6-3* shows.

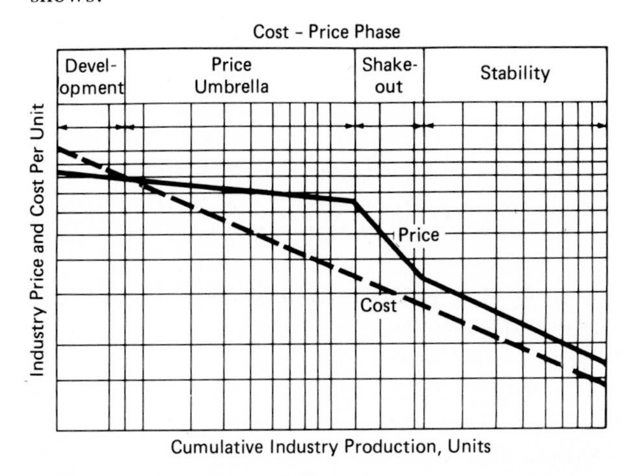

FIGURE 6-3 Typical Price-Cost Relationship

Source: Adapted from *Perspectives on Experience* (Boston: The Boston Consulting Group, 1972), p. 21

EXPERIENCE AND COMPETITIVE STABILITY

BCG's most important conclusion was that competitive relationships cannot be stable when one company has a large market share and manages it so that its incremental accumulated experience allows it to lower costs relative to the competition (BCG, 1968). Lower costs, of course, in simple terms, lead to market power and potentially to further market share gains.

BCG proposed that stable competitive relationships can only occur where price and cost closely follow the same pattern—that is, when prices and costs decline at the same rate and where all competitors are able to maintain the same relative cost positions, as indicated by stable market shares.

The implications of such an ''iron law'' of market share and market power are powerful, *if it holds*. It would mean that ultimately any market will be dominated by one competitor, so long as that competitor follows the BCG cost control prescriptions.

MARKET SHARE, MARKET POWER, AND SECURITY

A firm's performance from the pursuit of market share does not depend on *whether* the law of market share power holds, but rather the strategy will work *while* the law holds. Businesses survive so long as they are able to stay in touch with the market. Thus, it is not share that counts, but creating value in the eyes of the customer and being responsive to the customer's needs. Changes in taste or demographic shifts in the market, revised prices for substitutes or complementary goods, all influence demand for the product and the ultimate size of the market.

Remember, the strength that comes from having a low cost position can become a weakness if the market changes—for example, if consumers or buyers find their needs have changed or if some creative and innovative competitor, or new entrant, has found a way to satisfy these same needs in a way which offers the consumer more value. In such circumstances, the fixed asset commitments required to reach a low cost position in many markets can become a mill-stone around the corporate neck. Timex's efficient assembly operations had been the source of its competitive strength in the low-priced watch industry worldwide for over twenty years, but they became largely irrelevant when Texas Instruments (TI) entered the market with digital watches. On entry, TI probably enjoyed a lower cost position than Timex and the TI watch was an electronic product on which TI could anticipate a fast ''start-up'' cost decline—one that Timex's old technology could not duplicate.

The real point of BCG's theory, in simple terms, was that ultimately profit margin is a function of sustained market share. Essentially, however, that is a tautology, since it was share that yielded low cost and price power and further market share gains. It's akin to the ''buy low, sell high'' rule for stock market success—true, but difficult to practice, as BCG warned.

Market share is only an indicator of strength, not a security guarantee. A danger with strategies heavily dependent on the experience curve is that the people of the organization may become inward-looking, operations-dominated and myopic. An experience curve strategy is often erroneously believed to be a production strategy. Some managers forget that sensitivity to the market and customers' needs is necessary if they are to sell the product. Sustained willingness to buy is the only guarantee of an opportunity to double sales volume over any time period.

The cost declines promised by the experience curve are most germane during the start-up and early growth stages of the life cycle. Here accumulated volume grows quickly, almost certainly before substitutes are developed by competitors. And here costs can be expected to decline rapidly, if managerial emphasis is put on this objective. The puzzle for management is to take advantage of the opportunity to reach a dominant position without being trapped in a destructive competition by an overcommitment based on false expectations of continuing growth for an unchanged product.

A LESSON FROM WELFARE ECONOMICS

The reason competition based on aggressive price cutting is so destructive is that it is naive. It does not manage value effectively. Let us reflect for a moment on one of the concepts used by welfare economists, *surplus,* particularly the consumers' surplus, and use it to help us see how value can be mismanaged by short-sighted price cutting.

As time passes, an aggressive firm attempting to build market share and market power is likely to advertise and improve its product to increase demand. At the same time, it is likely to invest in new designs and new high-capacity equipment to lower its average cost position. However, these decisions give it higher fixed costs while cutting variable costs. Success, and the urge to build share, may lead the company to cut prices, too. Hence, the supply and demand charts at times 1, 2, and 3 in *Figure 6-4* reflect a successful marketer improving production capabilities and cutting prices to build additional volume and share.

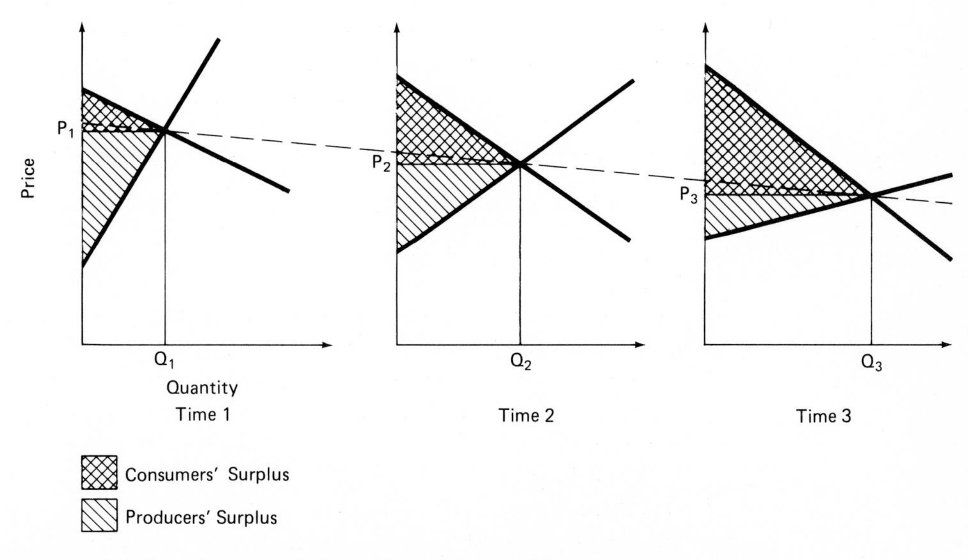

FIGURE 6-4 The Reallocation of Value with "Experience"-Based Pricing

Imagine that price cuts, new distribution channels, quality improvements and advertising combine to move the demand curve to the right and make it more inelastic, as *Figure 6-4* shows between times 1 and 2. Such success encourages the firm to expand its capacity and improve its operating efficiency again. Improved production capabilities and new capacity flatten the supply curve and move it to the right. Its aggressive competitive practices and its success are likely to prompt the firm to cut its prices again, ultimately reaching the situation portrayed as time 3 in *Figure 6-4*.

Obviously, prudent managers would invest in advertising and plant only if they believed there will be a return. This is likely, however, only if the demand curve stays up—that is, stays well to the right. Moreover, they should cut price only if they believe building market share is likely to be profitable and defensible once captured.

Yet price splits the value created by the product offering into two components: One, the consumers' surplus,[1] shown by the closely hatched area(s) above the market price between and to the left of the supply and demand curves; and two, the producers' surplus,[2] below the market price, between and to the left of the supply and demand curves. Note the reduction in the proportion of the value created by the producer but kept by the consumer, the consumers' surplus, versus that kept or captured by the producer, the producers' surplus, when the producer cuts prices.

Figure 6-4, therefore, illustrates one of the costs of building share with aggressive price cutting: the producers' retention of less and less of the value created within any time period as prices are cut. This means it will take longer and longer to recover the investments, and recovery is possible only if demand can be maintained. If for any reason this is not so, the cash invested may be lost and unrecoverable. Indeed, there are many "possible causes" of such a situation, including new product offerings by existing or new competitors. The dwindling producers' surplus also signals that profits are falling, leaving less money to wage marketing or production wars in the future.

Thus, whenever the value of market share is threatened or the certainty of having time to get capital out of a business is low, the experience curve is likely to be inapplicable. Abell and Hammond (1979) suggest that care is needed in using experience-based strategies in these situations:

- if value added is low;
- if competitors have low cost positions because of some non-experience-based resource or relationship;
- if technology is rapidly transferred among firms by equipment manufacturers or licensing, for example;
- when the effects of scale are low.

They warn that patents, as well as seasonal, and cyclical factors, can also complicate the use of the experience concept.

[1]The consumers' surplus is a measure of the value captured by those buyers who, although willing to purchase a good at a price above market, are able to buy at market. The market price is a "deal" in their eyes and the indifference between the price they were willing to pay and market is a surplus or benefit they enjoy—the consumers' surplus.

[2]The producers' surplus measures the difference between market price and a lower price at which some (efficient) producers are willing to supply.

THE ABUSE OF THE EXPERIENCE CONCEPT

Nevertheless, these warnings—like those of Alchian and Hirschleifer, Conway and Schultz, and later BCG—concerning the importance of the total market and the prospect of market saturation, have sometimes been ignored by management intent on achieving a low cost position. Some managers, in the interests of capturing the value of ''experience,'' have committed to expensive plants completed as the market was nearing saturation.

Management can be a victim of ''mob psychology,'' as McKinsey noted in 1932. Spurred by naive overconfidence, managers may pursue a growing market with plant additions without considering the implications of competitive plant expansions (and consequent potential loss of manufacturer power) in the market. The US color TV industry in the late 1960s and the US chain saw industry in the mid 1970s suffered this fate.

Similarly, managers may pursue cost reductions with such gusto that they lose sight of the danger in the (cost) advantage: reduced flexibility in the face of market or technological change. Henry Ford discovered this danger to his great chagrin in 1927 when General Motors' multidivisional strategy forced the discontinuation of the Model T and a twelve-month shut-down for retooling for the Model A (Abernathy and Wayne, 1974). Indeed, there are ''limits to the learning curve,'' as Abernathy and Wayne wrote.

SOME IMPORTANT CONSIDERATIONS IN MANAGING EXPERIENCE

Earlier we noted that costs go down because of the rate of output and scheduled volume and that these factors combine to create opportunities for commitments to scale (economies), technological progress, and learning. These appear to be the levers for cost management. Sultan (1975) estimated that the prices of steam turbine generators fell between 1904 and 1970 on an 87 percent experience curve—that is, the ratio of price decline per unit with each doubling of experience was 87 percent. As he explained it, if the total output of steam turbine generators on a cumulative throughput basis climbed from 6 million to 12 million kilowatts, the cost per kilowatt would decline from an index of 100 to an index of 87. However, he found that there were two principal components for this cost decline: a 93 percent curve for cumulative production experience, or learning, and a 93 percent curve for product technology. The effects are multiplicative, hence the 87 percent product experience curve (.93 × .93 − 87).

Figure 6-5 illustrates one of the critical issues in using the experience curve: it is important to define the area of investigation carefully. On the figure, the 87 percent slope applies to generating units of a particular size. Considering the total costs of generating capacity, a 70 percent curve holds, according to Sultan. Experience developed as the industry itself acquired the capability to produce increasingly large-scale units and took advantage of learning and technological progress.

In a study of the petrochemicals market, Stobaugh and Townsend (1975) reported on the effects of competition, product standardization, experience and scale as causes of lower prices. They summarized as follows:

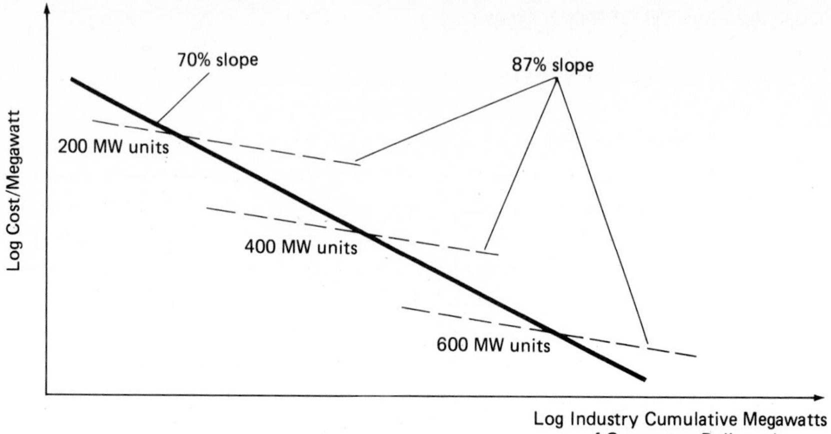

FIGURE 6-5 **Cost Experience for Steam Turbine Generators**

Source: Day and Montgomery, "Diagnosing the Experience Curve," *Journal of Marketing,* 47, Spring 1983, 47.

> Competition, product standardization, experience, and static scale are all significant factors in petrochemical price declines and act in the expected directions. They become important over the 3 to 7 year interval relevant for investment decisions. By the time a petrochemical has three or more producers, experience and the combined effect of the unidentified time-related variables generally have a larger effect than the number of producers, product standardization, or static scale. (p. 26)

They presented their findings on the price declines of eight petrochemicals over a five-year period as shown in *Table 6-2*.

Note that Sultan's and Stobaugh and Townsend's research was founded on price-based experience curves. Experience curves can be estimated for price or cost for products, for industries, or for companies, and they can be estimated across time or across companies or both. Each form of analysis presents its own insights and presents its own

TABLE 6-2 **Sources of Price Decline for Eight Petrochemicals**

Average 5-Year Change (Allowed) in Factor(s)	*Percent Relative Reduction of Real Price over 5-Year Interval*
40% more competitors	5%
Standardized quality	5
150% more accumulated experience	12
60% more output per producer	5
Other time-related factors over 5 years	12
All factors*	34%

*Again, individual factors are multiplicative, not additive. Thus, individual reductions multiply to give total reduction: (1-.05) (1-.05) (1-.12) (1-.05) (1-.12) = (1-.34)

Source: Stobaugh and Townsend, "Price Forecasting and Strategic Planning: The Case of Petrochemicals," *Journal of Marketing Research,* 12, February 1975, 19–29.

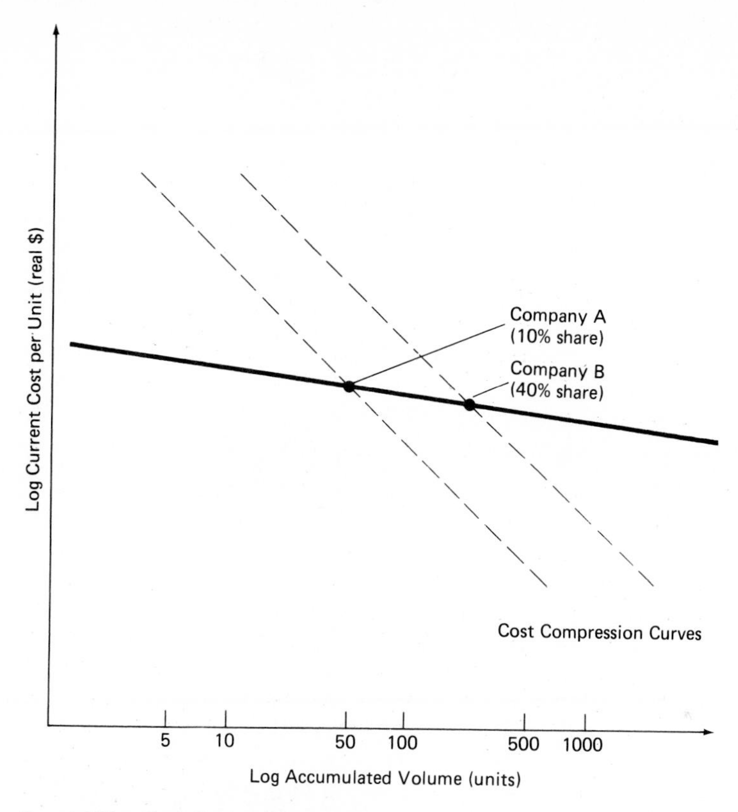

FIGURE 6-6 Competitive Cost Comparison Curves

Source: Day and Montgomery, "Diagnosing the Experience Curve," *Journal of Marketing,* 47, Spring 1983, 49.

problems. Day and Montgomery (1983) point out that the cross-sectional experience curves encompassing the output of many separate producers are likely to be shallower than curves calculated on the experience of a single decision maker. Biggadike (1977) reported that the real price per unit of a split-system central air conditioner has been declining on an 80 percent curve with each doubling of industry experience, yet a cross-sectional curve describing several major competitors' costs had a slope of 92 percent.

Figure 6-6 illustrates the difference between industry and firm experience curves. Day and Montgomery offer the following explanations for the steeper curves achieved by a corporation (when compared with an industry):

1 Followers may enjoy lower initial costs than the pioneer—if they can learn from the pioneer's successes and mistakes by hiring key personnel, or reverse-engineering its products, or by duplicating its manufacturing and distribution or service systems.
2 Followers may be able to leapfrog the early entrant by using new manufacturing technology or by building a plant to a larger scale, and by sourcing components from producers whose own experience is larger than the innovators'—that is, take advantage of shared experience.

TABLE 6-3
Experience and the Relative Contribution of Various Cost Components

	Cost Component									
	A (75% Curve; 1 Item Per Unit)			*B (80% Curve; 1 Item Per Unit)*			*C (80% Curve; 2 Items Per Unit)*			
Experience with the Product	*Component Experience*	*Cost Per Unit*	*% of Total Unit Cost*	*Component Experience*	*Cost Per Unit*	*% of Total Unit Cost*	*Component Experience*	*Cost Per Unit*	*% of Total Unit Cost*	*Total Unit Cost*
100 units	100	$70.00	70.0%	10,100	$20.00	20.0%	1,000,200	$10.00	10.0%	$100.00
1,000 units	1,000	26.92	47.8	11,000	19.46	34.5	1,002,000	9.99	17.7	56.37
10,000 units	10,000	10.35	28.4	20,000	16.05	44.2	1,020,000	9.94	27.4	36.34
100,000 units	100,000	3.98	17.5	110,000	9.27	40.9	1,200,000	9.43	41.6	22.68
1,000,000 units	1,000,000	1.53	11.7	1,010,000	4.53	34.6	3,000,000	7.02	53.7	13.08

Source: Abell and Hammond, *Strategic Market Planning: Problems and Analytical Approaches*, Englewood Cliffs, NJ: Prentice-Hall, 1979, p. 126.

SHARED EXPERIENCE

Shared experience is an important confounding factor in the interpretations of relative cost positions in nearly every industry. For example, a diversified wire producer making steel, copper, and aluminum wire might well have a considerable advantage over a specialist because of its ability to spread its development, marketing, and overhead costs over a larger sales volume.

While shared experience often frustrates measurement and has to be estimated, it is clear that a company which has produced 900,000 units has an advantage over two major competitors who have produced 700,000 and 400,000 units, respectively. But if this leading competitor's product incorporates components which are used in another related product with a 600,000 accumulated volume, it shares components with a total effective accumulated experience of 1.5 million, making it an even more formidable competitor.

The difficult question, as in many strategic studies, is the issue of what is a relevant market. Shared experience is relevant where the production process has built on earlier products' components and where costs are shared. A smart manager of a "first-in" competitor can confound potential entrants by his or her ability to produce innovative products at low cost, for example, by re-using tried components in innovative ways to create value in the marketplace. The relevant experience curves of such a producer concern components rather than the new product per se.

For companies which exploit shared experience within a product line which assembles components or modules or systems in different configurations, it is important to note that the strategic cost factor changes over time and as experience accumulates. The impact of cutting the cost of a particular component of the final product varies over time, as *Table 6-3* shows. Components have different relative cost impacts over time because the company's length of experience with each component varies. It is sensible that management's attention should turn towards the component where the current impact of a cost cut on overall production cost is the highest. And, when cost reduction is achieved on such a component, the manager's interest must shift to the next component where cost reduction can significantly affect the product's costs. In *Table 6-3*, the "critical" component is A at first, then B and finally C.

EXPERIENCE, PRICE, AND VALUE

Business decisions necessitate tradeoffs between objectives, such as profit and growth, short-term advantage and long-term security, and value creation and profit-taking. In evaluating the resource base of the firm, experience is a summarization of the firm's success at combining the critical functions of marketing, production and finance in a cost-efficient way. Effectiveness, however, is best represented by the value created in the market by the firm's product or service offerings, and a firm's ability to hold its sales volume *and* its prices and maintain its share of the market, especially when that market is growing.

Managing experience, too, means making tradeoffs. To illustrate, there is potential inflexibility in a capital-intensive production strategy. For example, a company which has integrated backwards to gain control of raw materials sources, in order to provide a greater percentage of the total value added in the industry chain, is less flexible than one which buys its inputs on the open market. Yet there is tremendous strategic flexibility in having a relative cost advantage. This strategic flexibility may be the ultimate advantage of experience-based cost reductions. The low-cost producer may or may not make a decision to lower price, but the option, at a profit, is always available to such a producer. Faced with the prospect of new entrants, for example, a price cut may deter entry. And with no new entrants, and the other competitors operating at higher costs, a strategy of price maintenance can pay handsome profits to the low-cost producer.

Experience, prices, and value are, as we have shown above, inextricably interconnected. Simple, generic strategies based on low cost or low price can be useful reference points during the strategy formulation process. However, business success rarely comes from the simple application of generic strategies. In this chapter, for example, we have seen the long-term inflexibility that may be the result of some cost cutting and value adding strategies.

Value added and profit, the share of the value added captured by the firm, are ultimately the firm's critical competitive resources. Value added stems from a concentration on the customers' needs. Profitability and, ultimately, profit stem from the firm's ability to meet these needs in a creative as well as cost-effective manner.

Experience, properly applied, creates value by meeting consumer needs, while continuing efforts to control costs promote efficiency. So long as the firm understands the necessity to be sensitive to changing consumer needs, a low-cost position can give it competitive (pricing) flexibility against new entrants or price cutting competitors who did not pay attention to *both* demand and supply.

CUTTING COSTS IS MANAGEMENT'S RESPONSIBILITY

George Santayana wrote, "Those who don't understand the past are doomed to repeat it." For all its truth, this maxim is largely honored in the breech by US managers who, as a group, sometimes seem to hurry toward the future (or the latest management fad) with little sense of the tremendous resource of their past experience and its relevance to their mission of cost control. Indeed, the recent vogue of factory "quality circles," where workers gather to suggest ways to improve quality, is an attempt to capitalize on the experience of those most closely associated with the production process and use that information to raise productivity and lower costs. It is difficult to move beyond the past and create beyond experience if you don't know how you came to the present.

While the quest for lower costs must be tempered with a realistic understanding of the future longevity of the market and the prospects of profit, ultimately costs will not decline unless management acts as if it believes a cost decline is possible. Simply put, this is because cost management is ultimately a social activity. Cost improvements are always possible if people are encouraged to seek them and rewarded when they do:

> The industrial learning curve thus embraces more than the increasing skill of an individual by repetition of a simple operation. Instead, it describes a more complex organism—the collective efforts of many people, some in line and others in staff

> positions, but all aiming to accomplish a common task progressively more efficiently. (Hirschman, 1964, p. 128)

Experience thus summarizes management's coordination of its own organization and, as well, requires an understanding of the forces at work in the industrial and competitive environment of the organization. We explore the firm's economic environment, the industry and competition, in Chapters 7 and 8.

chapter 7

The Industry Environment

INTRODUCTION

For managers, the purpose of environmental analysis is to understand the forces changing their industry. They have to understand the reasons for turbulence and the reasons for periods of relative stability and calm. Ultimately, they have to be alert to the forces of change. Some of these will undoubtedly come from within their own organizations, from dissatisfaction with present results or a realization that some corporate resource can be turned to greater advantage in the marketplace. Others will stem from the actions of one competitor or even many competitors in their industry.

Yet senior managers seldom study their industry. It is a time-consuming task, typically delegated to staff whose conclusions are tested against the experience of senior management.

Industry analysis should, therefore, result in conclusions which help managers evaluate and formulate strategies on the basis of reliable information. Reliable information is vital when critical tradeoffs have to be made between long-term and short-term profit—in other words, between short-term profit and current corporate growth. Analysis must help managers understand the forces driving change, anticipate the actions of competition and the consequences of those actions, and help them anticipate consequences of any commitments the firm might make to change.

Managers don't like surprises, and they don't like to be caught unaware. Consequently, they have to develop an understanding of their environment, the source of most surprises, and an ability to use that understanding. Fayol (1972) went so far as to say, "managing means looking ahead . . . to foresee . . . to assess the future and make provision for it" (p. 43).

We have split environmental analysis into three sections. In this chapter, we examine the industry, where the primary choice is what role to take. In Chapter 8, we examine how to compete, once you have chosen your industry role or have recommitted to it. And Chapter 9 discusses the greater environment which affects all industries, that is, society itself.

In this chapter, then, we deal with the industry environment. We have chosen an approach which is exhaustive, so that you'll have a reference point for any complete study you may wish to make. Indeed, a complete industry analysis will give less experienced people significant insights into the workings of both their industry and their firm. We caution you, however, that the scope of a complete industry analysis is well outside normal managerial experience. Typically, managers will select from this framework those pieces which they believe are likely to reveal the sources of change and the opportunities and problems which industry change presents for them. Experienced people tend to be more accurate in their assessment than those with less experience.

A complete assessment is most relevant in times of turbulence, where the strategic decision is to change or recommit to an historical industry position. If the industry is changing drastically, however, "all previous bets are off," and the strategist must take a long, hard look at the firm's industry and competitive position in it. At such times, the strategist seeks a target for reinvestment so that the firm can move with the times, preserving the value that has been created in the past and adding to it by investing in the center of future profit opportunity—for example, by taking a new role in the firm's traditional industry chain.

A comprehensive framework is invaluable, because it tells you where to begin and what to do, and it gives you confidence about completing the task. And, as your experience accumulates, the industry analysis framework will help you quickly pinpoint sources of vulnerability and opportunities evolving in the marketplace.

FUNDAMENTALS OF ENVIRONMENTAL ANALYSIS

When managers allocate human and capital resources to a project, they commit or recommit their oganization to a strategy they believe will succeed and will enhance the value of the firm. No matter what results have been achieved already, the firm's commitment is based on an expectation of future results. But results depend not only on what is done; they are also conditional on the future.

Because of this, prudent managers try to become aware of trends and recognize events which will make their jobs easier—*opportunities*—and those trends or events which will make achieving their objectives more difficult—*threats*. Opportunities exist when we are able to work with or use the environment; in sailing, being able to run with the wind is an opportunity. Threats exist in both management and sailing when the winds change against us. Yet even when the environment is threatening, so long as we know where we are and where we want to be, we may be able to move towards our objective, albeit slowly. In other cases, we may find the environment so alien to our cause that we have to alter some of our objectives and seek new ones, even if only temporarily.

The purpose of environmental analysis is to identify the significant trends—that is, those likely to affect our results—early enough for management to provide for them. Such an analysis relies on two principles: one, that the future will evolve out of the present from the past; and two, although the future evolves from the past, that the future world will be different.

Insight is required. Environmental assessment and the forecasting inherent to it are more than simply projecting or extrapolating current trends and results. What management must do is to interpret current events and discover their meaning for the firm.

A realistic view of management's capability for effective environmental assessment is also necessary. Only if change can be interpreted in the light of earlier experience will it be noted, have meaning, and be intelligible to management (Johnson, 1967). Sharing this view of management's limitations in environmental assessment, while still stressing the importance of environmental data, McKinsey wrote during the Great Depression:

> The human mind . . . cannot make perfect decisions with reference to the variable factors which affect our business actions. Although this is true, we should not be discouraged of doing as well as we can. . . . [We] should guard against mistakes by securing all the information we can as a protection from our inherent tendency to be guided by mob psychology. (1932, p. 8)

Good managers make a healthy skepticism work for them in environmental analysis. They use all the information available. They avoid being slaves to tradition and are not closed-minded. They think for themselves, realizing that they cannot know when specific events will occur nor how important they will be. By knowing their organization and their environment, however, they prepare their firms for the future. When the unexpected occurs, they are able to understand quickly its real impact on their firms' interests and act appropriately.

A STAKEHOLDER APPROACH TO EFFECTIVE ENVIRONMENTAL ANALYSIS

What are the significant trends? Traditionally, strategic managers have considered competitive, technological, economic, political, and social (including demographic) trends. The dilemma is where to begin. All these trends are important, because each affects the level of demand or the conditions of supply which the firm meets in its markets.

Supply and demand describe the conditions of exchange between the firm's products and its environment, and we can note that very few organizations can exist for long without some form of exchange of input for output (Williamson, 1975; Pfeffer and Salancik, 1978). Indeed, the impacts of the environment on the terms of exchange—that is, the market price and quantity produced—demonstrate the interdependence of the firm and its environment. The firm's performance is the result of its exchanges with its environment.

We have therefore come to use an approach to environmental analysis which focuses on the stakeholders of this firm-environment exchange. *Figure 7-1* illustrates the range of stakeholders in the environment of a typical larger US firm. A stakeholder is any individual or organization whose behavior can directly affect the firm's future but is not under the firm's control (Freeman, 1981). Such groups have a stake in the firm, relationships with it, and interests in its results, as well as direct and indirect influence on those results. In short, there is an exchange of goods or services for money, or of approval for results, between the firm and such groups. The exact number of stakeholders to be considered will depend on the organization, and the weight given them is likely to vary depending upon the issues at hand and the circumstances surrounding the issues (Freeman, 1981; Emshoff and Freeman, 1979).

It is obvious that this stakeholder environment is wide and the interconnections among all the participants are likely to be complex. To manage this complexity, and to allocate our efforts where the environmental effect on the firm is greatest, we will work selectively and sequentially through our stakeholder set. Focusing on one group of

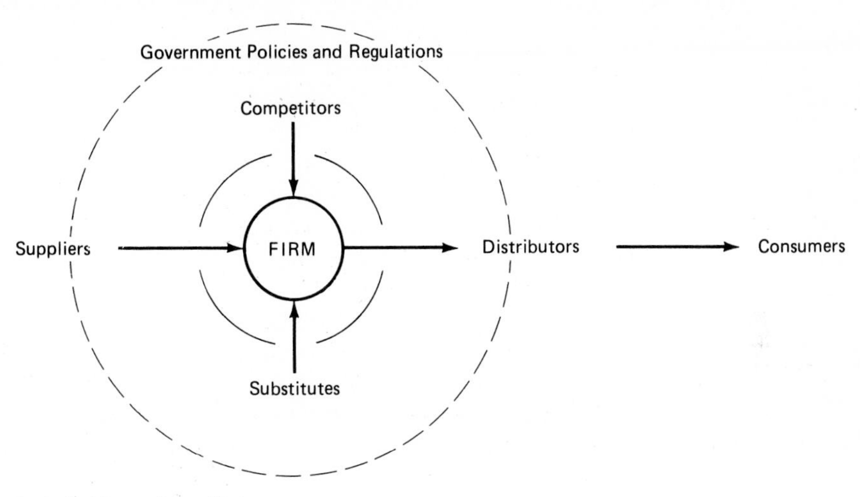

FIGURE 7-1 Stakeholders of the Firm

stakeholders at a time limits errors. The sequence helps make the relevant environmental issues clear and keeps the task manageable for those who have operating responsibilities in the organization.

Keep in mind that, in environmental analysis, our approach is to assess whether our strategy is consistent with the environment and to anticipate the future path of current events and their impact on our performance. Our objectives are to be realistic and to accurately distinguish minor change from structural changes, which are likely to have greater consequences for the viability of our strategy. The most important changes are those which:

1 affect the role of stakeholders and their power in our affairs;
2 alter the relative power of the players in our competitive arena; and
3 point to improved methods of operations.

These changes are likely sources of opportunities and threats. And whatever trends we identify, we must identify them in a timely manner because we want time to consider whether and how we should position our organization to take advantage of them, or, at worst, accommodate them.

Now, let us describe the order in which we analyze stakeholders to fully assess the firm's environment. First, we explore the production-distribution relationships in the industry, because these supplier and customer stakeholders have the most exchanges with the firm and therefore the most impact on it. Next, we move to competitors—indeed, competitors are stakeholders since their financial performance depends on the activities of the firm. Finally, we discuss the firm's social and political stakeholders, some of whom may have the power to forbid the firm to operate.

In this chapter, however, we will concentrate on the economic relationships between the firm and its stakeholders. Of course, some industrial stakeholders have social-political relationships with the firm, too. We will not deal with these here. This aspect of the industrial stakeholders as well as the firm's relationships with other, primarily non-economic, stakeholders will be discussed in Chapter 9.

THE INDUSTRIAL ENVIRONMENT

Although the firm is affected by many environmental factors, our analysis begins in the environment usually most relevant to the firm's operating and strategic decisions: its industry. We want a framework which organizes industry data to help us understand the basic economics of our industry and the behavior of our competitors. Amazingly, few firms have more than vague notions about their industry's structure and the future significance of their competitors' behavior.

The data we need are usually easy to collect, and, although there may be gaps, very rarely are these critical. Lack of information should not hamper industry analysis. Trade magazines and shows, customers, suppliers, and salespeople are all rich sources of information on industry and competitor performance. So, too, are annual reports, industry associations, and government statistics. Indeed, it is amazing how much information on a firm's industrial environment is available at minimal cost from government agencies, public libraries, or conversations with industry participants. Even small pieces of strategic intelligence can lead to important inferences about the industry and our competition.

STAKEHOLDERS IN THE INDUSTRY CHAIN

Every firm holds a position or *role* in the chain of activities necessary to convert natural and human resources into more valued goods or services and market them. The firm's role describes what it does—for example, it may be a miner, grower, manufacturer, distributor, or retailer.

Industrial power allows a firm to pursue its own objectives in its own ways. Firms without power are very dependent on those ahead and behind them in the industry's natural sequence of activities. To evaluate a firm's power in the industry, then, it is important to assess the interdependencies which exist between the firm and others in its chain.

The industry chain, also known as the commercialization chain, the production-distribution chain, and the value adding chain, is a subset of the firm's stakeholders, as shown within the dotted lines in *Figure 7-1*. The industry chain is illustrated separately in *Figure 7-2* and focuses attention on the exchanges between buyers and sellers—input/output relationships (McLean and Haigh, 1954). We will use the chain as the foundation of a framework for industry analysis.[1]

[1]While the graphics of the industry chain show suppliers and customers in a visually horizontal relationship to the firm, it is important to note that any merger between these parts is referred to as vertical integration, since the economist views the relationships from suppliers, through manufacturers, to customers as vertical. Similarly, economists refer to mergers between those competitors at the same stage in the chain—i.e., competitive manufacturers or competitive distributors—as horizontal. Following the tradition of strategic management, however, competitors are shown in a vertical relationship with the firm in *Figure 7-2*.

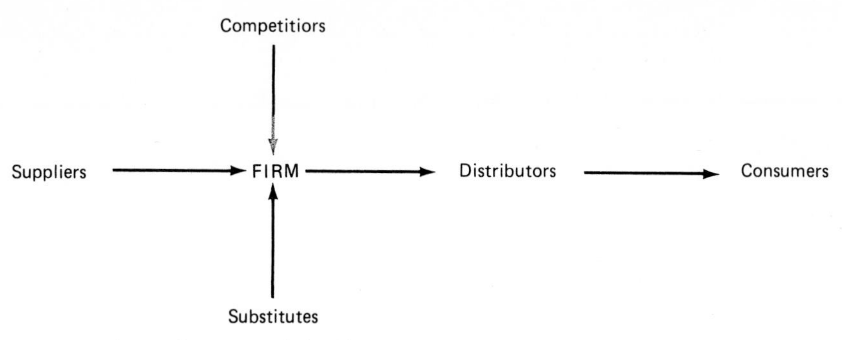

FIGURE 7-2 The Industrial Environment of the Firm

FRAMEWORK FOR INDUSTRY ANALYSIS

The Framework for Industry Analysis (*Figure 7-3*) organizes industry data so we can view the industry as a whole. The framework requires that we identify the major players in the industry and then collect data to describe its essential economics, competitive practices and trends, risk/reward structure, and the macroeconomy's impact on industry members. We will use this information to determine which roles have or promise greater relative power and to identify trends, and thereby the opportunities and threats, within the industry. A study of the industry and its structure is in fact akin to industry demographics: we are interested in corporate births and deaths, movement within the industry chain, geographical movements, and income and wealth statistics.

We begin by identifying the groups holding various roles in the industry and then describe the rest of the data needed for a very thorough industrial analysis. We simply work through the framework addressing each issue in turn. First, we need to know how many stages are in the industry chain and the identity of the key players and their relative importance. Then we need to know how they compete—what are the key economic characteristics and competitive variables, the results, the risks taken and rewards received at each stage as value is added.

The Players

Identifying the players requires us to consider who is in the industry, stage by stage. It is useful to record how many competitors there are at each stage and even how they are distributed by size or class. In most instances, it is useful to note the major competitors by name, and whether they serve a distinct or special market segment. Large corporations often play multiple roles with sister divisions acting as both suppliers and customers.

Suppliers, of course, include sources of raw material as well as manufacturers of intermediate goods. Ford, for example, buys tires but makes glass. Hence, it is a customer of Firestone and Goodyear as well as a buyer of silica sands. Prior to Polaroid's introduction of its SX-70 system, Kodak supplied instant film negatives to Polaroid.

Buyers include other manufacturers as well as wholesale and retail distributors and, ultimately, consumers. It is important to identify who the buyer is, and what type of demand influences sales. Sometimes the ultimate buyer may be strongly influenced by others. For example, although elevators are purchased by developers, architects usually

FIGURE 7-3 Framework for Industry Analysis

	Raw Material Supplier	Intermediate Goods Manufacturer	Final Manufacturer	Wholesaler	Retailer	Customer
The Players						
Names						
Number and size distribution						
Segments addressed						
Government's roles						
Entry/Exit trends						
Historical Elements of Competition						
Type of demand						
Product differentiation						
Price/Cost						
Quality/Service						
Value						
Capacity						
Timing of intense activity						
Likely changes						
Economic Characteristics (of operations)						
Growth						
Product life cycle stage						
Technology/Process						
Capital/Labor intensity						
Value added						
Fixed/Variable cost levels						
Breakeven volume						
Operating leverage						
Labor skills required						
Length of operating cycle						
Inventory position						
Receivables/Payables position						
Experience						
Macroeconomic Response						
Impact of business cycle						
Impact of fiscal policy						
Impact of monetary policy						
Inflation						
Robustness of demand						
Risk/Reward						
Profitability analysis						
Margin						
Turnover						
Leverage						
Profit share/Market share						
Sustainable growth rate						
Conclusions						
Risks taken						
Power, and rewards of power						
Problems						
Outlook						
Likely future competitive entrants						

make the specification decision. Because elevators have a derived demand function, sales occur only if developers expect a healthy primary demand for residential and commercial space. A peek inside a children's shoe store will show that, while parents purchase the shoes, even very young children have strong preferences which heavily impact the purchase decision.

Beyond identifying the players, an assessment of the profit impact of size may provide insights into the current and future importance of particular firms in the industry. Market share, or relative market share (your market share divided by that of your biggest competitor) is a useful measure of size and points to the market power of firms at different stages in the industry chain. Research by the Strategic Planning Institute and its associates on the Profit Impact of Market Strategy (PIMS) data base has pointed to a positive relationship between market share and profitability (Schoeffler, et al., 1974; Buzzell, et al., 1975), although others (Gale, 1972; Rumelt and Wensley, 1981; Hatten and Hatten, 1985; Woo, 1983) have challenged the general application of the finding.

Profits, profitability, and profit share all carry important information on the viability of a business. The crucial factor for management is not whether profitability and market share are correlated generally, but how they are related *in their own business*. The answer may help us evaluate alternative strategies, the adequacy of our present strategy, and the vulnerability of our present position in our industry. In fact, a firm's management should be alert to growing competitors who are earning profits greater than its own and holding a profit share greater than its own market share. Such companies are building not only market share but probably also cash reserves for additional expansion, productivity improvements and, thereby, increased market power (Hatten and Hatten, 1985).

In addition to identifying the major players and the size distributions of the industry's members, it is worth noting the multiple roles of government in the industry. In the auto industry, for example, government's role has changed over the years. As well as providing the legal structure for corporate activity via limited liability, the government has mandated safety and pollution standards and the 55 mph speed limit. It guaranteed the Chrysler bail-out loans and is a customer, tax collector, and source of information for the industry. Furthermore, government's fiscal and monetary policies can stimulate or reduce private demand for cars.

A knowledge of entry and exit trends can enrich our analysis and understanding of an industry's competitive environment (Porter, 1980). Entry to the ranks of a firm's suppliers may mean opportunity for lower-priced inputs. Exit may mean more power to the survivors, since competition is reduced. Additionally, entering and exiting capacity can signal efficient scale in the industry. Entrants can be presumed to be making their best commitments with plant design, and so point to currently efficient scale. Plant closures should point to size which is marginally profitable (Scherer, 1970).

Historically Exploited Competitive Weapons

Having identified who is in the industry, it is useful to consider how they compete. Many weapons exist: price, quality and service, value, capacity and availability, and product differentiation, to name a few. Porter (1980) says there are three generic strategies which are successful: cost leadership, differentiation, and focus. While we will defer our discussion of the firm's competitors until later, historic patterns of competition throughout the industry point to strategies that have worked at a particular industry stage in the past and to those that may be used again. Intense competition upstream at supplier stages may lead to lower manufacturers' costs. Intense competition downstream by distributors may lead to higher manufacturers' margins.

In considering competition in each stage, try to determine what events lead to outbursts of intense competitive behavior and whether these conform to any sequence or pattern. Knowledge of when competitive battles erupt or how they are timed may help you anticipate future competitive events in your stage elsewhere in the industry. For example, price wars afflict the soft drink industry early in the summer when Pepsi or Coke lowers prices. Awareness of this strategy and its timing is important to retailers who are dealing with other soft drink producers and planning their inventories to synchronize with price reductions and advertising in the industry.

Economic Characteristics

Economic logic suggests that certain industries work in certain ways. Understanding the economic rationale for industry behavior should help you develop your personal view of what the characteristics of a successful company in each industry role should be. For example, because iron ore is heavy and has a relatively low bulk value, the steel industry tends to concentrate or partially refine the ore before it is transported to the steel mills. The paper industry usually locates its mills near forest reserves, although the paper recyclers, like the scrap metal industry, locate near or in old urban centers where supply is plentiful and reliable.

Determining the basic economic characteristics at each stage of the industry chain is important, because that knowledge can help you develop an economic rationale for your own strategy. The characteristics of the industry tend to generate rules. For example, in the auto industry, some dealers use the following rule to control their used car inventories: "Don't let the sun set on a forty-five-day used car." Meat packers have an even more vivid inventory rule: "Sell it or smell it." Unconsciously violating industry rules often leads to failure. And innovations which consciously break with the conventional wisdom of the industry must be thoroughly analyzed and tested before commitment. McDonald's, for example, broke the traditional rule of the hamburger industry, "fresh to order," but Ray Kroc had the experience and success of the McDonald brothers' operation in California to bolster his confidence in the method and its product when he successfully automated (Kroc, 1977).

Certain basic data are needed to describe an industry and its economics. What type of demand drives the market? Farm equipment and fire engines may be favored by some buyers because the products are red or green or yellow, but they are certainly not consumer goods and are difficult to sell when farm income or local tax revenues are down.

Where are property, plant, and equipment located? Why? What is an industry's geographic scope? Bulk value of raw materials and transport costs, limited sources of supply, or the need for large energy or water resources may restrict some industry stages to particular locations. Food distribution, for example, tends to be a regional business. Brewing has developed a national scope as the US population migrated from the Northeast and Midwest to the West and South, as efficient scale rose, and as national advertising became feasible.

Capital and labor intensity, efficient scale, breakeven volume, and operating leverage available are all characteristics of the operating processes used by firms at every stage. They highlight the importance of volume and market scope, and their relative importance tends to change over time. Sometimes industries are surprising. Can manufacturing, for example, is seen as capital-intensive by many people. However, although can lines are costly, they are durable. An analysis of the costs of a can shows that, due to the high cost of setting up the line, the costs of line maintenance, and the skills required to do these jobs well, labor is the largest part of the value added in can manufacturing. Labor cost control is therefore more important in the can industry than most people believe, explaining why the industry has been known to accept a strike rather than a wage increase it believes is too high and explaining why modern canning plants often have idle lines set up for specific product runs. The lesser importance of capital also explains why the potential for entry is high. Many sources of competition exist, keeping prices low. The large brewers, for example, have their own canning operations, supplementing external capacity.

The operating cycle (days of inventory plus days of receivables) is another important characteristic because it determines how much working capital is needed to operate the business, that is, to synchronize its operations with those ahead and behind it in the industry chain. As cash is converted to inventory and inventory to receivables and receivables to cash, the business links itself to suppliers and customers and moves through an operating cycle. In some businesses, such as agriculture and leisure goods, the cycles are seasonal and therefore very long. In others, there are many cycles per year; for example, supermarkets have very short operating cycles.

Where the working capital is invested points to the security of the credit risk and the importance of the service role that the business plays in its industry. For example, brewers carry large receivables from their distributors. Iowa Beef faces the following credit cycles in the meat packing industry:

Farms to Iowa Beef	0 to 1 day
Iowa Beef to wholesaler	9 days
Wholesaler to distributor	26 days
Distributor to restaurant	45 to 60 days
Restaurant to patron	0 days (cash or credit card)

Note that for a distributor, working capital is needed to pay its suppliers (inventory) and finance its sales (receivables).

Typically, those with power command better terms and may receive credit and even on-time inventory delivery. For example, the Japanese auto industry uses the Kanban system where auto manufacturers receive inventory ''just in time'' for production, without the expense or risk of storing materials. Sears Roebuck and the large English retailer Marks and Spencer use their heavy buying power to gain much credit and service in their dealings with suppliers.

The Product Life Cycle

Growth is another important characteristic of an industry. Fast growth situations attract entrants, while slow growth promotes exit. One of the most powerful analytical tools in the strategist's armory, the Product Life Cycle, addresses growth directly and helps us speculate on the evolution of a product, market, or industry.

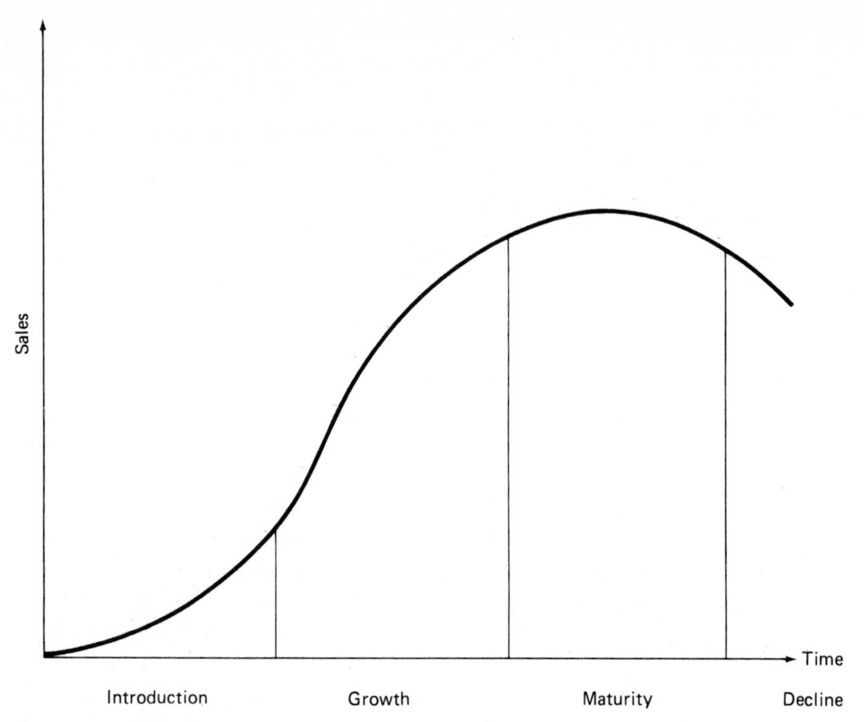

FIGURE 7-4 The Product Life Cycle

The life cycle model suggests that most product-markets develop along an S-shaped path (*Figure 7-4*) with slower early sales growth, faster midterm development, and tapering sales growth as the product saturates its market and competition appears. Common sense and experience suggest that management practices should change to earn the best possible results at each stage as the product moves along the life cycle.

But the value of the concept lies in the way it helps us anticipate industry evolution and the future track of most competitive variables. *Figure 7-5* illustrates this point by showing likely evolutionary paths for capital investment, profit, cash flow, competition, and innovation over the life cycle. Since businesses are economic systems, each element of the system is interdependent and must move consistently with the others. This systematic consistency gives the product life cycle its analytical power and explains its popularity.

In a discussion of the product life cycle, it is necessary to note that the classic S-shaped life cycle holds exactly for very few products (Gaston, 1961; Gold 1964). Gold tracked thirty-five single-product industries over a seventy-year-period, 1885 to 1955, and found that twenty-nine of them fitted four basic patterns: eight showed constant growth, nine showed slow growth, eight had growth followed by stability, and four had growth followed by decline. Although these basic patterns appeared to hold, he observed wide short-term deviations from the long-term growth path and argued that it is dangerous to use projections of recent experience in lieu of forecasts of future demand. He explained that managers try to overcome sales declines and to continue success, thereby altering the

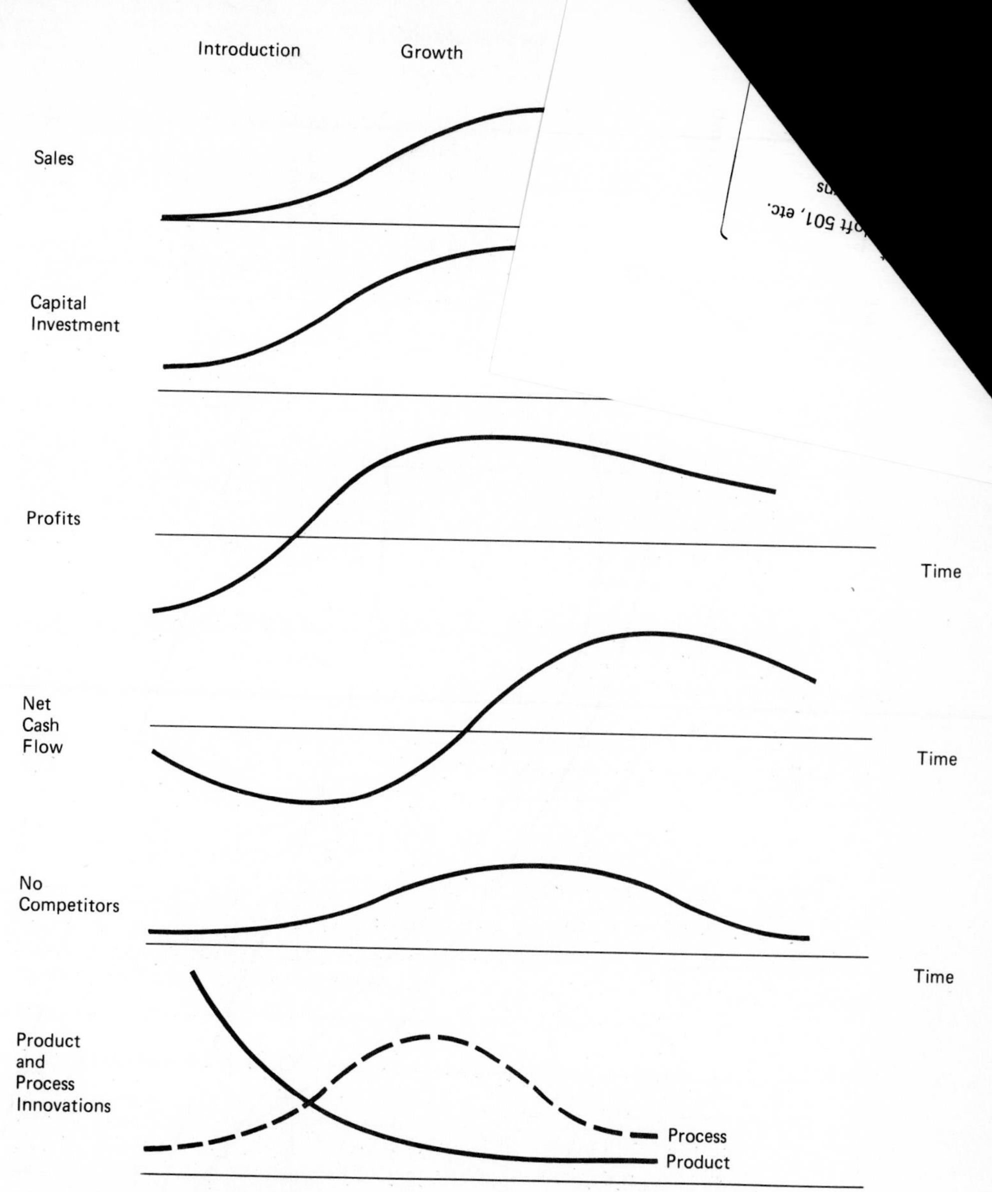

FIGURE 7-5 Impact of the Product Life Cycle

growth path. Managers elongate the 'S' pattern rather than allowing the product to decline as the model suggests.

Evidence of this type of behavior is presented by Yale (1964) and by Levitt (1965) in their discussions of the nylon industry. As *Figure 7-6* shows, nylon's sales were repeatedly revitalized as new uses and new users were found for the product. Each extension postponed the time of maturity. Cox (1967) in his study of the ethical drug

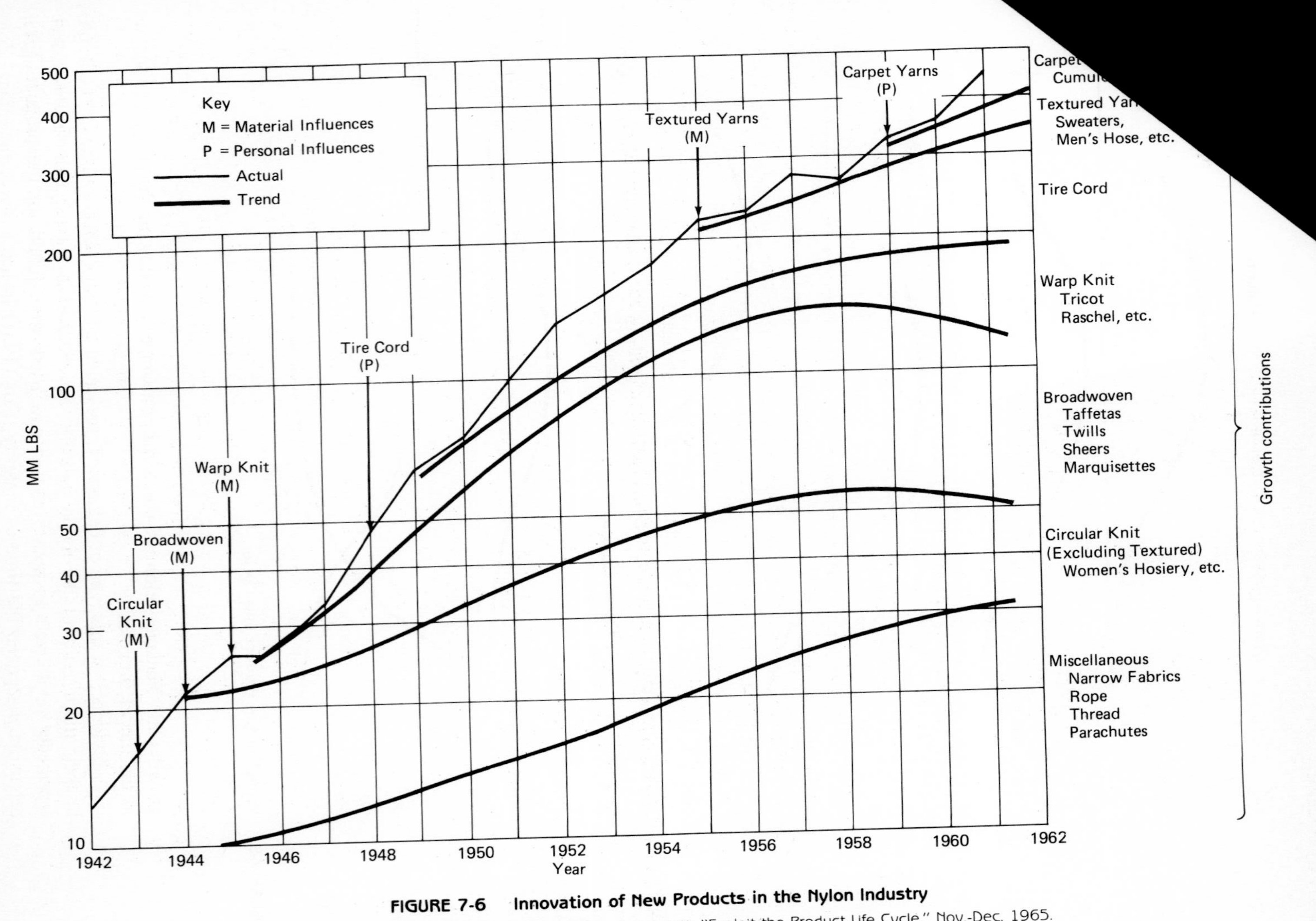

FIGURE 7-6 Innovation of New Products in the Nylon Industry

Source: Reprinted by permission of the *Harvard Business Review*. Theodore Levitt, "Exploit the Product Life Cycle," Nov.-Dec. 1965.

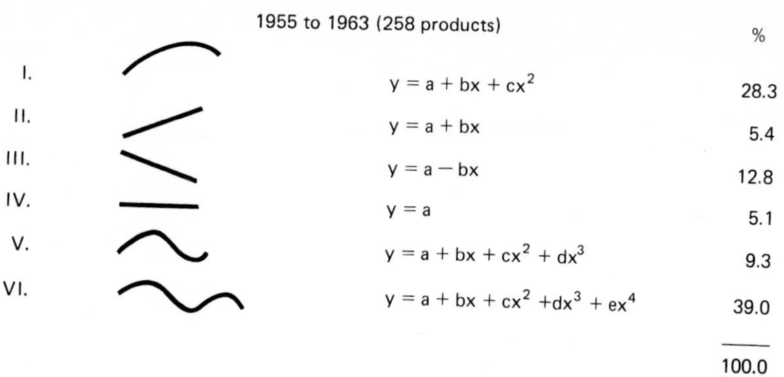

FIGURE 7-7 Growth Patterns in the Ethical Drug Industry

Source: Adapted from Cox, "Product Life Cycles as Marketing Models," *Journal of Business*, 40, 4, Oct. 1967. Reprinted by permission of the University of Chicago Press.

industry found six life cycle patterns (*Figure 7-7*). Note that most drug sale curves ultimately experienced decay, probably as more effective drugs were substituted for old.

Substitution of one product form for another is quite common, as is the substitution of one technology for another. Examples include water- and oil-based paint, electric furnaces replacing open hearth steel furnaces, and jet planes replacing those driven by propellers (Fisher and Pry, 1971; Lenz and Lanford, 1972).

Polli and Cook (1969) investigated 140 nondurables and made the following observations, consistent with Gaston's, Levitt's, and Cox's work:

1 Stability does not mean saturation unless no new product forms are possible with current technology or no new uses exist.
2 Several periods of decline may apply to a product form but are unlikely to apply to a product class.
3 A mature market may mask turbulence among product forms or brands.
4 The life cycle model fits more narrowly defined products better than it fits broad product classes and industries.

Bass (1969) and Nevers (1970) used an epidemiological model of first purchase behavior based on the first few years' sales experience of the air conditioning and color TV industries to estimate cumulative market size, peak sales, and sales rates. At the time, Bass predicted a decline in color TV sales, while the industry projected continued growth and committed to substantial new plant additions. Bass was right and the industry wrong; new plants were idle, draining the competitive strength of the industry and perhaps indirectly leading to the later successful Japanese entry to the US market. In beer, the life cycle is thousands of years long. In electronics, it is probably months long.

For us, the life cycle model should focus attention on change and the need for adaptation, as well as the likely character of the future market and competition. For the strategist, the issue is less likely to be short-run sales forecasts and product planning than it is plant size, capital commitments, and commitments to businesses themselves. Fast growth is increasingly difficult to sustain in any business, and it is in this context that the life cycle model raises useful questions and prompts us to be alert to signs of change.

Indeed, many industries run into trouble and overcapacity when their members assume current sales growth rates will be sustained forever. *Figure 7-8* shows a graph of projected growth of the personal computer industry done in 1983 (Stipp and Hill, 1983). This is a simple "northeasterly," where sales have been forecast as running up the northeast corner of the chart at a constant rate. Serious overcapacity and price cutting could occur if the personal computer industry did not grow as expected and, indeed, by mid-1985 this was the case. The industry was in decline and Steven Jobs, Apple's founder and chairman, was dethroned.

Growth also affects technology. As markets grow and competitors enter, the strategic problem shifts from product specification to process efficiency and perhaps to service capability. Utterback and Abernathy (1975) have described the parallel evolution of process and product innovation which highlights the reasons for change. As *Figure 7-9* shows, they hypothesize different innovation priorities as time passes and the product life cycle evolves.

Hayes and Wheelwright (1979) applied these ideas to process and product life cycles, advocating coordination. Note that there are some very fundamental economic pressures driving competitors in fast-growing markets toward standardized products and

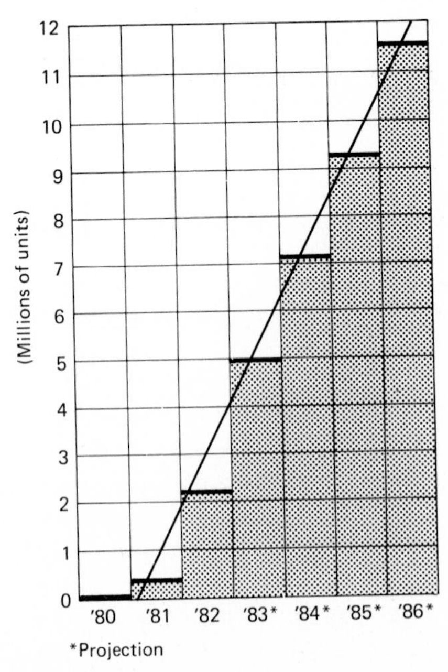

FIGURE 7-8 Sales of Home Computers Costing Less Than $1000

Source: David Stipp and G. Christian Hill, "Texas Instruments' Problems Show Pitfalls of Home-Computer Market," *The Wall Street Journal*, Dow Jones & Co., 1983. All rights reserved.

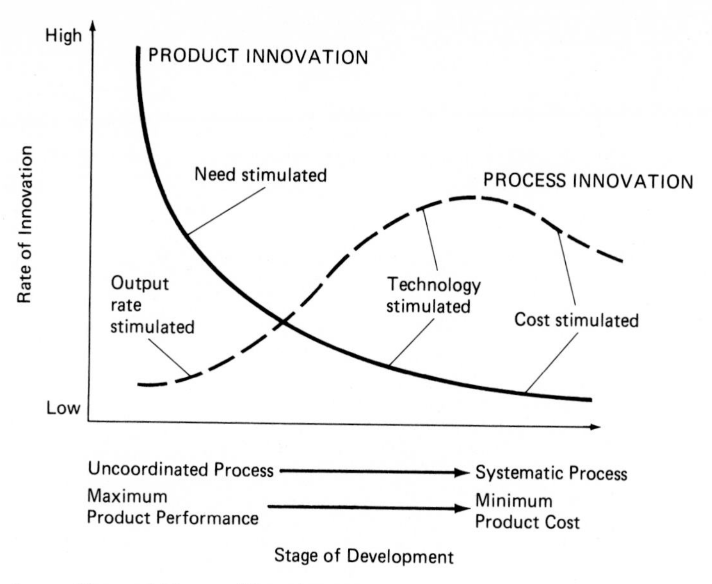

FIGURE 7-9 Innovation and Stage of Development
Source: Adapted from Utterback and Abernathy, 1975, p. 645

mass or continuous processes, as implied by the arrows down the diagonal of *Figure 7-10*. These pressures include:

1 Competitors' need to lower costs, particularly variable costs. With demand rising, investments in fixed assets appear supportable, and so fixed costs rise.
2 The immediate benefits of scale. As the Lang effect shows, the costs of a production facility do not grow as fast as outward capacity:

$$\text{Cost of new plant} = \text{Cost of old plant} \times \left(\frac{\text{Capacity of new}}{\text{Capacity of old}}\right)^{L}$$

where L, the Lang factor, is about 0.7. Costs rise with the surface area of materials used to build the plant and capacity with volume, hence the .7, roughly 2/3, power factor.[2]
3 The effects of experience and learning. Costs of production fall as managers and workers learn to improve production techniques.

Remember, though, that asset commitments imply risk, even in a period of growth. High productivity may be at a cost of reduced flexibility and innovative capacity. Competition from other industries and process changes by customers may severely affect the business (Abernathy and Utterback, 1978). On the other hand, of course, the rise of

[2]Compare the surface area of a cube, roughly proportional to its cost, with its volume. A cube of sides 1 has a surface area of 6 enclosing a volume of 1; a cube with sides 2 has surface area of 6×2^2 with a volume of 2^3 or 8. Hence costs increase slower than capacity, roughly measured by volume.

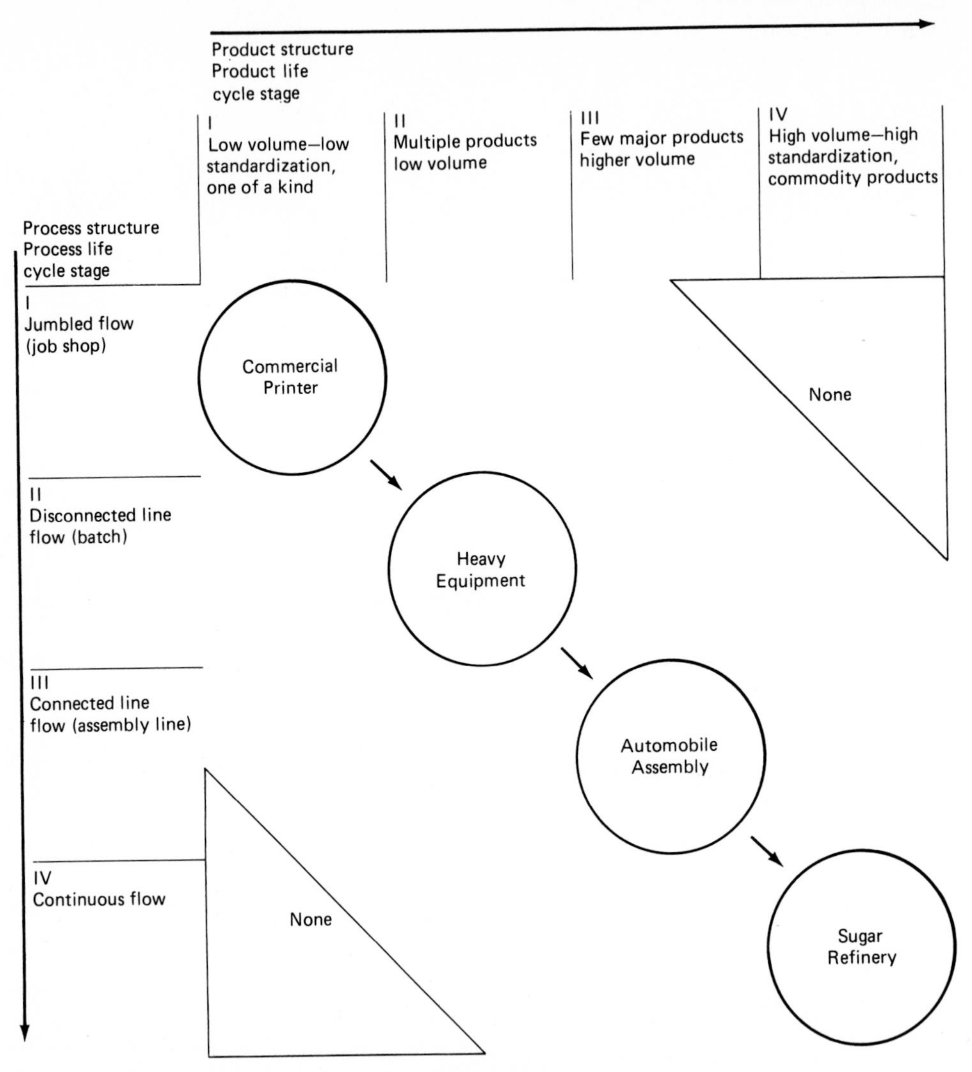

FIGURE 7-10 Matching Major Stages of Product and Process Life Cycles
Source: Hayes & Wheelwright, 1979, p. 128

world-scale plants, especially if demand is controlled by contract or vertical integration, may prevent competition from entering a market for many years, since competition at such a scale is enormously expensive. And if demand is contracted, a window of opportunity does not exist. Demand and market scope must be balanced with plant size; massive marketing efforts and research accompany the building of world-scale plants, to ensure that an efficient market exists and is tapped prior to such a plant commitment.

Value Added Analysis

Value added is another economic characteristic which we should investigate. Value added shows which parts of the industry chain make major contributions of value to the final customer and thus gain major rewards for their effort. Value added is the difference between the selling price and the costs of materials inputs for that stage (that is, it includes labor, plant and profit). For example, in the lobster fishing industry, the prices per pound at various stages of production might be (Uyterhoeven et al., 1977, p. 208):

Ex vessel	$1.08 per pound
To wholesale	$1.48
To retail	$1.88
To consumer	$2.49

and the percent value added for each stage is:

By fisherman	$1.08/$2.49 = 43% (includes fishing costs)
By dealer	$ .40/$2.49 = 16%
By wholesaler	$ .40/$2.49 = 16%
By retailer	$ .61/$2.49 = 25%

Value added is particularly revealing when compared with risk and gives insight to the power held by the major players. If both value added and risk are assessed at each stage, the favorable positions (high reward for low risk) and unfavorable positions (low reward for high risk) in the industry chain can be seen. In the lobstering example above, the fishermen have high risk while adding little value (when costs are considered), but wholesalers add much value at relatively little risk for themselves. The risk in the industry comes in finding supply, and this is obviously high for the fishermen while the wholesaler only sells what he can get. The economics of the lobster industry, then, supports the concept of independent fishermen operating at small scales with relatively low capital investment, because low financial risk is more appropriate in this low value added situation. Large companies operating capital-intensively at this stage with technology substituting for labor would actually raise the risk (with high fixed costs) and so be uneconomical in this industry. Effort on a larger scale might make sense if lobster farming (in tanks) were perfected to be a reliable source of supply; the risk of supply would be substantially reduced and could thus justify higher capitalization. Similarly, large-scale effort may be worthwhile in lobster wholesaling because the rewards are high and the lower risk factor can justify higher fixed costs.

Macroeconomic Sensitivity

The macroeconomic sensitivity of the industry refers to the effect of the business cycle (*Figure 7-11*) and macroeconomic policy on firm performance at different stages in the industry. Macroeconomic phenomena include unemployment, inflation, and interest rate

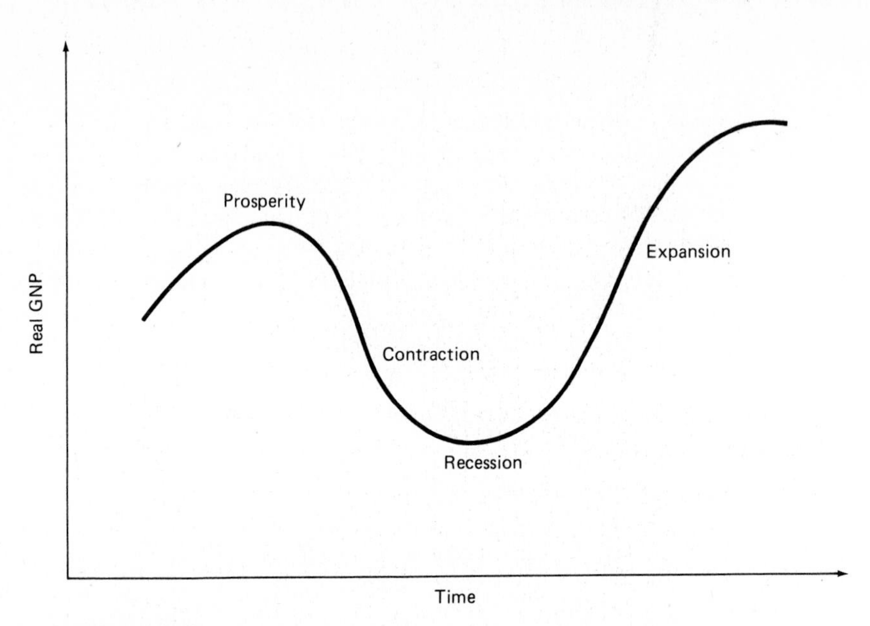

FIGURE 7-11 The Business Cycle

fluctuations which accompany the business cycle, and the monetary and fiscal policies which influence the cycle. The 1974 and 1981–82 recessions demonstrated that monetary and fiscal policies which had been seen as keys to extended post-World War II prosperity in the US were not a macroeconomic insurance scheme; the business cycle continues to have a severe impact on certain industries, an impact amplified by the industries' own purchasing and inventory policies as well as government monetary policy affecting interest rates.

The macroeconomy can affect different businesses' sales in a variety of ways, depending upon whether buyers see the good as discretionary or essential, a prestige or a make-do item. Cyclical goods are those for which demand moves with the business cycle; demand is strong during periods of prosperity and weak during recessions. Firms selling cyclical goods are more vulnerable in recession, although their performance is very strong in periods of economic prosperity. Automobiles are cyclical, as are large home appliances, carpeting, and Coke and Pepsi.

Countercyclical goods are those for which demand runs against the business cycle: demand slows in prosperity and increases in recession. Starches, such as rice and pasta, as well as movie tickets, moderately priced alcohol, and generic colas are countercyclical. Similarly, dry-cleaning and shoe-repair services are countercyclical, as people make do with the old rather than buy new clothes or shoes in recessions.

We shall term "robust" those businesses which can withstand the swings of the macroeconomy and enjoy stable demand throughout the business cycle. These goods include high-priced, prestige items, such as Mercedes-Benz automobiles, fur coats, and expensive alcohol, since the rich are generally less severely affected by recessions than blue-collar workers. Essentials, such as toothpaste, respond very little to small changes in GNP. Interestingly, Dr Pepper has had a history of demand apparently unaffected by recession, perhaps because its drinkers must have the "most original soft drink" no matter what the state of the economy.

Goods with a derived demand are those for which demand depends on the demand for other goods. If the primary good is cyclical, countercyclical, or robust, goods which have demand derived from it will be similarly influenced. Elevator demand, for example, is a derived demand from the primary demand for commercial or residential space; hence elevator demand is cyclical, as is construction.

If some firms are particularly vulnerable to certain macroeconomic situations, the likely effects of attempted macroeconomic stabilization policies of government and the central bank will be important for them. Taxation and monetary policies can seriously affect particular products' customers, and these must be monitored carefully by the managers of affected companies. For example, Chrysler's recovery was slowed and the fate of International Harvester made bleaker by the Federal Reserve Bank's high interest rates and the federal government's tight fiscal policies in the early 1980s, effectively restricting demand in Chrysler's and International Harvester's markets. Restauranteurs fear Congressional tirades against the "three-martini lunch" and expense-account meals when tax reform is debated. Construction is sensitive to both interest rates and the interest payment and depreciation expense deductions allowed by the federal tax system.

The macroeconomic environment affects industries on the demand side through the impact of the business cycle and economic policies on customers. Its impact is also felt on the supply side, as competitors enter or leave the industry due to prosperity or failures as the business cycle shifts. It is felt as capital becomes more expensive and less available when government borrows heavily in the capital markets and forces interest rates up. Also, unions become more powerful in prosperity and more aggressive in periods of inflation.

The manager must be aware both of how the macroeconomy affects his or her business directly, and also how it can or might shift power in the industry chain. For example, in a recession, a high fixed cost producer of a cyclical good has less power in relation to customers, since volume is essential for its survival. The power of cyclical goods producers rises in periods of prosperity, since supply may not match the exploding demand levels felt by their distributors.

Lincoln Electric, a manufacturer of welding equipment and consumables, provides an interesting example of a firm structured so that every phase of the business cycle can be used to enhance its business strength. Lincoln takes a proactive position in the macroeconomy and moves with the times.

Lincoln has a "no layoff" policy. It controls or limits its growth in expansionary times and so avoids overhiring. Its costs are constantly cut by serious management effort and with employee cooperation. With general prosperity, its sales of highly cyclical arc welding equipment soar. Lincoln turns down orders or accumulates a backlog, but it never raises prices to restrict demand. Nor does it hire extra employees to cope with short-term production problems. Indeed, it tries to lower its prices constantly as its costs drop. In recession, its low prices and competent technical services make it the preferred supplier and give it a robust position in its industry. Rather than laying off experienced people,

Lincoln sees recessions as periods of slack capacity and uses them to prepare for the next upswing. James F. Lincoln, a founder of Lincoln Electric, explained:

> Continuous employment is the first step to efficiency. But how? First, during slack periods, manufacture to build up inventory; costs will usually be less because of lower material costs. Second, develop new machines and methods of manufacturing; plans should be waiting on the shelf. Third, reduce prices by getting lower costs. When slack times come, workers are eager to help cut costs. Fourth, explore markets passed over when times are good. Fifth, hours of work can be reduced if the worker is agreeable. Sixth, develop new products. In sum, management should plan for slumps. They are useful. (*Civil Engineering*, American Society of Civil Engineers, January, 1973, p. 78)

Lincoln has actively limited its exposure to macroeconomic change. Most firms, however, are passive reactors to macroeconomic change, but that is their choice. An understanding of the macroeconomy's impact on firms at different industrial stages should help managers understand how and why their firm is affected and thereby help them take the first steps to limiting those effects by developing a strategy which uses the macroeconomic cycle to enhance their firm's competitive strengths.

Returns and Profitability Analysis

One of the great clichés of business is that business is about results, about returns at the "bottom line." And, of course, returns are the primary signal for entry and exit, for investment and divestment. Returns summarize the success of firms at each industry stage and reflect their robustness in the face of macroeconomic change.

Returns point the way of industry change. Stages with high returns may be attractive targets for future corporate migration; others, the low-return stages, may be reduced in importance. For decades, the oil companies have moved away from low-return stages and placed more resources in high-return stages (McLean and Haigh, 1954). Xerox, as another example, enjoyed very high returns in its copier business, a factor which ultimately made its markets attractive targets for Japanese competitors such as Savin and Ricoh and for re-entry by former competitors like Kodak.

Because returns point to the future, they must be thoroughly understood. Possibly the best tool for this purpose is Profitability Analysis founded upon the DuPont formula:

$$\text{Return on Equity} = \text{Margin} \times \text{Asset Turnover} \times \text{Leverage}$$

$$\frac{\text{Profit}}{\text{Equity}} = \frac{\text{Profit}}{\text{Sales}} \times \frac{\text{Sales}}{\text{Assets}} \times \frac{\text{Assets}}{\text{Equity}}$$

By applying this formula to the major players or class of competitors stage by stage, and by tracking the evolution of margin, asset turnover and leverage over time, we can learn not only how strong the stage is, but where its members may be vulnerable to competition and entry, and how they are changing their business.

As an example of the application of profitability analysis, notice that a strike would hurt firms where volume or asset turnover—that is, a large sales/asset ratio—is an important contributor to profitability. A price war could be started by a firm whose profits are founded in its asset turnover, hurting both competitors dependent on sales margin and their suppliers. Rising interest rates could severely affect a competitor or customer whose equity is highly leveraged with funds borrowed at variable rates.

Similarly, if return on equity (ROE) is stable while return on assets (ROA), and either margin or turnover or both, fall, the company must be leveraging up. This, of course, raises questions: why and how long can this strategy be sustained? A falling ROA, that is:

$$\frac{\text{Profit}}{\text{Sales}} \times \frac{\text{Sales}}{\text{Assets}}$$

may be a natural transitional cost of far-sighted expansion. On the other hand, it may be due to foreign competition. In the second case, prudence may suggest divestment and a reduction of equity investment. Hence, the company's increased leverage could be the owner's deliberate strategy to survive in a different competitive world.

It is important, therefore, to recognize how firms earn their profits in each stage of the industry chain. The components of profitability should relate to the economic character of the industry stage. Where sales are growing and returns are high, entry is likely. Where margins are high, turnover is likely to be low. Where turnover is high, margin is likely to be low. If ROA is high, debt may be used to accelerate growth. If ROA is low, the risk of leverage rises. Bankers try to lend only to those who will pay their loans off, to businesses they believe have low risk and high return.

For every business, this conservatism of financing institutions raises a question: How fast can we grow? John Chudley of Letraset, a British company, answers it this way:

> The long-term rate of growth that a company can afford under normal conditions is about two-fifths of the rate of return it earns on its capital employed. (1974, p. 81)

Chudley's personal experience-based response was founded on a British corporate tax rate of 40 percent and a 33 percent dividend payout, but there is a universally applicable formula for the sustainable growth rate which we can use in any corporation. The sustainable growth rate, g_S, is the rate of growth a firm can finance independently:

$$g_S = \frac{\text{Profit after Tax} - \text{Dividends}}{\text{Equity}} - \text{Inflation}$$

This calculation is based upon two implicit assumptions: First, that the firm's asset turnover is fixed (i.e., sales/assets is constant), and second that its leverage is unchanged (i.e., assets/equity is constant).

Quite simply, the sustainable growth rate is the ratio of new capital to capital employed, adjusted for inflation. Here, of course, the new capital is raised the old-fashioned way: It is earned *and* retained in the business, hence the name sustainable growth. Inflation slows real growth because it reduces the purchasing power of the dollars retained.

The sustainable growth formula gives us a simple way to monitor market power in our industry analysis. It also can help us identify opportunities and points of likely industry change. When a company has a sustainable growth rate which exceeds the growth of its industry or industry stage, $g_S > g_{industry}$, a company is financially capable of expanding its market share, integrating, or diversifying. The competitors who are threats may be in a high growth position or, conversely, desperately trying to escape from a low growth position. A low growth capability nearly always is due to low margins and limited market power. In family companies, it may be due to years of generous dividends.

Risk/Reward

The balance of risk and reward at each stage in the industry provides important data on the power and flexibility of the players in each industry role. Identifying where firms put their assets at risk and where they reap their rewards gives insights to their vulnerability or strength. Recognizing the ways in which a firm successfully controls the risks inherent to its position—by choosing to operate in a strong local market rather than risk costly national competition, for example—may indicate the future strategies which management believes are useful and those which are unthinkable.

The financial statements help us pinpoint where the firm is at risk. The balance sheet, for example, shows where fixed assets are heavy, how suppliers support the firm through its operating cycle, and how the firm serves its customers by providing financial support. A strong, low-risk firm will be integrated financially with its suppliers through large payables, for example, possibly cutting its own fixed asset exposure. A powerful firm will have small receivables, since its distributors will carry large inventories on their own books; its distributors view themselves as dependent on the firm.

As an example of a low-risk, high-power firm, consider AT&T, the old "Ma Bell." From 1956 until its 1982 settlement of a Justice Department suit, AT&T was the largest, if not sole, customer for certain telephonic products in the United States. Its suppliers extended substantial trade credit to AT&T, to the extent that AT&T's working capital was often negative. Indeed, AT&T's working capital need was reduced because of its access to its suppliers' working capital. A less powerful firm would not be treated so favorably by its suppliers.

Conversely, the terms which a less powerful firm received on raw materials would be shorter and more expensive; it would have to fund its own working capital. This is the situation in which Chrysler Corporation found itself soon after its brush with insolvency in 1980. To continue to operate, Chrysler had to generate its own working capital by selling fixed assets and entire non-automobile businesses; suppliers and bankers were understandably wary of Chrysler's ability to pay in its weakened condition.

A firm's choice of customers in the industry chain also influences risk. A small manufacturer selling exclusively to Sears Roebuck in the US is very dependent on Sears, and so is at risk should Sears redirect its purchasing. The small manufacturer may be asked to extend liberal credit, may cut its prices, or may even invest in plant rather than risk the loss of a large customer like Sears or General Motors. On the other hand, a speciality shoe manufacturer with one hundred equal-sized accounts can negotiate tough prices and payment terms with each of them, since the loss of any one customer's business represents only a small risk. The shoe manufacturer can limit its receivables and use the capital elsewhere in its business rather than bankroll a large customer.

Risk and reward are therefore important in determining what the viable opportunities and real threats in the industry are. Obviously, no firm will consciously choose a position in the industry with low returns and high risk, but if that is the reality of the present situation, then it must be recognized before management can correct it. Knowledge of the behavior of other players in the industry and the rewards and risks they take should help an organization improve its operating performance, either by imitating others in limiting risk or by gaining larger rewards in new markets where the returns are high.

An understanding of where returns are rising and where they are falling can be used to develop alternative strategies which move the firm toward more powerful roles or which reduce the risks or costs incurred with low-return activities. In the long run, risk/reward data should help strategists add value, by entering high-return businesses which have low risk, while cutting their high-risk/low-return operations.

SYNTHESIS: POWER, OPPORTUNITY, AND THREAT WITHIN THE INDUSTRY CHAIN

The data we have described as being used in the Framework for Industry Analysis are detailed and exhaustive; collectively, they give us an industry map which we can use to guide us in evaluating our current strategy and later to formulate new strategies. In practice, experienced managers will emphasize some parts of the framework at the expense of others in particular situations. Similarly, complete data are available in some case studies, while in others they are not. What we need to know is simple enough: What does the map mean for us? It will probably suggest focusing on some industry roles and some industry characteristics more than others.

The signs of industry power are revealed in the linkages, exchanges, and results of the industry chain. *Figure 7-12* focuses first on vertical integration, then on results and the industry's reaction to those results. It lists the signs of shifting industrial power. By focusing on the role(s) we play and comparing the data on our role with those on the others, we can judge who has power and who earns the largest rewards—they should be the same companies. Then we try to discern what present changes portend for the future success of our current strategy and for the likely development of competition in our stage (or stages) of the industry.

The locations of power in an industry can make or break a strategy; identifying them is therefore critical to strategic management. Are we making the best use of the power we have in the chain? Could that power be enhanced? Will the power of others block our strategy? Certain strategies will be aided by the power we have in the chain, while other strategies may depend heavily on other players in the chain and could be stymied by our own lack of power against them. Research suggests the obvious: market power, if managed properly, should enhance returns now, by raising revenue or controlling costs, or both; it should also reduce risk in the future, thereby enhancing value.

Likely future problems will emerge from a detailed study of an industry. Is entry by potentially strong competitors likely in certain stages? Have large players inappropriately evaluated the risks they have taken, making exits from some positions in the industry likely? Are certain companies ignoring the economics of their industry roles, and are their returns starting to slide?

After analyzing the industry, a strategic manager should have a better sense of likely

FIGURE 7-12 Linkages Within the Industry Chain

Vertical Integration
- Who does business with whom
- Ownership
- Contractual relationships
- Business linkages (e.g., inventory/credit support)

Pattern of Result
- Value added
- Risks taken
- Profits
- Growth

Reactions
- Asset deployments (signals ROA expectations)
- Entry/Exit/Migration
- New investments
- Capacity additions (signals demand expectations)
- Technology push
- Price shifts

Summation
- Who has power
- What is the outlook—problems/opportunities
- Likely future completion
- Key to future success

future developments in the industry. Insight into future developments reveals areas where opportunities or threats to our current strategy may lie. Perhaps, recently, one firm has successfully taken on a preceding or subsequent role in the chain; others may follow, leading to the integration and consolidation of a number of production stages. If an extended period of prosperity seems to lie ahead, some firms in the more cyclical portions of the industry will grow substantially stronger and become more powerful forces in the industry.

Your assessment of which stages of the industry chain are powerful and where there are opportunities to increase power can be corroborated by checking asset deployment of the major players at those stages. Resource deployments by industry members, if consistent with changing patterns of risk and reward, point to opportunities where additional rewards can be gained at low risk. Resource redeployment from certain areas may indicate threats where low rewards are accompanying high risk. You would expect assets to be invested where power is greatest, supporting strength and taking advantage of opportunities, and likewise that assets should be moved out of areas of weakness. If actual asset deployments are consistent with your power assessment, your assessment is shared by the industry and you are probably correct. If, however, asset deployments are different than you expected, there are two possible explanations: either the firms in the industry are misreading the environment, or they have additional information which leads them to a different assessment of emerging power, opportunities, and threats. Either explanation points to a need for further analysis before you complete your work assessing the industry.

Managers adopt strategies which conflict with the conventional wisdom of their industry only if they have good reasons to do so.

PREVIEW

Now, having taken the industry chain out of the full stakeholder set, limiting our focus to those stakeholders most closely related to the firm's operations, and having a sense of how the industry is evolving, we focus on competition per se. Hence, we put the firm's chosen industry role under a microscope, narrowing the breadth of the analysis and intensifying its depth. We focus on those who share that role, the competitors, and those who may share it in the future, potential entrants. First, we try to determine what their strategies and objectives are now and are likely to be in the future. Second, we explore what we might do to improve our performance. Finally, we examine how the results of our present or new strategy will be affected by our competitors' actions and reactions.

chapter 8

Competitive Analysis and Competing

OVERVIEW

This chapter focuses on competition, that is, on the activities of players in a particular industry role. It examines forces affecting the competition between organizations playing the same roles within an industry chain.

The selection of an industry role presupposes an analysis of where the firm can add most value with manageable risk and capture an appropriate profit. This done, the task is how to compete in your chosen role with others who have made similar role selection decisions. It is here, as we examine how other firms compete and anticipate how they will respond to competitive pressure, that competitive analysis can add value for the manager.

Competitive analysis and competing go hand in hand. It is virtually impossible to be an effective competitor unless you have a good understanding of your competitors' objectives, strategies, perceptions and resources. Without an informed sense of who your competitors are and what they are trying to do, you are managing blindly; sooner or later (probably sooner) you will be vulnerable to them.

The essence of competition is to focus strength against weakness. Competition places strategy against strategy. We must be able to move a little faster and a little harder than the competition. There are two principles to keep in mind:

1 *Focus strength against weakness.* Note, however, that smart competitors will focus their strengths against our weaknesses. Consequently, this principle is quite difficult to put into practice unless you thoroughly understand yourself and your competitors.
2 Before you seize an advantage or avoid a danger, *consider the danger in the advantage and the advantage in the danger.* In competing, the danger very often stems from vulnerabilities exposed by errors in attempting to do too much too soon with insufficient resources.

The objective of business competition is not so much to damage the competitor as to win the market. And we must remember the advice of Alfred Sloan, an early Chairman of General Motors: Companies compete with all their resources, not just specific products.

Indeed, all the fundamental tools of competitive analysis have been developed earlier in this book. You have to be able to look at your competitors as thoroughly as you look at yourself. You must understand their strategies, objectives, motives, perceptions and responses to pressure. You must identify their strengths and resources and understand the competitive arena where you meet.

To understand the competitive market, you have to understand your own role in the industry chain and the pressures that affect your competitive position. You have to work to develop your power in the marketplace and in this you will have to contend with the power of your suppliers and customers, those preceding and following you in the industry chain, as well as the power of your rivals, and the competitive strengths of substitutes and new entrants.

In this chapter, we will emphasize the nature of competition: its structure and the forces that enhance or destroy competitive advantage. These, indeed, are the forces of structural change and we shall discuss various ways to assess them. In doing this, we shall discuss strategic groups and competitive information and the ways in which alternative models can be used to formulate better strategies on the one hand, and to anticipate the consequences of competitive action on the other.

Competing is a mind game. We believe that, although industry structure may influence decision makers, essentially competition is about people, not structure. For this reason, identifying and understanding competing managements is a critical element in developing your sense of the competition and your ability to anticipate the likely course of future events.

DEFINITIONS OF THE INDUSTRY: THE COMPETITIVE ARENA

One of the principal difficulties of competitive analysis (and business) is determining exactly what the competitive arena is. There is always a risk in a competitive situation of defining the arena too narrowly. One way to avoid this error is to be alert to changes in the pressures stemming from those around you in the industry chain. It is particularly important to think about your product or service as satisfying certain consumer needs; then, look to consumer behavior to tell you what alternative ways they see to satisfy those needs.

Substitutes

Defining the competitive arena is the equivalent of defining the relevant market, and it is a matter where considerable debate is both possible and useful. Economists, however, have dealt with this problem for many years, particularly in the antitrust courts. They have developed an approach to determine substitutes: By calculating cross-elasticities, they judge which goods indeed substitute for others in the market. Cross-elasticity, ϵ_x, is calculated as:

$$\epsilon_x = \frac{(\%\text{ change in quantity sold of Good A})}{(\%\text{ change in price of Good B})}$$

that is, the responsiveness of the quantity sold of another good when your price changes. Obviously, if you increase your prices and consumers buy more of a good you had not considered a substitute for yours, the market has indeed spoken. Buyers apparently believe the other good satisfies about the same function as yours, and you must reconsider your definition of the competitive marketplace.

Competitive substitutes are those goods which fulfill the same consumer need. Recognition of the range of consumer substitutes can also give a manager insights to likely potential market entrants. We emphasize that what is a substitute is market-determined rather than based on the producer's perception alone. Indeed, a producer might emphasize product quality while failing to notice that quality is not a major factor for the consumer who considers goods of lower quality attractive substitutes. For example, a consumer might see a cheaper set of soft-sided luggage as a substitute for a longer-wearing, better-made line if he or she focused on the fashion aspects of the product rather than viewing it as "luggage for life," the term used by the producer.

Entry

Another purpose in defining relevant competitive scope broadly is to assess sources of likely entry, the sources of future competition. While not every firm is a potential competitor, it is helpful to think about where entry could come from. A firm making a separate product but sold in the same market as yours, or a firm with a good relationship with your industry's suppliers, has eliminated some of the costs of entering the market with a product like yours. A profit in its current business may provide capital for expansion, diversification, and entry to your business. A handbag manufacturer, for example, could readily introduce a line of casual soft-sided luggage, because it has access to the same suppliers and distribution channels as those already in the casual luggage industry. Other firms may integrate forward or backward to become new competitors in a particular industry role.

Let us consider an example showing an old industry subject to extreme competitive pressures from both traditional competitors and new entrants. For top management, this threatened a total change of the basis of competition and required fresh thinking about the definition of their industry. This was the situation facing Polaroid and Kodak when Kodak entered the instant photography market in 1976. Was the market "instant photography," or photography generally? Was it amateur photography, or all photography? We might have expected Polaroid to adopt a narrower definition because of its past successes in instant photography, while Kodak, because of its diverse activity as a chemically-based photography company, might have adopted a broader definition.

However, at the time Kodak was entering the instant photography market, Japanese manufacturers of 35 mm. cameras, such as Olympus and Canon, were beginning to drop the prices of their products. Basically, consumers had three choices: the traditional Kodak-type product using 110 film, the instant products exemplified by Polaroid, and the newly price-reduced 35 mm. systems. Further complicating the world of Polaroid and Kodak was the competition among Kodak's Super 8 movie systems, Polaroid's instant movie system (Polavision), and amateur video technology with Sony's Beta system.

Indeed, the growth segment in photography during the late 1970s and early 1980s was the 35 mm. market. Instant photography has been relatively stable since the end of the 1970s. Polavision was a commercial failure, although, in the company's eyes, a considerable technical success. Sony, the innovator with its Betamax system, did not become the industry standard; amateur video in 1985 was dominated by the VHS systems. Furthermore, the intrusion of Sony and video into photography heralded a change in photography from being a chemical-based industry to being electronic-based. The traditional dominance of Kodak, based on chemicals, is perhaps at risk because of the entrance of new competitors from outside the boundaries of the traditional industry, competitors whose technical skills are primarily electronic.

However, as these examples demonstrate, for top management the definition of relevant market is more than a strategic sleight of hand. For the strategist, the definition of market means a target of opportunity and a target of effort. Helicopters, for example, is a broad market, while heavy military helicopters is a more narrowly defined market with different requirements for success. Corporations which identify viable niches, those groups of customers who need special services or who cannot be served economically by larger corporations, have opportunities to survive profitably in markets seemingly dominated by larger competitors. If such a company has a strategy to pull business to it with superior differentiated service or product design, and coordinates this marketing effort with an efficient cost position based upon judicious sourcing and subcontracting, it can turn profit opportunity to reality.

THE FORCES OF COMPETITION: THE ELEMENTS OF MARKET STRUCTURE

Recall the Stakeholder Diagram, *Figure 7-1*, and the industry chain which we drew from it in *Figure 7-2*. *Figure 8-1* is nothing more than part of this chain, the part relevant for a firm focusing on one industry role. The forces of competition, described by Porter (1979), are the power of suppliers and customers and the threats of new entrants and substitutes, together with the rivalry between competitors within the industry.

Porter (1979) lists elements of supplier and buyer power which can be summarized by noticing that industry roles with few players have relatively more power than industry

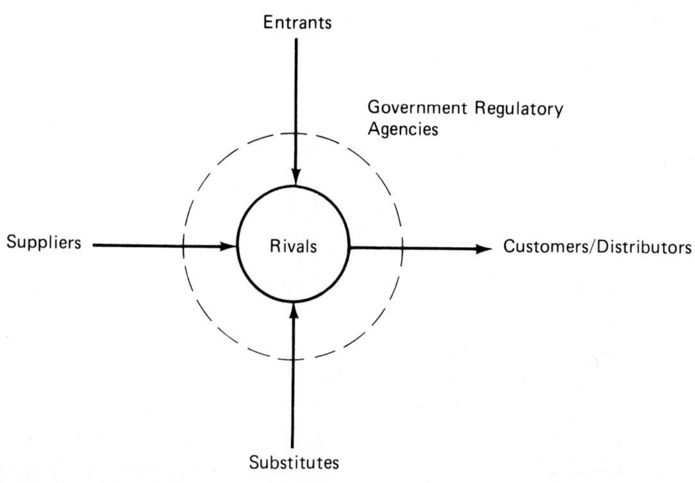

FIGURE 8-1 The Industry Chain

roles with many players. A few players are powerful. For example, a manufacturer with few customers must please them, perhaps setting prices to please them, or lose significant market share. Likewise, a firm with few suppliers has few alternative sources and so must often bear with price rises or quality downgrades or be unable to produce its product.

Let us recall some examples of market power. The old AT&T (''Ma Bell''), the regulated ''monopolist,'' nearly always operated with negative working capital as its suppliers were forced to give it favorable terms. The English retailer Marks and Spencer as well as the American Sears Roebuck have sufficient power in the marketplace that their suppliers realize that losing such a large customer would indeed be disastrous; such suppliers live with severe pressure on their own margins as a result of these retailers' power.

Porter, and Richard Caves (1964), echoed Joe Bain's work in 1956 and listed the important structural elements for competitive analysis as:

- seller concentration
- product differentiation
- barriers to the entry of new firms
- buyer concentration
- height of fixed costs and barriers to exit
- growth of market demand

As in all economic analysis, the players with the scarce goods have power. This notion characterizes Caves's first four elements, which refer to current market power. Information on the last two is useful in forecasting the sustainability of those who are currently powerful and the future location of market power in the industry chain.

Exit barriers are seldom discussed, but they can be relevant in some industries. For example, in the brewing industry, the substantial fixed costs of an efficient-scale plant limit entry and also force medium-sized brewers already in the market but operating with minimal profits to stay in longer than ROA alone might justify—the old plants have low market value.

As another example of exit barriers, the glass industry was substantially overcapacitied at the end of the 1970s, yet the large firms which owned much of the capacity were unwilling to write down their fixed assets and take a loss because of the expected negative impact on their share prices. Moreover, the potential buyers of some of these overcapacitied plants were foreign glass manufacturers who wanted the additional US capacity and customer relationships to compete in the glass companies' basic, still profitable markets. Both these factors meant that exit from unprofitable operations was nearly impossible, both financially and strategically.

THE STRUCTURE OF US INDUSTRY

Henderson (1979) argued that a stable competitive market rarely has more than three significant competitors, the largest of which has no more than four times the market share of the smallest. He argued that the ratio of 2 : 1 between the market shares of any two competitors seems to be large enough to keep the smaller one small. This is so, he believed, because substantial growth by the smaller players requires such high spending that it is impractical and so market structure is relatively stable. Henderson also said that any competitor with a relative market share position of less than 1/4 of the largest can hardly be effective.

This finding is based on the power of experience, discussed in Chapter 6. Recall that the basic theory of the value of experience goes something like this: A sustained high market share gives a company a larger accumulated experience than its competitors and, hence, if it is managed forcefully, a low cost position and, because of this, a potentially high profitability.

Subject again to the complexities of defining a market in any exact way, the Boston Consulting Group's position has been that where the number of competitors is large and where scale economies and opportunities for technological progress exist, a shakeout is nearly inevitable and, *by definition,* only those firms which grow faster than the market can survive. In the Boston Consulting Group's terms, this means, to all practical purposes, that the ultimate market structure will consist of only two large-share competitors who will be profitable while a few other firms will survive so long as they are prepared to live in a position of marginal profitability.

The research of Cooke (1974) and Cox (1977) as well as Bass (1977) and Miller (1977) is relevant here because it suggests industry-specific bench marks of relative competitive strength. Cooke, working with Cox, identified a structural relationship of firm market shares within industries, approximated by a semi-logarithmic function, so that the market share of the j-th firm is a constant percentage, c, of the next highest ranked firm:

$$s_j = c\, s_{j-1}$$

For the leading firm, this means the proportionality constant is the reciprocal of the relative market position it enjoys, and relative market share of the leading firm is 1/c.[1]

Perhaps more important is the significance of the relationship between c and the number of *important* firms in the industry. Bass (1977) reports that the leader's market share in what we will call a stable competitive equilibrium is approximated by the relationship:

$$s_1 = 1/\sqrt{n}$$

where n is the number of important firms. Also notice that, by definition, the total market must be 100 percent (or at least approximately so), so that:

$$1 = \sum_{j=1}^{n} s_n$$

[1] $\log s_j = k_0 - k_{1j}$
$c = \text{antilog } k1$
where s_j = the market share of the j-th firm in the market
j = the market share rank of the firms in the market, k_0 and k_1, are regression coefficients.
c is a proportionality constant, the transformed slope of a semilogarithmic function which describes the structural relationship of the market shares held by firms within an industry.

that is,

$$1 = s_1 \, (1+c+c^2+ \ldots +c^{n-1})$$

and

$$s_1 = 1/(1+c+c^2+ \ldots +c^{n-1})$$

which is the same as:

$$s_1 = (1-c)/(1-c^n)$$

so that we can say:

$$s_1 = (1-c)/(1-c^n) = 1/\sqrt{n}$$

Hence, knowing any two of the s_1 or n or c, we can estimate the other and then contrast the estimated structure of the industry with the actual.

When c is small and therefore the leading company enjoys substantial relative competitive strength, and when estimated structure is close to actual, we might consider the market in a state of "equilibrium." Where estimated and actual structures diverge, it seems likely that the competitive situation is unsettled. Under such conditions, efforts to build market share are likely to be more successful than attempts to take cash out of the business. Moreover, the leaders' market positions, in particular, may be in jeopardy. *Table 8-1* is a sample of s, c, and n statistics for a series of US industries in 1974.

When linked with the product portfolio in Chapter 16, this relationship between leader market share and industry structure gives you both a bench mark and a shorthand way of exploring the structure of the market, estimating relative market shares and the number of significant competitors. All these factors have a bearing on the attractiveness of

TABLE 8-1 Industry Structure and Relative Size

Industry	*c*	*Number of Important Firms*	*Cox**	*Leading Share $1/\sqrt{n}$**	*Actual '74*
Automobiles	.420	4	59.9%	50.0%	49.6%
Sulphur	.539	6	54.8	40.8	
Diesel engines	.566	6	44.9	40.8	
Ready-to-eat cereals	.599	7	40.8	37.8	41.0
Cigarettes	.735	6**	31.5	40.8	
Air transport	.785	11	23.1	30.2	
Steel	.812	16	19.5	25.0	
Trucks	.850	6**	22.1	40.8	36.1
Beer	.893	25	11.4	20.0	
Gasoline	.898	40	10.3	15.8	

*Estimates
**Cox notes these as exceptions to the direct relationship between c and n
Source: Adapted from Cox, "Product Portfolio Strategy, Market Structure and Performance," and Miller, "Comments on the Essay by William E. Cox, Jr.," in *Strategy + Structure = Performance*, Hans B. Thorelli, ed., 1977. Bloomington, IN: Indiana University Press.

market through supermarkets and drugstores (perhaps because its parent company, Bic, had experience in these channels), ultimately began to sell ''French'' hose retailing for a price roughly three times that of L'Eggs, through the department store and even boutique channels.

Note that a series of competitive maps like *Figures 8-3* and *8-4* would have made this development very obvious to all the competitors. It might have led some American hosiery manufacturers to renew their attentions in the department store market sooner, moving to a new strategic group, rather than allowing an additional entrant to take advantage of the gap in the distribution net. However, we can note that DIM was a world-scale producer in France and probably interested in incremental business, *not* a major market position in the US. Its interests and those of the US majors were asymmetric.

This kind of a map is very simple and can serve the creative and realistic manager well. And, indeed, competitive maps are sometimes very powerful in picking up the direction of change in a competitive environment. Most successful small companies use strategies that are variations on the simple theme of identifying and servicing an industry void, doing things large companies do not or will not do.

You will probably find mapping and a traditional policy focus on companies helpful in recording what people are doing and indeed what they may do next. Recall that strategic models are tools to help you organize business data. Also remember that certain models will capture different information in a more strategically meaningful form (for different people). Often you will identify the most useful information only when you have taken a number of different approaches to organizing industry facts.

USING STRUCTURAL ANALYSIS

The dilemma facing an executive who has developed a competitive map is to determine what the consequences of any pattern shifts are. For example, if there is an apparent gap, a sensible question is: ''Is it real or illusory?'' In the competitive environment, there is an ambient set of economic conditions that can be catalogued quickly. For example, use the Industry Framework of Chapter 7 to see what results deter competitive entry into the gap, as well as barriers to exit or entry. It is here that the structural models favored by industrial organization theorists can be of greatest value to the strategist, for they help us assess the consequences of collective corporate actions.

Take, for example, a simple mapping which suggests that a large number of competitors are beginning to turn from their traditional markets to a common, growing market, as the American chain saw manufacturers did in the early 1970s. Under these conditions, prompted by both external opportunity and, it seems, by the internal pressures of the large corporations which owned them, the US chain saw manufacturers began to chase the rapidly growing high-volume consumer market for chain saws. This market, which may have developed in response to the oil price shocks of 1973, had many signs of a market ''bubble''—for example, its rate of growth was over 50 percent per year. After four years, the market penetration had reached a level of about 20 percent of US homes; similar products, like lawn mowers, had penetrations of about 30 percent. Moreover, an executive considering the consequences of all this movement might have observed that the number of competitors serving the mass consumer market was beginning to increase and that these same competitors were adding capacity, apparently on the assumption of increased demand and increased market share.

A structural analysis would have pointed to:

1 Increased competition and therefore lower margins.
2 The prospects of declining growth rates promising intense competition and additional pressure on margins.
3 Lower margins which were very likely to be associated with higher fixed asset investments and, therefore, lower turnover.
4 A transfer of power from the manufacturers to the large mass market retailers such as Sears and Penney's.

The combined pressures of competition and higher fixed costs in a bubble market can be lethal when the bubble bursts and growth slows. Price discipline is likely to be nonexistent as some competitors begin to cut prices to preserve volume and obtain some contribution to their fixed costs.

The perceptive manager might have seen this migration away from traditional chain saw outlets toward the consumer markets as an opportunity, however. As in hosiery, a gap was opening in the market. Producers could serve those buyers who, being heavier users, needed service, parts, and more heavy-duty equipment than the consumer market. No US manufacturer deliberately made this choice. Due to a consent decree in an earlier antitrust case, McCulloch was prevented from moving further toward the mass market, precluding Black and Decker, its owner at the time, from using the company as it had planned. McCulloch, therefore, appeared to be a handicapped player yet to some extent was forced to behave in its own long-range best interests.

The real beneficiaries in the market, however, were the European manufacturers who for a number of reasons (primarily because of their commitments to growth in Europe and their highly integrated manufacturing strategies) stuck with their old, high-quality, service-supported dealer network in the US and in addition began to pick up the better capitalized and market-linked dealers of the American manufacturers. The result was that while the unit market share in the industry shifted substantially toward the American manufacturers, the profit share went toward the Europeans. Interestingly enough, the lifetime expenditure by a buyer in the higher-quality, heavy-use segment of the market—for both the initial equipment and consumables such as chains, bars, and other parts—was estimated at between five and ten times as large a dollar amount as the lifetime expenditures of the high unit growth consumer market. The US manufacturers appeared to have focused on share, not profit.

As we stated earlier, the industrial organization model popularized by Porter in the strategic management literature is most useful in anticipating just what the consequences of a collected competitive action will be. Corporate actions such as those we have described in the chain saw industry have consequences: industry structures change. And, with the structural changes come changes in competitive power. New entrants in the form of conglomerates pressuring growth in similar ways within one market segment dominated by a few retail chains, such as Sears, were the set of conditions that heralded a major transfer of power from manufacturer to distributor in the chain saw industry. The dealers serving the heavy-use market were ignored by their old suppliers while the consumer market became overpopulated with suppliers.

A COMPANY PERSPECTIVE ON STRUCTURAL ANALYSIS

In looking at a competitive environment, the strategist focuses on the competitors to determine what is likely to happen and on the structural model to determine what the consequences of their expected actions will be. It is, then, a matter of judgment: Are the competitors as well-informed and as diligent in analyzing the situation? What pressures will they respond to? Often managers suffering from short-run pressure for immediate results within their corporation will gain those results at the expense of their long-run competitive position and ultimately the long-run welfare of their company.

Indeed, a focus on earnings, perhaps prompted by the pension fund ownership structure of the US stock market, can have major long-run disadvantages. Ironically, senior management of the type which says, ''Get me the results today,'' and rewards short-term performance, itself magnifies the pressure for results with its strategically inappropriate measurement and reward systems. Smart people do what you pay them to do. These matters are discussed further in Chapter 15, but suffice it to say that a firm populated by smart people rewarded with inappropriate incentives can find itself in a great deal of (strategic) trouble.

STRATEGIC GROUPS AND STRATEGIC INFORMATION

A strategic group is an analytical tool used for purposes of investigation to group companies which pursue similar strategies with similar resources. The term was first used by Hunt (1973) and then by others studying a variety of industries.

Strategic groups have been used in two distinctly useful ways in the literature. First, primarily Harvard-based doctoral research (Hunt, 1973; Porter, 1974; Newman, 1978) has used the strategic group concept where the focus has been to simplify the industry structure, reducing the number of competitive variables considered to two and then mapping firms on those dimensions. Those firms with similar map positions are referred to as strategic groups. The alternative use of the term strategic groups is in the work of Hatten and others who used groups of firms to explore the strategies of individual firms. The Harvard research primarily addressed the question: What is the structure of the industry? By contrast, Hatten, Schendel and Cooper (1978) and later Schendel and Patten (1978) at Purdue focused on the strategies of companies and attempted to define those strategies in multivariate terms.

Although the simple bivariate map and group technique we described for hosiery and chain saws is quite powerful in the classroom, there are circumstances where it is insufficient and indeed could be misleading for a practicing manager. Getting data into high relief can be effective for analysis, but throwing away data by summarizing it too severely can be very costly for a strategist.

Indeed, the costs of data compression are highest when you are looking at ways *to creatively formulate a new strategy* to difference yourself from the competition. Formulation—asking, ''What next?''—requires much more information and it is here that multivariate methods, although expensive in terms of data and time required, have value.

Strategy formulation requires creativity which requires information—and often the critical information for the strategist is not similarities but rather differences. The group formulations using bivariate rather than multivariate data simply focus on similarities and do not provide sufficient information to allow you to pin down and evaluate new and different directions or options.

We can note here that the use of the bivariately defined strategic group stems from a number of factors—the first being the question asked in the original Harvard research, which was primarily concerned with structure itself and focuses on modestly capital-intensive industries where distribution played a very big role (white goods, bicycles, chain saws). Thus, their research correlated or mapped quality against distribution.

In contrast, the Purdue research pursued a different question: could strategy be modeled econometrically? This research began with a different premise, that strategy involves many variables and certainly at the business level encompasses more than one function. And there was a particular problem: the data available to model the firm in any strategically meaningful way are scarce and complicated—and strategic models are data-intense. One way to handle this problem was to pool the data to preserve information and study groups of firms which were alike but not exactly like each other, to establish a range across every variable. In this way, the researchers could look at the impact of manipulations of that variable on profitability or other performance goals over a reasonable range—for example, over a range of plant capacities or advertising expenditures per unit. This allowed them to highlight relationships so they could later *compare the results of the econometric investigation and the data* on all these companies, first, to test the validity of the model and, second, to determine whether manipulations of a particular variable indeed affected performance in ways that were both desirable and feasible for a particular company. Firms were grouped not because they were the same but because they were alike or comparable yet different.

Then, separate groups were formed to facilitate the analysis of the strategies of firms which were unalike because of size or strategy. Under these circumstances the researchers could then look not only at how different companies might compete, but how they might use the results and experiences of their competitors to enhance their own performance (see also McGee, 1982).

For example, only one strategic group in the beer industry studies, the regional brewers, shows multiple brands positively correlated with profitability. Yet an examination of the data on the separate firms being analyzed as a group showed that only one, Heileman, exploited multiple brands extensively and profitably. Note that in this use of the strategic group, it was the preservation of information and subsequent investigations or checking of empirical conclusions against data that led to:

1. Increased understanding of a competitor on a number of relevant competitive dimensions.
2. Asking whether other companies should try to do what a successful and different competitor did.

Another difference between the Harvard and Purdue research is that Harvard researchers tended to view a group as a competing unit rather than an analytical unit. This may have stemmed from the types of industries they studied, where, for example, the scope of the industry was national rather than regional with geographical restrictions. The key difference is that the Harvard formulation involves only companies that are competing with each other and this is not a general case, but a special one. It is, of course, a very powerful technique where the fit is perfect, but it is not so valuable for strategy formulation and the development of alternative strategies. Again, the critical distinction is really alternative uses of information.

The Purdue research used data on the beer market, a geographically dispersed market. In such a situation, it became obvious that groups did not have to be made up of companies which competed with each other or in any meaningful way as a cohort against a common larger rival. Indeed, groups were composed of members who were active in the market and competing against other market members—that is, small companies competing in different markets against the national-scale brewers. Information on companies competing like you, but not with you, may suggest alternative strategies for you—strategies such as those that companies similar to you have employed successfully against larger rivals.

COMPETITORS AND COMPARABLES AS SOURCES OF INFORMATION

Strategies are best evaluated in light of their results, both ours and our competitors'. An old adage illustrates this focus on results in competitive analysis: ''He who has the power has the gold.'' Indeed, conclusions on strategic history and forecasts of the likely locus of future strategic power can be drawn from competitors' financial results, that is, by analysis of the financial ratios of competing and comparable companies across the competitive spectrum of the industry. A powerful competitor will be one who is prospering, while less powerful players are likely to have a weaker cash flow.

Competitors leave a financial trail of success or failure in the marketplace which can point to potential improvements or problems in our own operations. Similarly, companies preparing to enter a market leave tracks which will be clear to astute managers who search for them. Using comparable profitability (DuPont) analyses, product life cycles, experience curves, and technology analyses, we can examine the results of competitors' functional activities in finance, marketing, and production, and later discuss how different values among competitors can affect future strategic choices and results. This requires considerably less effort than the econometric approach referred to above, although the skill needed to gain real insight is one that is slowly honed by experience.

Applying the DuPont formula to current and potential competitors can demonstrate how they are making money, where they are at risk, as well as how their sources of profitability have shifted over time. For example, brewing industry data shown in *Table 8-2* illustrate how Heileman's success depends on its extraordinary turnover relative to the national brewers, Anheuser-Busch, Miller and Schlitz. The explanation is that Heileman bought older, smaller breweries depreciated by their former owners; Heileman purchased these facilities after these companies failed or left the industry. Note, too, with high fixed costs and declining market share, Schlitz was also becoming heavily dependent on leverage as turnover slowed in the 1970s. Yet Schlitz's ROA was only 2.65 percent in a world of 12 to 20 percent prime rates; such high interest rates would make financial leverage still more expensive as time passed. As another example, Dr. Pepper had a much higher asset turnover than Coke or Pepsi in the past, but its desire to bottle more of its own packaged products severely affected its asset turnover and profitability.

Use of the *product life cycle* and estimation of *experience curves* and the impact of

TABLE 8-2 Profitability Analysis Applying the DuPont Formula, US Brewing, 1977

	ROE	=	*Margin*	×	*Turn*	×	*Leverage*
	Profit/Equity	=	*Profit/Sales*	×	*Sales/Assets*	×	*Assets/Equity*
Anheuser-Busch	13.5%		4.6%		1.43		2.06
Heileman	22.8%		4.5%		2.70		1.86
Miller	16.7%		4.3%*		1.62		2.40*
Schlitz	5.6%		1.7		1.56		2.04

*Assumes Miller's interest expenses and leverage are the same percentage of Philip Morris' corporate interest and equity as brewing assets are of the company's total assets, 41.8%

new technology (both process and product) for current or possible competitors can also indicate the likely strength of future competition and those firms' ability to control their costs. Timex controlled costs very well on its mature product, the pin lever watch, but Texas Instruments' ability to base a watch on semi-conductor technology lowered costs by a scale factor which Timex's more traditional methods could not match. Timex remained a watch manufacturer, but used its distinctive competence as an assembler, working for growing firms which had little manufacturing capacity, such as Polaroid in the 1960s and early 1970s, and more recently Sinclair Computer with their under $100 personal computer. Timex chose not to invest heavily in the watch business in the early days of semiconductors, when it was at a comparative disadvantage without electronic technology.

Competitors' experience can be used to enhance a firm's own experience, both in marketing and in production. Indeed, if the experience curve is considered for components as well as products, then identifying the competitions' sources of shared experience and their respective cost positions could provide a new entrant with clues to the technology and market expertise needed to be more efficient than the innovator. Zenith is a very good example of a smart "number two" which essentially has used the development efforts of RCA, the innovator in the television industry, as real-life market research. Repeatedly, Zenith has introduced its version of RCA's radio and television products after RCA, avoiding RCA's errors and capitalizing on its successes but without assuming the costly risks of the innovator. In the cigarette industry, too, Phillip Morris is not considered an innovator but rather a firm which follows the successful innovations of others. Phillip Morris brings to market products which are even more successful than those of the innovator, including Virginia Slims cigarettes for the women's market, Vantage cigarettes for the health-conscious smoker, and Miller Lite low-carbohydrate beer. Indeed, contrary to popular belief, Miller did not invent the low-carbohydrate concept in beer. Instead, Miller took market research which had been done on an early low-carbohydrate entrant and determined what features made it appealing to heavy drinkers in order to formulate its product and advertising strategy for Miller Lite.

COMPETING: THE MIND

Competition is not an analytical exercise—it's a matter of personal commitments. Analysis may shape those commitments, but analysis of organizations as objects rather than structures populated and manipulated by people is sterile.

A manager who sees an opportunity and says, "The limits are within myself," is likely to look for ways to change an industry and may even succeed. The manager who looks at an evolving competitive situation and sees all his competitors moving in the same direction, risking their power, and joins them because he can think of nothing better to do, merely subscribes to short-sighted competitive greed.

The game is one of minds. Bruce Henderson recognized that in 1967 in his article, "Brinksmanship in Business," which dealt with the advantages of being perceived as an irrational player. We can examine a modern example where the obvious may not be true. Coca-Cola and Pepsi surrounded themselves with subsidiary brands like Tab, Sprite, and Diet Pepsi and in the early 1980s introduced caffeine-free and non-saccharine sweetened diet drinks—a difficult competition. Then in 1985 Coca-Cola changed its Coke formulation to one, it said, which would be more appealing to Pepsi drinkers. Two months later, responding to what it said were consumer and bottler demands, Coke reintroduced "Coke Classic," splitting the brand and apologizing to its customers for its error. At last, Coke had taken an action that Pepsi could not publicly emulate in the short run; who would want to emulate an error? But it is the result that counts, not the decision. Coke's actions sparked interest in an old brand and perhaps gained shelf-space for two colas, their sugar-free and caffeine-free products, as well as Cherry Coke. In this example, Coke may, indeed, "be it."

COMPETITIVE SIGNALLING

Competitive signalling is the term strategists use to describe this kind of game. Competing on paper with signals about capacity and new products is used by the petrochemical and computer industries where the cost of adding capacity is enormous. In the chemical photography industry, Kodak has to inform its film competitors about its new products eighteen months in advance of their introductions, as part of an earlier antitrust decree. And it could be argued that when Polaroid produced its own film for its SX-70 system rather than continue to buy it from Kodak, Polaroid signalled Kodak to either leave the instant market or compete.

Ultimately, we have to keep in mind that competitors are people, too. They respond to pressure—pressures from inside their organization, pressures to perform and excel and to win quickly, the pressures of the marketplace, particularly the capital market. And they will respond to the pressure of competition.

Remember, a major purpose of competitive analysis, whether the comparable or structural approach, is to be able to anticipate your competitors' likely reaction to your strategy changes. Indeed, strategic action and reaction in the industry set off competitive signals, and the competitive signals sent by a firm can be managed in order to help create a favorable competitive environment for itself. A firm which has an elastic demand, for example, could drop prices and, while raising its own revenue, wreak havoc with firms who have built inelastic demands for themselves. Similarly, a firm with a strong inelastic demand could raise prices and make itself powerful financially, perhaps even increasing the prestige value of its product, while its competitors with more elastic demand suffered through lower prices with limited profits and minimal prospects for improvement. This last strategy was followed in the German automobile market by BMW and Mercedes-Benz, leaving Volkswagen's base products in a poor competitive position and probably putting pressure on it to strengthen its more luxurious Audi line.

Another interesting case of competitive signalling was the Pepsi Challenge taste test. The Coke-Pepsi cola market demand is elastic, since the substitutes are closely matched to most palates. The taste test represented Pepsi's signal for competition on quality rather than cut-throat competition on prices, in an industry where price competition is self-destructive for the major competitors, particularly the smaller Pepsi. Similarly, Dr Pepper's claim to being "deliciously different" and "the most original soft drink" represents a competitive signal to other soft drink producers. It removes Dr Pepper from being considered a cola substitute and thus allows it to charge higher prices as a soft drink whose unique flavor is the base of an inelastic demand.

Analysis of competitors (and substitutes) should also include an assessment of their own managers, whose experience and values may either preclude or emphasize certain kinds of reactions or strategies. Indeed, competitors are people, too. For example, the inventive Dr. Edwin Land at Polaroid was unlikely to compete with processed photographic developments at Kodak, even when 35 mm photography grew in popularity—he stood for instant photography. Baron Bich, who had made his fortune with the Bic ballpoint pen, was slow to develop felt-tipped writing instruments because he believed felt-tipped pens would not be used by consumers in a world of carbon-copy technology. Bic thus opened a "strategic window" (Abell, 1978) for the entry of Gillette into the mass pen market with the Flair felt-tipped pen. Swiss watch industry leaders, as precision jewelry manufacturers, probably found it ludicrous that Timex could sell $6.95 watches in American drugstores in the 1950s, and, again, that twenty years later Timex itself could be underpriced by a new electronic entrant to the watch industry, Texas Instruments. Most of the Swiss watch manufacturers chose not to compete with either "industry upstart," and thus opened a strategic window for Timex and, later, the electronics industry, to successfully enter watch manufacturing.

THE ROLE OF ERROR

The biggest cause of competitive failure is error—not what the competition does, but what you do as you respond to the wrong information, the wrong set of competitive signals, or the wrong pressures from your own organization.

In this context, the market share-profit relationship, often generalized as positive by structural analysts of industries, bears verifying in the industry's particular competitive environment. Looking at the historical market share-profit relationship and how it has changed over time, many managers, and too many strategists, assume that high market share will ensure profitability. Nevertheless, it is worth looking at competitive experience to validate this belief for a particular firm in a particular industry. While the PIMS data seem to indicate that a positive market share-profitability relationship holds for large, diversified firms (Schoeffler et al., 1974; Buzzell et al., 1975), this is not necessarily true for firms of different sizes or in particular industries. Hatten and Hatten (1985) found that the market share-profitability relationship varied substantially for different sized brewing firms, and the differences called for the small firms to gain profitability from very different competitive behaviors than those which brought profits to the larger firms.

A misunderstanding of their potential market share-profit relationships can be particularly dangerous for firms with a monopoly position in their industries, such as those

FIGURE 8-5 Evaluating Competitors

To evaluate a firm's competitors, ask:

1 Who are our current competitors? What is their strategy and objectives?
2 What kind of power do we have, relative to them?
3 What kinds of products are substitutes for ours? Would the consumer agree?
4 How much power do we have against substitutes?
5 Who are potential competitors?
6 What would make it attractive for the potential competitors to enter? What would be their entry strategy?
7 Are we powerful enough to keep potential competitors out, or be unaffected by their entry?
8 How can we enhance our power and use it to increase our returns?
9 What are our vulnerabilities?

with patented technologies. Such firms may feel that their high market share and profit levels are impenetrable by potential competitors. That feeling can blind them to substitute technologies or to international competitors who gain market share by paying more attention to cost control, service, and quality than the richer monopolist.

To sum up, the power of competitors must be realistically assessed for the firm to gauge the likely success of its strategic behavior. A powerful competitor may mean that certain strategies are not worth pursuing, and its presence may encourage a firm to seek strategies avoiding direct competition. Knowing your competitors is essential if you are to forecast the future environment of the firm responsibly.

Figure 8-5 lists important issues to be addressed in evaluating competitors, substitutes, and potential entrants. Indeed, the best way to avoid surprises from unexpected sources is to be aware of the motivations behind such unexpected, and possibly unwelcome, events. The firm's power in relation to its current and potential competitors must be assessed, since competitive power will facilitate certain strategies while weakness may make the success of some strategies impossible.

EVALUATION OF THE FIRM IN ITS COMPETITIVE ENVIRONMENT

Just as resource assessment required a listing of various kinds of resources before the critical ones could be assessed, environmental assessment encompasses various industrial, competitive, macroeconomic, and stakeholder observations as a prelude to evaluation. Here, the environmental evaluation criterion is overall fit with the probable world to come. The important question is, "Will the firm's current strategy work in its likely future environment?" In order for a firm's strategy to continue to perform well, the distinctive competence of the firm must remain relevant and advantageous in the likely future environment.

Both the distinctiveness and the advantage—that is, the firm's ability to perform on this critical dimension and its ability to leverage it—must be retained in the emerging environment. Advantage comes from differences. An environment in which many competitors have the same ability, or where it is no longer possible to do business in the manner in which the firm excelled, is hostile to the firm. The firm's strategy no longer fits in the firm's emerging environment.

Future strategic success requires that the firm's competences continue to provide distinction and advantage in the marketplace. Thus, full assessment of the competitive environment requires that the firm have answers to the following questions:

1 How will industrial power shift?
2 Will the distinctive competence still yield a competitive advantage?
3 Will the firm's competitive advantage still exist in its old markets?
4 Should new markets be sought where the competitive advantage can be claimed, or will the environment and competition change so that a new distinctive competence must be developed?

Economic relationships are interdependent by their nature. Cross-impacts of likely futures will exaggerate some vulnerable areas as well as strengths, competencies, and weaknesses. Complete environmental assessment should generate sets of opportunities and threats which strategists must consider if the firm is to successfully achieve its objectives.

SUMMARY: THE SILVER LINING OF THE BLEAKEST ENVIRONMENTS

A strategist may make an unpleasant discovery about the likely future, one which will hinder his firm; the firm may appear doomed in a crisis. In these circumstances, remember the Chinese character for "crisis," a combination of the characters for "danger" and "opportunity." Indeed, every environment is a source of both opportunities and threats. Management must design strategies which make and take advantage of opportunities while neutralizing threats in the environment.

Insight is often the key to responding to a seemingly hostile environment. Groups of knowledgeable participants may be able to engage in loosely structured (Delphi-type) discussions to brainstorm about issues which seem unworkable and unthinkable, to identify what or who could change an industry's structure to make it more conducive to the firm's strategic success. Vulnerability and cross-impact analysis can also allow more realistic assessments of the options and actions available and their effect in the likely future environment.

The environment itself is neither totally negative or positive. Keep in mind the advice of Ecclesiastes 9:11:

> Again, I saw that under the sun the race is not to the swift, nor the battle to the strong, nor bread to the wise, nor riches to the intelligent nor favor to men of skill, but time and chance happen to them all.

For success, analysis must be followed by action which capitalizes on opportunities and minimizes the risk of threatening situations.

PREVIEW: SOCIAL-POLITICAL AND INTERNATIONAL ENVIRONMENTS

Major changes in a firm's social-political environment, such as society's attitude toward the firm's products, or in the international environment, such as reduced tariffs or new import restrictions, will affect the firm. In contrast to changes in the industrial environment—which generally allow the firm to continue to operate—social, political, and international changes can have very abrupt effects, and may actually require a firm to cease operations immediately and totally. Examples of such immediate changes are the nationalization of the firm's subsidiary in a developing country or regulations which declare a firm's product outside safety or trade limits. Monsanto's plastic bottle (one of its major intended uses was as soft drink packaging) was for a time declared an unsafe receptacle for food by a government agency.

Social-political organizations and international political changes can affect costs, prices, and power in the industrial chain as taxes and regulation raise costs or as tariffs significantly raise prices to consumers and open or shut markets to producers. By forbidding or interfering with the sale of certain goods, constituencies of the firm can even break links in the chain and so represent a significant loss of market and competitive power.

Thus, social, political and international power, although it is apparently non-economic, can have severe economic consequences for the firm in its industry. Regulations, political power, and ethical considerations can shift their emphasis, so that the manager must constantly be aware of their changing economic implications. Stakeholder values and objectives—major aspects of the social-political and international environments, and sometimes basic causes of changing industrial structure—will be discussed in Chapter 9.

chapter 9

Stakeholder Analysis and the Organization's Objectives

INTRODUCTION: A DIFFERENT APPROACH TO OBJECTIVES VIA STAKEHOLDER ANALYSIS

Strategists have been known to develop plans which they consider logical, pre-emptive, and efficient in their use of resources and almost certain to succeed in the firm's future environment. But the plans have not worked, and the planners have scratched their heads and wondered why.

Sometimes plans do not work because the objectives or strategies could not win support. Indeed, strategists cannot simply concentrate on the rational elements of the organization—they must take its heart into account, too. And the organization's heart is revealed by its objectives and values, what it wants and the actions which its members will accept. Dill wrote:

> All efforts to move in new directions entail risks that important side costs and consequences will be overlooked, and that failure to consult and inform will breed resistance from those whose help is needed. (1976, p. 125)

Of course, social values and objectives will shift over time. Indeed, when an organization's objectives are being reviewed or developed, the issue is to synthesize and accommodate internal and external stakeholder interests appropriately. The firm's relationships with its stakeholders have to be managed in an interactive way. Cyert and March (1963) noted, "Organizations do not have objectives; people do," and the stakeholders of the organization are represented by people. Hence, stakeholder management necessitates developing relationships with people, some of whom act independently while some act as agents of others, for example, unions. Stakeholders may have stakeholders themselves! To be effective, management must earn stakeholder support, commitment, or acceptance for the organization's strategy (Bourgeois, 1980).

Internal stakeholders are those involved in the operations of the business—the employees, both blue- and white-collar, as well as outside members of the board of directors. They are the organization's personnel resource and the source of its human energy (Selznick, 1957). Their values, preferences and needs, and the firm's ability to satisfy them, are major factors in determining what is organizationally possible. Barnard wrote, "The life of an organization depends upon its ability to secure and maintain the personal contributions of energy necessary to effect its purposes" (1966, p. 92).

While the boundary between internal and external stakeholders is sometimes fuzzy, external stakeholders generally come from the wider environment first discussed in Chapter 7. Stakeholders evident from the industry chain include suppliers, customers, and bankers. Others are shareholders and competitors. External stakeholders also come from the social-political, macroeconomic, and internal environments and encompass the neighbors of a plant, local politicians and journalists, state and federal regulators, and even industrial policymakers in other countries.

The sensitive strategic manager must recognize the full range of actual and potential stakeholder pressures and identify their sources in the objectives and strategies of particular stakeholders. As in resource and economic environmental assessment, the full identification of the firm's current stakeholders, their objectives, and the firm's ability to satisfy them improves both the quality of analysis and the prospects of successful action. We can note, however, that not all who claim to be stakeholders are legitimate; some, in fact, may be opportunists attempting to use the organization to serve their own ends (Dill, 1976).

The first step to improved constituent or stakeholder management is fully identifying stakeholder interests and power. The second is to recognize their ongoing and changing contextual power. The third is to distinguish superficial differences among stakeholders from those that are fundamental (Andrews, 1980). This approach highlights the tradeoffs required to develop support for a particular strategy or set of objectives. Knowing the range of your stakeholders' interests and how they are changing allows a rational consideration of the noneconomic issues which can dominate or constrain strategy for very valid reasons (Murray, 1978). Understanding that the stakeholders of different firms are likely to be different implies that varying accommodations will be made by each firm, to some extent explaining the differences in chosen strategies within industries and across regional and national cultures. For example, it is likely that employees in the computer industry, who have prospered because of growth and innovation, are much more favorably disposed toward technological change than shoe industry employees whose experiences when automation displaced labor have made them more wary of innovation. As a result, innovative strategies are easier to pursue in the computer industry and more difficult to implement in the shoe industry.

STAKEHOLDER ANALYSIS

Analysis before action is the watchword of the strategist, as Sun Tzu wrote 2500 years ago: "With many calculations, one can win; with few, one cannot. How much less chance of victory has one who makes none at all!" (1963, p. 71). This is true in the societal arena, just as it holds in the industrial and competitive environments.

To manage our stakeholders effectively, we need to know ourselves and them. We need to learn how our strategy affects their success, and how theirs affects ours.

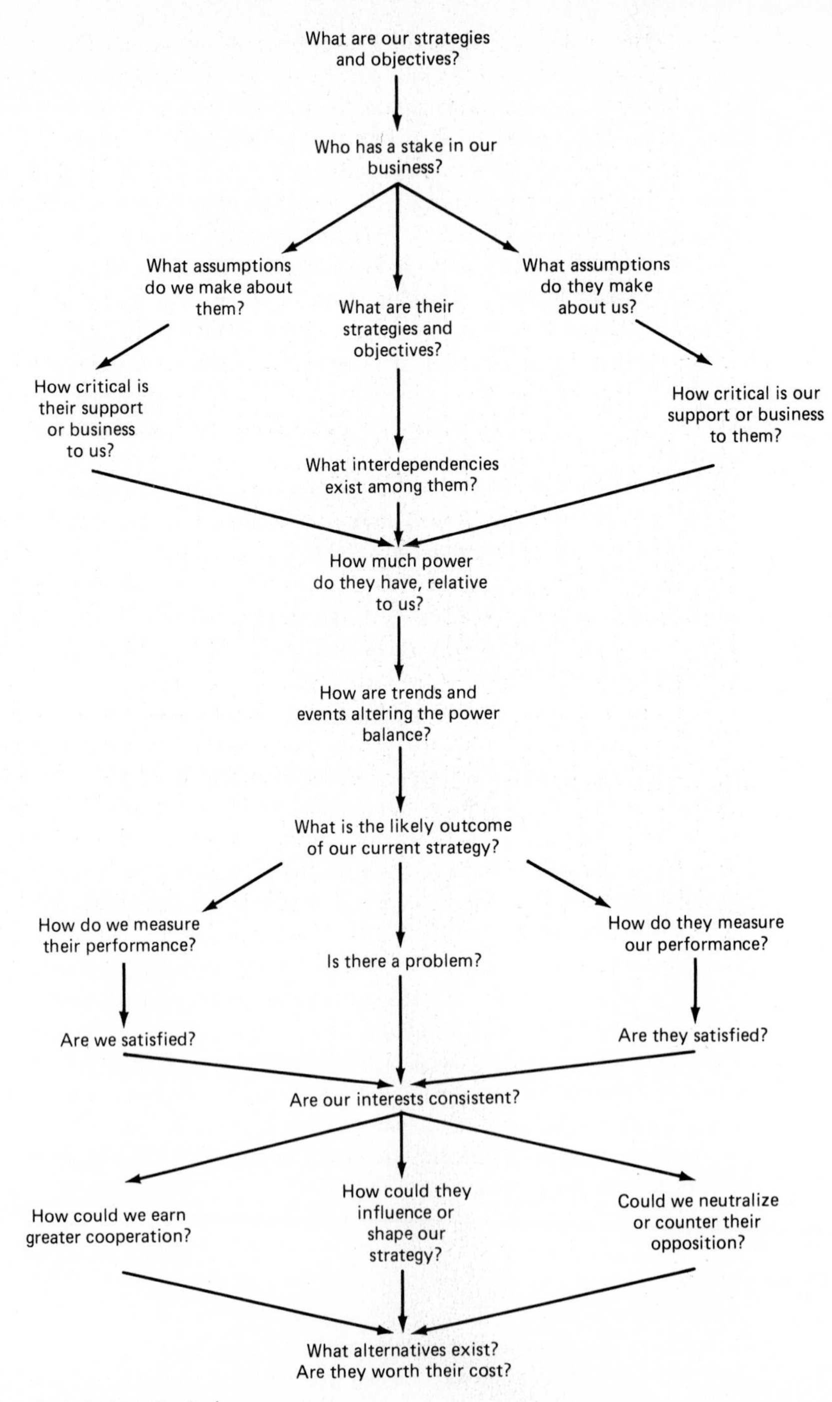

FIGURE 9-1 Stakeholder Analysis

Stakeholder analysis, like competitive analysis, requires us to be "other-centered" (Rogers, 1977) and to see the complementary nature of stakeholder relationships.

In a simple sense, our task is to collect data so that we can understand our stakeholders' objectives and behavior, recognize their power and use that knowledge and our creative ability to anticipate the stakeholder implications of our current strategy. Later, this analysis will help us determine what our alternative strategies are and which is likely to contribute most to our future success. *Figure 9-1* illustrates the flow of this process of analysis within the stakeholder environment.

THE STAKEHOLDER AUDIT

To organize our analysis, we need a framework which will lead us to an understanding of our stakeholders and their satisfaction with our performance as well as their power with respect to our organization. Following Emshoff and Freeman (1979), we want to recognize all our stakeholders, not just the highly visible ones. In addition, we want to develop a sense of the overall cooperative potential of our stakeholders and of our capability to deal simultaneously with several of them. Once we have evaluated our current strategy, our responsibility is to the future. Thus, evaluating stakeholders will lead to considerations of managerial action appropriate within the stakeholder environment.

Figure 9-2, The Stakeholder Audit, is an important framework to organize, investigate and analyze stakeholder interests. It focuses attention first on the nature of our stakeholders' interests in our current strategy and objectives. Then, it organizes what we know and believe about our stakeholders and our relationships with them, emphasizing the complementary nature of the relationships. The sequences and titles—Actions, Beliefs, Cooperative Potential, and Stakes—are designed to help us recall and use what must be considered—the ABC's of stakeholder management. We have to understand the ABC's in order to be effective stakeholder managers. Stakeholder analysis begins with identification of who the stakeholders are and which are currently most important. The stakeholder mix can be expected to change over time and from issue to issue so that stakeholder analysis is ongoing and dynamic. We can refer to *current* and *potential* stakeholders in every corporate action and for every corporate issue, and we can judge whether they are supporters or opponents.

Actions

For all significant stakeholders, it is important to examine their actions to determine what they are doing, what they want, and what they will tolerate. What they do may be more important for a manager than what they say. Some stakeholders want much and tolerate little divergence from their ideal, while others are more relaxed about their personal stake in the firm and will tolerate greater divergence, except perhaps on one or two sensitive issues which move them to activism.

We need to learn what stimulates stakeholder activism. Stakeholders are particularly important when they demand an active role in corporate decisions. Simon (1976) and Barnard (1966) believed that individuals and organizations who could affect the corporation had thresholds beyond which they became active participants rather than passive

FIGURE 9-2 The Stakeholder Audit

	Supporters (Active)	*Uncommitted (Nonactive)*	*Opposition (Active)*
Who are the stakeholders?			
Currently active?			
Not active?			
Potentially active?			
For or against?			
Actions:			
What are they doing, e.g., what pressures and procedures are they using, and what actions have they taken to get what they want?			
What are the thresholds between their indifference and activism? What has or could trigger their response? What are their sensitive areas?			
What are they asking for, or what will they ask for, and what do they want?—i.e., what are their objectives?			
Beliefs:			
What do their executives believe in? Is their knowledge of us accurate or inaccurate?			
What assumptions do they make about us? What assumptions about them are *implicit* to our strategy?			
How do they think we affect their success, and they ours?			
What is their power relative to us? What is our power over them?			
How do they measure our performance, and we measure theirs?			
What do we really want? Are these objectives legitimate? Are they satisfied? Are we satisfied? What do they really want?			
How will time and current trends affect their satisfaction, relative power, and activism?			
Cooperative potential:			
With which of our stakeholder sets are they related or dependent?			
What differences are there between them and us, or our other stakeholders? Are these differences fundamental or superficial?			
How could they be influenced, and by whom, at what cost?			
Stakes:			
What is their stake in us, and what is our stake in them? How important are these stakes?			
What is their real power in our affairs? Is theirs an *equity* interest, or is it economic? Do they seek influence for some other reason?			
What power do we have in their affairs?			

observers of corporate affairs. Because stakeholder activism can sometimes lead to major constraints on normal operations and because circumstances alter thresholds, we must identify the relevant thresholds between stakeholder indifference and action. While linked with the issue of what they will tolerate this also requires the strategist to think critically about the unthinkable: "What will they do if provoked? How could it happen?" A very simple example of the costs of threshold violation can be seen in the vastly different responses people receive if they ask, "May I step to the front of the line?" or if they barge in. The first approach respects the stakeholders involved, the second does not.

Stakeholders may have unstated as well as stated objectives, and the unstated objectives can have surprising and undesirable impacts on the success of future strategies. Here, an historical perspective on the stakeholders' patterns of behavior is important: What situation precipitated actions which were unexpected and inconsistent with their public statements and espoused values? What unstated values and objectives are implied?

For example, the flat administrative structure of a small firm may hinder an entrepreneur's much publicized attempts to expand, but his refusal to hire a general manager and share power is a very strong behavioral signal that one of his important values may be the maintenance of close personal control of the organization. Like the biblical tree, the entrepreneur must be judged by the fruit of his actions, as well as by his talk! Unstated and implicit objectives often have greater weight in management than highly publicized slogans. Actions alert us to stakeholder strategies and let us infer what their objectives are, with respect to us.

Beliefs

Beliefs—theirs about us and ours about them—play a large role in stakeholder relations. Beliefs may be founded in fact or in misinformation. Clues to the real state of affairs are usually found in the statements and memoranda of stakeholders and their representatives, and in their actions. Although we will have internal data for ourselves only, our experience and their public posture should enable us to say what we think their key people believe in and what they will find unacceptable. We can speculate on the assumptions they make about us, and we should be careful to look at the complementary assumptions we make about them.

The assumptions implicit in our strategy must be made explicit if we are to manage our relationships with our stakeholders; management is essentially a conscious activity. Typically, the assumptions which managers fail to specify relate to the real sources and scope of stakeholder power (or powerlessness), and to the respective objectives of managers and stakeholders. These assumptions apply to the criteria our stakeholders use to monitor our performance and what we use to gauge theirs. Politicians, for example, have a limited personal responsibility for performance in the marketplace; their currency is measured in votes at the polling booth. If we wish to understand our stakeholders, we need to learn how they measure their own performance and how they believe we affect it. We have to judge whether they are satisfied with us and determine whether we are satisfied with them. We must look at them through their eyes and not through our eyes only.

Cooperative Potential

In assessing the cooperative potential of stakeholders, note that most stakeholders should be expected to act in their own self-interest, ensuring that their contributions to the firm provide an appropriate benefit to themselves. It is management's job to ensure that cooperating with management and supporting its work is within the stakeholders' interests. This is particularly important when opposition could undermine the firm's vitality and reduce its options. Likewise, management has a responsibility to ensure that the firm's contributions to its stakeholders benefit the firm.

Every stakeholder can support, ignore, or oppose management's initiatives and programs, and vice versa. Because resources are scarce, management must determine how to allocate them among its stakeholders and their developing interests over time and in changing circumstances. Common sense and experience suggest that powerful contributors will demand a share in the organization's success and that some people and organizations will attempt to frustrate management at almost every turn in their efforts to achieve some tangentially related purpose of their own.

Between the extremes of active proponents and active opponents, there are likely to be many stakeholders who are indifferent and uncommitted unless mobilized. Mobilization may not be necessary for success on most corporate initiatives. But for those where opposition can be seen or anticipated, management should begin to seek its friends and identify its foes.

The factor which we should consider is whether interests are shared or are superficially or fundamentally different among stakeholders. For particular stakeholders, much will depend on the relationships between us and them, their real interests and ours. If they and we are highly interdependent and are threatened by the same forces, the cooperative potential will be high. If they are loosely connected to us and highly dependent on others, they will be less likely to support us in tough situations. Moreover, as time passes and events unfold, some potential coalitions are likely to break, while others may strengthen.

Grefe (1982) makes a practical and even finer distinction when he describes "family" and "friends" in the stakeholder context. "Family" matter most, share your interests, and will suffer or benefit with you; they are a loyal and usually constant stakeholder group. "Friends," according to Grefe, are merely allies and are likely to be less constant, shifting their allegiance to suit their permanent interests, issue by issue.

Stakes

Ultimately, the effort we put forth and the strength of our support or opposition will depend on the importance of the stake each group sees in us, and likewise the stake we see in them. Freeman (1981) uses the terms "equity, economy, and influence" to describe the nature of most constituents' stakes in a business enterprise.

Stakeholder analysis has a simple purpose. It is to help us construct a reasoned explanation of stakeholders' behavior and an understanding of their power in our affairs. It should help us distinguish between the legitimate stakeholders' demands and those of the opportunists who seek to use the organization. Government in some instances chooses the easy way and makes business responsible for the implementation of government objectives rather than using tax revenues to finance programs designed to achieve the same ends. Housing policy, highway safety, and pollution control are just a few areas where government has used business to achieve its social objectives, by mandating the availability of bank financing for certain construction projects and by requiring safer and less polluting automobiles.

We use stakeholder analysis to alert us to which stakeholders are satisfied with our performance and which are not. We have to look at the data, judge who is with us and who can be persuaded, and judge whether our present and potential support will outweigh that of any opposition by a sufficient degree to ensure organizational commitment and the ultimate success of our current stragegy. This evaluation done, we may have to develop a new strategy to manage our stakeholders. The key factors in our deliberations then will be: First, are our stakeholders content and satisfied with our performance, and we with theirs? Secondly, what is their real power in our affairs, and our power in theirs?

STAKEHOLDER MANAGEMENT

In a well-managed organization, objectives exploit the flexibility which current success gives in the interests of future vitality. Success is an opportunity to run the company as it should be hereafter (Bower, 1966). We will only have the opportunity to manage as long as our stakeholders are satisfied. This is why the audit of stakeholder satisfaction is important, and why stakeholder management is critical.

Stakeholder management is founded in performance. If our results and actions satisfy our stakeholders, we will have earned the right to manage our organization autonomously, we will have leeway, and we will be able to manage our relationships with our stakeholders to ensure the survival and vitality of our organization and the maintenance of an economic system that values such business-society relationships. Where we can anticipate problems with particular stakeholders, we can work to reduce them, resolve them, or maybe redefine them. We can use time and power to influence the process whereby they will be addressed, and the forum in which this will take place.

Knowledge of who has power and who may use it, plus an explicit consideration of how our current strategy is likely to affect our stakeholders, will lead us to seek strategies which eliminate difficulties. For any remaining, we may make tradeoffs consistent with both our own interests and our stakeholders' interests, or attempt to develop coalitions to help us get what we believe is best. Stakeholder analysis is essential to the rational, skillful use of power. Some examples illustrate the need to implement strategies with stakeholder interests in mind.

In the mid-1950s, Martin Halen, the founder of Green Stamps, successfully mobilized all the businesses which supplied the trading stamp companies with premiums as a powerful political constituency to head off legislative efforts to abolish trading stamps (Grefe, 1982). New England Telephone attempted to use a similar stakeholder strategy in its efforts to charge users rather than all subscribers for directory assistance calls (Emshoff and Freeman, 1979). New England Telephone identified stakeholders it believed could influence the Massachusetts Department of Public Utilities and then disseminated information to them, interacted with them, and accommodated to their concerns. The company also polled the public on the issue, finding support. In opposition, however, was the company's union which, through skilled political coalition-building in the Massachusetts House of Representatives, was able to block the change. Directory assistance is a labor-intense service and, despite the company's guarantee of job security, the union would not negotiate about it.

SOCIAL RESPONSIBILITY

Social responsibility issues typically arise when there has been a failure in stakeholder management. For example, a firm may have ignored or misread one or more external stakeholders and allowed the second-order effects of its operations or products to pass the threshold of community or political activism—perhaps allowing an offensive effluent to pass into an adjacent stream, or selling a car of questionable safety. Once aroused, stakeholder activism can threaten the normal operations of the firm. Such situations demand skilled stakeholder management.

We believe, like Ackerman (1975) and Post (1978), that the firm can operate more smoothly and effectively if its relations with its societal stakeholders are managed like any other function, such as production or marketing, before thresholds for stakeholder activism have been passed. Indeed, since responsibility issues arise at the shared boundaries of the organization and its social and political stakeholders, it is operations managers who are on the front line. Unless there is a responsive corporate culture supported by senior management to guide these people, the firm is likely to live from crisis to crisis in its relations with its publics (Simon, 1976). In fact, social responsibility issues are often simply signs of a failure of corporations to adapt to present-day realities of reasonable and legitimate stakeholder demands.

Milton Friedman writes that the only "social" responsibility of the firm is its fiduciary responsibility to maximize returns to shareholders (Friedman, 1962). The reality of today's business environment, however, indicates that poor management of the firm's important relationships with its constituents can affect operations and profits. A loss of flexibility, exorbitant legal fees, and the diversion of senior management time are all inefficient results of poor stakeholder management.

We believe stakeholder management is good business. Social responsibility is a responsibility of the strategic manager; Freeman goes so far as to say that "strategic management is building bridges to the firm's stakeholders" (1981, p. 20). It is not a matter of taste, nor is it just enlightened self-interest, to manage stakeholder relationships well.

Proactive Versus Reactive Management

Management can be proactive rather than reactive. Managers have choices about which stakeholders' interests to serve, whom to satisfy and whom to disappoint, and to what degree, and they can anticipate stakeholder interests. They must choose how to balance their organization's short- and long-term financial performance needs with critical social demands which, if ignored, may sorely affect its ability to do business (Barnard, 1966; Selznick, 1964; Andrews, 1980). Just as he or she prepares for an expected change in the industrial environment by altering variables such as prices, production methods, or debt source, so, too, in the societal arena, the manager can consider which stakeholders have priority, how interests can be balanced, and how the firm's actions on social issues or for specific stakeholders can be timed to do the most good.

Reactive managers, by comparison, tend to use strategies in the societal arena designed upon the base of their competitive experience. Managers who are exclusively reactive risk heavy costs in situations where the firm is allowed to drift into conflict with powerful stakeholders. Such issues could be quickly resolved or negotiated if they were identified and understood earlier. A crisis situation in a social issue has the same impact as an unexpected economic crisis: the manager loses flexibility.

One pharmaceutical company avoided the high research and development costs which characterize the industry by acquiring smaller companies with proven new products and then using its marketing and financial resources to stimulate growth and improve operating performance. They waited, watched, and reacted in the competitive arena, and did the same when one of their products became the target of drug abuse. By waiting to see what would happen next, they lost their ability to control their future. Their concern became news, and then a political issue. They found their product placed by the US Drug Enforcement Agency on the restricted manufacturing and sales list, forbidding its production or sale. What worked competitively failed in the world of societal and regulatory stakeholders (Schwartz, 1978).

The second-order effects of social responsibility situations can go substantially beyond the original issue as the situation evolves. Depending on the values and power of the affected stakeholders, social responsibility issues can create events and investigations which attract media, political, and government attention to a number of a firm's activities, sometimes virtually unrelated to the original issue. Enough managers have been caught flat-footed and open-mouthed by TV cameras to realize that Post's view of social responsiveness as a necessary, ongoing activity of corporate managers is reasonable. Insincerity robs management of credibility and influence.

If social responsiveness is treated as a managerial responsibility, a strategic view can enhance performance in dealing with sometimes seemingly intractable social issues and stakeholder demands. Cohen (1982) writes that information, time, power, and involvement are critical variables in every negotiation. It is useful, therefore, to evaluate our use of information, time, and power in our relations with our stakeholders—that is, to evaluate our stakeholder strategies.

Empathetic Management: Thinking It Through

Responsible management means knowing what effects our operations have on the well-being of employees and neighbors. It means anticipating or resolving issues before they are politicized and before new actors or stakeholders enter with additional expectations which have to be satisfied (Post, 1979). A firm should develop a system or process of self-governance to ensure that it knows what it is doing and that it is not knowingly violating the rights of others (Selznick, 1964; Dalton and Cosier, 1982).

It is important to consider the strategy, objectives, resources and environments of the stakeholders involved in a social responsibility issue, to recognize their power and anticipate their reactions to a firm's various planned (and implicit) stakeholder strategies. For example, immediacy, frequent coverage and relevance to a broad spectrum of the population are important objectives of the broadcast media. They have a particularly difficult time finding newsworthy items on weekends or over holidays. Ralph Nader certainly understood this when he called a press conference to describe the Corvair's failures late on a Friday afternoon, in the summer of 1963. His pronouncements were the most important event for the news reports of the weekend, and General Motors' executives did not offer a response until business hours on Monday. Understanding the strategic significance of Nader's timing would have made GM management more effective and responsive spokesmen in their company's behalf.

Similarly, government regulators have objectives which are important to them. And government officials have methods, such as the use of delays for permits or meetings, by which to achieve their objectives. Thinking through a regulatory agency's likely response to various strategies and the procedural actions available to it would improve the likelihood of choosing a strategy which could allow the firm to function effectively and with low legal costs.

Interactive Management

Interactive stakeholder management, where management realizes likely stakeholder reactions and responds to stakeholder interests and actions, is better than either reactive or proactive stakeholder approaches. Post (1976) writes that the best stakeholder management is generally interactive, since reactive management is rarely in control of the situation and a proactive stance may address the wrong problem. Interaction allows the firm to influence both the process by which an issue is resolved and the outcome of that process. While sometimes the firm has no choice but to be reactive, being reactive indeed limits the firm's choices.

Choices are enhanced and increased when stakeholder objectives can be thought through ahead, when time is available to handle issues interactively and to negotiate, and when you know how stakeholders measure your performance and you understand how you value theirs. Indeed, time and knowledge are both the most important results of anticipatory, interactive stakeholder management and so are the most valuable resources to carry out that management function effectively. Knowledge is a major source of power in social responsibility situations. Time provides the opportunity to use it.

TOWARD EVALUATION

In the last two sections, we have addressed not analysis per se, but analysis in a context of relationship management, linking analysis and action. This shift of emphasis is deliberate, for although we believe analysis is a necessary prelude to effective action, analysis and action are not totally separable. Analysis is most useful when the analyst appreciates the context of prospective action. Context for the strategist is the net of stakeholder relationships which exists and changes with success and failure, including failures of responsibility.

Before we act, we have to judge what the facts are and then what they mean for the organization. This last phase necessitates making value judgments—judgments about the significance of the facts for ourselves or our organization. Knowing what the facts are, we attach weight or significance to them and thereafter regulate our behavior (Vickers, 1965). Hence, our movement from facts for analysis to relationship management and responsibility is designed to focus attention on the need for judgment and the influence of values in strategic management.

Values matter in strategic management. Personal values give strategies vitality.

Indeed, how long do people support unprincipled leaders, or those without a cause? Sun Tzu wrote that the first factor in (military) success was the moral factor, explaining:

> By moral influence, I mean that which causes the people to be in harmony with their leaders, so they will accompany them in life and unto death without fear of moral peril. (1963, p. 64)

Arjay Miller vividly reminds managers of the importance of personal values and "doing good," when he advises that in thinking about the ethical, moral, and legal aspects of their decisions, managers should apply what he called the TV test and ask themselves, "How would I explain my actions on TV?" His advice is simple: Don't do anything you wouldn't be willing to explain on TV (Miller, 1980). The question demonstrates that while managers can choose both strategies and implementation methods, their responsibility and position place them in the public eye. They must be willing to live publicly with the results of their decisions. Results are generally easier to live with when they have been anticipated and judged appropriate *before* commitment, while there is time to choose courses of action.

THE MORAL FACTOR: JUDGMENT

What is moral judgment? Barnard (1966) defines morals as

> . . . personal forces . . . which tend to inhibit, control, or modify inconsistent immediate specific desires, impulses, or interests and to intensify those which are consistent with such propensities. (p. 261)

Judgment is a subtle quality. It is labeled by others as good or bad, responsible or irresponsible, insightful or pedestrian. Yet, the calculus of judgment is largely unknown, as Vickers notes:

> There is no means by which any of their judgments can be proved right or wrong—even, I shall suggest, after the event. Judgment, it seems, is an ultimate category, which can only be approved or condemned by a further exercise of the same ability. (1965, p. 13)

Despite this difficulty, managers and others agree that good judgment is restrained. While seeking, indeed creating, opportunity, it is not opportunistic. It is essentially moral, in that it seeks something greater than merely an immediate advantage.

Moral restraint is needed to promote and protect the best interests and well-being of the organization. Selznick calls the source of this well-being the integrity of the organization. Indeed, opportunism threatens integrity, and Selznick writes:

> To take advantages of opportunities is to show that one is alive, but institutions no less than persons must look to the long-run effects of present advantage. In speaking of the "long run" we have in mind not time, as such, but how change affects personal or institutional identity. (1957, p. 143)

Barnard (1966) eloquently presents the case for moral management. Responsibility gives dependability and determination to human conduct, and foresight and idealism to purpose (p. 260). Management's resources root it in the past, while the future is endless (p. 284). Foresight, high ideals, and long purposes are the basis for persistent cooperation in this context. Thus, the chief executive responsibility is to develop a capacity "to bind the wills of men to accomplishment of purpose beyond their immediate ends, beyond their times" (p. 283).

A critical responsibility for a leader is, therefore, to inculcate his or her organization with a moral code to guide its decisions. In Simon's terms, a good manager creates a moral culture (Simon, 1976). Indeed, this is not needed simply to avoid failure in some relationship or exchange; it is needed to create and protect the organization, its "self." "Do unto others as you would have them do unto you" is the essence of organizational morality which restrains and protects the institution.

OBJECTIVES

Ultimately, organizations exist because they serve a purpose: they have objectives which are worth winning. The essence of leadership is choice and the assumption of responsibility for a commitment to a particular path. Sometimes the leader must transcend disagreement and subordinates must follow (Andrews, 1980, p. 85).

Failure by leadership default very often comes from trying to avoid internal conflict or appeasing the illicit claims of some opportunist stakeholder. When businesses fail, it is often by default rather than error. As managers, we can, do, and will make errors. But we do not have to live with repeated errors. If we demand performance of ourselves, that is, if we have objectives, we can demand performance of others.

Selznick (1957) noted that without specific or legitimate objectives, organizations drift, "exposed to vagrant pressures, readily influenced by short run opportunistic trends" (p. 25). He attributes this type of drift to a failure of nerve and a fundamental inability to see what corrupts an organization and makes it vulnerable. As Andrews (1980) puts it, management can allow everyday pressures to rob it of a capacity for self-criticism.

EVALUATING STRATEGY AND OBJECTIVES

Since strategies are what we do to achieve our objectives, when we evaluate our strategy and its results, there is a legitimate question: What were our objectives? Remember, as managers, we may choose to modify our objectives, but it is necessary to evaluate them first. Were they ambitious, inspirational and far-sighted, or mundane? Were they feasible, or impossible?

These are vital issues and it is stakeholder behavior which is the best indicator of our success. Stakeholder behavior, commitment, and enthusiasm all point to stakeholder satisfaction. If there is no enthusiasm or if there is waning commitment, it could mean inadequate or unrealistic objectives or dissatisfaction with our strategy.

We need a capacity for self-criticism to answer the question, "What do the symptoms mean?" One way to find out is to seek meaningful patterns in the Stakeholder Audit

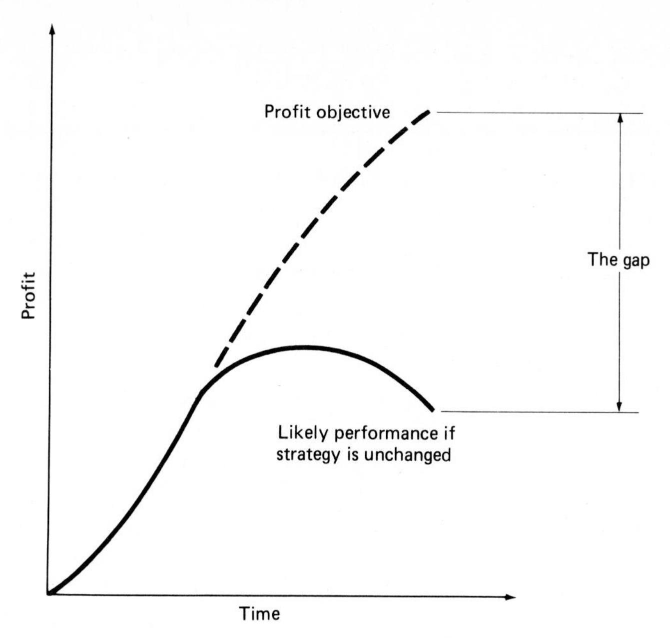

FIGURE 9-3 Gap Analysis

data. For example, we can identify any gap between our performance and our stakeholders' objectives. Secondly, we can compare our performance gaps with our stakeholders' power. Is there a pattern of satisfaction or dissatisfaction? Do the powerful or powerless receive satisfaction in return for their support?

Gap Analysis focuses management attention on the difference between what was wanted and what was achieved. Following Ansoff (1965) and Kami (1969), the identification of the gap is a stimulus for a strategy to close it. *Figure 9-3* describes a profit gap, and similar gap analysis can be done for other objectives. We will discuss gap analysis in more detail in Chapter 11 where we use it as an aid to develop alternatives.

Although normally restricted to financial and market performance, gap analysis can be applied to any performance measure, including the secondary and more remote effects of operations on the environment or stakeholder satisfaction. To do this, the more you know about your stakeholders and how they measure your performance, the better. Likewise, the more you are able to specify and measure your own performance, the better. Explicitness in gap analysis facilitates self-criticism.

SOME CONCLUDING COMMENTS

Just as the summary of the resources and environment of the firm moves the strategist closer to analyzing how they fit together and fit with the strategy, so, too, our concluding comments on objectives will focus on fit. Do the objectives of the firm which the strategist has identified fit with and synthesize stakeholder interests? Do they inspire the firm or constrain it? Do they represent tradeoffs and accommodations of extreme interests so that the firm can operate normally? If a firm's objectives run counter to a major stakeholder's interests, the "fit" is bad, and many strategies which may satisfy simple economic objectives may be unworkable. In practice, if the lack of fit is great enough, key stakeholders may act to constrain operations and remove management.

Indeed, objectives and constraints come from people's values. The heart operates differently than the head, and the heart is indeed an important component of the firm and of great interest to the strategic manager. In the context of stakeholder management, objectives may be considered positive imperatives, what the firm will do. Constraints, in contrast, are negative imperatives, corresponding to "will not do" (Simon, 1964). Both objectives and constraints are important, as the strategist seeks to satisfy the former and avoid violating the latter.

In evaluating our strategy, we consider the quality of the results it has produced and promises; we must blend analysis and synthesis. We have a view of the strategy itself and we have a perspective of the economic environment, the firm's resources, and its stakeholders and their values and objectives. Essentially, each view by itself is only part of the whole picture. In the next chapter, we put them together and gain the benefits from the many perspectives we have developed to evaluate our strategy as we move towards the future.

chapter 10

Strategy Evaluation

INTRODUCTION

Strategy evaluation is one of the most important steps in the strategic management process. Evaluation marks a watershed stage in our efforts to formulate strategy. Before evaluation, we collect and analyze facts. After evaluation, we synthesize new alternatives. Evaluation requires both analysis and synthesis, because it is the step in the process where we have to pull information together.

To evaluate, we look back and we look ahead. In evaluating a strategy, we set the stage for improvement and change. Evaluation requires judgment because evaluation precedes our determination of what to do next.

Evaluation permeates good management systems. Not only do managers evaluate their current strategy's performance, they later must evaluate alternative strategies. As part of their work, they must evaluate their competitors' strategies and the strategies of their organization's stakeholders. Moreover, each manager has to learn to evaluate his or her own performance and the work of others before supporting a new venture, promoting or rewarding subordinates, or considering a new position. Much depends on knowing how to evaluate strategy and people and being right—your career, the survival of your organization, and the jobs of the people who work for you and with you.

In the context of evaluation, what does "being right" mean? Simply put, it means ensuring that the actions you take, based on the evaluation, work out. It does not mean making the right decision. Managers do not just make decisions. Indeed, that is really a very small part of the job (Mintzberg, 1973), and, quite often, a number of alternative courses of action could give satisfactory results (Simon, 1976). Being right as a manager means getting the right result.

Evaluation forces us to look at multiple dimensions of strategy in the organization. *Figure 10-1* illustrates the complexity of the situation facing managers. Getting results is not simply a matter of evaluating the current strategy and selecting a strategy likely to be effective in the *future* environment. The strategy has to be implemented through the organization with its structures, systems, and people. Behavior—action—produces results. When results are unsatisfactory, therefore, the problem may not be the strategic decision. Problems may be due to structural or administrative errors, the personal actions of key people in the organization, or environmental changes.

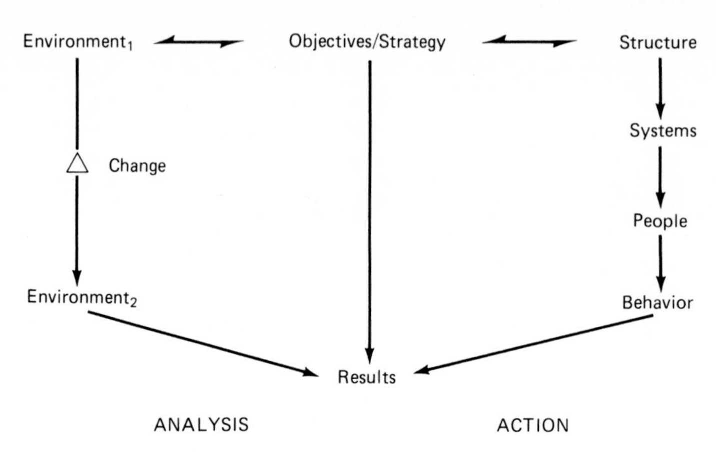

FIGURE 10-1 The Strategic Management System

THE NEED FOR JUDGMENT

Judgment is needed in evaluation because we are under pressure to be right. When we are under pressure, we are likely to pay too much attention to the present or to our prior experience and too little to the future. Moreover, it is never really clear what the facts available mean—for example, what are symptoms and what are causes of problems? Furthermore, as our planning horizon extends, our confidence in the details of any forecast declines. For example, managers of an electric utility face construction periods of five to ten years and an operating life of perhaps as much as fifty years when they commit to new generation and distribution facilities. They have to commit knowing that unexpected change is inevitable. Judgment is essential in these circumstances.

Judgment is required because evaluation leads to a determination of what to do next and where to intervene in the system. Should objectives or strategy be changed, or is it the organization's structure or administrative systems which need modification? Is it a person who must be replaced?

When we evaluate a strategy and take the first steps to determine what to do next, we address a situation marked by complexity and interdependence—and by uncertainty, because the future is uncertain. The effectiveness of the strategy is interdependent with each element in the system that is needed to gain the desired result. Evaluation—sorting out what is needed—requires judgment.

EVALUATION FROM MANY POINTS OF VIEW

To cope with multiple sources of complexity and uncertainty in the evaluation process, we need information and we must break with conventional ways of thinking which limit our ability to be insightful and put unnecessary bounds on our thinking (Simon, 1976; Williamson, 1975). We have to learn to evaluate the strategy from many points of view and we have to learn how to weigh our findings.

Each evaluation perspective we will use tests the strategy. Each test points to potential strengths or weaknesses, to opportunities and threats, to problems, to the benefits and costs of either a continued commitment to the current strategy or of a change. Note that few strategies will receive a perfect score on each dimension. It is the pattern as a whole which we have to use to guide us towards a judgment. The multiplex view, however, helps organize and integrate the information available to us, adds value to our evaluation effort, and, later, will help us generate alternative strategies and develop more efficient operations. The many perspectives and tests pull all the data together and thereby reduce the possibility of our evaluation being dominated by a single error of judgment. Ultimately, the multiple perspectives free us from conventional views alone and so help us intervene in the strategy-structure system more effectively and more efficiently.

EVALUATION AND TIME

Strategy is essentially a bridge between past and future. We stand in the present, straddling the past and the future. Thus, time is a critical factor in the evaluation process:

1. We use the track of performance from the past through the present to the future to judge the merits of a strategy.
2. Our judgment also may be affected by *when* we look.

To make sure the evaluation does not give undue weight to our own present, the evaluation process is more effective when it examines the results of a strategy in the past, present, and future. In this way, it gives weight to current trends, particularly to those originating outside the organization.

Moreover, strategy evaluation is not simply a matter of how results change over time. How the company or organization uses time and times its actions is a strategic choice and this, too, must be considered in evaluating strategies. The following excerpt from *A Book of Five Rings,* written in Japan in 1645, captures some of the subtle relationships between strategic success and time:

> In strategy there are various timing considerations. From the onset you must know the applicable timing and the inapplicable timing, and from the large and small things and the fast and slow timings find the relevant timing, first seeing the distant timing and the background timing. This is the main thing in strategy. It is especially important to know the background timing, otherwise your strategy will become uncertain. (Musashi, 1974)

Looking at past, present, and future results helps us develop insight to the quality of strategy design and its execution, and insight as to whether the strategic management process is becoming more effective. It helps us isolate the proven, real strengths and weaknesses in the business—the resources we have for future competition. Finally, it helps us judge whether the firm's management has been awake to opportunity, timely and far-sighted in its actions and thus building the organization's competitive strength—or short-sighted, wasting resources to create short-term but temporary success—or reckless, needlessly placing the organization's future in jeopardy for short-term, opportunistic gain.

It is worth noting here that the emphasis we give to past, present, and future in strategy evaluation is traditional in business. The accounting system provides us with data along that same time track. The balance sheet is an accumulation of the results of our past strategies. The income statement tells us how we are doing currently, while the sources-and-uses-of-funds statements essentially tell us where the firm believes its future lies, since the use of funds reveals the firm's investment in the future.

The DAAG Example

In this chapter, we will refer repeatedly to the DAAG example to highlight the critical elements of strategy evaluation; here we introduce it and illustrate the importance of the time element in evaluation. During the early 1960s, DAAG, the disguised name for the European division of a US multinational elevator company, adopted an aggressive growth strategy in the market for Class B elevators (those designed for three- to five-floor buildings). By standardizing its product line, initially in Germany and later throughout Europe, and by rationalizing its production operations, the company cut its costs. At the same time, however, it cut its prices even faster to build volume and market share. By 1969, DAAG had reached the point where elevator prices were below manufacturing costs, and questions were raised about the value of the strategy. Critics noted that it is usually possible to build volume if you give goods away. *Figure 10-2* illustrates the situation facing DAAG.

Remember that, for DAAG, 1969 was about half-way through the thirteen-year period which the managing director had believed necessary to complete the changes required to make his strategy successful inside DAAG and in the market. He had planned for losses on current sales and maintained his division's profitability by expanding and emphasizing his elevator service business. In fact, he may have used his losses on new

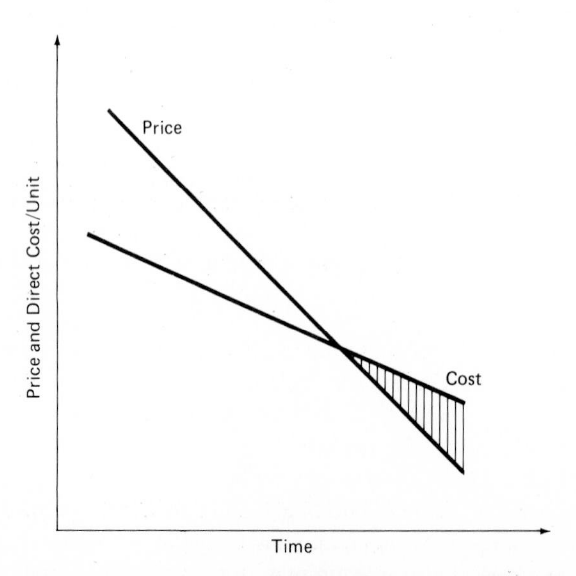

FIGURE 10-2 Price and Direct Cost of a Standard Elevator, c. 1963–69

elevator sales to force manufacturing efficiency on his company and change in his industry.

Because elevators are critical to convenient access to larger buildings, yet are a small part of total building cost, they add considerable value and enjoy relatively inelastic demand, although the level of demand varies with the fortunes of the construction industry. While the company's price cuts forced internal reorganization to reduce costs, the strategy stimulated industry restructuring as some competitors yielded share and sought less competitive niches, while others operated at reduced margins until they either left the industry or imitated DAAG's operating methods, albeit slowly.

Note how time can affect the evaluation of DAAG's strategy. In 1969, an evaluation which heavily weighed losses on new sales might have led to the abandonment of the strategy. A more thorough evaluation would have seen that the strategy was taking advantage of reductions of trade barriers due to the existence of the European Economic Community (the EEC or Common Market) and of the then-current building boom in Europe to develop an unusually robust competitor from a once very ordinary company. Four years later, in 1973, the company's profits demonstrated the success of the strategy and the good judgment of the parent board which had allowed the division to follow its strategy.

In 1969, however, this success was not assured, although the track over time indicated that DAAG's competitive strength was growing. By 1969, the company had been successful in moving its cost structure to a steeper experience curve than it had enjoyed earlier, a steeper curve than any of its competitors. As DAAG gained volume in its standardized lines, it achieved a new scale of production, exploited processes which allowed learning, and focused and rationalized its factories and selling operations.

Figure 10-3 illustrates DAAG's experience curve for its most successful model. Note the cost break around 1966 or 1967. A competitor tracking DAAG might have fitted

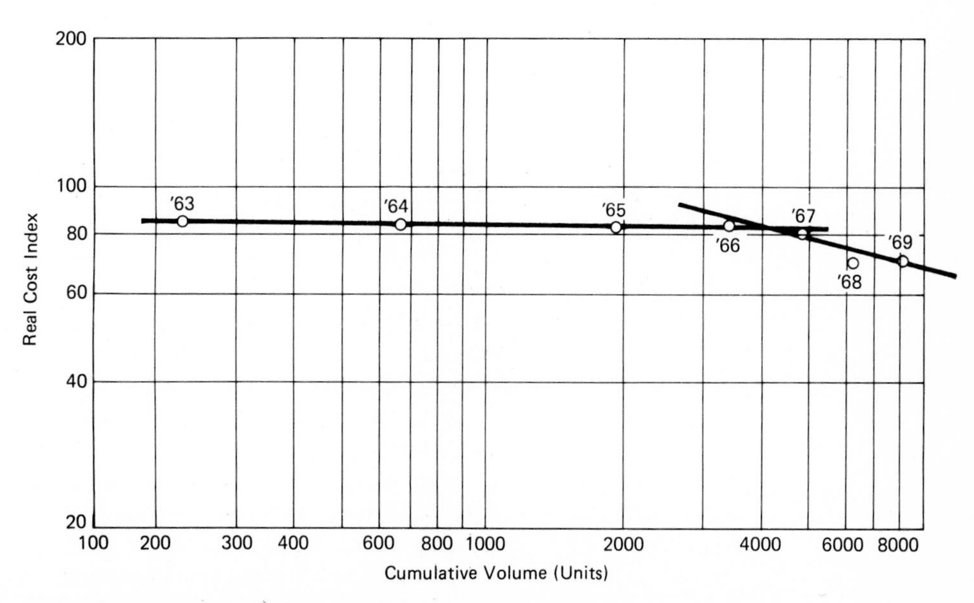

FIGURE 10-3 DAAG: Experience Curve MOD-5 Elevator (Log/Log)

a single curve to the company's cost data through 1969, reasoning that, like the other elevator manufacturers in Europe, DAAG had done nothing to improve its operations. This would have been a potentially very costly underestimation of a competitor whose scale of operations had changed dramatically.

Even in this abbreviated example, it is easy to imagine reaching a different conclusion on DAAG's strategy if we had evaluated the results in 1965 or 1966 when the experience effect had not been captured by DAAG, or if we took a different point of view—for example, that DAAG was out of control. But if we could foresee the longer-term benefits of the operating strategy then underway, would we have given support to the strategy? Indeed, evaluation requires the use of the tracks of many results over time.

SOME PRINCIPLES OF SUCCESSFUL STRATEGIES

While the past, present, and future track of results over time gives us one framework with which to evaluate strategy, we need others to widen our perspective and to enlarge our analytical armory. Let us use experience and consider what makes a strategy effective or ineffective.

First, *the strategy must be consistent with the environment.* It is tough sailing into the wind. It is easier to move with the environment than against it. DAAG, for example, standardized its product line and rationalized its production operations across national boundaries during a period when barriers to international trade were falling in Europe. Similarly, it expanded its Class B operations at a time when construction of three- to five-floor buildings was booming, making its entry to the market easier.

Second, *the strategies of the parts must be consistent with each other and the whole.* For example, marketing must be consistent with manufacturing. For many years, US farm equipment manufacturers such as J.I. Case and International Harvester sought volume in the market to help them cut costs, but marketing continuously broadened the product line, denying manufacturing any opportunity to reach efficient scale. The two functions, production and marketing, were seeking volume but at cross-purposes for the firm's profitability.

Third, *effective strategies focus resources rather than spread or scatter them.* Few weak companies have prospered by diversifying, for example. Some have made money by cutting back and focusing their energy on one market segment, however. Joan Fabrics, once a diversified fabric producer, eliminated almost its entire product line and specialized in upholstery fabrics for the auto industry in the late 1970s. The company has prospered as velour seat-covers have supplanted vinyl in US-made cars.

Fourth, *effective strategies usually focus strength against weakness, seize an advantage, and exploit their competitors' errors to limit costs.* DAAG, a large, well-capitalized multinational company, attacked not multinationals but small family-owned regional elevator companies. It used strategy to pressure these companies into error. If they held their prices, after DAAG cut its prices 9 percent from its former 10 percent premium to match the smaller companies, DAAG gained share. Its new low price, buttressed by its image as a quality international producer, gave DAAG the advantage. If its small competitors cut prices, DAAG saw them cut margins and underinvest in the future. Only a few could identify small, specialized niches out of the thrust of DAAG's strategy.

Fifth, *resources are critical.* Strategy is the art of the possible. Do what is feasible. Resource shortages lead to constraints and vulnerabilities. DAAG moved deliberately, constrained by the profitability of its service business.

Sixth, *risks should not be taken casually.* They should be limited, managed, and reduced—usually by using time rather than fighting it, and by finding others who will absorb the risk for a fee, a reward you can afford to pay if things work out. Resources and relationships can be used to absorb the costs of failure.

Seventh, *a good strategy is controlled.* Its success or difficulties can be anticipated and milestones defined to monitor performance. It should be "self-correcting": managers should learn from their successes and failures. Surprises are failures of control.

Eighth, *strategy should build on its successes.* Internally, success should be traded for autonomy. Externally, success should be used to manage effectively and build more success. Many companies pursuing growth and low-cost strategies see volume leading to cost efficiency and so to opportunities to lower prices again and stimulate sales, gaining more volume, and thereby allowing the cycle of success to continue. Once the strategy is in place, it strengthens itself until the environment changes, as it did for Timex when low-priced electronic watches were introduced to the market.

Ninth, *a sign of strategic success is support by the organization's stakeholders, particularly by top and middle management.* Support is not only a commitment, but a confirmation by others that the course is right.

CONSISTENCY CHECKS

Consistency is the most important characteristic of a successful strategy (Tilles, 1963; Andrews, 1980). In fact, consistency is the shared characteristic of all the principles listed above—consistency with the times and the external environment, and consistency within the firm, including consistent, focused functional strategies. Attacking weakness with strength and exploiting others' errors to limit costs is consistent with maintaining your resource base. Attempting what is impossible is inconsistent with resource maintenance, as it implies taking risks you cannot absorb.

External Consistency

Probably one of the most useful ways of evaluating a strategy is to focus on external and internal consistency. External consistency asks, is it timely? Does the strategy use the environment and ride the wave of change or fight it?

Another form of external consistency is robustness. Robustness refers to a strategy's competitive strength under different environmental contingencies. Strategies which build competitive strength under conditions of prosperity, stability, and recession, for example, are robust and may even be pre-eminent, since these strategies ensure competitive strength and therefore prosperity for the firm under all scenarios.

DAAG, the elevator company we described earlier in this chapter, built a Europe-wide organization using its existing plants for the most part, thereby limiting its capital commitments and so its risk exposure. It made standardized rather than custom elevators and sold them at low prices. Standardization led to volume production, scale economies,

FIGURE 10-4 DAAG's Strategy, 1969, a Robustness Test

Building Industry Conditions	*Major Customer Needs*	*Standardized Producer's Competitive Strength v. Unstandardized*
Boom	Delivery	High
Stability	Reduced construction time, service	Growing
Recession	Price	High

and new manufacturing processes which enhanced the company's existing capacity and lowered costs, as well as allowing faster service and installation time.

Figure 10-4 illustrates the robustness test for DAAG under different industry conditions. DAAG's customers have different needs in different industry conditions. The standardized producer's competitive strength is affected by those conditions. The company's competitive strength grew as it reorganized, reduced costs, and trained its field staff to work with and install the standardized elevators. Because it had not substantially altered its fixed costs, its relative competitive strength was robust in bad times as well as good. Moreover, in good times DAAG could deliver its standard product faster than any of its nonstandardized competitors. Again, it had a competitive advantage. The strategy was robust.

Internal Consistency

Internal consistency is a test focusing attention on functional operations, the business's internal components. If they are coordinated and if each serves the firm's strategy by striving for objectives which are consistent, the strategy of the business will be internally consistent. Adler of Bic used the analogy of business as a car to emphasize the need for coordination and balance within an organization; the analogy stresses the importance of internal consistency.

An organization in which the marketing staff's success depends on maintaining its size and stable relationships with its customers will probably fit with an operations group organized to deliver quality goods. Relationships with customers and internal relationships will probably be smoother in this case if price stability is more important than cost reduction. In contrast, an organization like Bic's emphasizes growth, volume, and volume-based cost reductions. Bic's strategy, too, is internally consistent and, operating cycle after cycle, it built the company's resources and competitive strengths.

Resource Adequacy

Another form of internal consistency relates directly to resources. Are the resources available when they are needed? Abundance allows flexibility and reduces the costs of error. Scarcity constrains freedom and intensifies uncertainty and internal conflict (Pfeffer and Salancik, 1978). A small brewery which aspires to growth is a typical example of a business which cannot afford success. If it promotes its product and fills capacity, the costs of additional capacity are high. If incremental expansion is impractical, the investment required for a new discrete plant is usually too big. New York's Schaeffer Brewing perished as an independent company because it did not have the financial resources needed to implement its strategy of converting its production operations to efficient scale. Although debt was available to the company, rising interest costs through the 1970s and intense competition combined to create losses, and the company failed. The resources were inconsistent with the needs of Schaeffer's strategy.

Consistency with Stakeholders

Consistency is also needed between the strategy and objectives of the firm and the objectives of its stakeholders. Inconsistency here is likely to lead to conflict and a lack of support for the strategy, and so to ineffective implementation. Persistent internal disharmony or conflict with major input-making or output-taking stakeholders is likely to lead to a lack of consensus at the top of the firm and to ambiguity and inconsistency in the market. Without support, top management has no clear power or mandate to do anything, and the organization typically begins to decay. Curtis Publishing Company was a company owned largely by the Curtis and Bok families. Although it published the *Saturday Evening Post,* a very successful magazine in its heyday of the 1920s, the company floundered because in the end, by the 1960s, no one involved in the organization had the power to act decisively and put the survival of the company before the survival of its products.

COMPETITIVE ADVANTAGE

Essentially, companies survive and succeed when they have a competitive advantage and fail when they do not. Even if the advantage is local (for example, a seaside hotel), or temporary (for example, a new but imitable product), the prosperity of the business depends on its ability to defend its relative advantage and on the abilities of its rivals to reduce it. And, we should remember that advantages are rarely absolute or permanent; they apply to a particular segment or niche or time.

Evolutionary theory suggests that niches are the result of a confluence of environmental conditions, have a finite capacity, and may close when the environmental conditions needed to sustain them change (Zammuto, 1982). When change occurs, companies have to learn to survive in a different world and use their resources and competencies to create a new competitive advantage. Timex's dominance of the watch industry ended with the advent of the electronic watch although it continued to use its manufacturing competence to assemble Polaroid cameras and, later, Sinclair computers. Coors's Western markets were isolated from competition by the Rocky Mountains and the Western plains as well as by taste distinctions, until the 1970s. Increased saturation of the Eastern and Midwestern markets led successful national brewers such as Anheuser-Busch to move west into competition with Coors, while Miller targeted its Miller Lite beer to compete directly with Coors. Hence, Coors lost its geographic niche and its taste advantage concurrently and has been unable to maintain its profitability and market stature, or to revive its product's distinctiveness, since that time.

Being the same is never enough. You have to be better than your competitors and different from them. It is your differences which allow you to develop an advantage (Henderson, 1979). The issue as we evaluate our strategy is: What are the differences between us and our competition? Does our strategy exploit those differences to give us an advantage?

Later, we will have to find ways either to enhance our advantage or to start new businesses, in which our competitive profile, our resources, can be used to create an advantage. It may include upsetting an existing competitive situation by entry, acting to induce competitors to avoid us, or deliberately avoiding competitors. We will discuss the generation of alternatives based on a firm's competitive advantage in more detail in Chapter 11.

RISK AND REWARD BALANCE

A principle which permeates strategic management is that *risks must be balanced by rewards*. Managers should strive to increase rewards and cut risks. In the framework of conventional finance theory, a generally upward sloping relationship is posited between risk and reward. One version shows return on assets plotted against β, relative variability of market price, a proxy measure of risk, as *Figure 10-5* shows. The dots[1] under the curve show the investment options facing a portfolio manager who can choose between a treasury bill with a steady return (if held to maturity) and other investments. An efficient investor will mix a portfolio between treasury-bills with low relative risk and the most efficient investment in terms of reward for risk taken. The only ways to increase value are to increase reward or cut risk, or both.

Theory and the realization that value is enhanced when reward is increased or risk is cut should lead us to examine the risk/reward balance of our strategy. Where are the risks? Can they be reduced by different operating procedures or different strategies? Can the rewards earned justify the investments in money and time required?

Are risks taken adequately rewarded? This should be a major concern for management. What risks are inherent in the current strategy? There are many possibilities because some risk is associated with every balance sheet and income statement account. Risk relates to what may happen in the future, and any of these accounts can change due to risk. Of course, the financial statements themselves describe situations of little risk, since financial data rely primarily on historic or market costs.

The Sources of Risk

What are the risks? Liquidity means foregoing the opportunity to invest. Accounts receivable involve credit risks; inventories may carry a fashion or obsolescence risk, as well as the possibility of disaster, theft, or deterioration. Fixed assets expose a company to the technological risk of obsolescence and even nationalization in some cases. Short-term

[1]It is interesting to note that the feasible set of investments (the dots in *Figure 10-5*) are mostly losers who took too much risk and so destroyed value.

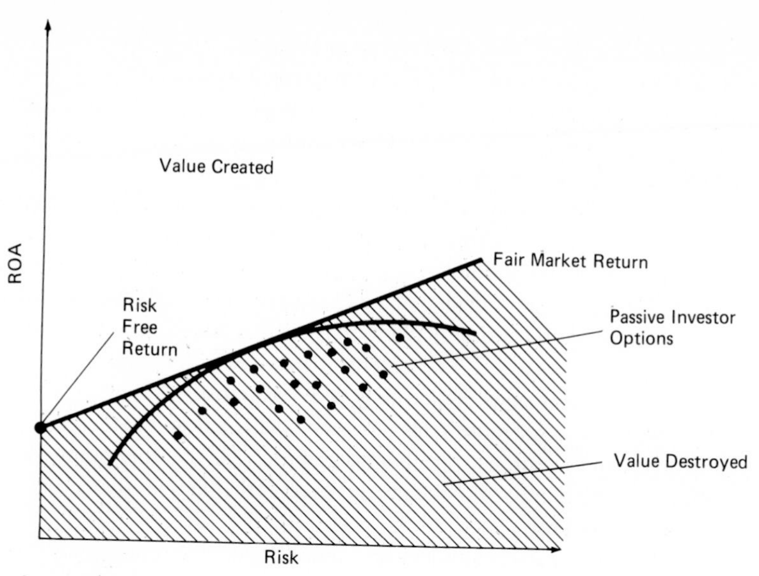

FIGURE 10-5 Risk and Reward

and long-term debt carry the risk of insolvency and negative leverage. Poor equity placements may lead to risk of control.

There are risks of short supply from scarcity, strike, or breakdowns in the plant which interrupt business. Risk is also associated with demand. Product failure or tampering, such as Tylenol experienced in 1982 and 1986, and promotional failures such as Schlitz experienced in the late 1970s with its ''Drink Schlitz or else'' campaign, are examples of demand-related risk.

Risks are popularly seen as environmental contingencies which carry potential loss, that is, financial risk. But risks also exist within the organization and for its people. For example, the risk that failure will lead to a loss or diffusion of power with the organization is a very real problem with some strategies, making future action more difficult.

The point here is not to be exhaustive about strategic risks, but simply to note that in business there are many sources of risk. The more you are able to specify and identify the risks you take, the more likely it is that you will find ways to manage them explicitly and the fewer risks you will overlook.

Reducing Risk

How can risks be reduced? Managers can use time instead of fighting time, and accumulate resources. Managers can also develop relationships or commitments which not only share the risk but, in doing so, reduce it. In real estate and in major petrochemical projects, for example, risks are reduced by prior commitments. In a shopping center or commercial development, a signed commitment by a leading tenant—for example, a major department store chain—substantially reduces the risk of the venture. In the petrochemical business, ''take or pay'' contracts from major customers have the same effect, since the customer essentially guarantees payment in all cases by signing such a contract—the customer must take it or pay for it anyway.

DAAG provides us with superb examples of risk management over time. DAAG's managing director limited his own and his organization's risk by taking one step at a time and making each step work out before taking the next. First, he had his engineering staff design a B-class elevator which he called "standard." Then he sold the elevators. Not until he had sold more than 200 did he need anything, and then he asked the parent for a dedicated plant for the now-proven product. (Remember that, until this time, European elevators were custom-designed.) Next, he found an acquisition target in the B market and bought it, saving 2 years of plant construction time and picking up a 15 percent market share, giving DAAG a 35 percent share, about 800 units per annum. The next year DAAG's elevator sales in Germany rose to almost 1500 units, where they plateaued. The next request was for more sales territory, so the parent put the managing director in charge of European operations, but there was little risk. By this point, the strategy was proven and it remained only to replicate and exploit the competitive strength already established, country by country.

By being patient and by using time to accumulate results, the managing director was able to limit risks. Because each move was predicated by business success, each move was reversible at only minor incremental cost. Moreover, each additional commitment increased the company's competitive strength, making it more robust. The timing used to implement the strategy reduced the risks attached to the strategy.

Willingness to take risk varies with individuals and with situations (Luce and Raiffa, 1957; Swalm, 1966). A full assessment of the risk/reward profile of a strategy thus requires that the "who" and "under what conditions" inherent in the risk component be clarified. "Who" may reinforce the notion that certain important stakeholders in the business may be sources of support who could reduce the perceived risk of the strategy. And "under what conditions" may also reveal resources, strengths, weaknesses, or critical experiences which may alter an initially simple risk/reward assessment. Indeed, since risks are viewed more subjectively than most rewards, the values, resources, and risk tolerance of key stakeholders are most relevant when we evaluate a strategy, our own or another's.

CONTROL

One factor which tends to reduce stakeholders' perceptions of risk is control. People will support a strategy which requires substantial investment and operating losses if management comes to the pump for money once, can live within an initial budget, and can sustain itself. Smart managers learn this early since they know that when you ask you have to give, and what you give up for the privilege of using other people's money is autonomy or independence; control and constraints come along with the money.

Another aspect of control is "controlled" results. DAAG's strategy was to sell at prices set in anticipation of later cost efficiencies—a practice followed in many industries. For example, in airplane manufacturing, and in the electronics and auto industries, prices are set based on costs estimated on forecast unit sales. DAAG's strategy was questioned in 1969 when prices fell below manufacturing cost, yet the company had lost money on elevator sales every year from 1966 to 1969. What reassured the critics was the fact that the average loss per elevator had stayed close to 100 Deutsch Mark (DM), falling as low as 90 DM and rising as high as 108 DM. Because the company retained over 80 percent of its elevator customers as service customers and earned a 10 to 12 percent margin on service, and because elevators need regular service, the small loss of 100 DM, or about 1 percent of sales, gave little cause for alarm. It could be recouped within a reasonable time by the service business which was generated by sales growth. DAAG's total strategy was under control.

ACHIEVEMENT AND GAP ANALYSIS

As we have noted already, managers, strategies, and organizations are judged by the results they produce. But there are more kinds of results than the commonly measured profit, growth, and market share, for example. Results are generated in all the exchanges that occur between the organization—that is, its stakeholders—and its environment.

For example, the ability of an organization (and its management) to achieve its objectives and satisfy its stakeholders is a key test of a strategy and the organization. DAAG's management had a solid record of accomplishment to reassure its stakeholders:

1 management had standardized the company's product line so that 80 percent of DAAG's sales throughout Europe were accounted for by only five different models;
2 it established a European organization and engineering group;
3 it cut costs by almost 20 percent in six years;
4 it captured 25 percent of the European market in units (18 percent in dollar volume);
5 it rationalized manufacturing across Europe;
6 its installed base grew significantly, spreading the fixed costs of their service over higher volume;
7 it earned profit each year.

Top management won the support of its parent company, its peers and its subordinates for what had been viewed by many as a controversial and risky strategy.

Although past achievement is important and gives us confidence in the worth of a strategy, the future is more important. Will the company be able to achieve its objectives, develop or maintain a competitive advantage, and satisfy its stakeholders? Declining advantage and growing stakeholder dissatisfaction should be alerts that the longevity of current profitability, market share, and growth rates is suspect. Even if current results are good in numeric terms, their quality is poor if advantage is declining. The cost of maintaining current earnings is sometimes to sacrifice the organization's future.

An analytical tool which can help us focus new attention on management's investment in the future is Gap Analysis. We introduced the gap concept in Chapter 9, in the stakeholder context. Gap analysis leads us to question not only our likely future achievements, but also our aspirations for the future (Ansoff, 1965). Are our results likely to be adequate? Are we working hard enough? Are we overreaching? Should our strategy or our objectives be changed? Gap analysis is usually applied to an organization's principal objectives and interests. But it can be extended to apply to competitive advantage and the firm's critical stakeholders.

As *Figure 10-6* indicates, gap analysis compares achievement and aspiration, specifically expected (forecast) achievement on an explicit objective against what is required. In this example, the future sales of the organization, if it pursues its current strategy unchanged (the bold line), appear likely to fall, although management is intent on very substantial growth (the dotted line). The gap is the difference between target and likely accomplishment.

If the gap is negative, as in *Figure 10-6,* we may wish to consider whether our resources, including our competencies and competitive advantages, are up to the task. A more modest ambition might be more rewarding and less risky, because it is feasible. Alternatively, we might seek projects, programs, and strategies to close the gap, as Ansoff (1965) suggests. If the gap is positive and performance exceeds aspiration, we should consider the merits of greater ambition and upwardly revised objectives.

Gap analysis forces managers to measure their performance and to audit their gap-closing capabilities (Kami, 1969). Indeed, if you apply gap analysis to nontraditional objectives, such as the satisfaction of explicit stakeholders or stakeholder groups, or to competitive advantage, the analysis forces some hard thinking about measurement. What do stakeholders want? On what dimension is our competitive advantage? Specificity is often the first step towards better management and better results, even with nonfinancial or nonmarket objectives.

The identification of a gap of any substance allows management, for example, to identify and prioritize their on-the-shelf growth projects. How many are there? Kami suggests that a successful organization is *unlikely* to be successful on more than 30 percent of its growth programs; he argues for programs with a total potential of three times the gap over five to ten years. In making that self-assessment, management is advised to monitor

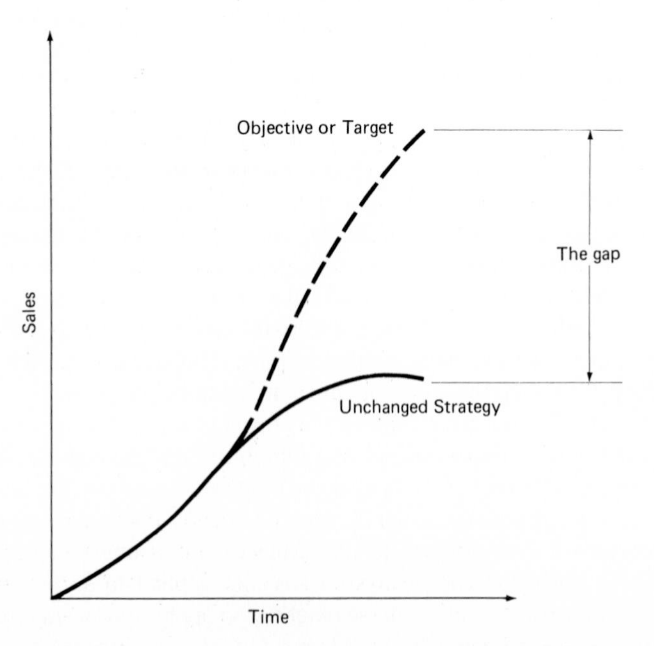

FIGURE 10-6 Gap Analysis

and review the track record of past new ventures (Crawford, 1966). How many were successful? How capable is management of tracking their success and setting practical milestones to measure performance? Kami (1968), after experience at IBM and Xerox during their periods of high growth, suggested that forecasts which were essentially extrapolations typically exceeded actual performance by 100 percent, that is, a factor of two!

Obviously, finding a gap forces a search for both gap-closing strategies and more realistic objectives. Ansoff (1965) broke these two alternatives into two principal classes, expansion and diversification, either internally or by acquisition. We shall deal with these again in Chapter 12.

AN INTEGRATIVE MULTIPLEX VIEW

Multiple assessments, done simultaneously, are necessary for a full and competent strategy evaluation—a multiplex approach—because there are so many aspects to consider. The track of time from the past, through the present, to the future, sets out trends. Trends alert us to opportunities and threats more quickly and reliably than data from a single period. We judge performance by results or achievements; these are the ultimate merits of a strategy. Risks must be reduced and rewards increased to create value. To gain competitive advantage is almost always the reason why we strategize; prosperity in business stems from creating and exploiting an advantage.

Understanding the need for a multiplex perspective, how can we put all these issues together so that busy managers can make a preliminary evaluation of a strategy with reasonable prospects of success? Tilles (1963) used six criteria: internal and environmental consistency, resource adequacy, risk acceptability, the appropriateness of the time horizon, and workability. Under "risk," Tilles emphasized the time and size of the commitments required; "workability" refers to the future. Andrews (1980) used nine different criteria: identifiability and explicitness; the extent to which the strategy uses opportunity (gaps in the market are vulnerabilities); consistency with respect to competence and resources; internal consistency; feasible corporate and personal risk; consistency with values of management; level of contribution to society; stimulus to organizational commitment; and early signs that the strategy works in the market.

These writers, as well as experienced managers, make it clear that many criteria are needed to fully evaluate a strategy. There are many sources of uncertainty and vulnerability in business. Each point of view we take in evaluating strategy adds to our understanding of the situation facing management, although a particular point of view or form of analysis may have limited immediate value.

Strengths, Weaknesses, Opportunities, and Threats

What we strive for is a synthesis of all our information, a view of the whole situation which will help us bring the critical factors into high relief. By focusing on the critical factors, we create a shorthand way to send the most relevant information to management and so expedite action, where it will pay off. Two sets of ideas which have stood the test of time as summary statements of a strategy evaluation are strengths and weaknesses, opportunities and threats. Some writers use the acronym SWOT to describe the combinations. They are, of course, a matched set, since strengths can be used to take advantage of opportunities and threats can be made more serious by weaknesses.

Strengths are the characteristics and resources that give a company power in the market and make it uniquely capable in specific ways. Weaknesses limit the organization and make it vulnerable to attack. While closely related to resource evaluation, strengths and weaknesses have a dynamic and time-specific character; they relate to the competitive environment ahead and to what the firm needs to succeed. Strengths may include high brand recognition and consumer perceptions of product quality and value in an industry where branded products have premium prices, or perhaps a cost advantage due to scale or process efficiency. A weakness could be a temporary or chronic overdependence on debt during a time of rising interest rates, intense competition, and an imminent need for capital to maintain a competitive cost position. Both strengths and weaknesses are situation-specific and occur in time. They wax and wane as competitors and the world change, sometimes converting strength to weakness and leaving management with the task of creating strength again.

Opportunities and threats seem more linked to the external environment than strengths and weaknesses, but this is not always the case. Opportunities for improvement and new ventures exist within the organization and threats can come from within, too. An overcompetitive battle for succession, for example, may leave the company with an exhausted victor, a divided board, and a decimated senior executive cadre.

What are opportunities and what are threats depend on the resources available and uncommitted. Liquid companies can weather different and more severe storms than overextended organizations. An opportunity may be the discovery that the firm's products have a different consumption pattern with a particular market segment. After Miller Brewing acquired a small brewing company primarily to recapture an important Chicago Miller distributorship, an alert manager noticed an unusually heavy consumption of low-calorie beer in the blue-collar town of Anderson, Indiana—an observation which ultimately led to the phenomenally successful Miller Lite beer. A threat may be the actions of a regulatory agency or a competitor which seem likely to interfere with our normal way of business.

Strengths and weaknesses ultimately must be matched with opportunities and threats to generate alternative strategies and select among them; hence the name SWOT analysis, because all four factors are important. However, we should keep in mind the value of comparative and competitive analysis in identifying each component. Not only do they help us appreciate our industry position and how it may shift, but the collective experience of other organizations is available to us to test our ideas, to learn from, and to confirm or refute the conventional wisdom of our industry.

AN EVALUATION FRAMEWORK

Figure 10-7 shows a matrix which collects and summarizes the major concepts used in strategy evaluation. Vertically, it shows how strategies are evaluated by their results over time. The horizontal dimension lists the many components of the firm and its environment which must be addressed. The matrix suggests the use of comparability to evaluate past

FIGURE 10-7 An Evaluation Framework

Track Record	Company Objectives	Your Stakeholders' Objectives	Company Resources	Industry	Competition	Environment	Stakeholders
Past			Comparables				
Current Near-term Future			Control and Risk Exposure				
Long-term Future			Consistency, Robustness, Gap Analysis				
Strengths							
Weaknesses							
Opportunities							
Threats							

results; risk exposure and control for current and near-term performance; and consistency, robustness, and gap analysis for the long-term future environment. In addition, *Figure 10-8* suggests a series of pragmatic evaluative questions. Note that strengths, weaknesses, opportunities, and threats appear on both of the figures to summarize the evaluation process.

By looking to the past, try to determine whether performance is improving or decreasing and why, in addition to how well resources are used. In looking at the most recent cycle, try to see what problems are being created by your actions and what opportunities lie in underutilized resources. Looking to the future, try to determine whether the concepts and assumptions that underlie your strategy are likely to be valid and consistent with the trends of the environment and robust under likely contingencies, including competitors' responses and initiatives. In addition, ask whether your assumptions are consistent with stakeholders' values for future activity and performance.

Consider what the past performance of your strategy has been, what results you have achieved, and why. Consider the consequences of your current mode of operating—for example, what are the results of undermaintaining your facilities or replacing professional staff with less experienced or less capable people in order to hold costs or salaries down? Finally, consider how well your current strategy will function in the environment you see ahead.

By contrasting your most recent results with your earlier record, you can see where your performance has slipped and where you are doing well. In contrasting your results with your objectives, you can see where improvements are needed and where you can proceed confidently. Examining the record of comparable and competitive organizations and contrasting their record with yours, and asking a simple question—"Why?"—you may identify new opportunities, potential improvements, and sources of useful information.

FIGURE 10-8 Strategy Evaluation Questions

	Your Track Record	*Your Objectives*	*Your Stakeholders' Objectives*	*Performance of Comparable Organizations*	*Forecast Environment*	*Resource Base*
Past Performance	Where have you done better or worse and why?					
Current Operating Performance	Are the trends positive or negative?	Are you meeting your objectives, and why? What are they?	Who is satisfied? Who is not? Are thresholds violated?	Who is doing better or worse, and why?	Are you creating future problems for yourself? Are you moving with or against the environment?	Are you fully utilizing your resources? Consistently?
Expected Performance in Future Environment		Is there a gap? Are your objectives achievable or can they be modified?	How will your current strategy affect your stakeholders? Their power, their relative power, and activism?	What will these and competing organizations do to counter your efforts?	What trends will hinder you and which will help you achieve your objectives?	Do you have the resources to succeed in competition?

Strengths
Weaknesses
Opportunities
Threats

Evaluate your current strategy against the environment you see ahead. Can it succeed, substrategy by substrategy? Will your strategy do the job for you in the future world you see ahead? Do you have the resources you need to make it a success?

Evaluation requires systematic thinking. Inconsistency is typically the signal of problems, the alert. Inconsistencies between results and objectives, resource needs and capabilities, between what we are doing and what will be needed, are likely to appear. Evaluation is necessary so that we can determine what to change.

To conclude the evaluation, decide what you think your problems and opportunities are. Typically, your sense of problems will come from a failure to meet objectives, from organizational strife, from inconsistencies you identify, from a sense that your competence has been declining, perhaps in marketing or service delivery, or from a sense that your organization is losing its competitive or financial vigor. These are all symptoms, however. It is important to determine why these symptoms exist, if you can, so that your future actions can be more effective. By contrast, your sense of opportunities will come from your successes, the enthusiasm which organization members have for particular programs, your identification of unserved needs which your communities or competitors have ignored, and your realization that you have discretionary funds available to invest.

THE PRACTICAL BENEFITS OF EVALUATION

Managers who do not manage well always seem to be surprised. Their best-laid plans appear to go astray, or, as one president of Scripto said, ''I lie awake all night wondering how things will work out.'' The president of another company told a consultant, ''If only we'd called you in sooner.'' Bottom-line blindness had led that company to monitor profit closely, but poor asset deployment had allowed the company to put too much money into its inventory, and the inventory was obsolete. A multiplex evaluation would have uncovered that strategic flaw. A rigorous strategic evaluation can head off surprises and insomnia, since a strategy evaluation can flag potential problems while they can be successfully handled, before they become real problems.

Strategic evaluation allows the manager to anticipate responses to expected problems. It is a necessary step before generating alternative strategies, because alternatives responding to specific problems and needs are likely to be more valuable than alternatives based on gazing into a crystal ball. And strategic evaluation is an ongoing process. The continuous evaluation of the results of an implemented (alternative) strategy creates an opportunity to constantly refine and improve the strategy.

Management has to develop sufficient confidence in its analysis and evaluation to act, but management must also expect change and understand the need for reaction. If the objectives of the organization are far-sighted, management can change its strategy in small and even large ways, but stick to the course selected.

The task is never easy. Strategic success comes from creating a situation where your organization has an advantage over its competitors and then acting to exploit that advantage to achieve your objectives. Mastering the situation requires information and hard thinking: evaluation. Remember, the only competitive situations you should enter are those you can win and defend. Otherwise, why invest resources?

PREVIEW: DEVELOPING SOLUTIONS, NEW OR IMPROVED STRATEGIES

Once you have a sense of what your organization's problems and opportunities are, it is your job to develop potential solutions. In developing these solutions or responses, you are moving to modify your current strategy, improve your performance, and turn your organization toward new opportunities. These are the subjects of Chapter 11.

chapter 11

Generating Alternatives

INTRODUCTION

Generating alternatives, the strategies and actions organizations could take to exploit their opportunities or resolve their problems, is a challenging and exciting part of every manager's work. The task holds the challenge of making organizations work better and the challenge of resolving an organization's really difficult problems. Freewheeling creative thinking and participation in the definition of an organization's future can be very exciting.

Once you have developed a deep understanding of a business's current strategy, the alternatives you need will often come to mind quickly. This is natural, because strategic analysis is a problem-finding process (Ansoff, 1971; Bower, 1967, 1982). With the organization's situation defined as strengths, weaknesses, opportunities and threats, solutions develop as natural responses to each type of problem. In most instances, the alternatives which fit this natural response category exploit traditional or standard strategies which are evolutionary rather than radical.

For most successful organizations, the outcomes of a strategic audit are minor changes to the existing strategy, fine-tuning of operations, and limited trials of a new strategy. Successful performance implies maintaining what works. In successful organizations, management is concerned with preservation of what it has and with continuity rather than change, so change is slow and adaptive. Braybrooke and Lindbloom (1970) and Quinn (1980) call such changes logical incrementalism, since they build from a successful base in ways which improve performance still further.

Yet even in a world where continuity is valued highly, sometimes radical change is required. When the problems or opportunities facing the organization are too large, complex, or intractable for incremental and evolutionary solutions, radical solutions may be needed. But we must determine the real cause of management's difficulty in certain situations so that we do not undertake the risks of radical solutions needlessly. Narrow-mindedness, tunnel vision, or a loss of flexibility in management's thinking may be blocking the creative elements of the strategic management process. Alternatively, perhaps the change ahead in the environment is truly large and does have grave consequences for the organization. In this case, developing a response is indeed a major challenge not readily amenable to normal approaches. Radical solutions and significant strategic change may be necessary.

The purpose of this chapter is to help you generate alternatives effectively and efficiently and help you understand the role you can play in defining your organization's future. Alternatives are best generated with an attitude which is opportunity-seeking rather than problem-solving. We will describe the generic strategy options that are available to every organization. We will then suggest what "blocks" mean in the process of generating alternatives and how to get out of them. We will also outline ways to deal with more extreme situations where major change is required. Finally, we will illustrate how all levels of management must contribute to the process of generating alternatives if the organization's strategic performance is to improve significantly.

SELECTION OF PROBLEMS TO SOLVE

As we begin this chapter, we should note that although the strategic audit process which encompasses strategy identification and evaluation often "finds" problems, and although many of them can be addressed quickly and at low cost, this is not always so. Nor is the problem always the best starting point for generating alternatives. Indeed, we do not have to solve problems simply because we find them.

In management and administration people must learn to stop solving problems indiscriminately and start thinking about addressing problems selectively to create value and keep it. Very little time in our society is spent determining which problems warrant effort. We honor problem solvers and our education system institutionalizes the myth that problems should be solved. Indeed, "good" students are often thought to be those who solve the most problems during their education.

The job of management is not to solve problems, nor is it to define problems for others to solve. At its best, managing is an opportunity-seeking activity (deBono, 1977). Problems are nothing more than opportunities to act and thereby achieve our objectives.

Indeed, because management's job is not to solve problems but to define and achieve objectives so that the value of the organization is enhanced, management must be selective. Managers must select from among the problems and opportunities revealed by strategic analysis (and day-to-day events) those few which warrant attention. Managers must select problems which, if addressed, will move the company furthest toward the accomplishment of its objectives. Selectivity is key: Management must choose which problems and opportunities to address, which to ignore, and which to monitor.

So before working hard to exploit opportunities or to reduce the number of problems facing an organization, reflect on the outcome of your work to identify and evaluate your firm's strategy. What is the firm's business and what is making the greatest contribution to its success or impeding its progress most severely? Put your effort where the payoff is likely to be greatest. Address both strategic and operating problems and opportunities. Not every problem is inherently strategic, and neglected operating problems can lead to corporate failure.

BEGINNING THE PROCESS OF GENERATING ALTERNATIVES

Strategy evaluation provides us with opportunities to understand what we do now and to do it better, as well as time to prepare and provide for the future. It tells us what is working and what is not. Evaluation alerts us to the likely future course of events and to the need to modify our objectives. Therefore, evaluation is the logical starting point as we seek to generate alternatives.

Either our business is working well and is properly positioned for the future, or change is needed. If we have a successful strategy and understand the reasons for its success, we should most probably follow this advice: "If it works, don't fix it!" If our strategy has problems, our efforts to identify a response should be guided, first, by the source of the difficulty, and then by the fact that useful strategies have common characteristics.

Each component of our analysis contributes issues to be addressed in the process of generating alternatives and points toward solutions. Strategy identification, for example, focuses attention on internal consistency, competence, and competitive advantage. If there is inconsistency, we can seek ways to reduce it. If our competence is unclear or declining, we can attend to it. In evaluation, the principles introduced in Chapter 10 define the characteristics of successful strategies: internal and external consistency, focus, strength against weakness, feasibility, control, and support. Does our strategy have these characteristics?

As we attempt to respond to issues coming from the evaluation process, we should make our moves deliberately. Remember that the least change is often the best change, and almost always it is the least costly and has the lowest risk. The results of small changes are easiest to monitor and control.

GENERIC STRATEGIES AND STANDARD ALTERNATIVES

The more extensive the problem, the more thought and insightfulness seems required to solve it. Yet, in addressing this task of designing a new strategy, remember the advice of Ecclesiastes 1:9:

> What has been is what will be and what has been done is what will be done; and there is nothing new under the sun.

Management need not innovate in every aspect of its strategy to succeed. Imitation can be very helpful (Levitt, 1966), and generic strategies suggest approaches known to improve performance.

So much of what people herald as new is simply something, once forgotten, which has been rediscovered and repackaged. In business, for example, the profits of the old product line have always been the primary source of funds for new ventures, long before the concepts of "cash cow" and "wildcat" were conceived and popularized by the Boston Consulting Group (see Chapter 18). Many sophisticated dictums are basically simplistic, although not necessarily simple to implement. For many years now, our neighbor, a successful stockbroker, has heard his mother-in-law's parting advice after every visit: "Remember, Mel, buy low and sell high." Obvious, of course, but correct—simple to say and difficult to do.

So it is in strategic management. Generic strategies such as Porter's differentiation, overall cost leadership, and focus (1980), and Utterback and Abernathy's performance maximizing, sales maximizing, and cost minimizing (1975), are little different from the buy low, sell high advice our friend receives from his mother-in-law.[1] They each point to ways to raise revenue or lower costs, both sure-fire methods to increase profits!

Typically, the generic strategy's emphasis on one or two variables maximizes its visceral impact and intuitive appeal, but complicates its use. Business-level strategies by their nature are integrative; they encompass many variables. "Overall cost leadership" is a dangerously flexible strategy definition. But the question, "How could a company attain overall cost leadership?" should provoke useful thinking. Often the value of generic strategies lies more in the questions they provoke than in any simple effort to implement them independently.

Other standardized strategic options come to mind. A company might choose between a change in its strategy and no change. Changes could include liquidating all its assets or part only, perhaps to specialize in one particular industry role by harvesting (slowly liquidating) its activities in another business. Alternatively, it might diversify. Vertical integration is another option. Growth may be by business development, emphasizing product or market expansion, and market expansion might be regional or international.

Figure 11-1 suggests the large number of options available to the strategist. To change or not to change, of course, is a very basic choice. But change may encompass contraction (liquidation), growth via specialization after consolidation, or diversification. Whether liquidation is fast, via divestment, or slow by harvesting over time, may depend on factors such as potential buyers or shared facilities. Consolidation, or narrowing scope, may occur with or without integration. Joan Fabrics, for example, began its consolidation strategy by moving out of all its former markets except the automobile upholstery fabrics market. It then integrated its auto fabrics activities by becoming involved in more stages of the production process.

We have included market scope and research emphasis as other dimensions of generic strategy development in *Figure 11-1,* but we have certainly not exhausted the sources of generic strategies. Each managerial dimension adds flexibility to management's choices, helping managers differentiate their company from its competitors. Such flexible thinking ensures that the strategy ultimately adopted has the greatest promise of serving the organization, since it has resulted from thoughtful combinations of strategy options. Henderson (1979) emphasized the importance of differences among firms when he wrote that advantage stems from differences and, unless there is an advantage, we note there can be no real economic profit.

Liquidation

Liquidation refers to decisions to leave a certain business or product sector. Divestment is a single-step liquidation and refers to the sale of a business. Harvest is the term frequently applied to a slower liquidation process in which the business continues to function but in a contracting form. In a harvest, little additional investment is made in the business, and resources are typically removed from the business and redeployed.

[1]See Galbraith and Schendel, 1983. These options could be used concurrently. Combinations of generic strategies may be helpful, e.g., a low-cost position in one segment to maximize sales, accompanying cost reductions on another product line. Marketing, production, and finance variations of the generic strategies create many potential combinations which can differentiate one company from another.

FIGURE 11-1 Generic Alternatives

GENERIC STRATEGIC ALTERNATIVES	
No Change	Options
Change:	
Liquidate	Harvest or Divest
Specialize	Consolidate or Integrate
Diversify	Product or Market

GENERIC TARGETS FOR DEVELOPMENT	
Market	Operations
Niche	Product
Segment	Process
Regional	Purchasing
National	Service
Multi-National	Cost
Global	

For example, if change appears necessary, a company may choose to specialize by consolidating in a regional market, perhaps reevaluating its purchasing strategy and deciding to assemble components rather than self-manufacture.

Liquidation is popularly seen as the result of poor business performance, something which necessarily happens to losers, rather than as an active approach to improving performance. However, the liquidation strategy simply implies that some activities have been found to be more attractive than others. These attractive activities warrant more of the firm's resources, which are sensibly redeployed from low-return businesses to those with higher earnings. Ultimately, the liquidation strategy should improve overall corporate performance. The harvest or partial liquidation strategy represents a very deliberate attempt to improve performance by limiting, rather than ending, commitment to certain low-return businesses. If, as is hoped, rates of return improve when less capital is devoted to the business, the harvest strategy will successfully demonstrate that resources were being used inefficiently in that area.

Integration

Integration into other components of the product-distribution chain can be an attractive alternative for managers who feel their objectives would be better served if they had more control of their suppliers or customers. Forward integration moves the firm's activities toward the consumer; for example, adding distribution to manufacturing capabilities is forward integration. Backward integration involves the firm in supplier activities in addition to its own. Both forward and backward integration are examples of vertical integration in the terminology of industrial organization economists. Horizontal integration, by contrast, refers to buying competitors at the product-distribution stage in which the firm is already operating. This strategy can be used to gain access to supply or distribution components which a competitor has and the firm itself wants; its purpose may really be vertical integration.

Classic vertical integration is costly and may not earn an appropriate return. Yet, integration need not be by ownership; fixed assets can be rented or coopted as well as owned. Contractual arrangements for input or output or for operating services can also accomplish the objectives of integration—that is, control and power—with much lower fixed cost commitments. Contracts, for example, can provide supply or distribution rights with less risk than the suppliers or distributors themselves carry. Sears and the Japanese auto makers are examples of powerful firms whose contracts with suppliers give them power with less risk than the suppliers themselves carry. Cartels are contractual arrangements dividing markets among a number of suppliers, and are thus an example of a contractual approach to horizontal integration. Cartels are common in business dealings outside the US; they are illegal restraints of competition in the US.

Integration can result in interdependence as well as power. Williamson (1975) rationalizes integration by describing the reduction in transaction costs between integrated components as more than compensating for less independence. The integrated oil industry is an example of a situation where the interdependencies between integrated components probably provide more effective, faster signals of market movements and so better responses than the independent components could generate individually.

McLean and Haigh (1954) take the example of integration still further as an alternative when they note that US oil companies have continuously changed positions in the chain, even jumping stages rather than simply moving one stage forward or backward. Changing position can be a valuable strategic alternative. In addition to investing in the most rewarding industry stages, an industry participant changing positions may bring valuable information, contacts, and experience which could raise the rewards and lower the risks of entry. For example, many of the surviving large shoe manufacturers in the US are now major retailers and importers, apparently using their traditional and tested fashion and distribution skills more profitably in merchandising imports rather than American-manufactured shoes. Such experience can be a source of synergy in the new position in the chain, enhancing performance beyond the level historically expected or available to other new entrants. And it may be a very appropriate way of transforming a company or revitalizing it—for example, in consolidating industries which no longer provide opportunities for the number of participants currently operating.

Diversification: The Product-Market Matrix

The product-market matrix shown in *Figure 11-2* provides a frequently overlooked framework for assessing served and neglected potential markets. In the matrix, customers define the market; product encompasses the current product, a simpler version of the same product, related and more technically advanced product forms, and unrelated product technologies. The results of the interactions of markets and product technologies when a

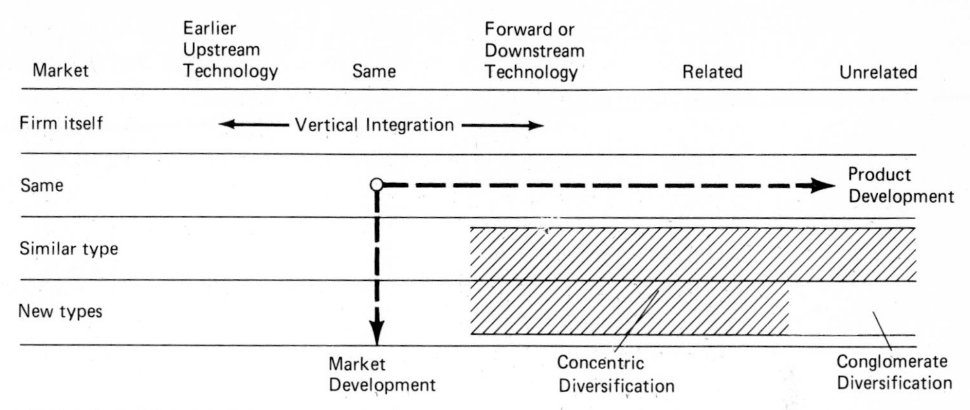

FIGURE 11-2 The Product-Market Matrix

firm is serving its own supply needs include integration and point to improvements in its own operations.

Product development occurs when the firm serves the same customers with an expanded product line. Market development uses the current technology to service additional markets. Concentric diversification is Ansoff's (1971) term for attempts to service additional markets with expanded technology offerings. Conglomerate diversification refers to business strategies offering unrelated products to new, unrelated customers.

The product-market matrix suggests directions for single-business expansion. In cases where no profitable potential markets or related technologies are apparent, it can point to diversification away from a single-business focus as a major strategic alternative—the single-business commitment may be considered too risky, while it seems that risk may be reduced by diversification.

MANAGING THE PROCESS OF GENERATING ALTERNATIVES

Creativity, Flexibility, and Timing

While we have described types of alternatives, we have thus far said little about the process of generating alternatives. Yet the process is a delicate one, and careful management of the process is likely to improve its results.

Probably the most important thing to remember about the process is that the likelihood of generating good-quality alternatives is increased if many alternatives are considered (DeBono, 1968; Janis and Mann, 1977). Few alternatives often indicate a stymied, nonproductive situation. Consider the following list of possible alternative types:

1 Status quo—"business as usual" is always an option.
2 Generic strategies to raise revenue and lower costs.
3 Actions which may alter stakeholder support and power.
4 The unthinkable—those actions that violate conventional wisdom.

Each of these strategic types holds a number of actions open to the firm. If they are never explicitly listed, they are unlikely to be adopted—and a very good approach to an opportunity or problem may be lost.

The objective of the process is to develop strategic alternatives which differentiate an organization from its competitors. Often the best alternative may integrate elements of some apparently inappropriate alternatives. Inhibiting creativity during the process—for example, by committing to an idea or evaluating it too soon—will limit the number and quality of suggestions with useful characteristics. Avoiding hasty evaluations and judgments which induce you to discard alternatives will allow you to rethink, rework, or combine them to make them more attractive. The practice of discarding suggestions too soon inhibits the creativity needed to develop alternatives. Nevertheless, creativity is needed to generate a relatively large number of alternatives, although the need for originality can be tempered if we realize that alternatives which represent strategic improvements are likely to have certain characteristics and comply with the principles described in the evaluation process (Chapter 10).

As we seek advantage and try to employ our resources as distinctively as possible, flexibility is important—call it adding degrees of strategic freedom, if you like. Flexibility to see things freshly and an ability to question current practice are important skills, yet they are difficult to maintain in practice. Familiarity, pressures for action and results, and other factors lead to an inability to think flexibly and insightfully.

Some flexibility is truly creative, although sometimes necessity is its mother. Indeed, many entrepreneurial ventures are successful only because the new owner "did not know it could not be done and had nothing to lose anyway" (Uyterhoeven et al., 1977, p. 49). Yet, expertise and market dominance can often lead to blindness, just as wealth can turn venturers into conservatives. People may fail to see the significance of current events or be unable to respond to them appropriately.

For example, many technological innovations have been made outside the bounds of the industries they have later captured. Presumably the incumbents had too large a commitment to the old way. As Cooper and Schendel (1976) found in their studies of technological threat, in mature industries, the outsider is likely to be the innovator; management and users alike are distracted by the new product's minor characteristics; managers rarely identify what it will take to succeed with the new technology; and established firms rarely make the right commitment early enough and large enough to win. Management was simply too inflexible to rethink the product, or found the situation too complex to handle well.

Timing is another variable sometimes neglected in the process of generating alternatives. Some alternatives will not work as expected without prior groundwork, and staging their implementation in steps can increase the probability of success as well as management's control. Management can react to results if those results unfold slowly rather than cataclysmically.

Thus, alternatives are best considered as actions to be taken at certain times, rather simply than as actions—with no sense or control of timing. Argyris (1977) writes of our need to monitor success, and this is facilitated if timing is a managerially controlled variable. Indeed, a limited early commitment provides results to guide further action.

Mental Blocks

Although many of the changes managers make to their strategies and operations are clearly straightforward responses to problems found in a strategy audit, these are usually minor in scope and are essentially a fine-tuning of the organization's strategy and the

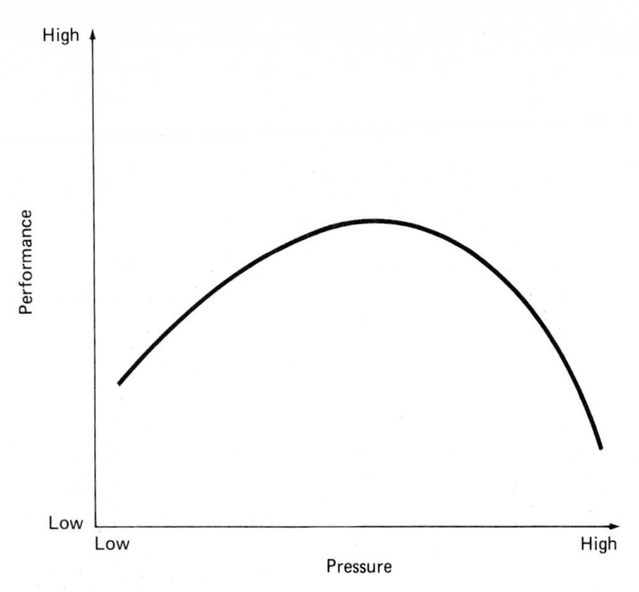

FIGURE 11-3 Pressure and Performance

operating systems which implement it. When larger changes are called for, generic and standardized ''cookbook'' strategies can often be adapted to serve the needs of the organization—raising revenues and lowering costs generally raises profits!

Sometimes, however, management is blocked. Being blocked is usually experienced as a feeling before it is recognized as a fact. Nonetheless, the feeling is usually a real sign that something is wrong in the process. Despite hard work and the passage of time, the company can find no way to improve its position and resolve the problems it sees.[2]

Mental blocks typically occur when the pressure is greatest. In fact, it is precisely when we need a broad perspective and some flexibility that we seem most prone to narrow our vision and find ourselves trapped in a mental block (DeBono, 1977; Ohmae, 1982). Although a little pressure prompts successful effort, too much quickly becomes dysfunctional and performance tends to falter, as the conceptual diagram of *Figure 11-3* suggests.

The block phenomenon is so pervasive that it warrants explicit attention. You are probably blocked when:

- you feel pressured and you are simultaneously unproductive;
- you recognize growing intolerance of others' points of view and an instinct to defend your point of view, a pattern repeated by your colleagues;
- priority is given to the loudest and most insistent voice, although you feel something is wrong but cannot specify what it is.

To some extent, these symptoms apply whether you are working alone or with others.

[2]The same thing often happens to students working on a case. Despite continued effort over time, progress is elusive and their frustration with the case and their colleagues grows.

FIGURE 11-4 Behavior Blocking New Thoughts

1. "Tunnel vision," when all attention is focused on the wrong response, like a wild animal frozen by the headlights of an oncoming car.
2. "The all-or-none fallacy," when management defines its options as a 0:1, go–no-go situation—for example, defining action against competitive entry as a success if the entry is completely prevented and as a total loss otherwise. It might be possible to take advantage of the entry by a competitor to have the overall market grow while preserving a powerful market position. Essentially this is a perverse form of greed.
3. "Perils of perfectionism": an unwillingness to commit to action until even subtle and often irrelevant details are attended to. An example might be to delay market entry until a totally pre-emptive strategy is developed, although you have developed a strategy which promises a relative competitive advantage.
4. "Loss of perspective": focusing on the details to the exclusion of the key factors that truly make a difference—for example, worrying about the costing details of a TV advertising campaign while your manufacturing costs substantially exceed your competitor's.
5. Failure to challenge constraints, especially self-imposed constraints. For example, consider the plight of a product manager, who controls only the marketing strategy for his product, confronting a corporate pressure for higher margins. Not controlling overhead or fixed or variable manufacturing costs, he feels trapped but does not consider price or service charges which may help sales and margins, at least in the short run.

Source: Adapted from Ohmae, *The Mind of the Strategist,* New York, NY: McGraw Hill, 1982.

Different types of blocking observed by Ohmae (1982) are listed in *Figure 11-4*. In all these circumstances, management's thinking is inflexible. Typically, under pressure, people are blind to opportunity. To break out of their own personal boxes, managers need to take a different point of view, perhaps their boss's or their customers', and change their perspective. They should use the new point of view to add new variables and flexibility to their thinking.

Recognizing the block is the first step toward a cure and possibly the way to a breakthrough. Blocked problems tend to be "we can't do's" seeking solutions. Ohmae says that a "can do" attitude is needed; DeBono says we should focus on the benefits of opportunity. One way to gain perspective is to concentrate on the key factors of success and drop the detail—that is, administratively delegate the less urgent and focus on the most important.

Essentially, blocks are not simply cognitive failures. They involve cognitive, social, and emotional factors (Emshoff, Mitroff and Kilman, 1978). They involve self-centeredness rather than other-centeredness, for example, a focus on operations rather than on the customers, or on divisional operations rather than on the corporate strategy.

Breaking Mental Blocks

Breaking blocks requires hard work and smart flexible thinking. Remember, Edison said invention is 98% perspiration and 2% inspiration. Moreover, we should not be content with a satisfactory solution. We should strive for flexibility, new perspectives, and choice.

More alternatives provide an opportunity for wiser and more confident choices. Having choices means we have degrees of strategic freedom, an ability to follow variations on strategic themes to achieve our objectives. Such freedom does not come from the presence of slack resources alone. Choices can be provided by insightful and creative management, too. Sometimes an abstract concept of the business promotes innovation, although most businesses begin with very tangibly defined products and services and never change. Levitt (1975) addressed such conservatism and the potential costs of a narrowly defined and inflexible concept of the business in ''Marketing Myopia.''

A New Concept of the Business

The Bic Pen Corporation is a good example of a flexible company whose self-concept changed. It began making ballpoint pen refills and gradually expanded its product line to include disposable ballpoint pens, retractable pens, and porous-tip pens. Later, it added cigarette lighters, pantyhose, and disposable razors. In the process, management changed its self-concept from ''pens'' to ''writing instruments,'' then to ''manufacturers and marketers of high quality, everyday disposable products distributed through writing instrument channels,'' and next to a ''marketing company.'' Management moved from tangible to abstract in its concept of its business. The test of such a concept is its productivity: Does it lead the company to new products? *Figure 11-5* illustrates Bic's conceptual evolution.

Adaptation and flexibility such as Baron Bich's at Bic is often a result of exerience. When logic does not work, try intuition to develop a new approach—intuition is your collective experience at work. The work of the Applied Research Center at the Wharton School of the University of Pennsylvania, for example, emphasizes stakeholders and stakeholder interests as opposed to the strategic and environmental analysis we emphasized. A focus on customer, competition, and company is a three-phased check list which Ohmae (1982) uses to generate ideas. The test, of course, is always productivity.

Exploiting Analogy

While it sometimes pays to be very detail-oriented, identifying key factors and restructuring them in the light of simple widely shared analogies is offen productive. This particularly is true of one-on-one competitive situations.

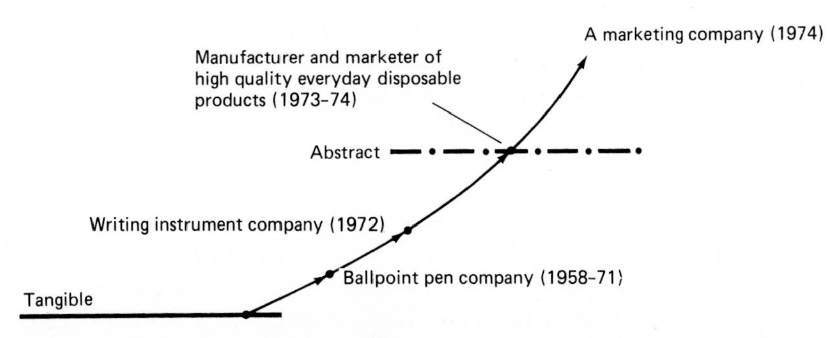

FIGURE 11-5 Conceptual Evolution of a Business: Bic

FIGURE 11-6 Relative Advantage: Polaroid vs. Kodak

	Polaroid	*Kodak*
Marketing		+
Product technology	+	
Brand	+	
Operations		
Short-term	+	
Long-term		+
Finance		+
Management		+
Edwin Land	+/−	

When Kodak entered the instant camera business in 1976, observers rated Polaroid and Kodak as shown in *Figure 11-6* on each of seven factors (the plus signs indicate advantage). Kodak was judged to have a more experienced and accomplished marketing force, with more numerous and more loyal outlets than Polaroid. Yet many felt that Polaroid, as the innovator in instant photography, had product technology as well as brand recognition on its side. In 1976, Polaroid had its SX70 operations running profitably at about 40 percent capacity, producing 2 million units per year, while Kodak was not yet producing instant cameras or film in commercial quantities. Kodak had broken with its traditional practice of simultaneous national and worldwide new product introduction—the company planned a phased North American rollout beginning in Canada in May and later in Florida. Also, many felt Polaroid had a short-run advantage in its manufacturing operations that Kodak would ultimately erode. Kodak was about five times larger than Polaroid and so had the financial advantage. Polaroid had Edwin Land, a brilliant inventor but an apparently inflexible man, as CEO. Kodak had professional, institutionalized management and had managed succession well.

Focusing on the details and attempting to develop options quickly is an overwhelming task. However, focusing on the skeletal outline of relative advantage can be quite productive. Putting ourselves in the shoes of Polaroid's managers, we could apply the principle of strength against weakness, which would suggest a Polaroid assault head-on against Kodak's new product, avoiding Kodak's marketing and financial strengths.

Using an analogy from the martial arts and self-defense, we might begin to think of ways to actually use Kodak's money and marketing muscle to Polaroid's advantage. A military analogy would tell us to attack when Kodak enters the instant-camera market and before its presence is well-established. A lesson of the fairy tale of "The Three Little Pigs" is that wolves shouldn't climb down chimneys but work in the open range where their strengths give them an advantage. What is Polaroid's range? Is it technology? Could Polaroid manufacture and supply the market in advance of Kodak's entry and cut price either to stimulate its own sales and Kodak's response, and thereby delay Kodak's achievement of breakeven, or else to gain sales in a growing market stimulated by Kodak's introductory advertising? The point here is not to be exhaustive or detailed, nor do we intend to explicitly consider Kodak's and Polaroid's responses and reactions.

Rather, we have briefly demonstrated how analogy and focus on a few key factors can quickly stimulate the development of useful strategy alternatives in a tough situation.

A New Perspective: An Industry Focus

While our focus in the Polaroid/Kodak situation was on companies, sometimes our concentration should shift to the industry. The paper industry is capital-intense and employs very large-scale plants. The biggest producers, like International Paper, are vertically integrated back to the forests and have their own fuel supplies. How could a small company operate in this industry? How could it position its plant close to its source of materials and overcome the large companies' scale advantage? One company, Clevepak, entered the industry as a manufacturer by using scrap paper as its raw material. Clevepak created a supply advantage by locating not in the woods but near its supply in the city. It countered International's cost economies due to scale by choosing value-conscious small markets characterized by relative price inelasticity. It then buttressed its position with unusually generous service. It developed a niche by servicing not the large paper-users but small specialty-goods manufacturers who needed small numbers of special packaging boxes and cardboard containers which could not be supplied economically by the largest paper manufacturers. Clevepak, a small company, recognized every characteristic of the major players in its industry and found a way to neutralize or duplicate each characteristic's competitive impact.

Intractable Problems

Clevepak's strategy, systematically creating competitive capability in an industry by overcoming the rules of the game, is an example of the experience-founded thinking required when a strategic problem is truly difficult, but sometimes problems arise which are outside our available experience. For example, large environmental changes which threaten the continued viability of the organization may develop or are foreseen. What to do then?

When normal methods do not work, we must take a different tack and turn from logic, or vertical thinking, to what DeBono (1968) called lateral thinking. He describes it:

> Instead of proceeding step by step . . . you take up a new and quite arbitrary position. You then work backwards and try to construct a logical path between this new position and the starting point. (p. 15)

Emshoff, Mitroff, and Kilman (1978) offer advice in the form of a question we might use to get us started with lateral thinking in a business context: ''How would you redesign your organization and its environment so that it is perfect or ideal?'' They term this approach ''idealized planning.''

Idealized Planning: Strategic Assumptions Analysis

Such an approach to intractable problems discards the constraints which block thinking, drops details that confuse things, and focuses attention on the whole organization. The purpose is to identify new solutions or opportunities and then find strategies to realize their potential. By specifying an ideal and then the implicit assumptions needed to support that ideal, we may be able to develop a framework which is consistent with those assumptions and reality, and so form the basis for a feasible new strategy. This approach has been formalized by Mitroff and Emshoff (1979) in the strategic planning context as Strategic Assumptions Analysis and will be discussed in detail in Chapter 16.

Various techniques can be used to develop a vision of a perfect world. We can simplify complexity and reduce the number of factors we have to deal with simultaneously. We can brainstorm—accept spontaneous thoughts and even absurd ideas from members of a group, and work off them in every way we can. We can use analogy, approximation, or the distortion of a dominant constraint, we can bridge polarized ideas to help everyone see things differently, or even take exactly opposite points of view to help us see things freshly.

It is not a matter of working hard and long on intractable problems in order to achieve results. Rather, it is important to create a climate of trust so that people can explore their environment and their strategy and envision a better future. Once that future is seen, a path can be built back to current reality, and then direction can be reversed to achieve the desired future.

Organizations need the inspiration of radical change when the apparent alternatives fail the test of evaluation and when the portents are bleak. If management sees this need early it can prepare, test alternatives, and develop the organization by conditioning it for change.

No Apparent Problem

If there is no problem, DeBono (1968) wrote, there is no chance of progress, either. One function of management is to shape problems, even to create them. When the absence of widely recognized problems looms large, the ingenuity and energy of general management is needed most.

Andrews (1980) refers to the role of general managers as ''architects of strategy.'' By serving as architects of the possible future and as proponents of a vision which they can use to shape problems and opportunities, garner support and guide action, general managers make one of their major contributions to their firms. Vision, plus the energy, patience, and sense of timing to implement it, add up to success.

EVERY MANAGER CAN CONTRIBUTE

The excitement and the responsibility of generating alternatives is not the exclusive province of top management. Top, middle, and functional managers all have roles to play and contributions to make.

Generating alternatives is followed by evaluation, commitment, and implementation. The first three of these steps encompass the resource allocation process (Bower, 1970), a process which requires the interaction of many managerial levels. To advance through the resource allocation process, a proposal or an alternative has to be given definition and then impetus. *Definition* refers to fleshing out an alternative, giving it substantive content and the technical details which differentiate it from others. *Impetus* is the outcome of committed support within the organization, the phase when the alternative's merits are argued and advocated to move it towards approval.

During the resource allocation process, the *context* of the organization will be felt. Context determines what is acceptable and influences both definition and impetus. Context results from the culture and practices of the organization. It is affected by the way strategy is articulated, by the way work is organized and controlled and rewarded, and by the example set by top management. DeBono describes how two contributors to context, rewards and example, can thwart innovation in many large companies:

> You almost have the paradox [in large companies] that anyone intelligent enough to innovate is intelligent enough not to, because the chances of success are pretty small and if you make a mistake it can hang around your neck for the rest of your career. (1977, p. 57)

Addressing the roles of managers in developing alternatives, Bower (1970) notes that in most mature organizations lower-level managers define the problem while middle managers give it impetus and top management sets context. At the lowest level, specialists and functional managers confront specific problems and use their expert knowledge to solve them. At the second level, the middle managers who are the generalists integrate the work of the specialists they supervise and so give impetus to alternatives by:

1. deciding which proposals will go forward for approval;
2. providing liaison between senior management and specialists, clarifying corporate purpose for the specialists, and abstracting and translating technical detail for senior managers (Uyterhoeven, 1972);
3. accepting personal risk by staking their own reputation on proposals, that is, underwriting them.

These roles illustrate practice, but are not necessarily normative guides.

In reality, managers at every level must play a part in definition, impetus, and context development, depending upon their expertise, their interest and the strength of the management resources of the firm. For example, in small firms, one person may take every role. In rapidly growing firms, there may be few experienced managers to give a proposal impetus. Other mechanisms, including involvement of board members and consultants, will have to be used to test ideas and underwrite them.

Participation in developing alternatives is part of every manager's job, for it is only through the alternatives it generates that the organization implements its strategy and moves from analysis to action. Here, we have introduced the ideas leading to implementation to make the point that there are many roles that must be played in developing an alternative strategy for an organization or one of its parts. We will extend the administrative aspect of our discussion later in Chapter 14.

PREVIEW

The Strategic Management System, *Figure 11-7,* reminds us that strategic management is more than strategy formulation alone. Although our work thus far has focused on the left-hand side of the model, emphasizing the results of strategic action in a changing environ-

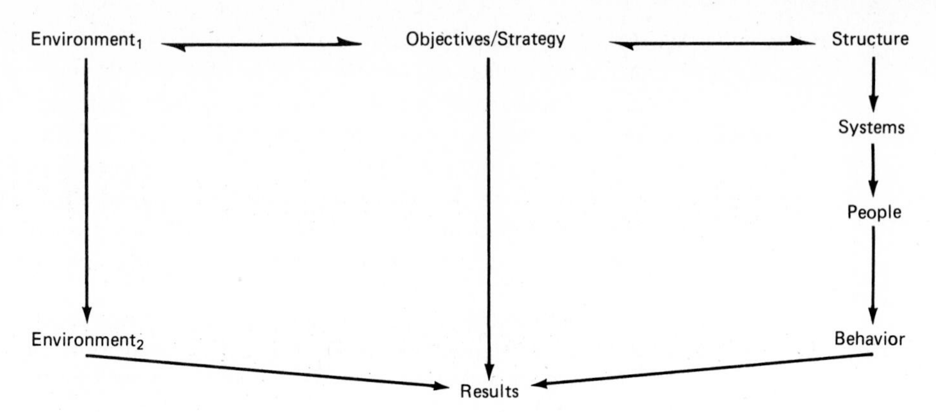

FIGURE 11-7 The Strategic Management System

ment, the results earned are not only conditional on the future but also on the behavior of the people in our organization. When evaluation points to problems, there are many possibilities for adjustment within the organization, short of a strategy change. These include the structure, systems, and people of the organization. In all these change sites, of course, less change is normally less costly and quicker. Indeed, the problems worth solving in the firm may be primarily administrative rather than strategic. We will discuss administrative aspects of the firm in detail in Chapter 14.

chapter 12

Evaluating Alternatives

INTRODUCTION

Evaluating alternatives is similar to evaluating a firm's current strategy, since we must consider how each alternative fits with the firm's resources, environment, and stakeholder objectives and values. But, unlike a strategy in use, new alternatives do not have a history, a track of results, to give us confidence in their future success. For this reason, the evaluation of new alternative strategies is more uncertain than attempts to evaluate a firm's current strategy, and so there is a greater risk of error.

Because a wrong course puts the firm's resources, its gain from earlier ventures, at risk, a commitment to the wrong strategy can be costly. Management may miss opportunity by conservatively sticking with an old strategy too long. The opposite type of error is adopting a new strategy which a more thorough analysis could have proven unfeasible. Whether we are too conservative or too casual in our evaluation, the sources of error lie in our own capabilities and in the uncertain future environment.

As we evaluate our alternatives, we must deal with the consequences of perceived uncertainty and limited information and with the fear that a competitor knows something we do not. We may feel internal discord stemming from personal limits and desires for personal advantage, gaps in our information base, uncertainty about the future, and the possibility that we are wrong. We may have misunderstandings and conflict over resources with powerful adversaries, and the possibility exists that we have oversimplified our world in the search for alternatives.

Strategists have recognized these problems for many years and have learned to live with and even enjoy uncertainty. Robert Price, then President and Chief Operating Officer of Control Data Corporation, wrote:

> Contrary to conventional wisdom, however, uncertainty is a positive force. Consider a world with no uncertainty—that is, perfect knowledge of everything. What would business look like? Every market would be dominated almost completely by one major supplier. That supplier would have no effective competitors because it would be making every decision with perfect knowledge. . . . Uncertainty gives rise to opportunities. (1982, p. 3)

Uncertainty, information gaps, and opportunity go together. Uncertainty leads to errors, and errors to opportunity. People see the future and interpret the present differently, so they act differently and get different results. DeBono (1968) points out that problems and opportunities ''jolt us out of the smooth rut of adequacy.'' In this sense, problems are the gateway to progress, and alternatives are the keys to opportunity. In this chapter, we discuss ways to evaluate alternatives which limit the risk and reduce the attendant uncertainty while creating viable opportunities for the firm.

COPING WITH UNCERTAINTY

The Importance of Choice

Probably the most important characteristic of the effective decision making process is choice: a larger list of alternatives will normally include more good quality alternatives than a brief set. Indeed, Janis and Mann (1977) make a ''wide range of alternatives'' the first of their seven ideal procedural criteria for quality decision making. When you have more choices, the evaluation process will give you more confidence that you have selected the best, because the ultimate choice won out over so many.

Such confidence is particularly important for organizations facing a need for radical strategic changes, changes for which there is no relevant history or experience. Radical changes are inherently riskier to implement because of the organization's lack of relevant experience, so selecting an alternative which has prevailed over many others increases our ability to ''sell'' it to the organization. Confidence stemming from a broadly based comparison process can actually induce greater commitment from those who would otherwise have been indifferent or hostile to major, untried change. DeBono wrote:

> Confidence in a decision does not depend on the lack of any alternative, for that might only indicate a lack of imagination, but on the ability to see many alternatives, all of which can be rejected. (1968, p. 149)

If management has compared a new strategy with many alternatives, we may safely say that although the prospective change may be untried, it certainly cannot be criticized as untested.

Thoroughness

Thoroughness in evaluation is especially important when considering future alternatives, because fit with a firm's resources, environment, and stakeholder objectives and values constitutes the sole source of evaluatory information. Without historical experience, we must be confident about fit. It is tempting to skip steps in strategic management, but skipping steps in the evaluation of alternatives can have dire consequences because already minimal information is further reduced.

Thorough evaluation must encompass the resources needed to support the alternative. While uncertainty about the future and risk are ever-present in untried alternatives, it is foolish to put the firm at risk because its strategy cannot be supported by the firm's resource base. Indeed, defining resource requirements is one part of evaluating alternatives which can be done with virtual certainty. Evaluating resource adequacy thus is an important, although frequently overlooked, test which can increase confidence in a chosen alternative. With adequate resources, the risks of a new strategy are somewhat reduced. Resources ensure that the firm can operate in the future. Strategies supported by inadequate resources endanger the firm, because they may destroy the firm's financial independence.

Unfounded Optimism

Thorough evaluation can remedy one of the most common errors of alternative evaluation: unfounded optimism. It has been vividly described by Hirschman in his study of international economic development projects:

> People typically take on and plunge into new tasks because of the erroneously presumed absence of a challenge, because the task looks easier and more manageable than it will turn out to be. (1967, p. 13)

Hirschman found that when planning their activities, people have a tendency to overlook threats to the viability of a strategy and a complementary tendency to overlook remedial actions which could be taken if a threat materializes. He called this ability to implement remedial actions the work of the ''Hiding Hand,'' which actually protects the outcome of the strategy. He warned that the champions of innovation (see Schoen's article, 1969) and new ideas tend to exaggerate the benefits of the strategy and discount its difficulties. Hirschman alerts us to typical errors:

- Pseudo-transferability: imitation of well-known successes elsewhere. If it is said to be like other successful ventures, we believe we understand it and that it has low risk.
- Pseudo-comprehensiveness: solving all the sponsor organization's problems in one fell swoop.

Hirschman concludes that individuals really do not believe in creativity and so see it as a surprise when it occurs. He says we essentially underestimate ourselves and tend to limit ourselves to problems we think we can solve, thereby falling into error—and occasionally opportunity.

Hirschman suggests a simple remedy for these errors: thorough identification of vulnerabilities and interdependencies, and the specification of the steps and results along the way. Thorough evaluation allows the interdependencies inherent in any strategy to be tested early and the outcomes of change to be monitored while adaptation is still possible.

Henderson (1979) cited three advantages of a rigorous and objective examination of a problem, that is, of a situation where something has gone awry: the discovery of invalid assumptions underlying the strategy; the discovery of neglected interactions resulting in suboptimization; and, finally, the discovery of a new, more powerful conceptual framework to explain the source of the problem and the likely impact of change. This third point suggests the opportune nature of strategic problems and links us again to Hirschman's ''Hiding Hand,'' bringing successful strategic results.

Contingency Plans

Contingency planning is another way to cope with uncertainty. It is based on an explicit recognition that the situation may not proceed as desired. Contingency planning prepares managers for uncertain situations and gives them practice in adapting to an unfolding reality.

Contingency plans specify actions needed to achieve our objectives if the original plan does not work out. Contingency planning is appropriate when alternatives are under evaluation. Alternatives which achieve desired objectives even with contingencies are superior, since they are robust across a wider variety of situations.

Using Intuition in Evaluation

Along with being as thorough as possible, do not devalue the contribution of intuition in the evaluation process. Intuition is experience at work. In an apparently irrational way, but in fact almost super-rationally, an experienced manager's intuition will give him or her insights to the overall effect of an alternative strategy by testing it against all his or her previous experience.

Intuition is usually active at the beginning and end of the strategic management process. Intuition is initially used to select problems worth pursuing, and intuition is finally used to synthesize all the evaluation information generated into a judgment and a decision which can be implemented by the organization. Henderson (1979) writes that consensus plays an important role in tapping the intuitive skills of management, because consensus is founded on "the wisest intuitive judgment of diversely experienced people."

Consensus and Support

Consensus building garners intuitive experience from many and so is a form of political thoroughness. As well, it has the side benefit of facilitating action. To cite Henderson:

> Implementation . . . is difficult if discussion and consensus have not been continued long enough to make the relationship between the overall objectives and the specific action seem clear to all who must interpret and implement required policies. Otherwise, the intuition of those who do the implementation will be used to redefine the policies which emerged from analysis. (1979, p. 45)

One CEO described his way of enforcing consensus development during his twenty-two-year term as president:

> If you're responsible for an area of the business and you report to me, you have all my authority to make decisions. The only requirement is that after the fact you have to convince me that you have thought through the rationale of your action, and that you had discussed it with everybody in the company who would be affected or who, on the basis of past experience, could contribute to your decision. You talk to me only if you aren't sure about your rationale for a decision, or you aren't sure who you ought to talk to.[1]

[1]Fletcher Byron of the Koppers Co., quoted by Myerson and Carey (1982).

Consensus about both means and ends, strategies and objectives, deserves consideration. Bourgeois concluded his study of the strategic decision making in twelve non-diversified public corporations of the Pacific Northwest as follows:

> Consensus on means always yields higher performance than disagreement on means, while allowing disagreement on less tangible goals tends to be associated with better performance. Also, the worst performance results come from goals agreement combined with means disagreement—i.e., when a firm agrees on where it wants to go but can't agree on how to get there! (1980, p. 243)

Because successful performance requires implementation, consensus on means is critical.

OPPORTUNITIES TO REDUCE UNCERTAINTY

Although managers must always cope with uncertainty when dealing with the future, some types of evaluation thinking and planning can reduce the level of uncertainty and so increase confidence that the alternative chosen will perform as expected. Methods to reduce uncertainty include careful analysis of assumptions and evaluation of stakeholder interests. Thinking about how to time implementation and how to monitor results over time also reduces the unknowns in the implementation process and allows adaptation to achieve the desired results, as Hirschman pointed out.

While the historical track of an alternative strategy cannot normally be evaluated, the assumptions underlying its expected future can be analyzed. Such analysis serves to reduce uncertainty because the outcome is more likely to be as expected if the assumptions seem plausible. Strategy which depends for its success on unsupportable assumptions is very dangerous and cannot be recommended.

Careful evaluation of stakeholder interests can also reduce the uncertainty stemming from unknown stakeholder reactions. Any strategy needs stakeholder support, particularly that of stakeholders within the organization. Thus, the strategy most likely to succeed should accommodate and build on stakeholder interests. Alternatives which violate important stakeholder values are in for tough sledding, and alternatives which require the formation of different stakeholder values carry more risk and require more managerial effort than those which build on current values. An understanding of stakeholders' interests gives us insight to their likely reactions under pressure; thus the uncertainty due to unknown reactions is limited.

Strategies are implemented over time, and so can be evaluated over time. This allows the firm's commitment to be limited and the period of uncertainty shortened, making the situation easier to understand and handle. If we evaluate an alternative strategy's likely implementation sequence, we can interpret results that vary from the expected and develop contingency plans to get back on track.

To emphasize the value of experiments, trials, and market tests, note that time and results achieved over time help build organizational support for a new strategy. Certain values, such as pride in a distinctive competence, can be nurtured and developed over time to ensure success. But when we evaluate an alternative, we must weigh the managerial costs in time and effort to build consensus support against the likely rewards of success.

EVALUATING ALTERNATIVES: A SUMMARY

Good managers don't just make strategic decisions; they make chosen strategies work. *Figure 12-1* provides a set of questions to test alternatives. These questions are organized within the resources–environment–stakeholder framework to address internal uncertain-

FIGURE 12-1 Tests to Evaluate a Future Strategy

Internally Focused: Resources and Internal Stakeholders

RESOURCES

Resource Adequacy/Feasibility

Does the company have the resources to succeed?

Can it afford the risks of the strategy?

Flexibility

Will the commitment necessary preserve the company's flexibility?

Are the risks taken warranted by the rewards expected?

Can the decision be reversed, and at what cost?

Controllability

Can the company afford to succeed?

Does management know how to gauge whether the strategy is working?

What problems will be resolved? What will be created?

INTERNAL STAKEHOLDERS

Stakeholder Adequacy

Will it satisfy internal stakeholder objectives?

Value Compatibility

Will the organization's critical stakeholders go along with it?

Impact on Management Harmony

Who opposes the strategy commitment?

What is the organizational and personal cost of commitment?

Externally Focused: Environment and External Stakeholders

ENVIRONMENT

Competitive Advantage

Does the strategy enhance the company's competitive strengths?

Is the company competitively early, late, or "on time"?

Is it far-sighted or merely expedient?

Does the strategy create and exploit a situation of imbalance—i.e., does it focus maximum resources against minimum opposition?

Does it preserve the firm's distinctive competence?

Is it robust?

Conventional Wisdom

Does the strategy violate conventional wisdom?

How do you know it will work?

Contingency Tests

What assumptions are implicit in the strategy? Are they viable—e.g., does the success of the strategy depend on an economic upswing?

EXTERNAL STAKEHOLDERS

Reactions

Does the strategy assume that the company's competitors are smart?

Does it allow for intelligent reactions by the competitors? Does it allow for irrational or emotional reactions by the competitors?

Vulnerabilities

What are the strategy's vulnerabilities?

Could it be caught in cross-impact?

The Ultimate Test

Does the strategy provide value to the ultimate customer?

Is the strategy consistent with the reality of the industry chain?

Does it acknowledge the real power of competitors, suppliers, distributors, customers, and regulators?

ties within the organization and external uncertainties originating in the environment. They test the strength of the strategy in relating the firm and its environment. The ultimate test, of course, is whether the strategy will create value.

With the information of *Figure 12-1,* the manager can anticipate problems or spot signs of trouble, monitor trends which herald their occurrence, and plan for contingencies. Evaluation provides managers with information on their chosen strategy before they commit to it. For example, it should identify potentially troublesome issues likely to affect the success of the strategy.

Time is a manager's ally. By understanding and using the flexibility that time gives, the manager can adapt and change resource commitments to keep the organization in phase with its developing environment, opportunities, and resource base. It is, of course, better to ride trends than to fight them. The latter is a risky approach while the former, by using the environment, accepts reality and turns it to advantage.

An evaluation of alternatives will identify areas of bad fit between strategies and the firm's resources, environment, and stakeholders. Using this information, the manager can modify and rework any alternative he or she believes is an opportunity, using the better elements of one option to reinforce the positive characteristics of another, and using other elements to neutralize the negative characteristic of otherwise acceptable strategies. The result can be a ''super option'' whose results in terms of value creation will surpass the original, and with lower risk.

Unless the manager is confident that a strategy will work within the constraints of the firm's resources, environment, and stakeholder values, the strategy should not be implemented. Companies and careers should be bet on ''very likely'' results, not ''maybe's'' or ''possibly's.'' This is why the most commonly implemented strategic alternatives are modifications of the original strategy with which the firm has experience and so less risk. Vickers (1965) wrote of the need for judgment in the strategic management process; judgment is obviously necessary when alternative future strategies are being evaluated.

chapter 13

Reading the Corporate Culture: Prelude to Executive Action

INTRODUCTION

Throughout this book we have stressed the importance of fact-founded decision making, that is, making decisions in the light of facts and what we believe those facts mean. With this chapter, we turn from analysis to strategy implementation, and our principal concern becomes the design of the administrative strategy. In the design of that strategy, again the facts of organizational life matter.

In particular, in this brief chapter we want to attract your attention to the informal organization and to behavior that is not defined in any formal way. Experience demonstrates that practice varies from design in most organizations, sometimes supportively and sometimes not. In designing an administrative strategy, organizational practices and beliefs must be honored: The realities of organizational life must be the foundations of executive action. For this reason, we now examine ''culture,'' an umbrella concept which encompasses all the actual behavior and beliefs of the organization, and the role of culture in administration.

CULTURE

Organizational culture has many faces or manifestations in every organization and is important to every firm. Schwartz and Davis (1981) say that culture ''. . . may be the most accurate reflection of why things work the way they do, and of why some firms succeed with their strategies while others fail.''

What is culture? Marvin Bower's (1966) simple definition, ''it's the way we do things around here,'' expresses the informal nature of culture. Attempts to change an organization and its strategy that are incompatible with "the way we do things" are likely to be met with resistance, confusion, and ultimately failure.

Another definition of culture that fits with our strategic concerns is that of anthropologist Clyde Kluckhohn. Culture is

> . . . the set of habitual and traditional ways of thinking, feeling and reacting that are characteristic of the ways a particular society meets its problems at a particular point in time. (1949)

The words "habitual" and "characteristic" point to patterns of behavior which reflect the shared attitudes and values of management and, as Schwartz and Davis (1981) point out, particularly reflect the values, beliefs, and norms that served top managers and their company well during their own rise to power. Citing another anthropologist, C.S. Ford (1967), Schwartz and Davis note that culture is "composed of responses that have been accepted because they met with success." They add, "It is these choices that continually reaffirm the corporation's culture and reinforce the expected behavior across the organization" (1981, p. 35).

Culture, then, is a manifestation of deeply rooted behavior. Ultimately, it may become an almost instinctive behavioral characteristic of an organization (and its management). It defines what is expected of the members of the organization in every situation and is transmitted from manager to manager informally, that is, by example.

STRATEGY AND CULTURE

Learning to understand organizational culture is important to fit in, create change, and even break the norms effectively on occasion. You need to be able to read the organization quickly and accurately if you are to:

1 formulate strategies that fit the organization;
2 implement them efficiently and effectively; and
3 survive within the organization and prosper.

Our strategies and personal actions must be consistent with the organization's culture, or we signal that we or our ideas do not fit. Consequently, only if we have the power and resources to sustain a very extended commitment can we consider taking the risk of culture change. Schwartz and Davis write:

> All steps must be prefaced by strong top leadership creating the pressure for change coupled with new top management behavior that sets the example. It is also necessary to have a united front at the top for the sake of sending consistent messages to other managers. The pivotal word is commitment—the commitment to initiate the cultural change and the staying power to see it through. (1981, p. 44)

Nevertheless, however, what Deal and Kennedy (1982) call "outlaws" can be tolerated in an existing strong culture. Usually very competent people, outlaws deliberately violate cultural norms, and survive. Their survival stems from the contributions they make, such as contributions to continued organizational evolution, new product development, or even the relief of pressure, as the jester did in the king's court. Even so, they satisfy the main requirements of the culture—their loyalty is never in doubt.

To illustrate the concept of the outlaw in the organization, Deal and Kennedy (1982) cite a story told about Thomas Watson, Jr., the son of the founder of IBM, and himself its chairman. "The duck who is tame will never go anywhere anymore," he said. "We are convinced that business needs its wild ducks and in IBM we try not to tame them." The story continues to describe an employee who once told Watson, "Even wild ducks fly in formation." Watson added this characteristic of organizational outlaws to his analogy, noting that their contributions were in a single (corporate) direction.

Culture is founded in shared values and indeed is a manifestation of those values. Culture affects the people and people affect the culture. The culture supporting the underlying values largely controls behavior in such organizations as Hewlett Packard, Lincoln Electric, and McDonald's. Indeed, we can note that:

> The main point of reference for analyzing the structure of any social system is its value pattern. This defines the basic orientation of the system (in this case the organization) to the situation in which it operates; hence it guides the activities of participant individuals. (Parsons, 1956, p. 67)

Thus, culture is a key element of strategy implementation and is anchored in the values of the organization's internal stakeholders.

IDENTIFYING CULTURE

The pattern of values gives us a ready handle on an organization's culture, and vice versa. If we can identify these values from what the company says are the reasons for its success, from the myths and analogies used to describe it, and from the behavior it is organized to encourage, we will be able to trace the values' influence throughout the organization.

A fruitful avenue for culture indentification is to track the powerful. Can we identify those who really succeed? For example, are they generalists or specialists? What career tracks pay off? What managerial roles are powerful? How long have the top people been with the company? What was the critical organizational problem which they solved? These questions point to patterns which reveal the corridors of organizational power which top management believes serve the organization well.

By identifying powerful organizational roles and by tracking the careers of those who hold them, we can learn how power is gained and lost. If we want to do so and have the self-discipline to persist, we can use this information to guide our own success. Moreover, by understanding how power is networked and structured in the organization, we may be able to influence its locus and even change it, if change is needed and we have sufficient power to do so.

A definite parallel exists between organizations in industries and the managers in organizations. Success in both contexts depends on a capacity to mobilize power. Given its industry role, an organization's success depends on its power to accumulate and use resources to achieve its objectives. Within an organization, a manager, too, has a role and must develop power to mobilize resources and achieve objectives.

In the earlier chapter on industry analysis, we examined the firm's role and power and used that knowledge to formulate business strategy. Here we advocate the use of the concepts of managerial role and power to analyze the organization and ultimately mobilize its resources. Reading the culture and understanding roles and power in the organization are first steps toward developing effective administrative strategies and successful executive action.

READING THE CULTURE

Given the two concepts of role and power, how can we use them to read the organization? We have already suggested the identification of superordinate objectives and tracking the careers of those who are powerful. Moreover, our earlier chapters evaluating strategy emphasized results. What are the actions and results that reveal how the organization works?

Culture is revealed by shared, repeated, and habitual behavior—that is, by the patterns of action—while the organization's reactions to the results which those actions deliver reveal what is valued. Hence, to read culture, we must study how managers work; how they work through, with, and around others to get results; and how they use those results to increase their autonomy and power.

How are critical problems defined, critical relationships formed, and tasks carried out? Schwartz and Davis (1981) suggest identifying the ways critical management tasks are carried out in the context of particular key relationships and tasks, and offer a simple Culture Matrix, shown in *Figure 13-1,* to assemble the data. In *Figure 13-1,* each line

FIGURE 13-1 Corporate Culture Matrix

	Relationships			
Tasks	*Companywide*	*Boss-subordinate*	*Peer*	*Interdepartment*
Innovating				
Decision making				
Communicating				
Organizing				
Monitoring				
Appraising and rewarding				

Source: Reprinted by permission of the publisher, from Howard Schwartz and Stanley M. Davis, "'Matching Corporate Culture and Business Strategy," *Organizational Dynamics,* Summer 1981, pp. 36, 38.

describes how a critical task is managed in the context of particular relationships. While serving as a check list, the table highlights interactions and can help you give meaning to the anecdotes or corporate myths and legends which convey organizational norms. *Figure 13-2* summarizes the culture matrix for the international banking division of a large US bank and suggests the kinds of data needed to understand how things are done. The data for such an inventory could come from company interviews or documents, the business press, or simply from your observations of the company at work. Note, however, that Schwartz and Davis restrict both matrices to internal matters. In some organizations, relationships with outsiders, such as suppliers and customers, are managed culturally—that is, the relating is culturally consistent and fits the organization's sense of self.

FIGURE 13-2 Summary of Cultural Risk Assessment (international banking division)

Relationships	*Culture Summary*
Companywide	Preserve your autonomy. Allow area managers to run the business as long as they meet the profit budget.
Boss-subordinate	Avoid confrontations. Smooth over disagreements. Support the boss.
Peer	Guard information; it is power. Be a gentleman or lady.
Interdepartment	Protect your department's bottom line. Form alliances around specific issues. Guard your turf.

Tasks	*Culture Summary*
Innovating	Consider it risky. Be a quick second.
Decision making	Handle each deal on its own merits. Gain consensus. Require many sign-offs. Involve the right people. Seize the opportunity.
Communicating	Withhold information to control adversaries. Avoid confrontations. Be a gentleman or lady.
Organizing	Centralize power. Be autocratic.
Monitoring	Meet short-term profit goals.
Appraising and rewarding	Reward the faithful. Choose the best bankers as managers. Seek safe jobs.

Source: Schwartz and Davis, 1981, p. 38. Reprinted by permission.

ROLE VERSUS JOB: THE USE OF POWER WITHIN A CULTURE

Strategy is implemented through others, that is, by people with particular roles in the organization's culture. For effective implementation, we must distinguish between roles and jobs. People in certain jobs may not take the role nominally associated with the job, but role-takers—that is, those who control resources and influence perceptions in the organization—are critical to the success of strategy implementation.

Separating reality within the organization from job description in a personnel file is critical for a strategist considering effective implementation. For example, an executive education director, by the impact he or she has on the thinking of powerful people in the organization, may be a more important force in the ongoing strategic management of a firm than someone who holds the job of strategic planner. A marketing vice president may make only promotional decisions, while product and pricing decisions are really made by the manufacturing manager.

A realistic perception of power within the organization's culture is important, too. Power is not formal authority. Morris West, in *The Clowns of God,* provides interesting definitions of power and authority:

> Power implies that we can accomplish what we plan. Authority signifies only that we may order it to be accomplished. . . . By the time it [the order] gets to the people who have to do it, it loses most of the force of its meaning. (1981, p. 342)

West's insightful view highlights the strategist's problem: Power is needed to effectively implement strategy, and formal authority is rarely sufficient to the task. We organize, as Parsons (1956) put it, to mobilize resources to achieve an objective. Yet, once organized, we are frustrated by our inability to keep things working.

Some people, however, gain the power to get things done. Moreover, the best corporations have learned to identify these people. They test managers by making their responsibility greater than their authority. Only those who can garner power, who can extend their authority by negotiation and trading while managing personal risks, succeed. And, because negotiation requires understanding the needs of those around you and trading things you do not want for things you do, the ability to gain power requires a highly developed understanding of what makes resources relevant and valuable, and what makes the environment threatening.

Ironically, managers worry about the costs of exceeding their authority. In reality, to satisfy the responsibilities of their job, they must extend their formal power informally (Uyterhoeven, 1972). Only if they succeed in integrating their actions with those of others around them in the organization can they earn the formal mantle of power which comes with senior management and facilitate the implementation of a chosen strategy.

CULTURE, ROLE, AND POWER IN ACTION

Changing culture is never easy, but sometimes cultural norms thwart necessary strategic change. In such cases, roles must be changed and power realigned to change long-standing institutionalized habits. Ineffective cultural beliefs must be exposed in such a way that those who hold them have an opportunity to change with their dignity intact.

Consider a large and today very profitable US shoe manufacturer. Originally a family company, its management believed its flagship brand shoes could be made only in its own plant to maintain their quality. Some years ago, it purchased a manufacturer of cheaper shoes in a deal that gave the owner a large block of stock in the parent company along with executive and board positions. This man had learned from his own salesmen that the quality of the parent company's flagship brand's quality was slipping, placing his own financial future at risk. After some weeks of investigation, he had his own factory make a set of flagship brand shoes and presented two racks of shoes at the next board meeting, those he had made on one rack, and the parent company's on the other. He simply asked family members to identify their own company's shoes. Looking at the two racks, they unanimously pronounced one definitely inferior and the other obviously up to their quality standards—picking the shoes made at the acquired company's factory as their own! Today, all the company's brands are made in factories best suited to their production, with desired quality and large profits.

A few months before the rack demonstration, this same man had won the confidence of family members by advising them against a buy-out offer from a conglomerate which itself later merged with the failing Penn Central Railroad. Thus an outsider gained power beyond his role with timely advice. He then used that power to violate the norms of the family board meeting and ask some very difficult questions, revealing the existence of a major business problem caused by an adherence to an ineffective way of doing business, an ineffective culture. His merger advice had demonstrated to family members that his interests in the company's financial future were the same as theirs, and he used his resulting credibility with them in the two-rack demonstration to vividly portray the faltering of their base business. Today he is CEO of the large company and on his windowsill is a brick carrying the words, "Why not?"

SUMMARY

Strategy works through organizations, and culture has an important impact on how organizations work. Culture can be the boon or bane of an organization's strategic future, facilitating or impeding performance. The strategist has two choices: Select a strategy which will achieve the desired results within the organization's culture, or work within the culture to earn and develop power which can be used to make certain aspects of the culture more hospitable to the selected strategy. Either way, culture must be recognized before the strategist can gauge the likely success of strategy or the best way to implement it within the organization.

chapter 14

Administration: Using the Organization's Structure and Systems to Implement Strategy

OVERVIEW

In Chapter 13, we introduced culture to alert you to the importance of the informal rules of corporate life. Culture can serve to align the shared power of the organization so that it will be more effective in strategy implementation. But strategic changes which are essential for a firm's health sometimes need to be implemented in organizations where the structure and culture will not facilitate, and may even hinder, administration. In this chapter, we discuss how one administrative concept, structure, can be used to develop an organization in which strategy can be successfully implemented and, if necessary, changed.

Of course, structural change is an additional and difficult step in the strategy implementation process. Biologically, and apparently organizationally, there is no growth without crisis. The administrative changes required to build an organizational structure to implement a chosen strategy illustrate that crises can indeed facilitate growth.

ADMINISTRATION

Administration has one basic purpose: to implement strategy. ''The corporate strategy must dominate the design of organizational structure and process,'' says Andrews (1980), emphasizing his point with the statement that the principal decision criterion in organizational design should be "relevance to the achievement of corporate purpose." Thompson put it this way:

> Perpetuation of the complex organization rests on an appropriate co-alignment in time and space not simply of human individuals but of streams of institutionalized action. (1967, p. 147)

Co-alignment is an important concept. Co-alignment does not require the standardization of action across the organization; it necessitates a strategic focus. Thompson explains that administration

> . . . is not a simple combination of static components. Each of the elements involved in the co-alignment has its own dynamics. Each behaves at its own rate, governed by forces external to the organization. (p. 147)

For example, marketing is influenced by customers and competitors; operations is influenced by suppliers, customers, and technology; finance is influenced by fiscal and monetary policy.

The co-alignment of streams of action suggests an analogy which may help make the point that we administer to focus our energy. In the *Art of War*, a commentator writing on the disposition of troops on the battlefield explained:

> The nature of water is that it avoids heights and hastens to the lowlands. When a dam is broken, the water cascades with irresistible force. Now the shape of an army resembles water. Take advantage of an enemy's unpreparedness; attack him when he does not expect it; avoid his strength and strike his emptiness, and, like water, no one can oppose you. (Sun Tzu, 1963, p. 89)

Administration means channeling the energy of the firm's separate parts so that they come together to create an irresistible force in the marketplace. Each specialized part of the organization has its own life and its own role to play. However, the combined effects of the parts create competitive power.

Skilled administrators accept and exploit the forces that motivate the different specialized parts of their organizations. By manipulating the strategic variables that produce co-alignment, they ensure that what is good for the whole organization is done, rather than what is best for one part.

THE STRATEGIC VARIABLES

What are the strategic variables? Barnard wrote:

> Now, if we approach this system or set of circumstances, with a view to the accomplishment of a purpose, . . . the elements or parts become distinguished into two classes: those which if absent or changed would accomplish the desired purpose, provided the others remain unchanged; and the others. (1966, pp. 202–3)

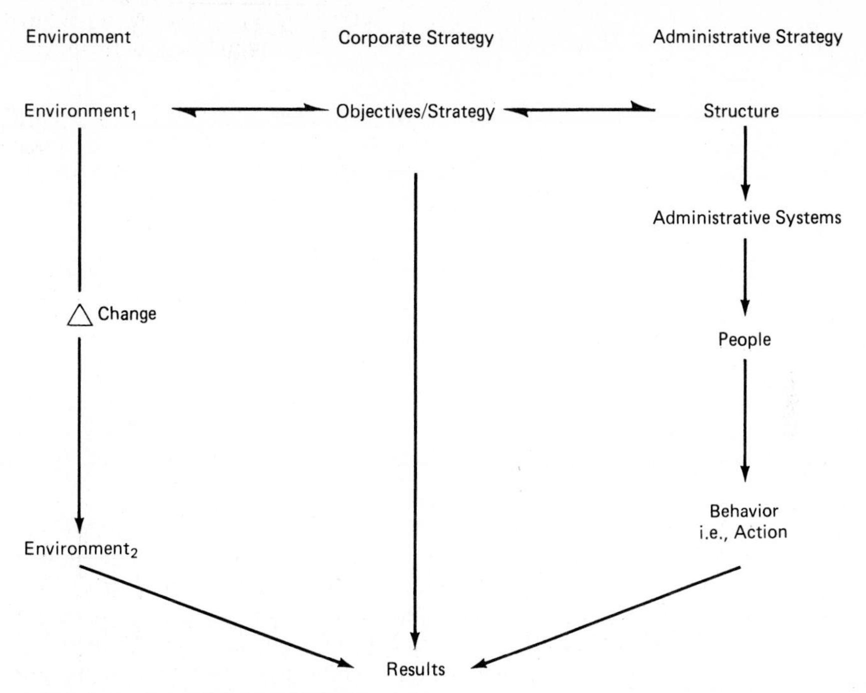

FIGURE 14-1 The Strategic Management System

The first set he called the limiting or strategic factors—"the ones whose control, in the right form, at the right place and time, will establish a new system or set of conditions which meets the purpose" (p. 203).[1]

Collectively, then, the literature alerts us to the importance of purpose in administration: we organize for a purpose and administer to achieve it. We administer both resources and action. Co-aligned actions maximize our impact, just as channels focus running water. In channeling or co-aligning our actions, we strive for economy, intervening as little as possible in the administrative system, but as powerfully as we can by manipulating the few elements that really matter, the strategic factors.

The model of the strategic management system introduced in Chapter 11 and illustrated in *Figure 14-1* puts strategy and results in the center to emphasize the importance of strategy in explaining performance. However, it gives prominence to the conditional effects of the environment, environmental change and the key elements of administrative strategy in the development of those results. Furthermore, double-headed arrows illustrate interdependencies between the environment and strategic decisions; between strategic decisions and administration; and, by implication, between the environment and the first element in the administrative strategy, structure.

[1]This concept anticipates the search for strategic factors and new strategies in Strategic Assumptions Analysis, which we referred to in Chapter 11 and which will be discussed in Chapter 16.

STRATEGY, FORMAL STRUCTURE, AND THE STAGES OF GROWTH

Structure is the configuration of the organization's human, financial, and physical resources used by management to coordinate action within the organization so that the firm's objectives are attained. Strategy and structure are interdependent.

Although we subscribe to the view that the purpose of administration is to implement strategy, we believe that strategic design flexibility should be constrained by what the firm's organizational capabilities or organizational resources are. Hence, although strategy influences structure, existing structure likewise influences our strategic decisions.

Chandler (1962) in his study of the evolution of a number of large American corporations, including DuPont, General Motors, Standard Oil (New Jersey), and Sears Roebuck and Company, advanced the thesis that structure follows strategy. In large measure, he believed that in the United States, demographic changes, prosperity, and technology led to new opportunities to employ existing resources more profitably:

> Expansion of volume led to the creation of an administrative office to handle one function in one local area. Growth through geographical dispersion brought the need for departmental structure and headquarters to administer several local field units. The decision to expand into new types of functions called for the building of a central office and a multi-departmental structure, while the developing of new lines of products or continued growth on a national or international scale brought the formation of a multi-divisional structure with a general office to administer the different divisions. (p. 14)

Essentially, Chandler observed the evolution of managerial specialization to cope efficiently with growth and complexity, just as Adam Smith's pin factory illustrated the benefits of manufacturing specialization in 1776.

In a later book, *The Visible Hand* (1977), Chandler gives great importance to the development of professional management in the evaluation of American industry. Vertically integrated and geographically diverse companies could not evolve until industry developed its administrative specialization, the managerial hierarchy. Chandler thus implied that structure influences strategy.

The problem is that structure has two faces. The face apparent outside the organization is the competitive or customer service side of organizational structure, while the face seen inside the organization emphasizes coordination and control. Researchers such as Lippitt and Schmidt (1967), Salter (1970), Scott (1971), Greiner (1972), and Clifford (1973) have all reported on the need for an appropriate match between the inside and outside faces of the organization—a consistent personality or identity. If there is a mismatch, dysfunctional behavior tends to develop.

Greiner (1972), using developmental psychology (Erikson, 1963) as well as Chandler's research, posits a "predictable" developmental track for the growing organization with periods of stable evolution culminating in revolutionary crises which are critical growth stages that few companies escape. In Greiner's model, organizations face critical experiences from time to time. As with people, the choices made are both effects of the previous phases and causes of the next phase's crisis. Greiner's phases of growth are

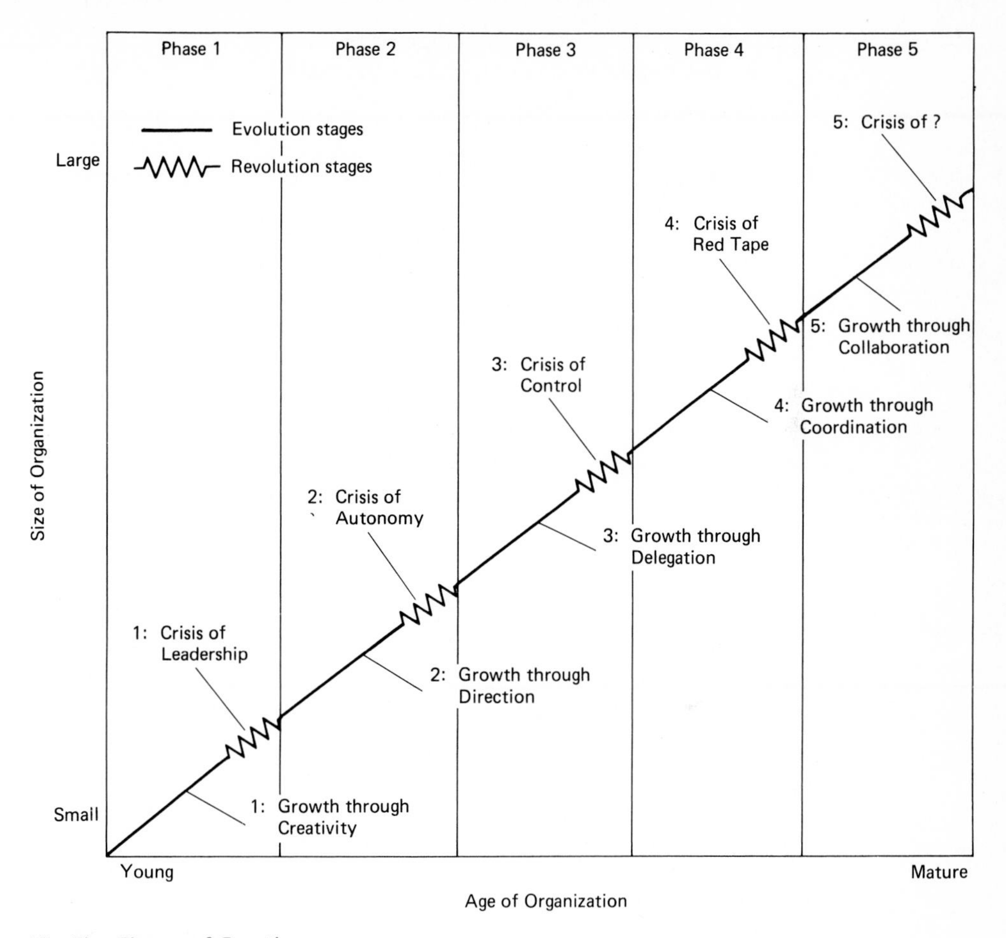

FIGURE 14-2 The Five Phases of Growth

Source: Reprinted by permission of the *Harvard Business Review.* Larry E. Greiner, "Evolution and Revolution as Organizations Grow," July-Aug. 1972. Copyright © 1972 by the President and Fellows of Harvard College; all rights reserved.

presented in *Figure 14-2*. The dominant component of this theory is, of course, that continued growth depends on management's ability to weather crisis.

As *Table 14-1* suggests, continued growth implies changes in strategy and structure as well as in the administrative systems used to coordinate the organization. Moreover, Greiner points out that we can anticipate and be alert for the next crisis if we recognize our present stage of growth. Typically, with size and age come new product markets and increased product market scope, formalization, specialization, and conflict between management's need for control and information and its ability to stay informed at low cost. Integration is a straightforward effort to reduce the organization's dependence on the external environment. Hierarchies and decentralized management are direct attempts to put decision making where the information is.

TABLE 14-1
Organization Practices During Evolution in the Five Phases of Growth

Category	*Phase 1*	*Phase 2*	*Phase 3*	*Phase 4*	*Phase 5*
Management Focus	Make & sell	Efficiency of operations	Expansion of market	Consolidation of organization	Problem solving & innovation
Organization Structure	Informal	Centralized & functional	Decentralized & geographical	Line-staff & product groups	Matrix of teams
Top Management Style	Individualistic & entrepreneurial	Directive	Delegative	Watchdog	Participative
Control System	Market results	Standards & cost centers	Reports & profit centers	Plans & investment centers	Mutual goal setting
Management Reward Emphasis	Ownership	Salary & merit increases	Individual bonus	Profit sharing & stock options	Team bonus

Source: Reprinted by permission of the *Harvard Business Review.* Larry E. Greiner, "Evolution and Revolution as Organizations Grow," July-Aug. 1972.

MESHING STRUCTURE INSIDE AND OUTSIDE

The organization's external world becomes more complex—so more uncertain as the organization makes decisions to diversify and as externally generated change occurs. Thus, the organization must develop specialized internal capabilities to relate with that world in a controlled way. The crises Greiner describes all occur when those relationships become uncontrolled, usually because simple choices were made naively in the glow of earlier success. Hirschman (1967) observed that people take on difficult tasks, thinking they are easy and then something goes wrong. He argued that from the crisis that follows comes the opportunity for growth and development—the principle of the hiding hand. Hirschman's "hiding hand" is never too far away from the successful manager.

The structural choices facing management always have two sides, internal and external. On the side of internal structure, or control, is centralization or decentralization, each with its specialized management roles. On the side of external structure in the market, the external relationship and strategic choice, comes diversity and interconnectedness, interdependence and, ultimately, integration.

Figure 14-3 relates the two dimensions of structure and control and makes the point that while there is no simple prescription for the right degree of centralization for every strategy, there are some highly probable mismatches, here represented by the empty zones. In simple terms, more integrated businesses with centralized internal structures appear more controllable than diverse organizations. Diversified organizations, being highly differentiated in the marketplace, require a differentiated management structure, that is, one which is decentralized.

Of course, if the environment becomes more complex and less stable due to interconnected industry chains, small numbers of competitors, scarcity of resources, or be-

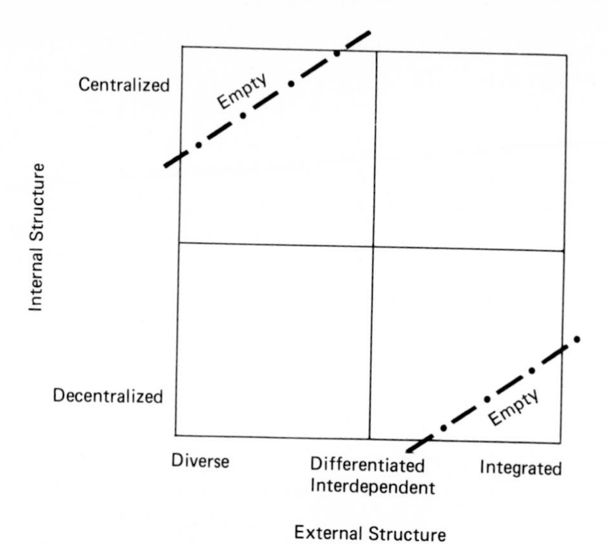

FIGURE 14-3 Matching Competitive and Administrative Structures

cause of governmental action, or technological or demand changes, our choice of external structure becomes complicated. Thompson's (1967) work suggests the following simple prescription: As our environment becomes more complex and less stable, we should move to even more independent and decentralized organizational units, adding layers of specialized management (for example, the groups or sectors at General Electric) to coordinate the parts into a responsive, purposeful whole. *Figure 14-4* points toward likely choices of structural design within various environments.

The issue for the manager is how to develop an organization capable of adaptation

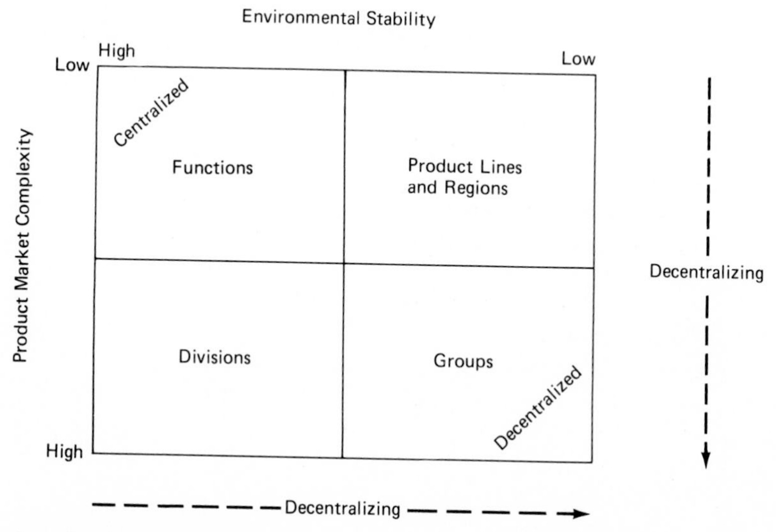

FIGURE 14-4 Organization Design Focus

to the marketplace on one hand, while maintaining operational efficiency on the other. A complex and unstable environment requires boundary-spanning activity to search for information and interpret it. Efficiency, however, requires commitment and sheltering the organization from change—hence the typical tension between marketing, as a differentiating, boundary-spanning unit, and operations, the efficiency-driven technical core. As in many other areas of management, Thompson's prescription presents a paradox and creates an administrative tension: Management must reduce uncertainty to maintain its operational efficiency and implement its strategy, yet it needs flexibility to change that strategy at every level if opportunity or crisis warrants it.

Matrix Organizations

The matrix organizational form which some organizations have adopted addresses these concerns directly. The matrix is an organization that abandons the principle, "for any action whatsoever, an employee should receive orders from one superior only" (Fayol, 1972), in favor of a multiple command system (Davis and Lawrence, 1977). Individuals in a matrix organization explicitly serve two masters. Concerning the matrix form of organization, even Davis and Lawrence advise, "If you don't really need it, leave it alone. There are easier ways to manage organizations" (p. iv).

Matrices penetrate only the top layers of the hierarchy, as *Figure 14-5* suggests, with the bulk of the structure outside and below the matrix. Essentially an integrating device for upper and middle management, matrices may suit situations where there is a

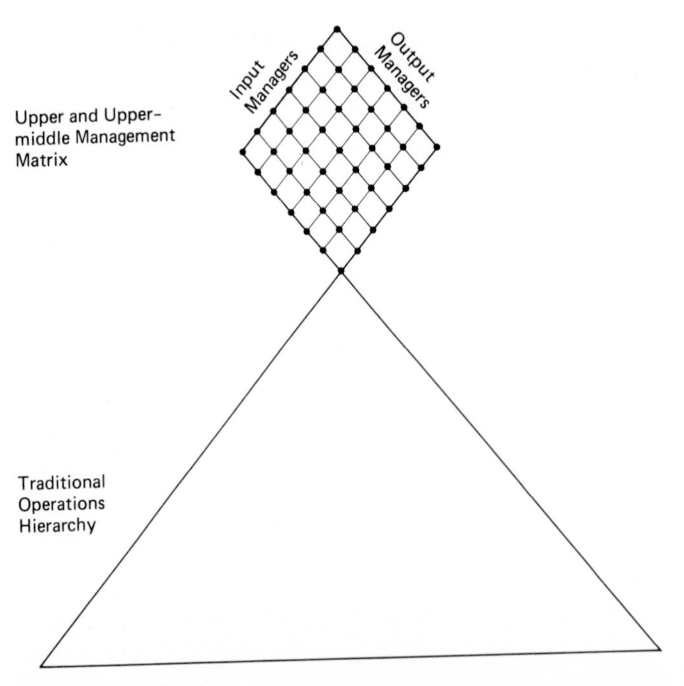

FIGURE 14-5 A Matrix Organization

Source: Adapted from Davis and Lawrence, *MATRIX*, Reading, MA: Addison-Wesley, © 1977.

very large need for information. For example, managers need information when external uncertainty exists and when their roles are highly interdependent. Likewise, information is needed where multiple and critical boundary-spanning functions exist within one organization and many resources are shared. Finally, we believe that information is highly valuable where there exists an imperative to isolate operations from the world because of the technological or security demands placed on them, for example, in the aerospace industry or international banking. Matrixing an organization requires its own supportive culture and administrative system, including simultaneous, overlapping information processing and resource allocation, outside arbitration to limit conflict, and dual personnel and reward functions.

THE INTERNAL CONTEXT: THE INFORMAL ORGANIZATION

So far in this chapter, we have offered a rationale for administration and some broad prescriptions for structuring organizations. Now we move to the inside, that part of the organization concerned with coordination and control. First, let us explore the context of the internal organization.

The decisions managers make and the actions they take occur inside the organization. Such decisions are founded on information, but not perfect or complete information. Williamson (1975) points out that in the face of uncertainty, managers often find themselves in an ''information impacted'' state, meaning that they are blocked, with only limited capacity for ''rational action.''

In these circumstances, people make the difference. They interpret information using their experience to intuit not only its meaning but its significance for the future, and for their fellow managers. Yet, their interpretations and judgments are likely to be idiosyncratic (McCaskey, 1982), especially when uncertainty is great and the pressure for action and better results is high.

Keep in mind the relationship between pressure and performance, shown in *Figure 14-6*. Managers should understand their own responses to different types of pressure and the reactions of others with whom they interact, so they can accurately evaluate the information received and respond appropriately—that is, in a way that gets the result needed.

For us, these observations set the stage for a particular view of the inner organization. Organization is not simply a structural design but a framework of formal and informal relationships among people. External complexity forces differentiation; internal interdependence necessitates communication, coordination, and hierarchies. Formal organizations reflect the outside face of the organization; they typically are rational designs that exploit specialization and hierarchy, and specify policies to control and guide action.

Informal organizations rely on interaction and behavior and example and exist wherever formal organizations exists. Barnard noted that ''An important and often indispensible part of a formal system of cooperation is informal'' (1966, p. 120). Barnard explains that the informal organization facilitates, speeds, and increases communication within the organization, promotes its culture and cohesiveness, and maintains individual feelings of autonomy and self-respect. In fact, formal and informal are not two organizations, but one (Hunt, 1972). We separate them, conceptually, for convenience, but inevitably manage one organization only.

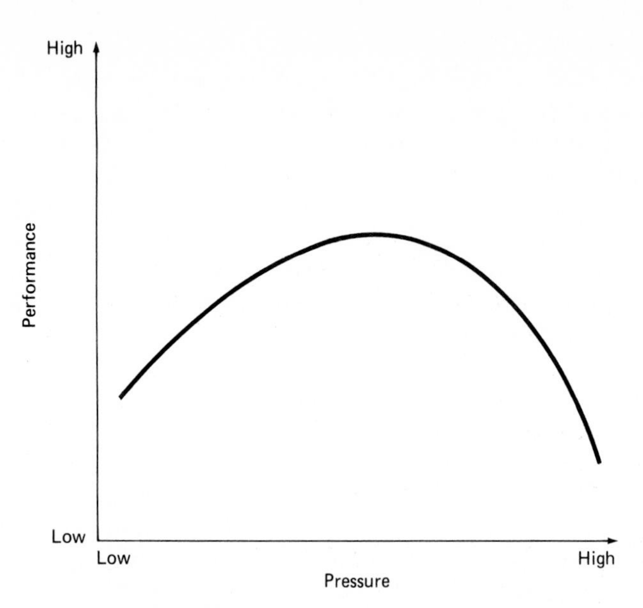

FIGURE 14-6 Pressure and Performance

These views are consistent with research on the job of the general manager, which reveals the importance of the informal organization in administrative success. Initially, successful general managers create an agenda for their area of responsibility, drawing on their knowledge of the business and organization, their intelligence, relationships and interpersonal skills and

> . . . using an ongoing, incremental largely informal process which involved a lot of questions and produced a largely unwritten agenda of loosely connected goals and plans. . . . They used those same personal assets to develop a network of cooperative relationships, above and below them, inside their organization and out, upon whom the job and their emerging agenda made them dependent. (Kotter, 1982, p. 127)

After six months to a year, Kotter reports, these successful managers began to spend more time seeing that their networks implemented their agendas rather than establishing new agenda items or new relationships.

There is, of course, no map of the informal organization complementing the formal organization chart. Each manager has to identify the relevant people for his or her job success. Each manager must build the relationship network and a power base to get the job done.

While authority can be given formally with the position, it is confirmed informally by those around you, above you, next to you, and below you in the organizational hierarchy. Wise managers therefore build personal relationships within the organization and learn to understand how people feel and what their behavior means. Climate is an encapsulating concept which describes this collective feeling—it reflects how people's expectations are being met (recall that culture defines what is expected).

DEVELOPING POWER IN THE ORGANIZATION

The purpose of all this activity within the organization is to develop the general managers' power to do their job. Control of resources gives power, and more resources tend to be allocated to higher performers. Some resources are scarce and have more value and create more power than others.

Just as some types of performance are more highly valued by the organization, information can be valuable, too, especially if it makes others dependent on you. Relationships can give you credibility, especially if they are with more powerful people. They can give you an opportunity to create a sense of obligation or encourage others to identify with you or your ideas (Kotter, 1979).

Kotter reports on the actions one manager took in a critical turnaround situation to quickly take charge and create a climate of dependency on him. Arriving at the division on two hours' notice in a large limousine with six aides, he immediately called a meeting of the top forty managers, outlined his assessment of the situation and his strategy. He fired the top four managers in the room, telling them to be gone in two hours, and stated he would dedicate himself to destroying the career of anyone who tried to thwart his turnaround effort. He ended the sixty-minute meeting by announcing that his assistants would schedule appointments for him with each manager beginning at 7 a.m. the next day.

We can note the manager's quick action and the use of formal position, supplemented by informal action to create dependency, and imagine how those managers left must have felt. Turnarounds sometimes necessitate seemingly draconian methods. The severity of the crisis and the short time available for change sometimes force an exaggerated use of formal and informal power. Managers have to use both the formal and informal trappings of power to be effective and efficient.

Now, having made a case for the importance of the informal organization, particularly as a source of the power for the manager who seeks to implement strategy, let us take a fresh look at the organization. Structure will vary with the environment and the job to be done. It must contribute to the satisfaction of the people who work within it and it will have formal and informal aspects. All these affect the manager through his or her position in the organization.

A MODEL FOR DIAGNOSIS AND DESIGN

A practical model which captures these key factors is illustrated below; it is adapted from Hunt (1972). *Figure 14-7* shows the organization in its environment and then breaks the organization into its major components: formal structure, informal structure, task technology, and individual needs. In *Figure 14-7,* we have emphasized the letters FIT'N, which help us remember what the key factors are: formal and informal structures, technology, and needs. All of these influence the manager's role and can be manipulated by the manager to some degree. Whatever configuration is adopted, however, it must fit the situation and the strategy, and it must fit the parts together purposefully.

For example, consider a company where technology is highly interconnected across its businesses. The technology, with its machines and processes, imposes a pace on operations and demands on the manager. It may be programmed and highly dependent on

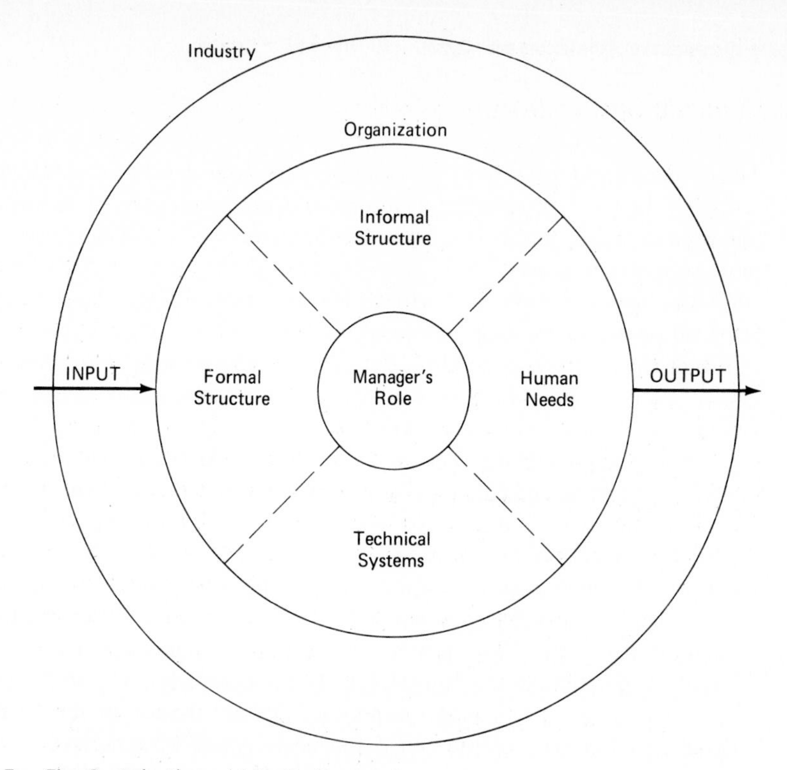

FIGURE 14-7 The Organization and Its Environment
Source: Adapted from Hunt, *The Restless Organization,* Brisbane, Australia: John Wiley & Sons, 1972.

scale for its operating efficiency. If these conditions hold, the technology itself makes the organization slow to adapt, since it is comprehensive and requires a large capital commitment. If this organization is administered through a very formal organization structure, with strict hierarchical divisions, tight controls and evaluation and compensation systems that are used to measure and punish deviation from plan, the manager is likely to have little room for initiative. Here, the organization will probably have an intense informal organization which its members use to humanize their work but not to achieve corporate objectives.

As described, the technology and formal structure stiffen the organization. If the environment becomes unstable and a change of strategy becomes necessary, the organization is likely to fail from simple inflexibility and nonadaptiveness. From the lower and middle managers' points of view, the task of the job is largely technical with very little strategic significance. For them, work is a matter of following orders and serving the "machine." Such managers are unlikely to cope successfully with external change.

THEORIES X, Y, AND Z

In the context of this discussion, it is interesting to examine McGregor's Theory X and Theory Y organizations (1960) and Ouchi's Theory Z (1981). McGregor describes the Theory X model as a "carrot and stick" organization which works so long as people are highly dependent on authority for the means to satisfy their basic needs. He believed that, with prosperity, organizations which relied on this principle would fail. The people in them would be indolent, passive, and unwilling to accept responsibility; they would resist change, follow demagogues willingly, and make unreasonable demands for economic benefits—which were all they received for their work. In our model, the Theory X organization would be highly formally structured, seek productivity through technology and the substitution of capital for labor, and deny the existence of all but the most elemental human needs. Such a business—a traditional US business, McGregor believed—would fail due to lack of adaptiveness.

McGregor described Theory Y as founded on an assumption that people are self-directing and self-controlling in the achievement of organizational objectives to the degree that they are committed to those objectives. In a Theory Y organization, authority is used less and is used less overtly. Theory Y organizations gain commitment by rewarding performance, allowing ego satisfaction and self-actualization. In our model, formal structure would be reduced in the Theory Y organization, and informal structure would take its place, moving control from the organization to its members. A less stiffly structured organization would result which would be inherently more adaptive and innovative, because whatever flexibility and adaptiveness exist in an organization stem from its people. Managers in the Y type organization have roles which extend beyond the technical towards the strategic and so have experience in adapting to change.

Ouchi (1980) in his *Theory Z* contrasts a classic American type of organization with a classic large Japanese organization, and then introduces what he calls the Type Z organization. As *Table 14-2* shows, Type Z's dominant characteristics are very similar to the Japanese model, varying mainly on the locus of responsibility and on length of employment—essentially accommodations to the "ecology of US industry and US culture." Ouchi's examples of Z-like companies included Hewlett Packard, IBM, Rockwell International, Dayton Hudson, Procter & Gamble, Eli Lilly and McDonald's. Ouchi makes the point that they are not all Z companies but share many Z characteristics.

Applying our model of *Figure 14-7* to the Z organizations which are high-technology companies, we can note that they have highly competitive and technologically unstable environments. Yet their own technologies are rigorous taskmasters. Companies

TABLE 14-2 The Theory Z Organization

	American	*Z*	*Japanese*
Term of Employment	Short	Long-term	Life
Frequency of Evaluation and Promotion	Frequent and Rapid	Infrequent	Slow
Nature of Career Path	Specialized	Nonspecialized	Nonspecialized
Explicitness of Formality of Control Mechanisms	Explicit and Formal	Implicit and Informal	Implicit
Type of Decision Making	Individual	Collective	Collective
Locus of Responsibility	Individual	Individual	Collective
Scope of Concern for the Person in the Organization	Segmented	Wholistic	Wholistic

Adapted from Ouchi and Johnson, "Types of Organizational Control and Their Relationship to Emotional Well Being," *Administrative Science Quarterly*, 23, no. 2, June 1978, 294, and from Ouchi, *Theory Z*, Reading, MA.: Addison-Wesley. © 1981.

in the computer industries have difficulty retaining the most able contributors to innovation—they can leave and do it themselves with the assistance of eager venture capitalists. The Z organizational type helps these companies retain their all-important resource, their people.

Generally, a highly formal X-type structure would be inflexible and inhospitable to innovators. Placing the control mechanisms in the informal arena maintains a more flexible and hospitable world that is likely to attract and retain the technologists these companies need. Hence, the Z organization with its consistent culture and long and stable employment satisfies corporate needs and employee needs, too.

IBM is formally structured and tightly controlled, of course, but its strategic diversity, technological leadership and dominance of its industry are legend. Yet matching its formal structures is an equally imposing, harmonizing informal culture which further strengthens IBM's control of its operations. IBM is a rigid defender of its technology in the courts. People think carefully before migration from IBM with technology learned inside. Size and diversity necessitate hierarchy, but the combined impact of formal structure and technology on the people of the organization is ameliorated, without reducing control, by IBM's career-oriented, company-loyal culture.

McDonald's, with its massive franchising operations and its part-time labor force, is a special Z organization; the organization the public sees is well outside of the corporation itself. Because McDonald's must deal with so many independents, held to it by contract and culture, informal relationships are used to keep things moving, avoid conflict, and maintain uniformity. McDonald's motto, "Quality, Service, Convenience, Value (QSCV)," is its culture. Again, a Z-like form, with stable employment at the top and a culture founded on simple, constantly communicated values like QSCV, appears to suit the needs of the situation well.

Our organization model focuses attention on the environment and the organization when the control systems are being designed or attuned to the needs of a particular strategy or strategic change. The elements of the organization have to fit together to serve the strategy. If the strategy places severe task demands on the organization, and if the environment is uncertain or unstable, management must carefully locate its control systems. Keeping the needs of the individuals who work in the organization in mind as you balance formal and informal is an important part of that organizational design activity.

STRESS AND PRESSURE WITHIN THE ORGANIZATION

The formal structure pressures managers for results, but the stress caused by this pressure is lessened if a consistent informal structure exists and allows the manager to develop the extra power necessary to get results. Inconsistent informal structure or a weak informal structure can turn pressure into dysfunctional stress.

Stress itself stems from our uncertainty about what to do and about how we will be judged. Thus, in a dysfunctional stress situation, a major real or perceived difference exists not only between responsibility and authority, but also between opportunities available to develop power informally and the power necessary to do what must be done.

Pressure is received by a manager and can be passed through to subordinates to raise their responsibility levels and so pressure them to gain power and use it. Good managers control pressure as they control resources, using it to increase output. Managers choose how much pressure to absorb and how much to pass through to their subordinates. Too much pressure retained or too much passed on, however, can be dysfunctional. Indeed, managers who let pressure become dysfunctional for themselves or their subordinates, who feel stressed or contribute to stress in those below, are not using their human resources well.

Good organizational structures place resources and pressure where they should be, while testing the people who must use them. You earn the next job (and demonstrate yourself to be ready for it) by getting the people below you ready for your job and integrating yourself into the next level, by using your resources *and* power to make your boss's job easier. Failure to delegate and failure to promote yourself are both deadly. Results must be traded for increased autonomy—that is, power must be used continuously to extend authority.

CHANGING STRUCTURE

Minimum change has the least organizational cost. The resulting strategic aphorism is: ''If it works, don't fix it!'' And the corollary is that if you don't understand the organization well enough to anticipate reactions and costs, you're doing the strategic equivalent of shooting bullets into a crowd when you attempt strategic implementation. ''Ready, Fire, Aim!'' doesn't work. A responsible manager minimizes organization costs as well as resource costs, and acts so that no cost is blindly incurred.

The costs of change are high. For example, as Barnes and Hershon (1976) have shown within the family company, strategic change usually requires a change in power, because those formerly in power had developed and supported an earlier strategy. This is also true in large organizations since people are influential in maintaining the status quo (Mintzberg, 1978). In larger firms, however, strategies are not always as closely linked with a single personality as they are in family firms. In this context, it is important to remember that a change in power is always evident on the organization chart, since it requires a change of people, of their roles *or* of their resources. We can add that for the formal and informal structures to be consistent components of a new administrative strategy, the organization chart recording the formal organization *will* change, if not by people's names and levels, then by job titles and classifications.

To consistently link the formal and informal structures, the formal structure will change to make role changes (that is, power changes) binding. Greiner (1972), for example, discussed the kinds of structures which firms will find most effective in different growth stages, noting that there are likely to be common kinds of administrative failure at thresholds between different growth stages. At these thresholds, the old power structure has become dysfunctional, since it serves the old strategy rather than the evolving strategy of the firm and so constrains performance. In family businesses, the essence of this conflict is summarized by the question: ''What is family and what is business?'' People may not change as the business changes; the thresholds between types of organizations illustrate how specific managers have failed to develop with the organization and so have constrained the organization's growth.

Along with formal structural changes, the reporting systems must be modified to support on administrative change. For example, suppose a marketing manager reports to a powerful production vice president. Perhaps appropriate when the firm was developing a new technology, this reporting relationship now gives the firm a dull market reputation. The breadth of its product line is limited because the production vice president controls costs by standardization although the competition offers a differentiated and fuller product line. If the marketing manager is given the title vice president and budget responsibility, while still reporting to the production executive, power has not changed. The problematic production dominance is likely to continue until both production and marketing vice presidents report independently to the CEO.

Quinn (1980) writes of strategic incrementalism, where strategic change is effected slowly. The concept is indeed a strategic adaptation of the economic concept of marginalism: small improvements improve the whole, and results at the margin indicate where further actions should be directed. Marginal actions which have negative results should be halted and those which provide positive results should be expanded. At different points in their history, GM, Timex, and Polaroid all needed to learn what customers' reactions to new, nontraditional products would be. Learning improved their ability to serve emerging market needs over time.

The concept applies inside the organization, too. Time is among the most important managerial variables. One of the best ways to control the costs of organizational change is to do it gradually, review results, and adapt while there is still strategic flexibility. Setting strategic mile-stones at definite time points is an appropriate way to avoid organizational shock and maintain control of change. Actions spread over time minimize risk and allow any losses that arise to be absorbed gradually.

SUMMARY: USING THE ORGANIZATION TO ACHIEVE RESULTS

How best to achieve results in an organization? As a manager, it is important to know your role and the roles of others. Consider how the formal and informal structures and the technical systems affect your role, and the skills needed to fulfill it, and how they satisfy your needs as well as those of others. Also, consider how parts bind the company together and facilitate its strategic success in its own environment. In this way, you will be able to define strategic roles for your managers, and put them in a logical, formal organizational context.

Knowledge of the organization requires seeing, listening, and learning. Observe the signals, spoken and unspoken. Learn by observing what risks are taken and how, particularly by the successful. Normally, successful managers take few risks, and, when they do, limit their exposure to carefully chosen dimensions along which they can absorb any possible losses. Do likewise. Only risk those losses you can absorb. And remember, a diverse set of organizational interests can help you absorb losses on one dimension while maintaining your power in other areas.

Middle management is a testing ground to develop organizational implementation skills. At the middle-management level, ambiguity is high due to the tension between the demand for results and low levels of formal authority. But those who can gain power and manipulate pressure to get results will demonstrate their ability to implement strategy at the higher levels of the organization. Middle managers who cannot do this find pressure becoming stressful.

Since power is important in implementation, managers must be aware of their positions in the informal organization. It is important to trust personal feelings, since they are the best and only documentation of your place in the informal system. A good rule for evaluating your position in the informal organization is, ''If you don't know you're in, you're out'' (Jennings, 1980). And being outside the important formal structure can severely limit your power and so limit the success of your efforts. In these circumstances, it may be time to find a new job and recapture the feeling of power that comes to those who are in.

chapter 15

Human Resource Strategy

INTRODUCTION

Human resource management is the humane side of enterprise in too few organizations. In many, there is neither humane administration nor effective human resource management, in spite of the nearly universal conclusion of corporate annual reports in which the "contributions of our most valued asset, our employees" are acknowledged.

People are important, and, in the best organizations, they are valued. People, however, are not corporate assets. They are willing to work for pay, given authority over the organization's assets, and given the responsibility to create value.

Some corporations recognize the importance of having the right people in the right positions and have a strategy to attract and retain them. Consider for a moment the following two statements, one from Walter Wriston, then Chairman and CEO of Citicorp, one of the largest US banks, and the other from Alan Zakon, at the time the newly elected chairman of the Boston Consulting Group, BCG. Wriston said:

> I believe the only game in town is the personnel game. . . . My theory is that if you have the right person in the job, you don't have to do anything else. If you have the wrong person in the job, there's no management system known to man than can save you. . . . The selection of the people that hold the key jobs is a principal function of the chief executive officer.[1]

Zakon wrote:

> BCG is a people business. Our creativity, our effectiveness with our clients can be no better than our staff. It is they who build our intellectual base and they who apply it. We are dedicated to recruiting the very best people. We are committed to maintaining an internal environment which encourages their rapid personal growth.[2]

People are important. And, as these two senior managers have stated, top management has to recruit and select people for particular jobs and create a structure and system that helps them do their jobs successfully and with enthusiasm.

[1]Wriston, as quoted in Foulkes, Fred K. and E. Robert Livernash, *Human Resources Management: Text and Cases*, Prentice-Hall, Inc., Englewood Cliffs, NJ, 1982.

[2]Zakon, BCG 1981 *Annual Perspective*.

Organization charts can describe positions and formal relationships between positions, but only people can make an organization come to life and use it to implement strategy, and only people can innovate. Rudyard Kipling put it this way:

They copied all they could follow
But they couldn't copy my mind
And I left 'em sweating and stealing
A year-and-a-half behind.[3]

People are valuable because of their minds. The job of managers is to get them to use their minds for the organization.

AN EARLY HUMAN RESOURCE CONSULTANT

Human resource strategy is, on the surface of things, simple: identify the tasks that need to be done and the skills required to do them; provide enough talented people to complete the work; place these people in the right jobs; and make each individual productive for the organization. In practice, this is a tall order, a difficult prescription to follow.

Jethro, Moses' father-in-law, paid him a visit during the Exodus and observed a classic failure to delegate. Jethro asked Moses:

> "What is this that you are doing for the people? Why do you sit alone, and all the people stand about you from morning till evening?" And Moses said to his father-in-law, "Because the people come to me to enquire of God; when they have a dispute. . . ." Jethro then said to Moses, "What you are doing is not good. You and the people with you will wear yourselves out, for the thing is too heavy for you; you are not able to perform it yourself alone. Listen now to my voice; I will give you counsel, and God be with you! You shall represent the people before God, and bring their cases to God; and you shall teach them the statutes and decisions, and make them know the way in which they must walk and what they must do. Moreover, choose able men from all the people such as fear God, men who are trustworthy and who hate a bribe, and place such men over the people as rulers of thousands, of hundreds, of fifties, and of tens. And let them judge the people at all times; every great matter they shall bring to you, but any small matter they shall decide themselves; so it will be easier for you, and they will bear the burden with you."

Jethro, perhaps acting as a management consultant, understood the limits of his role and his own capabilities. He recognized he was a counsellor and not the decision maker, and, notice, he wished Moses "God be with you," whatever his decision. He then laid out the principles of organization, in what is perhaps one of the most succinct and effective consulting reports ever. He defined Moses' role and the need for policies to guide everyday affairs. He specified the attributes required for the position of judge and established a hierarchy of positions. And he defined the central principle of delegation—"let them judge" according to the rules, with Moses making the decisions in exceptional cases.[4]

[3]From "Mary Gloster" by Rudyard Kipling.

[4]Our attention was drawn to the managerial significance of this biblical passage (Exodus 18:14–22) by Marvin Bower in his *Will to Manage*, p. 123.

Jethro said it all. Successful human resource management hinges on defining the roles of each level of management and creating a context so that managers know how to make a decision and which decisions to make. There has to be a supervising hierarchy and the people hired have to be able, qualified for the job, and capable of doing it responsibly.

Essentially, tasks are set by the strategy of the firm. What is it that has to be done to implement strategy? Where should responsibility for that task be placed so that the probability of a successful outcome is maximized? Is the task large enough to attract talented, high-calibre people? One question must be kept in mind whether you are accepting a new position or designing it: Is the job or the task to be done worthwhile? If it is not, then it is a poor choice for all concerned.

Remember, the mix of skills needed changes as people are advanced to higher managerial responsibilities. Initial appointments primarily require technical skills with only limited managerial and strategy skills to support them. In the middle-management positions of most enterprises, managing—that is, supervising and motivating others, translating abstract requests into explicit, tangible, coordinated, sequenced action—is more important. In top management positions, strategic management skills become most important. Indeed, some of these strategy skills are quite subtle, for example, the ability to identify the few key elements in the unwieldy flow of information that point the way of future strategy, or the ability to see how isolated minor incidents can be used to contribute to the well-being of the whole organization.

SELECTION

Strategic priority should be given to the well-being of the organization whenever a personnel appointment can contribute to the maintenance and development of the firm's distinctive competence or its superordinate goals, the values that define its culture. Moreover, such appointments warrant top management's attention. Selznick explained:

> When selection must take account of more than technical qualification, as when leading individuals are chosen for their personal commitment to precarious aims or methods, . . . where the social composition of the staff significantly affects the interplay of policy and administration, personnel selection cannot be dealt with as routine management practice. (1957, p. 57)

With the tasks defined and with a sense of what the critical appointments are, recruiting—that is, attracting qualified candidates and selecting the best—is very important. This is a difficult job. As Homer warned in the *Iliad,* c. 700 BC, skills are widely dispersed:

> You will certainly not be able to take the lead in all things yourself, for to one man a god has given deeds of war, and to another the dance, to another the lyre and song, and in another wide sounding Zeus puts a good mind.

The key to success, of course, is to identify the skills people have and the values they live by, and give them responsibilities that suit. The problem of matching people and task is as old as man and organization. Chang Yu, a commentator on Sun Tzu writing during the Sung Dynasty, explained:

> Now the method of employing men is to use the avaricious and the stupid, the wise and the brave, and to give responsibility to each in situations that suit him. Do not charge people to do what they cannot do. Select them and give them responsibilities commensurate with their abilities. (Sun Tzu, 1963, p. 94)

Chang Yu and Sun Tzu before him were writing about war. But, note, the quotation refers to the fit of both skill *and* personal values to the job and specifies the character of a successful match between person and responsibilities: ''Do not charge people to do what they cannot do.''

In management, board members are advised to select executives whose personalities and experience match both business conditions and the explicit objectives of the corporation. Suggesting that things have changed very little since 500 BC, Gerstein and Reisman present a senior executive's simple statement on selection:

> Some people are better at starting things up, some are better at squeezing the most out of them once they are running, and some are better at fixing them when they go wrong. Right now, the start up is complete, and it's time for a new man. (1983, p. 33)

During the early growth stages of a business, market definition may be the primary strategic problem; later it may become capacity balancing. Still later, in the mature stage of the life cycle, aggressive differentiated merchandising may be crucial to success. And, if a decision is made to get out of a business or to harvest it, cost control may be seen as the big issue. A close match of person and mission would suggest an executive with an entrepreneurial marketing orientation in the first position and a cost-conscious accountant in the latter. However, few companies have taken their senior middle management selection process to a stage where it is *formally* committed to making such a close match between corporate or business objectives, such as growth or liquidation, and the personal management orientation of particular men and women (Govindarajan and Gupta, 1981).

Rather, companies consider personal orientations *intuitively* when making senior assignments. Although senior managers will always prefer to put implementation into the hands of those most likely to succeed, there is at least one simple reason why personal orientation is dealt with intuitively and not always weighted heavily: the technology available to type managers is ''primitive'' (Stybel, 1982). Furthermore, although matching executive personality and mission may make sense, carried to an extreme it could deny the organization access to generally experienced people at the top should things change. Unless some of the firm's managers have weathered storms, experienced high growth, and learned how to cut costs in a crisis, it is difficult to see how they could direct a multi-business enterprise with any aplomb as top management. A firm subscribing too narrowly to type-matching would be shortchanging itself and its managers by failing to provide them with opportunities for executive development.

''Life cycle'' management selection at the top of the ongoing divisions of a large diversified business places specialists in delivering certain objectives, not generalists, near the apex of the managerial hierarchy. Such selection practices suggest three probable consequences:

1 there will be few proven internal candidates for advancement to the leadership position of the corporation whose businesses are in different life cycle stages;
2 the significance of differences across the firm will be emphasized, rather than common bonds and integrative internal relationships, reducing management flexibility;
3 if taken to its extreme, such close matching of manager and managed is unlikely to hold talented people within the firm when times change. Their prospects of advancement will have declined.

Moreover, such selection practices suggest that the objectives of business units will not be changed for some time and cannot be changed without a senior management change. Top management's ability to adapt to changing circumstances and opportunities is thus reduced.

TENSIONS AFFECTING HUMAN RESOURCE STRATEGY

There are obvious tensions between the short-run needs of an explicit situation and the long-run welfare of an organization, and between each of these and the career needs of a particular person, the executive, or candidate. These tensions have to be addressed. If their existence is acknowledged, any selection process can be monitored and refined based on experience.

The tensions in the selection process are not dissimilar to the tensions between the need for executive autonomy and the need for central coordination—each is a valid principle of organization (Sloan, 1963). Yet ultimately the cause of the tensions must be addressed. A decision to act has to be made by those involved, trading off the anticipated benefits and costs on each side of the spectrum. Here, experience is likely to outweigh science, since it is confidence rather than theoretical rigor that is telling in determining how to satisfy the long run needs of the organization.

In 1983, Ralph Lauren, the designer and also the founder of a clothing and cosmetics company with 1983 sales volume of $450 million, told the story of his experience in selecting a president for the company seven years earlier when its volume was $12 million:

> I trust my gut feelings about everything. . . . I picked the president of my company, Peter Strom, against the advice of experts. He's a low-key guy, doesn't come on like dynamite. He's got the kind of personality that grows on you. He's not a one-shot personality, someone who immediately convinces you he's going to take over the world. . . . The experts asked me what I saw in this guy. I told them: "He's the kind of guy I'd like to say hello to every morning, someone you *know* will be on your side, no matter what. That's saying a lot."[5]

Lauren appears to have weighted shared values higher than technical skill or "market orientation." Knowing intuitively that the personal relationship between the new presi-

[5]Quoted in the *Boston Globe*, Sept. 24, 1983, p. 10.

dent and himself would shape the future of the firm, Lauren selected a man who would help him create the kind of company he wanted. Ralph Lauren wanted as president someone with whom he could cooperate and a person who would cooperate with him rather than become his competitor. That's what we believe "on your side, no matter what" means. And, we agree, it is saying a lot.

CLIMATE: COMPETITION AND COOPERATION

Lauren hit upon one of the big issues of human resource management, the issue which ensures that you and your co-managers are productive. And that is fit. Strom fit with Lauren to make a cooperative team at the top. Lauren's intuition told him that he and his company would fare best with a cooperative internal climate in the highly competitive environment of the fashion industry.

Cooperation is necessary to co-align the actions of the firm to maximize their external impact. Other organizations might make different choices. For example, a more competitive internal climate might protect an organization from the slow draining of vitality which often afflicts monopolies, protected regulated businesses, and many governmental and charitable organizations, all of which are insulated from competition (at least in the minds of their managers and administrators).

Consider an observation which poses a dilemma for human resource management: If the climate created is too competitive, cooperation is diminished and the organization's best people will destroy each other; if the climate is too cooperative, the best are likely to be suffocated and the stimulus of their initiative snuffed out. Managers have to judge how competitive and how cooperative a climate is needed, given the organization's environment and its strategy. This relationship between competitiveness and cooperation is just one more tension which has to be manipulated with administrative skill to effectively implement strategy.

"Success in business is in almost exact ratio to the calibre of executive talent at management's command," was the conclusion reached by Marvin Bower after a long career at McKinsey and Company. But, he added, ". . . to be effectively at management's command, this executive talent must be working productively" (1966, p. 157). Management has the responsibility to make sure this is possible, that is, that managers can succeed. The culture, climate, and administrative systems of the organization have to be designed and managed so that they help managers do their jobs better, and thereby help the organization attract and retain high-calibre people.

ADMINISTRATIVE SYSTEMS: CHANNELS OF COMMUNICATION

Delegation is vital to the organization, and every executive has a critical responsibility to see that the organization's communications systems are established and maintained to aid delegation (Barnard, 1966, p. 218). Most people relish autonomy. Given a choice (in an organization that has policies delegating authority and lives by them), they prefer to be more than mere order-takers and to make decisions for themselves if they know what decisions they can make—and, we argue, if they know how they will be judged. Although management typically recognizes this priority, the number and power of the available channels of communication are often overlooked.

Administrative systems are communications channels. Recall that administration means co-aligning action. The communications sent through the administrative systems, therefore, should help the organization's managers co-align their actions—and note that "co-align" implies cooperation, not coercion.

Climate and Systems

The example of top management, the hierarchy of objectives and strategies used to focus action, the organization structure, the policies that guide day-to-day decision making, the financial information and control systems, systems for performance measurement and evaluation, and compensation and reward systems—these are the tools of administration and the threads, fibers, and lines of the communications system which management uses to influence the cooperative and competitive behavior of the people working in the organization. Their effects are interdependent. What is decided in one system influences the choices available in others and the ultimate effectiveness of the whole administrative strategy.

Management has to communicate its policies so that most people know what they can do. Example is probably one of the most powerful communicators in this regard. Another is the resource allocation process. Management delegates authority when it gives the custody of resources to specific managers. The allocation of resources makes authority tangible.

To ensure that there is a shared view of what is appropriate and correct, management designs a financial measurement system to emphasize what specific people are responsible for and what they should worry about. The explicitness of the financial system limits ambiguity but does not eliminate it. Ambiguity itself necessitates interaction and so stimulates more communication between managers. Its purpose is to promote a dialog between managers, not to make their lives uncomfortable. Now, let us see how the administrative systems work and what types of communications each system best fits.

Authority, Accountability, and Ambiguity

As we have noted already, one of the ways coordination is achieved without suffocating initiative is to design tensions into the administrative systems of the organization: authority and accountability is one of those tensions. Increased size and increased diversity both necessitate specialization of management and choices of how and where to allocate resources and how to coordinate action throughout the organization. When managers delegate, they maintain some control. They give authority—the physical custody of some corporate resources—to subordinate managers, but they hold their subordinates accountable for certain results.

Figure 15-1 demonstrates the sources and outcomes of the tension between authority and accountability, and the resulting ambiguity. The diagram puts policy first, since policy in our view is the sole foundation for delegation. On the next line, we see delegation which gives authority, subject to accountability for specific results. In structuring the organization, position by position and office-holder by office-holder, authority

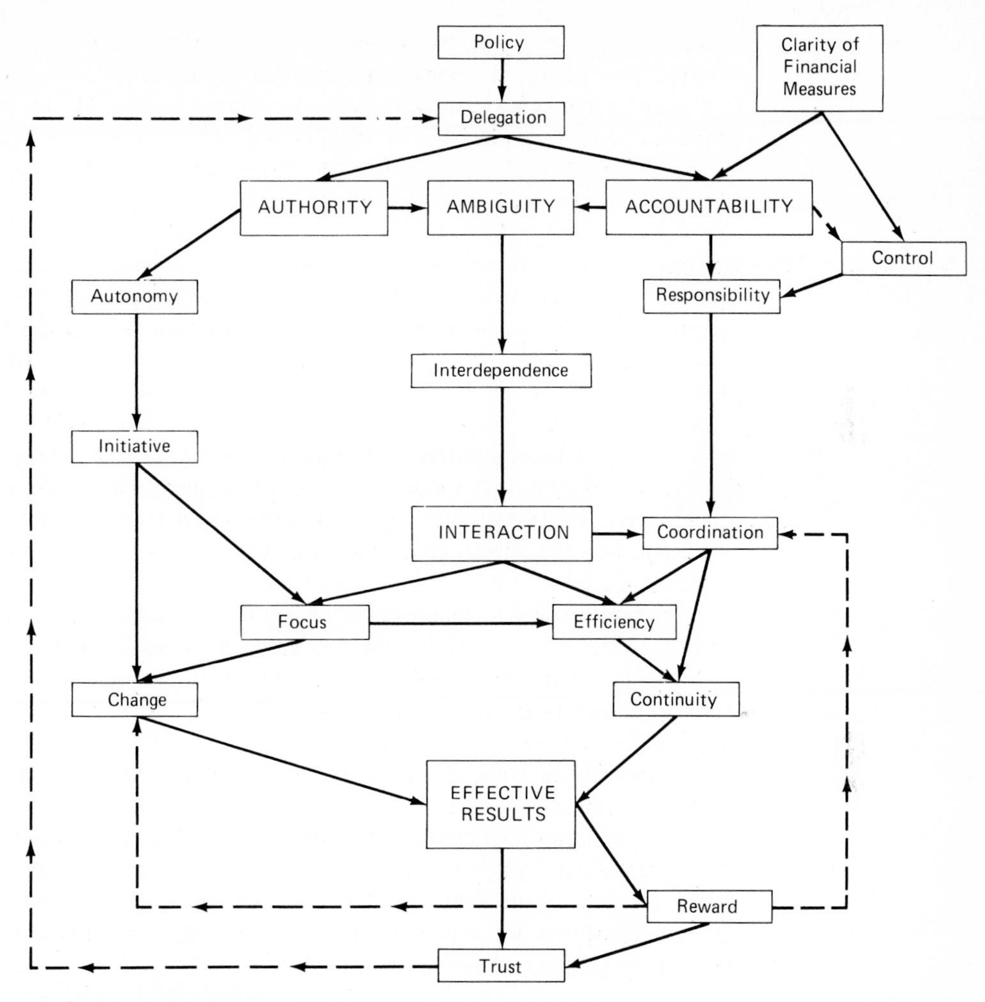

FIGURE 15-1 Authority and Accountability

over resources is given and accountability specified in reporting relationships. Authority, on the left side of *Figure 15-1,* promotes autonomy, which leads to the taking of initiative and to a search for possibilities for change. Accountability, on the right side, facilitates control and promotes both responsibility and coordination throughout the organization.

Now, consider how authority and accountability interact. For managers below the top, authority is usually less comprehensive in scope than the results required by the accountability system. Hence, the junior or middle manager's autonomy is restricted and he or she does not have custody of all the resources needed to succeed. The result is ambiguity.

Ambiguity, seen in the center of *Figure 15-1* under Delegation, stems from the fact that the activities and ultimately the results for which the manager is accountable exceed the capability of the resources in his or her custody. He or she is therefore dependent on others and, since the manager cannot simply make things happen by allocating his or her own resources, he or she has to interact with others to get the job done. Ambiguity therefore leads to interdependence and interaction. These interactions will include negotiation and attempts to influence others, for example, but in all their forms they force communication.

The Purpose of Ambiguity

Because the burden of accountability without autonomy often causes frustration, which leads to stress and career blocks for inexperienced managers, it is important to recognize the purpose of ambiguity so that you use it rather than suffer from it. Some managers incorrectly see accountability without authority as an impediment to their progress, rather than as a signal to talk. They try to work alone and fail, instead of working *through* others to succeed.

The result of delegation is not dysfunctional conflict between the accountability system and the authority system, the right- and left-hand sides of *Figure 15-1,* but rather effectiveness. The two systems are not in conflict but in tension, a tension which promotes communication and a focus on efficiency on the one hand, and a focus on the things that matter on the other, and so, ultimately, leads to effectiveness.

Authority leads to initiative-taking and accountability leads to coordination and efficient resource use. Together the two systems promote effectiveness stemming both from changes made for the sake of the future of the organization and from continuity which maintains the values of its resources. These resources are, of course, the building blocks for the organization's future.

Ultimately, it is the quality of the managers' contributions both to change and to continuity which establishes trust between managers, justifying rewards and further delegations of authority with increased autonomy to the achieving subordinate manager. The speed and certainty with which additional responsibility and authority are won will depend on the practices of the firm and its needs—for example, its growth and the degree to which advancement is competitive. The certainty with which reward follows results will influence any manager's subsequent behavior.

With this overview of the authority/accountability tension in mind, let us examine the roles of policy, delegation, and control, and the importance of trust within the administrative system. This done, we will examine measurement, appraisal, and compensation from a strategic viewpoint and conclude the chapter by summarizing how human resources shape strategy and are shaped by it.

Policies and Delegation

Policies are the foundation of delegation. If position in the managerial hierarchy is assigned on the basis of the organization's strategic needs to those with requisite knowledge, skill, perspective, and experience, and if authority is specified in light of the calibre of the human resources available, then each manager can act confidently within the scope of the authority delegated to him or her, and, importantly, with the confidence of the boss.

As *Figure 15-1* shows, policies are necessary whenever decision making is decentralized. Decentralization creates centers of initiative where specialized or informed managers can act in a timely and responsive way. Delegation specifies the authority of the managers of the decentralized unit so that they can take the initiative and succeed. Yet, if there are no policies to guide their decisions and to ensure them that they share a view of what is right with top management, delegation is a sham, initiative is reserved for those at the top, and all decisions of moment are centralized.

If managers are not allowed to decide, or if they are uncertain about what they can do or how their actions will be judged, survival dictates that they take orders and power is concentrated at the top. However, if policies exist which specify and communicate what decisions executives in certain positions can take, and if top management's practice or example is consistent with those policies, subordinate or junior managers can act confidently within the scope of whatever authority is delegated to them. They can use their minds for the organization.

Good practice is to act consistently with what you say and say what you believe. That is good example. Organizations have to let their members know what the limits of their authority are, what types of decisions are appropriate in various prescribed circumstances, and how the results they achieve will be evaluated. Inconsistent rhetoric and action are bad communicators and lead to uncertainty, shrinking confidence and a limiting of people's willingness to take the initiative. People learn quickly how their organization deals with success and failure, and change their behavior to attune themselves to the reality which is practice.

Delegation and Trust

The shared confidence underlying delegation and action is based on *trust:* delegation is a relationship which is, in essence, a contract. The terms of the contract are specified in large measure by policy, so that management as a whole is coordinated and discriminating in deciding what is the right thing to do. The contract is administered personally and develops on each side through interaction. Learning and results on both sides —that is, experience—accumulate to build either trust and confidence or mistrust (Barnes, 1981). Cooperative self-discipline on each side of the contract builds trust. Furthermore, the results achieved by the subordinate and the rewards given by the supervisor cement their trust in each other.

The paradox is that trust is only developed or extended when initiative is allowed and both executive capability and the relationships between supervisor and subordinate are tested. Policies are the framework within which this testing and executive development can occur at tolerable risk to all parties to the delegation contract, each member of the organization, and the organization as a whole. Policies in fact provide what Bower (1966) termed the backbone of the organization and the executive "will to manage," since they help all members understand what the values and plans of the organization are and adhere to them.

Control by Policy

Putting policies explicitly in place allows people to act confidently and with dispatch and to exercise initiative consistent with their capabilities and the organization's confidence in them. Allowing policy to evolve from practice, however, reduces management's control of action within the organization.

Control by policy makes good organizational sense. Control is needed to manage initiative, not to limit it. For example, the organization will be more effective if it focuses its efforts on specific targets of opportunity rather than dissipating its resources on many. It will be less exposed to risk if the scope of authority throughout the organization is matched with executive capability so that the cost of potential failure is personally and corporately absorbable.

If not consciously based on strategy, the facts of the situation, and organizational needs, policies which set out "how to do things" evolve out of practice. For example, subordinates tend to assume that their supervisors will act or make the same decisions as they do, if not advised otherwise (that is, controlled), and those below them will watch and do likewise—thereby establishing *de facto* policies. Such informal policies are likely to suit the parts of the organization better than they serve the whole and thus constitute an abdication of authority rather than delegation to serve the organization's needs. Such practices allow the dissipation of authority and weaken control.

"Loose but tight" is a term coined by Peters and Waterman (1982) in their book, *In Search of Excellence,* to describe how control by policy works. "Loose" refers to our freedom to act and use our judgment. "Tight" refers to doing what we do the "company way" in accord with policies so that our actions are focused on implementing strategy. Controls must be loose to allow action which is timely and responsive. They must be tight to ensure that decisions are made with the best available information and are co-aligned throughout the organization rather than being idiosyncratic. The concept is also found in other books on administrative practice, including those by Barnard (1966), Selznick (1957), and Bower (1966).

Policies and Administration

Policies enable delegation and control and so are a pervasive element in the administrative systems of the firm. These systems are like a light harness which helps the people of an organization pull together in the same direction. Policies promote efficiency, because they promote responsible self-coordination and allow people to act quickly in certain matters, and because they allow managers to discriminate between regular or routine circumstances and the exceptional. Policies provide a framework of criteria for managerial decision making.

Policies should be based on strategy and serve it, linking plan and practice. They should, therefore, be founded in the past and its experience but not stuck there. They should point to the future by laying out how certain things should be done in prescribed circumstances, as, for example, how employees, suppliers, or customers will be treated.

Policies should be simple and brief, focusing on the key factors rather than the minute—delegation means not doing the jobs of the people you supervise. Simplicity aids communication and promotes clarity and focus, since it reduces the need for individual interpretation and change. Simplicity also facilitates control, especially self-control, the least onerous form of control, thereby giving policy its administrative power.

THE ADMINISTRATIVE PURPOSES OF FINANCIAL MEASUREMENT SYSTEMS

Once management has established policies and decided to delegate authority, it has to communicate its intentions to the organization. There is a problem, however: how does management ensure that the message intended is received? In addressing this problem, the financial measurement system makes one of its less visible but crucial contributions to the welfare of the firm. Our discussion of financial measurement here will be administrative in spirit. We are concerned with communication between top and middle management, rather than with their respective reactions to the results of the current operating cycle.

With authority, the manager is given physical custody of some of the organization's assets. Custody makes the scope of the manager's autonomy explicit and tangible. By making the manager accountable for the use of those assets, the stage is set for a review of his or her stewardship. The financial measurement system should specify what the manager is accountable for, in a way which is:

> . . . consistent with, but more detailed than, the charter which describes his business responsibility. By deciding whether or not to assign a portion of the operating costs and asset values of shared resources to a profit center manager, corporate managers convey their intent about his or her need to be concerned with the effective utilization of those resources. . . . The design of the measurement system helps to ensure that the message gets through, reminding the profit center manager periodically whether and to what extent he should be concerned with the management of shared resources. (Vancil, 1979, pp. 129–30)

The exactness or specificity introduced by the financial measurement system is like a lens focusing management's attention on things that count. The administrative signals from the financial measurement system are important because they flesh out the fundamental contract between the manager and his or her boss. The measurement system also ensures that managers will establish a basis for a continuous dialogue about their collective use of the firm's resources, so that the benefits of any interdependency between profit centers or businesses are not lost. The ambiguity inherent in the administrative system is, therefore, nothing more or less than an alert signalling both the need for interaction and the possibility that tradeoffs between differing interests and objectives may be needed.

A secondary administrative function of the financial measurement system is to supply data documenting the outcomes of the continuous series of decisions which test the mettle of managers in every organization. This is important, because most organizations can only adapt by changing the authority and power of their managers (Barnes and Hershon, 1976). They can only do this if information on management's current performance and experience is available.

Administrative Signals from Financial Results

Current results give obviously powerful signals—probably the most difficult signals management receives if results are below expectations or if there is an unexpected loss. Note the words "expectation" and "unexpected." The delegation contract is violated by surprise, and surprise often leads to precipitous intervention by top management. "You help where you can," says top management, although such actions often reduce the autonomy of profit center management, focusing effort on the short run—since if you can't survive the short run, the long run doesn't matter.

Results are actually a mixed signal, however. They reveal something of how the market received our offerings and how we fared against our competitors, as well as something about how effectively and efficiently we operated our business. Thus, they have to be interpreted with care. In a crisis, or when they're surprised, managers are likely to overreact and the care needed in the situation is rarely given. Robert Uihlein, President and CEO of the Joseph Schlitz Brewing Company from 1961 to 1976, said when he took office, "The first thing I'm going to do is to give some fo the men around here a chance to make a mistake." What he was unable to foresee at that time was how he would react under pressure when a mistake occurred and what the net impact of encouraging rhetoric and discouraging follow-up action would be.

In the context of reacting appropriately to signals from the financial measurement system, we can note that, although some managers believe that a focus on details keeps them "on their toes," focusing on details can create a downward series of misallocations of management attention, interfering in the operations of those below and risking a failure of delegation. In general, the supervising manager should work with less rather than more detail because then the signal on subordinates' performance is clearer and there is less temptation to take on subordinates' problems, unintentionally usurping the authority delegated earlier.

Indeed, doing their subordinates' job is a common failing of anxious, newly-promoted managers who, instead of integrating themselves further up into the organization, return to whence they came—where they have mastery and feel less ambiguity. They do their old job, denying their subordinates the opportunity for development and themselves the opportunity for advancement. Rather, managers should react to the signals relevant to them, focus on the things that count, those things that contribute to the implementation of strategy, to the success of their own job, and the evaluation of their subordinates.

HUMAN RESOURCE EVALUATION: DEALING WITH SUCCESS AND FAILURE

The USCO-Euroco Example

Some years ago, while working with two separate companies each with sales substantially in excess of $10 billion, we had opportunities to learn how middle managers saw the possibilities for personal reward in the light of their companies' reactions to success and failure. The results for USCO and Euroco, as we will call them, are shown in *Figure 15-2*. The score, positive or negative, indicates the size of reward or penalty which managers believed they would receive when right or wrong.

Figure 15-2 shows that in USCO, if the manager was right in a judgment of what to support and what not to—that is, if the ultimate result favored the manager's decision—he or she was rewarded, but *only if* the company won. He or she got very little if the company was simply saved from losses. If the manager was wrong, he or she suffered and in fact was often fired. In Euroco, managers were rewarded differently. *Figure 15-2* shows there was a premium for being right at Euroco, but also a reward for championing a new venture.

In USCO, risk-taking was promoted by top management's speeches, but only winners were wanted. Full responsibility for failure was placed on individual managers. In Euroco, risk-taking was promoted at the top, but responsibility for results was shared. Because commitments to its new ventures were viewed as organizational as well as

EUROCO

Management Action	Outcome: Success	Outcome: Failure
Go	8	3
No Go	0	1

USCO

Management Action	Outcome: Success	Outcome: Failure
Go	3	−5
No Go	−1	1

FIGURE 15-2 The Payoff for Success and Failure

individual commitments, management viewed short-term results as a signal that their internal or operating procedures needed review. They assumed, to start, that the decision to enter was right.

USCO was fast of foot, while Euroco was a little slower, since consensus was needed for action. The European company viewed businesses as commitments which, if worth initiating, were worth persevering in. Its ventures were precision rifle shots while USCO's were shotgun blasts. USCO's ventures were initially more numerous, but they were also less focused, received less early corporate support, and had a high failure rate. Ultimately, because failure was followed by firing, venturing at USCO slowed and its rate of innovation declined. Poor results severely test management's commitment to delegation.

REACTION TO POOR RESULTS

The handling of poor results affects an organization's ability to innovate and change. If venturing is punished, venturing stops. In too many organizations, the evolution of a new venture follows a deteriorating path, because of the way management deals with failure. Initial enthusiasm for the venture is followed by disappointment when the first results are reported. ''Disappointment is relieved by a search for the guilty, although the innocent are punished while honor goes to the uninvolved,'' is an observation made by the Director of Research of a large British company. It seems to fit US experience, too.

When results are poor, how they're handled is less a matter of style than a matter of confidence and responsibility. A simplistic view suggests that either you intervene or you let the managers on the spot find their own way out of the dilemma. Another choice is to put pressure on the manager in trouble.

Management at Marks and Spencer,[6] the famous UK retailing firm, seems to disagree with such simple approaches. Management's policy for dealing with poor results is founded on two guiding principles:

1 external conditions do not justify results below plan;
2 departments where performance is smooth are closely monitored; in the face of difficult problems, pressure is relaxed.

Senior managers explain that their policy is founded on an assumption that good performance will deteriorate if not continuously pressured. Problems, however, necessitate effort and a clear head. Marks and Spencer's management believes that administrative pressure is unlikely to help the managers keep their heads when the going is tough and they are under the pressure of the problem and their own needs to succeed. At Marks and Spencer, they believe their human resource assignments are sound and that delegation means letting the manager on the spot solve the problem, drawing on (the experience of) others for aid as he or she needs it.

Of course, intervention may be necessary—for example, if a quick remedy is needed to ensure the welfare of the firm—but even in such a circumstance, managers should consider the signal they send and the way any intervention on their part will be received. Too early an intervention violates the delegation contract, too little may threaten the organization. Allowing too much pressure to reach a manager may stimulate errors rather than effectiveness. Indeed, crises reflect not only upon the manager on the scene but upon the wisdom and judgment of those who put the manager there and the quality of their supervision.

PERFORMANCE APPRAISAL

Performance appraisal or evaluation, salary determination, promotion, demotion, and termination often rely on the financial information system for much of their primary data. Managers similarly use the financial information system to help their subordinates assess where change is needed and to motivate them to change. Thus, the financial measurement system is used as a primary source of information for other administrative purposes besides communication of the intent and results of delegation.

Douglas McGregor (1960) made some observations about performance appraisal which are still valid. First, he noted a tendency for salary administrators to unconsciously discriminate to much finer levels than "outstandingly good," "satisfactory," and "unsatisfactory," and he charged that this was unrealistic. He maintained that different people used different standards, some were biased and prejudiced, and, moreover, each person's performance is ". . . to a considerable extent a function of how he is managed" (p. 83), all factors which make fine distinctions of performance impossible.

[6]Marks and Spencer, Ltd (A), ICCH 9-375-358.

McGregor found that when appraisals were used simply as a basis for consultation between superior and subordinate, they were more honest than when they were used for salary and other administrative decisions. However, he noted how difficult it is for any of us to hear and accept criticism: Too general and the subordinate finds it difficult to correct his or her behavior; too specific and the subordinate will argue that specific extenuating circumstances existed. Moreover, McGregor believed the effectiveness of the communication is often inversely related to the subordinate's need to hear—he even wondered whether people really wanted to know how they were doing—and that this tendency is exacerbated by making an event out of the appraisal interview.

Indeed, although we call it performance appraisal, the fact is that it is a personal appraisal. It is rarely an objective activity but a social-emotional one, quite subjective in most circumstances. At the top of the organization, where time horizons are longer and the job more complex, completely objective and certain evaluations are often impossible. Because appraisal leads to promotion or to termination, it is costly to individuals and organizations both. It must be made informed and equitable. Precedents exist for court intervention if this is not so.

Illustrating the frequent subjectivity of performance appraisal and one of its organizational costs, Bower wrote,

> Although I can't prove it, I believe that the insider who seems 65 percent qualified for the job is likely to outperform the typical outsider who seems 90 percent qualified, because the weaknesses of the insider are known, while those of the outsider are hard to learn accurately in advance. (1966, p. 170)

The insider, about whom more is known, faces a harder standard on the performance appraisal, while the outsider fares better. The organization, of course, is the loser as it opts for relative inexperience.

Multiple sources and multiple dimensions are needed to evaluate senior managers. Because strategies unfold over time and because results accumulate slowly, the overall pattern should normally outweigh one aberrant result. Strategic concept, control, achievements, risks taken, and support within the organization all point to the quality of executive performance. A wise boss turns the appraisal into a source of information for the manager being evaluated and motivates him or her to better performance.

MOTIVATION AND DEVELOPMENT

The shared purpose of appraisal, motivation, and development is to identify and communicate the need for change, to encourage the acquisition of knowledge and skill, and to develop the attitudes and perspectives that people need to do more comprehensive jobs. Semiannual or annual appraisal is not a particularly effective motivator to change. This is true, first, because most appraisal sessions focus on the need for improvements and what's wrong, and, second, because they occur too late. McGregor wrote,

> People do learn and change as a result of feedback. In fact, it is the only way they learn. However, the most effective feedback occurs immediately after the behav-

ior. . . . Three or four months later, the likelihood of effective learning from the experience is small. (1960, p. 87)

The One Minute Manager (Blanchard and Johnson, 1982) offers a prescription for fast feedback. The "hero," the one minute manager, tries to "catch" people doing good and praises them for it so they will learn what good management practices are. He manages by example. When reprimands are warranted, he gives them briefly and as soon as possible. He waits to let the reprimand sink in so that they can feel how he feels and then reassures the subordinate that he or she still has the boss's respect and support—touching (by shaking hands) to authenticate the full exchange and to end it.

The theme of *The One Minute Manager* is consistent with McGregor's advice that fast feedback motivates best. Fast feedback reinforces useful behavior. It deals one at a time with dysfunctional behaviors so that it is clear what behavior is being criticized and that it is the inappropriate behavior which is to be eliminated, not the person. In most corporate settings, managers eliminate people because it's easier—especially since they let a person's negative score accumulate until their frustration is so great that they take the simple way out and fire him.

Most executive development occurs on the job (Livingston, 1969). Such development occurs because a mentor or coach is on hand to reinforce discipline and to encourage. Deutsch (1983) describes what a mentor does, noting that if you turn the organization chart upside down, then your responsibility is to help those persons above you. Zaleznick (1977) says this was the concept motivating Donald Perkins, Jewel Tea's innovative president during the 1970s. Simple praise, notes, phone calls, and other acknowledgements of purposeful behavior can modify behavior if used consistently and insistently, especially early in the association when flexibility exists. The contribution of an effective mentor or coach is to bring forth what protégés have not discovered for themselves—the potential to do better—and to help them fit themselves into the organization.

Development is finally self-development. The classic transformation of the flower girl, Eliza Doolittle, to a lady in Shaw's *Pygmalion,* is an example of potential realized through coaching, although, as you may recall, the pupil ultimately had to fight for her independence. Like Eliza, executives ultimately have to be independent. Only independent minds are likely to innovate, for example.

The organization should be managed to give us the opportunity to develop ourselves. We have to integrate ourselves into the organizations we join and learn to discipline ourselves so that we are effective members. Ultimately, we are each responsible for our own development. As Kotter (1982) said, we have to set our own agenda to define our job and we have to build our own networks to facilitate our work. We have to think for ourselves since our minds and the minds of our employees are the ultimate sources of value and the sources of the satisfaction that should be associated with purposeful action and organizational membership.

From a corporate point of view, executives need to find ways to help managers develop themselves and test their mettle. Job rotation, including movement across organizational boundaries and between units, reduces barriers to communication and leads to new knowledge, skills, and perspectives. Communication and familiarity help free bottlenecks and reduce dysfunctional conflict. Temporary assignments to higher positions, during vacations, for example, allow testing and observation of performance at modest risk for all concerned. This is, however, a sadly neglected practice if potential successors and understudies are not identified for all general management positions.

Such trial and error learning experiences as those we describe can go a long way towards limiting the influence of the "Peter Principle," the observation that executives ultimately are promoted to the level of their incompetence where they become either failures or afraid to act. The incentives for promotion must be real. Compensation and the threat of termination are both used to encourage self-development and self-confidence throughout the organization.

COMPENSATION

Compensation is a difficult matter, probably handled too mechanistically in most firms. Here, our interest is in implementing strategy, and compensation is one of the most powerful communicators in the administrative armory.

Compensation cements the contract between employer and employee, between managers, no matter how humble or exalted. When you compensate or reward someone, you have a significant opportunity to reaffirm what your intent is and what your priorities are. The way you pay them tells them what is really important.

Figure 15-3 contrasts two views of salary, one of the most basic forms of compensation. One view is mechanistic, the other strategic. Possibly both are artificial, because practical salary schemes necessarily share characteristics of each. The key point we wish to make, however, relates to attitude. Salary is either market-driven—that is, it merely pays in some equitable way for services rendered—or it (and indeed all compensation) is an incentive to tune the organization to more effective strategy implementation. The mechanistic view is pedestrian and only partially relevant to the strategist, while the strategic view is challenging. Note, in *Figure 15-3,* that the needs of the firm are given

FIGURE 15-3 Alternative Views of Salary

Mechanistic	*Strategic*
1. Sets salaries systematically to divide a fixed pie.	Must convert salary payments to incentives.
2. Sees salary as a payment for job done.	Uses salary to reward past and present effort and to encourage future contributions and cooperation.
3. Sees salary as a monthly payment.	Uses salary to influence relationships among peers. Considerations of relative status and salary are keys to "perceived" peer group membership.
4. Tends to award salary on technical factors, for example: —contributions to profit —number of personnel supervised —nature and impact of decisions made —market availability (or replacement cost).	Must decide what kind of competitive or cooperative environment is wanted and use salary to create it. Hence will give weight to the relationship of the job to the distinctive competence of the firm in determining salary level.

greater prominence under "strategic." The strategist takes a different time perspective, emphasizing future contribution to a greater extent.

If the strategy of the firm is to have priority, management will design its full compensation scheme to communicate its purpose, to support its efforts to promote competitive and cooperative behavior throughout the organization, and to focus attention appropriately on the time horizons, long or short, of particular actions. For example, peaked salary structures promote competitiveness, while flat structures promote cooperation. The rate at which the structure narrows, whether there are a few steps or many steps or smooth transitions, signals whether internal competitiveness or cooperation is important.

Consider which of the three patterns of compensation in *Figure 15-4* is likely to be associated with the most internally competitive organization. Which do you think will be the most cooperative organization? In our view, the second (or mid) pattern is likely to be most competitive, because compensation narrows at precise points creating sets of "equals"—particularly near the top in ranks 2 to 5. Remember, money in the corporation confers status. On the other hand, the third or bottom chart is most cooperative. There are few large gaps and few gates between levels.

BONUS

Bonus is one of the classic compensation devices used in industry. It, too, allows the strategic manager an opportunity to focus management's attention on specific factors and to fine-tune the reward system. To illustrate this point, let us examine how some companies have designed and used their bonus systems.

At Analog Devices, a Massachusetts-based high technology company, management believed that no simple, one-dimensional bonus plan could satisfy its needs. As Stata and Madique (1980) tell the story (being Chairman and President, and former Vice President, the authors are primary witnesses), management settled on two dimensions, return on assets (ROA) and sales growth, to focus attention on the critical factors of profitability to fund growth and growth itself—a short-term factor and a long-term factor.

On the growth dimension, management used a twelve-quarter moving average. The period chosen matched the time it typically took Analog to realize the potential of a new product, and related to the typical tenure of an eligible executive in a single position or assignment. Shorter periods would have been too close in time to judge; longer periods would probably be too long and too distant from the perspective of an executive.

On the other hand, Analog expected its managers to adapt to changing conditions and make things work. Hence, it adopted a three-quarter average on the ROA dimension. This gave managers one quarter to pick up a result, one to change operations, and one to judge its effects.

To focus attention on the competition, Analog set its goals on each dimension to match industry peer performance—25 percent growth and 23 percent pretax ROA for the "better" semi-conductor instrument and computer companies over the prior three years. To help ensure that the company's financial strategy (funding its own growth) was feasible, management weighted the bonus in favor of ROA. As *Figure 15-5* shows, a full

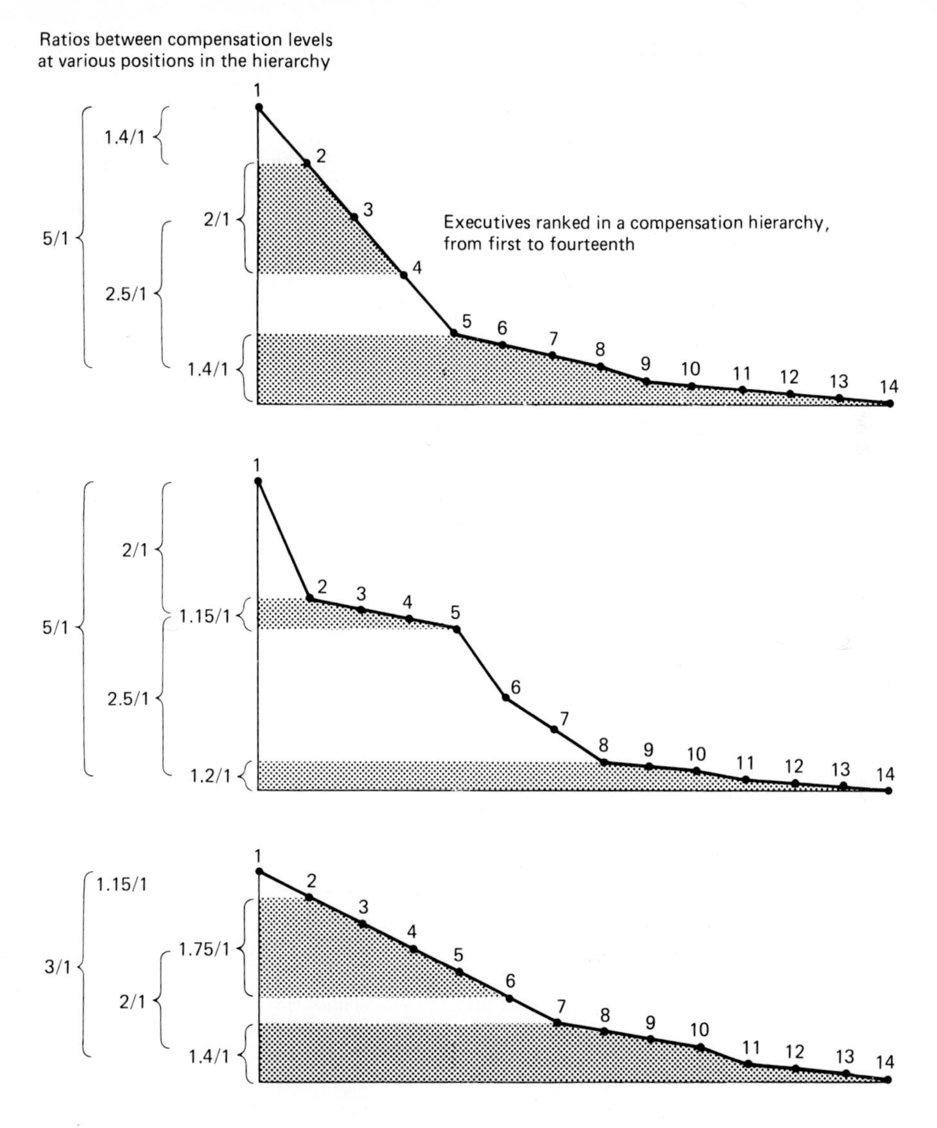

Note: These patterns are plotted on a semilogarithmic scale, such that the slopes of any one pattern may be directly compared with the others.

FIGURE 15-4 Three Patterns of Compensation in an Executive Hierarchy Having 14 Levels of Personnel

Source: Andrew Towl, "Patterns of Executive Compensation," July/August 1951. Reprinted by permission of the *Harvard Business Review*.

bonus would be paid only if goals were met. But for those who exceeded goals, bonus eligibility jumped very quickly indeed.

Analog further tuned its compensation strategy by varying the potential salary and bonus mix by rank. Those at the top could earn a bonus of up to 100 percent of salary, while those three levels below could earn only 10 percent of salary. Stata and Madique report Analog's management believed that although outstanding corporate results de-

3-quarter average return on assets as biased ↓		12-quarter average sales growth rate* → 14.9% Poor	15%	20%	25% Goal	30%	35%	40%	45% Outstanding
16.9%	Poor	0	0	0	0	0	0	0	0
17.0%		0	0.29	0.29	0.41	0.56	0.75	1.00	1.00
19.0%		0	0.29	0.41	0.56	0.75	1.00	1.30	1.30
21.0%		0	0.41	0.56	0.75	1.00	1.30	1.67	1.67
23.0%	Goal	0	0.56	0.75	1.00	1.30	1.67	2.12	2.12
25.0%		0	0.75	1.00	1.30	1.67	2.12	2.66	2.66
27.0%		0	1.00	1.30	1.67	2.12	2.66	3.29	3.29
29.0%		0	1.30	1.67	2.12	2.66	3.29	4.04	4.04
31.0%	Out-standing	0	1.30	1.67	2.12	2.66	3.29	4.04	4.04

*The bonus payout factor can be calculated from the following formula:
Bonus payout factor =

$$K = \left(\frac{\text{ROA\%} + \text{bias} + .4 \text{ sales growth\%}}{33}\right)^{4.5}$$

Note: The payout is deliberately nonlinear, generating higher incremental payoffs at higher levels of performance. Note the "cut-off" and "saturation" levels. The bias factor allows management to adjust the expected payout from year to year to compensate for unusual circumstances, for example, a year in which deliberate, heavy strategic expenditures are committed that will depress operating ROA. The bias factor is set at the beginning of the year-coincident with the annual plan-and then held constant through the planning period.

FIGURE 15-5 Bonus Payoff Function for 1979

Source: Ray Stata and Modesto Madique, "Bonus System for Balanced Strategy," Nov.-Dec. 1980. Reprinted by permission of the *Harvard Business Review*.

served an outstanding reward, junior managers should not risk such a large percentage of their compensation because higher-level decisions affect their performance, sometimes negatively. Analog paid its bonus quarterly in an effort to co-align management and stockholder interests.

At General Electric in the 1970s, management developed a three-factor bonus system to focus management attention on different factors across divisions according to their corporate missions, that is, the objectives set for them in the light of GE's corporate strategy. Invest or grow managers were more heavily rewarded for actions and programs geared to future benefits than for short-term results. Harvest or divest managers were rewarded more heavily for short-term earnings, as *Figure 15-6* shows.

Other schemes exist which incorporate more factors in bonus compensation. Stonich (1981) refers to a scheme using four factors—ROA, cash flow, strategic funds programs, and market share increase—with each factor rated differently according to the SBU (Strategic Business Unit) category of a particular operating entity. Strategic funds programming is a specific effort to emphasize long-run efforts in product development, innovation, and management development, for example, by separating normal operating expenses from ''expendable'' investments in the future well-being of the firm.

Stonich also refers to an income statement where the top part relates to operations and the bottom to strategic funds, so that operating and overall performance are

Market Growth
Market Size
Segmentation
Cyclicality
Nature of Demand
Ease of Entry and Exit
  Number and Size of Competitors
  Capacity in Place
  Scale Economies
  Break Even Positions
  Length of Operating Cycle
  Profitability
Roles of Price, Quality, and Cost
Product and Process Life Stage
Contingent Liabilities and Risks
Social Impact

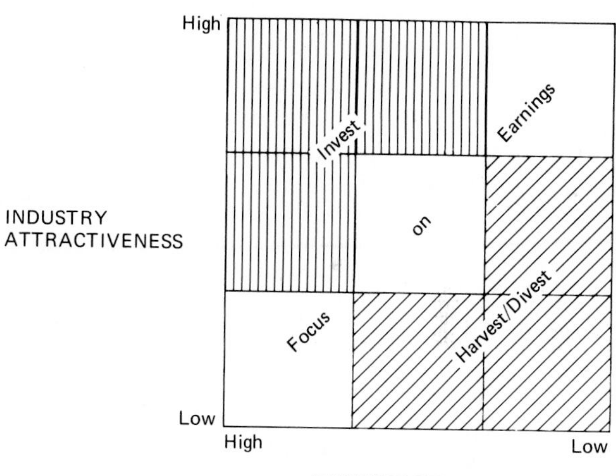

BUSINESS STRENGTH

Market Share	Management
Product Technology	Labor Productivity
Process Technology	Plant Capacity
Price Premium	Cost Position
Product (Brand) Image	Flexibility and Service
Sales Force	Material Cost
Distribution Strength	Environmental Impact

Matching Bonus to Business Mission

	Bonus Weight (measure)		
Objective	*Current Financial Performance*	*Competitive Position Future Performance*	*Other Factors*
Invest	30%	60%	10%
Focus on Earnings	50%	40%	10%
Harvest/Divest	70%	20%	10%

FIGURE 15-6 Business Unit Assessment

TABLE 15-1 SBU P & L Segregation of Strategic Funds

Sales	$12,300,000
Cost of sales	−6,900,000
Gross margin	$5,400,000
Operating SG & A	−3,700,000
Operating ROA	$1,700,000 or 33%
Strategic funds	−1,000,000
Pre-tax profit (ROA)	$700,000 or 13.6%

Source: Stonich, "Using Rewards in Implementing Strategy," *Strategic Management Journal,* 2, 351. © 1981 by John Wiley & Sons.

monitored. Note the placement of strategic funds below the operating ROA in Table 15-1. Stonich comments:

> Using the strategic funds deferral method, managers can be given incentives to invest strategic funds where, under a conventional ROA measurement, the incentive is to hold them down in the same way as operating expenses. Managers can be encouraged to follow their natural inclination to manage to the "bottom line," where, in this case, current operating ROA is the measure. Thus, current operations of the company can be made as profitable as possible at the same time that critical future investments through strategic funds are encouraged. (1981, p. 350)

Hart Hanks Newspapers specified objectives on six dimensions of performance for its subsidiary, Independent Publishing of Anderson, South Carolina, in 1975,[7] specifying for each objective "must," "good," and "outstanding" levels of performance. No bonus was to be paid until "good" was reached on "managerial margin." Thereafter John Ginn, the Independent's publisher, received a personal bonus which varied according to the number of goals achieved out of the total possible. He, as all Hart Hanks managers, received a corporate bonus based on corporate performance ranging up to 15 percent of salary, while the individual bonus could amount to 20 to 35 percent of base salary.

In all these examples, the effort to use compensation to focus effort on specific objectives is deliberate. Note the use of standards so that the quality of performance is essentially rewarded contractually. These examples show the use of multiple objectives which encourage managers to make the right tradeoffs for the organization.

CONCLUSION: HUMAN RESOURCES SHAPE STRATEGY

The theme of this chapter is that administrative systems are communications systems. Signals have to be clear and clearly received to help the people of the organization work together.

Sun Tzu wrote:

> When one treats people with benevolence, justice, and righteousness, and reposes confidence in them, the army will be united in mind and will be happy to serve their leaders. (1963, p. 64)

[7]Hart Hanks Newspapers, ICCH 9-377-062.

He also stated:

> Generally, management of many is the same as management of few. It is a matter of organization. And to control many is the same as to control few. This is a matter of formations and signals. (p. 90)

These ancient prescriptions are still applicable. There is no justice in asking people to fail. Selection must be informed and careful. Confidence necessitates mutual trust founded on results. Thus, assignments should be used to give people, high and low, opportunities to build experience and trust. Benevolence is a principle of doing to others as you would like them to do to you. As Chesterton said, it isn't that it's been tried and found wanting, it simply isn't tried.

James F. Lincoln a co-founder of the Lincoln Electric Company wrote:

> Competition means there will be losers as well as winners in the game. Competition will mean the disappearance of the lazy and incompetent. . . . It is a hard taskmaster. It is necessary for anyone, be he worker, user, distributor or boss, if he is to grow. . . . There is not danger from a hard life. . . . Danger is from a life . . . made soft by lack of competition.

Yet he also stated:

> The worker (which includes management), the customer, the owner and all those involved must be satisfied that they are properly recognized or they will not cooperate, and cooperation is essential to any and all successful applications of incentives.[8]

George E. Willis, Lincoln Electric's president in 1971, explained how Lincoln could simultaneously promote competitiveness and foster cooperation:

> If our employees did not believe management was trustworthy, honest and impartial, the system could not operate. . . This ties back to a trust and understanding between individuals and all levels of the organization.[9]

In a world where competitiveness is honored on the playing field, in the classroom, and in professional life, it is easy to overlook the need for cooperation. When we join an organization, we should recognize that we will have to work with and through others and that most of our interactions are fundamentally cooperative.

Size and diversity in organizations typically necessitate a specialization of labor and choices of where and how to allocate resources. But such divisions necessitate coordination and a coordinator, and so a hierarchy of managers. Hierarchy and specialization each imply selective recruiting and development and mechanisms to influence behavior. Managers will use universal and individual incentives to influence behavior, rewarding what is functional rather than dysfunctional, making allied decisions about the use of pressure and the scope of delegation based on both the needs of the situation and their personal styles.

[8]Lincoln Electric Company, ICCH 9-376-028.
[9]*Ibid.*

Concluding, we want to stress the needs of the organization for initiative and change and for coordination and continuity. We stress the use of competitive and cooperative behavior to implement strategy, noting that managers do not work alone but together, subject to their being individually responsible (to each other) for results. The organization needs initiative and change as well as coordination and continuity.

chapter 16

Planning and Control

INTRODUCTION

Planning at its best institutionalizes strategic management. With an effective planning and control system in place, management periodically reviews its current situation and results, looks ahead, and acts to position the firm for the future. Planning may be ineffective where management has failed to act, out of timidity for example, or because management has failed to use its results to improve its plans and control its actions.

Keep in mind as you read this chapter that planning is useful only if it helps us manage. The besetting sin of planners is to give undue importance to planning, plans, and the planner. Planning is not an end in itself, but simply an institutional approach for strategic management.

Planning means not only foreseeing the future but providing for it (Fayol, 1972). Control means predicting the outcomes of our actions, collecting information on performance, comparing plan and performance. Where our decision or action proves inadequate or successful, we can use control to correct the one and reinforce the other (Ackoff, 1970).

Describing a business plan in 1916, Fayol wrote, ''The plan of action is, at one and the same time, the result envisaged, the line of action to be followed, the stages to go through, and the methods to be used'' (1972, p. 43). Today, we would use the words, ''the objectives sought and the strategies to be used to achieve them,'' but Fayol's principles are relevant. Action is needed. We also note the importance Fayol gave to timing and the fact that he recognized that planning is costly, difficult, necessitates control, and must be repeated:

> Compiling the annual plan is always a delicate operation and especially lengthy and laborious when done for the first time, but each repetition brings some simplification and when the plan has become a habit the toil and difficulties are largely reduced. Conversely, the interest it offers increases. The attention demanded for executing the plan, the indispensable comparison between predicted and actual facts, the recognition [of] mistakes made and successes attained, the search for means of repeating the one and avoiding the other—all go to make the new plan a work of increasing interest and increasing usefulness. (p. 49)

Planning is important but not easy. Introducing his book, *A Concept of Corporate Planning,* Russell Ackoff eloquently describes the difficulty:

> Planning is the design of a desired future and of effective ways of bringing it about. It is an instrument that is used by the wise but not by the wise alone. When conducted by lesser men it often becomes an irrelevant ritual that produces short run peace of mind, but not the future that is longed for. (1970, p. 1)

Hunsicker (1980) quotes a typical executive complaint which suggests that Ackoff is right:

> We spend an awful lot of time planning but I find it hard to point to a clear case where our business is better off or even substantially better off for it.

Paradoxically, this same executive said the process worked ''reasonably well'' (p. 8).

DOES PLANNING PAY?

Despite management's occasional doubts, managers do plan, and researchers have generally concluded that over time the objective evidence is that planning pays. Using an extensive questionnaire to survey the acquisition practices of ninety-three US manufacturing firms over the twenty-year period 1946 to 1966, Ansoff and his colleagues (1970) concluded, ''the firms that exhibited extensive planning of their acquisition programs significantly outperformed the firms that did little formal planning'' (p. 5). Thune and House (1970) found that, when considered as a group, companies that engaged in formal long-range planning historically outperformed a comparable group of informal planners. However, Thune and House found differences in the efficacy of planning across industries and concluded:

> Successful economic results associated with long-range planning tend to take place in rapidly changing industries and among companies of medium size. . . . It is most likely that formal planning is a characteristic of a well-managed firm rather than the single cause of successful economic performance. (p. 87)

Thune's and House's work was extended by Herold (1972) who found that, collectively, formal planners' sales and profit growth outperformed informal planners' in the two industries he studied, drugs and chemicals. Reinforcing Thune and House's view that planning is associated with well-managed firms, Herold showed that the R&D expenditures of formal planners were greater than the informal planners'. Herold argued that planning and increased R&D expenditures each contributed to the increased success of the planners over comparable nonplanners and that this, too, was evidence that well-managed companies planned.

Although the research cited is not conclusive that planning per se pays, the evidence is that well-managed companies plan and outperform many others. However, in interpreting the research literature, recall that planning is only one of the administrative systems

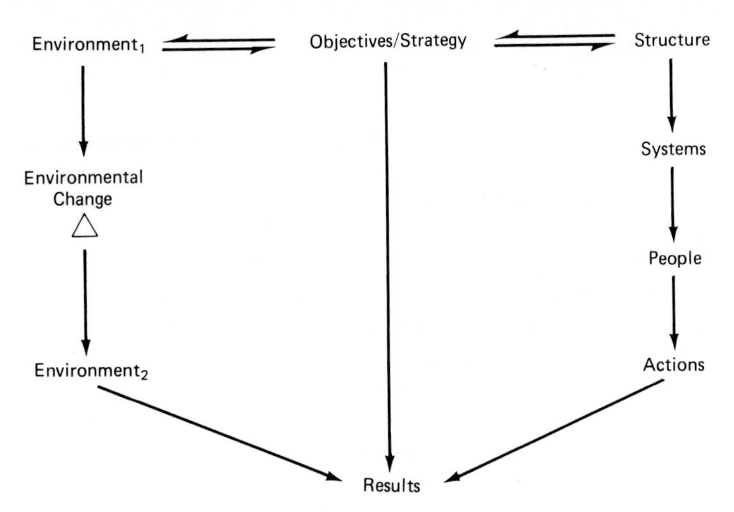

FIGURE 16-1 The Strategic Management System

management has at its disposal to enhance corporate performance. Our model of the Strategic Management System, repeated here as *Figure 16-1,* points to the separate but interdependent influences of the environment and the organization on the results earned by a particular strategy. And, although Ansoff and colleagues, Thune and House and Herold controlled for ''time'' and the environment, they did not have data on ''good'' and ''poor'' plans, control systems, nor the quality of the organization.

It is surprising that the research is as conclusive as it is, given the complexities of the full administrative system and the influences of the environment. Armstrong (1982) concluded in his review of the research on planning that planning is useful. He added, however, that the research to date says little about how or when to plan.

We believe planning is best when it is anchored in reality, when management ''owns'' its plans—that is, commits to them—and when top management uses its experience to add value to the corporation by strengthening the plans of separate business or business units in a thorough review process. Furthermore, plans are only useful when they promote commitment for coordinated action. Agreement on strategies is more critical than consensual objectives in the short run (Bourgeois, 1980), while organizations which promote and ultimately live consistently with superordinate objectives, appear to outperform all their competitors over time (Pascale and Athos, 1981; Peters and Waterman, 1982).

PLANNING PRACTICE

Formal planning for business was advocated by Fayol in 1916 and given a substantial boost in the United States by the consulting work of James McKinsey in the 1930s (McKinsey, 1932) and by his successors at McKinsey and Company and A.T. Kearney (Wolf, 1978). Since the 1960s, when ''having a plan'' became fashionable, management has wrestled with the wisdom of planning and the difficulty of doing it right. Wrapp questioned the wisdom of having a specific detailed plan at all:

> The top management must think out objectives in detail, but ordinarily some of the objectives must be withheld, or at least communicated to the organization in modest doses. A conditioning process which may stretch over months or years is necessary in order to prepare the organization for radical departures from what it is currently striving to attain. (1967, p. 95)

Plans are only tools. Wrapp, of course, advocated thinking about the future, although he cautioned managers about "published" plans. Used ineptly, plans can promote a set and inflexible position. Used well, they can promote coordination and focused effort. Wrapp warned management about the sacred character plans can acquire when they are seen as more than tools, and about the holy "hands-off" mantle which planners can gather about themselves in a large organization.

For example, during the 1960s and 1970s planning staffs bloomed in many large corporations, a growth aided by the availability of corporate computer power and econometric modelling techniques. While available today to planners and line managers alike, the computer languages available in those years preserved and enhanced the power of the planning staffs at the expense of line management and in some companies isolated the planners from action. In fact, although the Arab-Israeli wars in 1967 and 1971 foreshadowed dramatic structural shifts in the US economy, it was only after the 1974 oil embargo and recession that line managers began to regain influence in the planning process.

In 1976 Naylor and Schauland reported that econometric and financial models were often developed as the bases for corporate plans. Yet by 1985 some of the largest corporations, including General Electric which largely disbanded its corporate planning staff, had reduced their reliance on econometric and other planning models and put the responsibility for planning back on line managers. Although models are now used extensively to explore the implications of various strategic options, the turbulence of the late 1970s led companies to put responsibility for planning closer to the marketplace where current data and managerial experience can play a greater role in determining strategy.

In making this change to line-dominated planning, however, there is a risk. The older planning models placed great weight on analysis, but very little on synthesis. The danger is that the line-dominated approaches may place too little weight on the need for quality analysis as the foundation for the plan.

Mintzberg (1976), drawing on the research of neurologists and psychologists, noted that analysis and synthesis are two very different processes and rarely highly developed in one individual. He then proposed that there is probably a similar difference between formal planning and informal managing. Planners appear to work in a logical and orderly manner, while Mintzberg argues that many effective managers are intuitive and work with relatively little order, noting, "They tend to underemphasize analytical input that is often important as well" (p. 58).

In a speech before the Conference Board's 1981 Marketing Conference in New York City, John F. Welch, Jr., then Chairman and CEO of the General Electric Company, explained his views on why planning practice has turned, for now, back to line management and away from staff:

> At financial planning, at resource allocation . . . , the internalities, . . . strategic planning did well . . . but not too well at marketing, . . . the crucial externality. Comfortable with quantification, strategic planning mapped the external world beautifully—market size and share. It made huge contributions to resource allocation . . . but strategic planning didn't, or couldn't, *chart a market course*. . . . It didn't navigate . . . it didn't lead . . . and, unfortunately, too often it was seen to replace marketing. (1981, p. 3)

A sense of buyers' needs, ultimately seeking opportunity and creating value, is often lacking in formal planning practice. Planning promotes continuity rather than innovative change.

PLANNING PROBLEMS

As we will see, the problems that beset planning are simply a subset of those which afflict management, because planning is, as noted earlier, nothing more than one of the tools in management's administrative armory. As a result, the steps management might take to eliminate the problems of planning are likely to simultaneously facilitate and enhance the quality of planning and the effectiveness and efficiency of management as a whole.

Planning rarely works if top management does not support it. It can't work if insufficient resources are allocated to the job. Nevertheless, experience suggests that the law of diminishing returns quickly sets in if too many planners are put to work in one organization. Plans, like actions, must be founded in reality. The process used should be tailored to the needs and experience of the firm and its management rather than being abstracted from a planning text or workbook. The process will function more effectively if its results are monitored and if "good" planning is rewarded. Planning will be more fruitful if the process is modified from time to time to stimulate fresh thinking and to focus attention on different issues. Finally, planning will get results only if it is enacted—that is, if commitment follows plan and action follows commitment—and if the results of those actions are fed back into the thinking that occurs in subsequent planning cycles. Unfortunately, this rarely happens if a "planner" prepares the plan.

Consequently, an effective planning system should not rely too much on professional planners, or use too much of top and lower management's time. It should not cost too much to staff, and it should help line management day to day and thereby earn its keep. Remember, managers, not "planners," are ultimately responsible for results, including short-term results.

Top Management's Role

Probably the most critical audience for formal planning is top management. In most companies, if top management will not demonstrate support for a formal planning system, for whatever reasons, the system will be devitalized and will degenerate to empty ritual. A sure sign of a lack of top management commitment and a ritualistic planning system is middle managers who say, "We've finished the plan. Now let's get back to work." Indeed, George Steiner says:

> There can be no effective comprehensive corporate planning in any organization where the chief executive does not give it firm support and makes sure that others in his organization understand his depth of commitment. (1969, p. 2)

Steiner adds, "This principle should be obvious, but it is not."

Since it is usually CEO's who initiate planning and whose support is critical, why do they sometimes withdraw that support? The answer is unclear, but often it comes from frustration with the time consumed and the difficulty they meet when they try to use the planning system to address their big problems. Recognizing a hole (problem), they allow the digging (planning) to continue because planning is supposed to be good for a company.

Instead, they should follow Taylor's First Rule of Holes: When you know you're in a hole, stop digging! Bruce Taylor, Executive Vice President of the Greater Boston YMCA in 1983, introduced us to this "law." When applied to planning, it suggests a cure: if your present approach doesn't work, change it. Harold Henry (1977) wrote, "If one solution doesn't work, others should be tried. There is no cookbook ingredient which can be applied in every firm, but the most important ingredient is to find or develop managers who want to do a better job of managing" (p. 45).

The problem, as we warned earlier, is in treating planning as a sacred art rather than a tool, and planners as priests. This can be changed. Lorange and Vancil (1976) note that an effective planning system requires "situational design" appropriate to the organization's circumstances and resources.

Planners Are People Too (and Vice-Versa)

Of the resources affected by planning, it is the human resources that are most critical. People are responsible for planning, for its inputs and its outputs. People are accountable for the plan, the effect the process has on those involved, and ultimately for the actions taken and their results.

Remember, although planning appears to be a realistic, logical and intellectual activity, it is a social and emotional activity too. As Reichman and Levy (1975) point out, planning "prompts illogical, irrational emotional responses that actually inhibit" it (unless these responses are recognized and used, for example, to generate widely different alternatives as Emshoff, Mitroff and Kilman (1978) report).

Lyles and Lenz (1982) in their survey of planning practices of six regional commercial banks found that managers were aware of a large number of behavioral problems afflicting their planning efforts. We have classified the critical subset of these problems into three groups in *Figure 16-2,* reflecting our diagnosis of the types of people likely to behave in the ways Lyles and Lenz describe. The "incapable," perhaps because of lack of native talent or timidity, try to plan it safe. The "gamesmen" try to use the planning system for their personal gain, to play it for all it's worth. The "priests" play planning for its own sake. For the incapable, training may be necessary. For the gamesmen, top

FIGURE 16-2 Critical Behavioral Problems* in Planning

Incapable or Afraid

- Project current trends rather than analyze the future for opportunities
- Resist changes in the status quo
- Fear making mistakes
- Avoid thinking beyond short-run, day-to-day activities
- Are uncertain about the expectations of upper-level managers
- Become bored with the planning process

Gamesmen

- Primarily bargain for resources rather than identify new resources
- "Pad" their plan to avoid close measurement
- Resist the discipline that planning requires
- View their part of the organization as more important than other parts
- Comply with rather than being committed to goals

Priests

- "Pad" their plan to avoid close measurement
- File their plan away until next year and do not look at it
- Are judged on the basis of their credibility in the organization rather than upon reaching planned objectives

*A critical problem was shared by 65 percent or more of 72 managers in 6 regional banks with assets ranging from $1.8 to $2.3 billion, who, on a 1 to 5 scale (1, no reduction in effectiveness of planning, to 5, great reduction), gave it a score greater than 3.0.

Source: Adapted from Lyles and Lenz, "Managing the Planning Process: A Field Study of the Human Side of Planning," *Strategic Management Journal*, 3, 105–18. © 1982 by John Wiley & Sons.

management review and example are likely to effect a cure, while for the priests there may be no remedy within their present employer's organization.

CAUSES OF POOR PLANNING

Planning problems are merely symptoms. What are the ultimate causes of poor planning? Bales (1977), then a principal of McKinsey and Company, cited three reasons why senior executives become dissatisfied with the results of their strategic planning efforts:

1. superficial analysis;
2. monolithic planning;
3. inadequate review.

Superficial analysis means that important environmental and internal input to the planning process is ignored or overlooked by those who define the plan. Monolithic planning implies centralization, a standardized format and a process that suffocates thought and denies managers a right to commit personally to the plan—after all it is not theirs. Inadequate review, as with the other symptoms, suggests an uninvolved or an inappropriately involved top management and a poor administrative context.

Superficial analysis occurs when form masks substance, when people omit steps in the process and create plans without a firm fact-based foundation. Its symptoms are static business definitions and casual segmentation schemes, an internal rather than a customer or competitive view, simple extrapolations of past trends, "hopeful hockey stick" forecasts of future performance improvements (that is, beginning next year, but every year being one more year forward on a longer sloping stick, promising turnaround after an ever-lengthening history of decline). A continuous record of unrealistic forecasts, time horizons frequently varied waiting for a particular result, and undifferentiated plans and planning formats in use across business units, similarly signal superficial analysis.

Most planning problems can be remedied if there is a *review process* where experienced managers or board members focus on the key competitive factors and ask how results will be earned and how competition is likely to affect those results. If reviews during the planning process are used to develop managers and educate them about their business, rather than as a lever to extract commitments, top management can participate in the process, broaden the definition of issues and add the value of its experience to the planning effort of the organization.

Monolithic plans tend to the "top-down" variety and, as Pennington (1972) said, few plans that are handed down are carried out. But the suffocating climate of the monolithic plan is usually the result of a dysfunctionally overformal process and sometimes of overabundant central direction, either from top management or staff planners. Too many forms or the "we're done planning—now we can get back to work" comment are other symptoms.

If the forms are too numerous, or the nature of the plan review is too detailed or spread over too long a time, or if responsibility for the plan is dissipated, line management will be driven out of the planning process. Perversely, the situation will then get worse as "staff" fill the gaps left by the withdrawing managers, hastening their flight with plans that are irrelevant to operating management.

Ultimately, it is top management's responsibility to change things and make the planning process work. But the task is not always easy to accomplish. We plan to manage, but to use Marvin Bower's phrase, "the will to manage" is easily sapped. A cursory review devalues the planning process while too close an involvement by top management brings its own problems. Bower described this condition well:

> Either giving too-detailed instructions in advance or making a too-detailed review after action has been taken results in poor delegation. Any subordinate already has certain automatic performance guides: policies, plans, and budgets. If, in addition, his superior tells him step by step how to take action, the subordinate feels too much like a puppet. His freedom to think for and learn by himself is limited, and his opportunity to learn through mistakes is denied. The results are virtually the same when the subordinate knows his actions will be subject to detailed review: instead of using his own judgment, he will then try to learn or guess what the superior would do. (1966, p. 176)

Bower's conclusions are supported by Lyles and Lenz's (1982) research. When operating managers' perceptions of behavioral problems were compared with top management's, one of the few problems identified only by lower management as having a large, deleterious effect on planning was ''a fear of mistakes''; perhaps this fear was due not to a failure of courage but to too detailed supervision.

Ultimately, we must emphasize ''managing.'' Planning is itself uninteresting. We plan to manage better. If managing is kept paramount, few planning problems cannot be solved. Planning problems persist when planning takes on a life of its own and becomes independent of managing and management.

DESIGNING THE PROCESS

Problems in planning are often similar to the problems which firms have in adopting a strategic management perspective. The solutions are generally the same kinds of things which would improve most firms' strategic performance: Start from reality, think through how proposed actions will be implemented, monitor results, and use a strategic management process tailored to the context of your firm rather than generalized approaches abstracted uncritically from a planning guide or text.

To formulate strategy, we must weigh and integrate the current strategy, the state of the environment, the resources available, and the values, objectives, and commitments of key stakeholders. In designing a planning system, the critical decisions concern who will be responsible for which tasks, how the separate roles will be coordinated, and when and how information will be communicated to other participants in the planning process and other members of the firm.

Structure

In a decentralized organization, most of the critical decisions that are inputs to strategy definition will be pushed down in the organization to a point where relevant information is available and understood. In a centralized organization, many more factors will be determined at the top.

Here we should note that Alfred Sloan, a member of General Motors board for forty-five years and its CEO for twenty-three years, and Ralph Cordiner, once CEO of General Electric and the architect of its initial decentralized organization structure, both recognized an inherent contradiction at the crux of managing a decentralized organization. The contradiction lies between profit center or business unit managers' needs for autonomy and the corporate need for control. Many years after drafting his principles of organization at General Motors, Sloan described the contradiction as follows:

> I am amused to see that the language is contradictory, and that its very contradiction is the crux of the matter. In point 1, I maximize decentralization of divisional operations in the words "shall in no way be limited." In point 2, I proceed to limit the responsibility of divisional chief executives in the expression, proper control. (1963, p. 58)

Sloan continues by saying that one aspect or another is given priority or asserted at different times. "Interaction is the thing," he adds, presumably between executives negotiating a proper balance in the light of the facts defining the situation of each part of the organization and the whole.

Hence, one of the crucial inputs to the design process will be corporate need. If the corporation is in crisis, perhaps precipitated by external factors, a top-down approach is likely and subordinate managers' roles are probably restricted. When the corporation is doing well, a more decentralized competitive process is likely to be used, since internal risks are more affordable.

Things to Consider

Lorange and Vancil (1976) make some simple prescriptions for system design based on the typical managerial capabilities and environmental complexity of small and large companies. *Table 16-1* focuses on the nature of the goal-setting process and the explicitness with which objectives or goals are usually communicated to the organization. In the small company, face-to-face contact reduces the need for explicitness. In large, diverse companies, top management has limited ability to judge the appropriateness of the match between corporate objectives and divisional capabilities and so is likely to make less explicit statements of objectives at first and more explicit statements as planning experience accumulates and the organization itself matures.

Scanning the environment is typically centralized in small companies where only a few managers cross the organization's boundaries. In a large, diverse organization, however, the various transactions and relationships of the organization cross many boundaries, forcing top management to rely on middle management for information which describes the different environments in which the firm operates.

Lorange and Vancil's other issues reflect on the roles played by middle managers and staff planners as company size is increased and as planning experience accumulates. As the company matures and becomes more complex, Lorange and Vancil observed that

TABLE 16-1 Approaches to Planning System Design Issues

	Situational Settings		
Issues	*"Small" Companies*	*"Large" Companies New Planning System*	*"Large" Companies Mature Planning System*
Communication of corporate goals	Not explicit	Not explicit	Explicit
Goal-setting process	Top-down	Bottom-up	"Negotiated"
Corporate-level environmental scanning	Strategic	Statistical	Statistical
Subordinate managers' focus	Financial	Financial	Strategic
Corporate planner's role	Analyst	Catalyst	Coordinator
Linkage of planning and budgeting	Tight	Loose	Tight

Source: Adapted from Lorange and Vancil, "How to Design a Strategic Planning System," Sept./Oct. 1976. Adapted by permission of the *Harvard Business Review.*

strategic decision making is increasingly delegated and the staff planners' direct influence on the process declines.

How quickly should the process reduce options, fix on objectives, and convert high-level strategy to an explicit and committed budget? If fast, there will be little time for innovation and change. What should happen first?

The decision is, we believe, contingent upon the situation facing the organization. Let us note that planning follows the simple thought process set out by Dewey (1933) and includes steps which identify:

1 objectives
2 problems
3 alternatives
4 choices
5 actions

But the order is not (necessarily) fixed, although most plans are presented in a sequence such as that shown above. In some circumstances, it may pay to differ from Dewey's sequence and start the planning process at a different point. Our view is that where control and continuity are important, objectives can be set early. Where change is needed, objectives can be set late to allow time to develop options and evaluate them, to rework the best, and develop support within the organization.

SOME ADDITIONAL PRACTICAL CONSIDERATIONS

Strategy is converted to action through a hierarchy of interlocked plans of increasing specificity. Corporate strategy and objectives influence the content of investment programs, changes in business strategy, new projects, and ultimately precise operating budgets.

Sometimes the influence of strategy is direct and the planning sequence is logically developed to implement strategy directly, but most of the time it is not. Top management uses corporate strategy, the formal structure of the organization, the administrative systems that support it, and its own example to set the rules by which decisions are and will be made. In all but the smallest firms, where no middle-management level exists, it is middle managers who put their personal energy behind projects and new strategies to win corporate approval, thereby giving them impetus in the corporation. For the most part, explicit projects are largely defined by junior managers and technology specialists (Bower, 1970).

The decision process is therefore more likely to flow from bottom to top rather than top-down. The development of new computers illustrates the typical process well. In *The Soul of a New Machine,* Tracy Kidder (1981) describes how recent graduates essentially created the architecture of a new Data General computer in 1979. Tom West, the project manager, coordinated their efforts but, more importantly, motivated them with encouragement and underwrote the project by putting his career on the line. Top management's role was to set the context. Thus the project team could predict how top management would judge the new venture and they could develop and shape it to win.

As Thompson (1967) indicated, administration means channeling the ongoing actions of the separate parts of the organization so that they serve a common purpose. Planning, budgeting, and the decision process that is part of planning help managers focus the actions of the firm. The more steps there are between strategy formulation and the budget, the more time there will be for participation and innovation, and the more the process will contribute to the development of general management skills within the firm.

Managers have other design parameters at their disposal, too. Shank and his colleagues (1973) pointed out that management can influence the output of the planning process by modifying the linkages that exist between the various plans management creates. The more links there are, the tighter the control management exercises. Shank and his colleagues argue that control trades creativity for practicality, and so they recommend care in making these linkages.

Content linkages are potentially numerous. They may be as simple as the levels of financial detail and numeric rounding used in strategic plans and the budget. Are differences allowed—a loose link—or is a tight linkage necessary, with identical numbers required? How many years' data—none, or one, or more? Again, more links will restrict the innovative range of the plan. Do the strategic plans and the budget draw on the same data sources or not? What time horizons does each employ?

Content links are joined to organizational links to modify the range of the plan. If plans and budgets are reviewed by the controller, practicality and control are likely to have priority. Are plans and budgets prepared for the same units? In some organizations, administrative organizational units budget while plans are prepared by separate planning teams in an effort to encourage innovation.

Timing, too, is important. Which plans are prepared first? If the budget precedes the strategic plan, we can predict that the plan itself will be conservative and at best evolutionary. Timing of plan and budget initiation and approval will also influence the type of plan produced. As with the other links, more links give more control and constrain the forward reach and innovative scope of the planning effort.

INTRODUCING PLANNING TO AN ORGANIZATION

Unfortunately, planning is often introduced to an organization as an extension of the budget. This usually fails; it doesn't solve the big problems. Each linkage between plan and budget makes planning like budgeting. For example, if plan and budget are subject to similar reviews (although this may suit the purposes of organizations caught in a cash crisis) it is unlikely to make planning itself a useful tool for change. This is not surprising, of course; organizations have to stretch and change to handle their big problems and they have to learn their business and how to plan before they grapple with the big issues.

Experienced executives have suggested repeatedly that planning should be introduced simply with limited initial objectives. "Start small and make it useful" is their advice. Demonstrate that planning can earn its keep. For example, in a primary planning effort, management might focus on a study of its market, build understanding, and mount a new segmented marketing strategy because it senses the need for both change and an opportunity for growth and cost efficiency.

In a second round of planning, the focus of data collection and analysis might turn to operations, product costs and prices. The outcome could be rationalization and a focused new product development effort. In later cycles, when the process is working smoothly and knowledge of the business and its market is more extensive, more comprehensive planning can be initiated. Comprehensiveness becomes possible simply because data and experience accumulate as we plan and act. When we plan, we learn, and when we learn, we change things.

Kami (1968), who worked in planning at IBM and Xerox between 1952 and 1967, writes, ''Anybody can plan five years ahead; it takes real management to leap from crisis to crisis.'' Offering some useful guidelines for planning and for plan review, he emphasizes that plans are never perfect—for example, few plans are entirely credible. However, he implies that this is not a problem. Based on his experience, Kami suggests that reviewers seek proposals promising at least three times the dollar volume the organization needs to close the gap between current performance and its objectives. He has learned to expect that estimated costs and time needed will double, while the market will rarely be greater than half the initial projection. Yet he advises managers to make the necessary adjustments privately: ''But don't say anything out loud—that will kill the project. Just watch carefully that it's growing in the right direction.''

All this implies constancy to purpose (Bower, 1966). Senior managers have to develop a sense of purpose in their organization and direct their organization towards it, albeit indirectly. Constancy is necessary to maintain focus. The Theory of the Big Wheel explains why. An organization, Kami (1968) says, is like a set of interconnected gear wheels. The efforts of every senior executive, a big wheel, are multiplied by the efforts of those below. But if the big wheel makes half a turn, the people at the bottom, many wheels below, are likely to be revolved twenty-six times. In every organization, there is only a limited ability to adapt. The more change is needed quickly, the greater the effort required, especially from top management. The puzzle is that continuity promotes efficiency and change destroys it, although change is often necessary.

AN ALTERNATIVE PLANNING MODEL

Planning is, as Bower (1967, 1982) and Ansoff (1971) say, a problem finding process. But what if the problem cannot be solved? What if, after repeated planning meetings, research and discussion, the corporation is faced with an insolvable problem? What do you do if experience assessment methods (based on current strategy identification and evaluation) fail?

Following the advice of DeBono (1968) and Henry (1977), we change the way we plan. All planning mechanisms cycle through the steps described in this book, that is, through an assessment of the current strategy, the organization's resources, and its stakeholder objectives, coupled with a forecast of the likely future environment. But some alternative planning processes change the order of the steps, beginning with elements other than reality. In some circumstances, for example, when you are blocked by an intractable problem, planning can fruitfully begin with idealized solutions. A vision of the future may be more fruitful as a starting point in developing new strategies than an understanding of the present.

One method for solving unstructured and intractable strategic problems, which

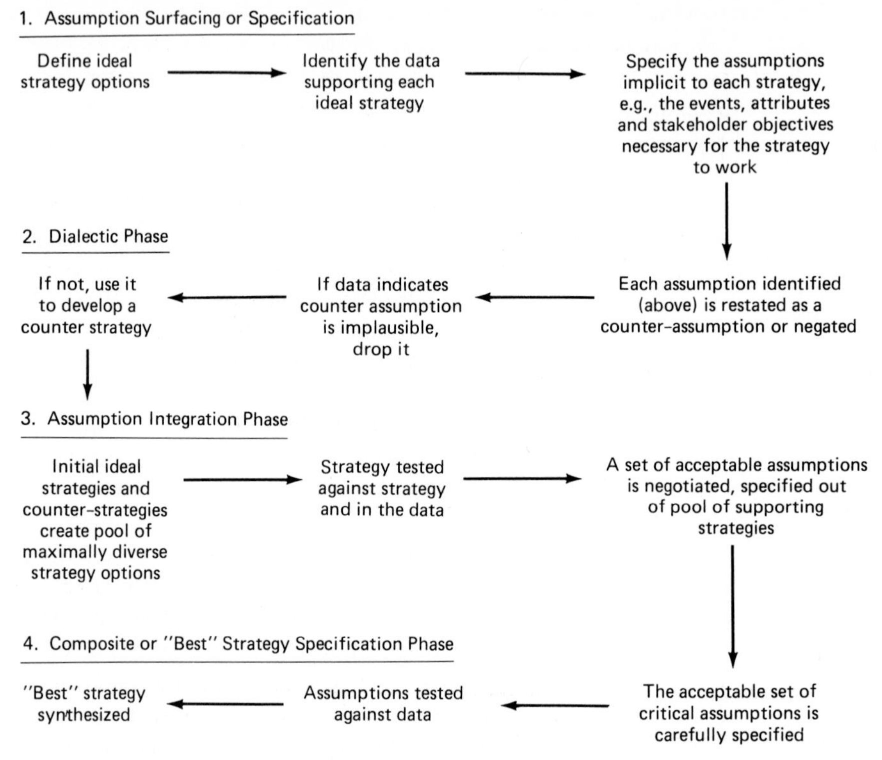

FIGURE 16-3 The Four Basic Steps of Strategic Assumptions Analysis

Source: Mitroff and Emshoff, "On Strategic Assumption-Making: A Dialectic Approach to Policy and Planning," *Academy of Management Review*, 4, no. 1, 1979, 5.

exploits this approach, is Strategic Assumptions Analysis (SAA). This has been advanced by Emshoff, Mitroff, and Kilman (1978)[1] and Mitroff and Emshoff (1979) who argue that their approach ensures that:

1 strongly different strategic options are considered;
2 thereby, the force of continuity, tradition, and organizational inertia is countered; and
3 the analysis that results is deep and so the organization is less vulnerable to non-penetrating thinking, which allows it to fall victim to unconsciously-made yet critical implicit assumptions.

The thinking behind the assumptions approach is that unless a strategy is tested against maximally challenging alternatives, it is likely to have undiscovered flaws.

As Mitroff and Emshoff (1979) describe it, the process has four phases, as illus-

[1]Strategic Assumptions Analysis and Dialectic Inquiry Systems have been described in a series of papers authored by Emshoff, Mitroff and Kilman, (1978); Emshoff and Finnel, (1979); Mitroff, Emshoff and Kilman (1979); Mitroff and Emshoff, (1979); Mason and Mitroff (1979) and Mitroff and Mason, (1980). Cosier and Aplin (1980) and Cosier (1981) offer criticism of the approach. Further comments are contained in Mitroff and Mason (1981) and Cosier (1981a).

trated in *Figure 16-3*. It begins with an assumptions specification stage which specifies "ideal" or uncompromising strategies. This is followed by a dialectic phase which exploits counter-assumptions to those underlying the initial strategies in order to develop an inventory of new strategies. In Phase 3, the pool of strategies and assumptions is purged of the irrelevant, the implausible and the unimportant, and finally effort it directed to identifying a practical best strategy in Phase 4.

The appeal of Mitroff and Emshoff's approach is that it breaks the block of the unsolved problem. Essentially, it is a planning methodology that takes advantage of one of DeBono's lateral thinking approaches, the use of direct opposites. Likewise, it relates to "double-loop learning" described by Argyris (1977), because it promotes challenges to conventional wisdom within the organization. SAA explicitly uses an Hegelian dialectic to test strategies and assumptions—strategy against strategy, assumption against assumption.

The originators of SAA, or idealized planning as it is sometimes called, warn that it is a difficult planning methodology in practice. Explicitly, they recommended its use only if experience assessment methods have been blocked. In addition, they point out that unless the initial strategies are dramatically different, the power of the approach wanes.

To obtain maximal initial divergence, they recommend the use of groups whose psychological characteristics or commitments are known. Groups of individuals are selected to represent different points of view. Each group would be composed of people of like persuasion (for example, supporters of a high or low price strategy or make or buy strategy), or of people sharing a similar psychological bent (optimists, pessimists, pragmatists, abstractionists, intuitive or logical decision makers). The point is to select groups likely to develop extreme positions.

Each group is then given the assignment to specify an ideal strategy and future environment, and to specify the assumptions underlying them. The following questions are illustrative of those used to initiate the process: What resources do you need? What environment will be most hospitable to your plan? What have you been assuming about the stakeholders or what have you had to assume about them so that if you started with these assumptions you would be able to develop your strategy?

With this done, the groups separately or together try to understand each others' points of view (not to reach consensus) and develop a set of opposite or negative assumptions. They then consider whether these negative assumptions imply a need for change in their strategies. If one of them does not, that original assumption is regarded as possibly irrelevant rather than critical.

Attention is then focused on the critical nature and certainty of the remaining assumptions and effort is directed to reduce the pool of assumptions as we noted earlier. (For example: in the circumstances shown in *Figure 16-4* research might be used to help specify the impact of Assumption C because it is both "critical" and "certain." A and B, being neither critical nor certain, appear to need little research and might be dropped from consideration for the time being.) Then, the pool of assumptions left is used to develop a "best strategy." Effort at this point is focused on integrating the robust elements of each separate analysis.

Emshoff, Mitroff, and Kilman (1978) suggest the need for an experienced facilitator to manage the dialectic and to help prepare an organization for the experience. Because groups are used one against another, trust is needed and unless this exists within the organization, no outsider is likely to develop it. For this reason, SAA is not for all.

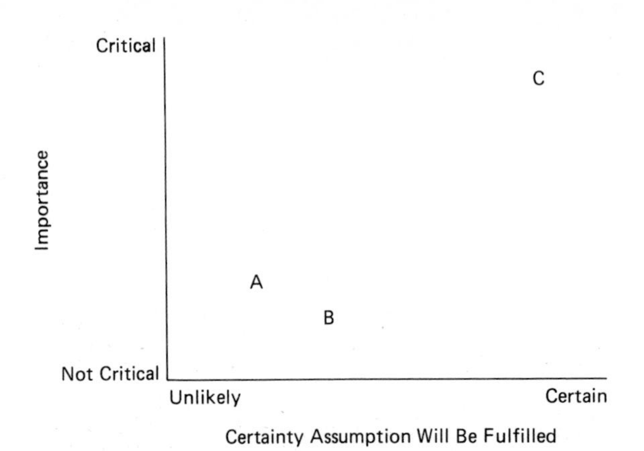

FIGURE 16-4 Importance-Certainty of Assumptions
Source: Emshoff and Finnell, "Defining Corporate Strategy: A Case Study Using Strategic Assumptions Analysis," *Sloan Management Review,* Spring 1979, p. 48.

CONCLUSION

Top management must promote innovation and renewal as well as control the organization. Rigid formal planning systems do not innovate, since increased formality tends to generate inflexibility, while innovation requires flexibility. Planning systems therefore need some flexibility to encourage innovation and generate creative insight.

Yet, if top management must both control and innovate in the planning process, exactly how do these apparently contradictory tasks get done? The answer is leadership and an administrative system that communicates top management's leadership and example throughout the organization.

Both analysis and action are necessary for success. Action is a sign of effective planning. Performance is a sign of good management. Continued and growing performance is a sign of good planning and control. Thus, the current organization's definitions of its strategy, resources, and environmental assumptions are important. But the impetus to action must also be considered; the context and culture of the organization are an essential aid to implementation. Strategies which are properly implemented get results. And attaining desired results is the goal of successful strategic management and effective planning.

To conclude our discussion of alternative planning models, it is appropriate to mention that Jack Welsh, soon after his election as GE's Chairman, refused to publicly define GE's corporate strategy. He instead articulated a series of objectives. This, of course, does not mean that GE has no corporate strategy. Rather, GE's management has found its old centrally administered formal planning process no longer relevant for its needs. GE wants new products and new ventures and needs people "behind" the company's ideas. It has therefore changed its planning practices to encourage initiative, corporate flexibility and personal responsibility.

chapter 17

Corporate Strategy in Diversified and Integrated Multibusiness Firms

INTRODUCTION

Corporate strategy defines the scope of the firm's operations and how the management allocates or deploys its resources to make the whole firm a vital, competitive enterprise. The whole firm must be "vital" and "competitive"; unless the organization can function as a whole, with corporate management adding value, it is difficult to justify keeping all the parts under one corporate umbrella.

Indeed, corporate strategy is concerned more with the question of where to compete than with how to compete in a particular business—the latter is the province of business strategy. At the corporate level, the issues are what businesses to be in and how to deploy resources between them, what kind of organization to become and how to use the firm's resources to create value.

The management of the multinational health care company, Becton Dickenson, once explained:

> A large corporation is like an army: Without a clear strategy, its divisions can easily aim toward several different objectives at once. The principal challenge confronting the managers of a corporation—like the generals of an army—is to define a strategy that enables each component unit to contend effectively against its competitors, and then to array their divisions so that the entire organization marches toward the overall objective.[1]

Becton Dickenson's statement makes the point that the job of corporate management is to develop objectives and a corporate strategy that dominates, and so integrates,

[1]Becton Dickenson Annual Report 1978.

the operating business units of the corporation. Within a multibusiness firm, each business should have its own strategy and objectives so that it can contend effectively against its competition while serving the interests of the corporation. From time to time, the interests of the corporation may be best served by changes in the objectives and strategies of one or more of the businesses which it controls—the corporation must be more important than its parts.

The principle that corporate objectives and strategies must be made to dominate the parts is central to our view of a multibusiness organization. Corporate management can only do its job and add value if the parts serve the whole. Only if the parts, the business units of the firm, are managed as resources to be used now or developed for later use by the corporation, will corporate management have an enacted strategy and the opportunity to use its accumulated experience to create value.

To distinguish corporate strategy from business strategy, the discussion in these three chapters on diversification is restricted to multibusiness firms where the corporate level is distinct from the business level. This distinction is clearer when separate or separable businesses have to be managed simultaneously. Hence, our focus is on multibusiness firms, particularly those which have diversified. We will explore diversification and the basic strategic options which diversity allows. We will examine US business practice, the rationale for diversification and its relationship to risk, and the results achieved by diversified companies.

In Chapter 18, we examine portfolio analysis and see how portfolio models can be used to track the firm's resource deployments and thereby the objectives of the firm's operating (business) units. The technique of Business Analysis is introduced in Chapter 19 as a tool for corporate strategy identification and is illustrated with the history of the Bic Corporation. The discussion of diversification will conclude, in Chapter 20, with multinational and global businesses and the administrative dilemmas faced by their corporate managements.

WHAT IS DIVERSIFICATION?

In simple terms, strategy is what you do to get what you want. Corporate strategy is what corporations do to achieve their objectives. What have they been doing? During most of the twentieth century, the largest corporations have been diversifying, and the extent of diversification has been increasing, particularly in industries based on newer and more sophisticated technologies (Rumelt, 1974).

The product-market matrix which we introduced in Chapter 11 and have extended into the international sphere in *Figure 17-1* illustrates the basic options available. As a company diversifies and moves away from a simple commitment to one product (or product line) for one market, a number of alternative directions is available. Note that *Figure 17-1* could be expanded by adding simple price and channel distinctions, or process technologies, for example.

The basic choices are simple. A movement from the ''same-same'' cell to the upper left of *Figure 17-1* implies vertical integration, forward or backward depending on whether the product technology is upstream or downstream in the industry chain. A

		Product or Service Technologies					
		Related					Unrelated
		Constrained				Linked	
	Markets	Upstream	Same	Downstream	Cored		
Domestic	Firm	Vertical Integration					
	Unchanged		Market Development ↓		Product Development →		
	New Geography						
	New Users				Concentric Diversification – Market-based + Technology-based		
	Unrelated Users						
International	Multinational						Conglomerate Diversified
	Global	Integrated International Operations/Competition					

FIGURE 17-1 The Product/Market Matrix

movement towards the bottom of the figure implies a market development strategy, while a movement to the right implies a product development strategy. Simultaneous addition of new markets and products and technologies amounts to diversification (Ansoff, 1965).

When diversification strategies are pursued, the character of the strategy is important. For example, is it concentric or conglomerate? If the diversification is distinguished by a *common thread* which relates past, present, and future markets and products so that insiders can guide the future development of the organization and outsiders can see where it is going, the diversification is concentric. A conglomerate is a firm where product market choices are unrelated (Ansoff, 1965).

Since Ansoff's work on diversification, researchers have focused their efforts on understanding the significance of product-market relationships within the diversified firm and have divided the related and concentric diversification category into two types: constrained and linked. A constrained diversification is characterized by a dominant core,

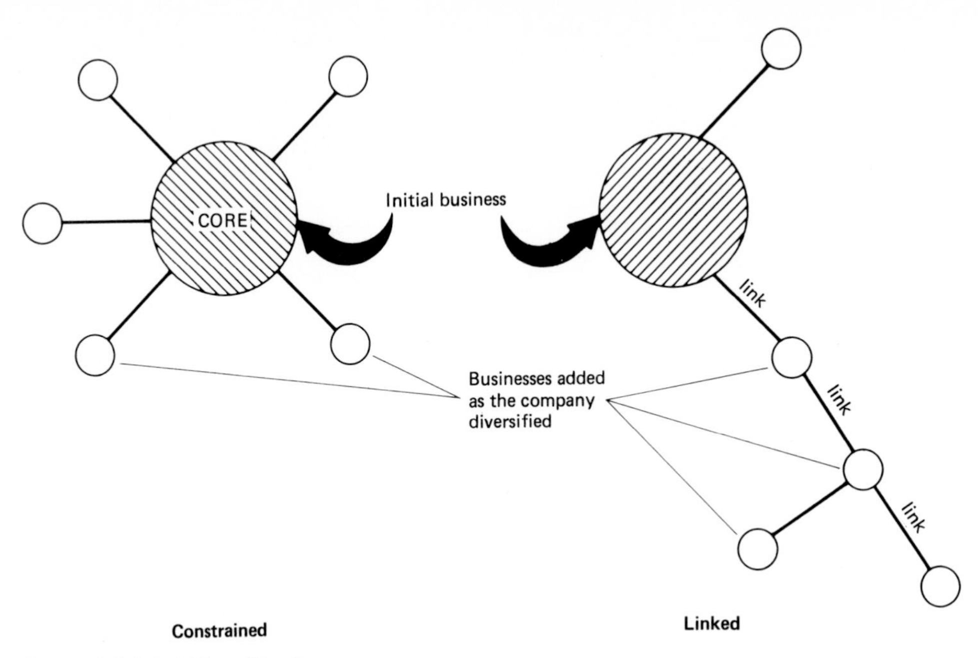

FIGURE 17-2 Types of Related Diversification

either market- or technology-based, while a linked diversification is characterized by simple links between one business and another. In simple terms, the archetypes are illustrated in *Figure 17-2*. The constrained firm has a core, the linked firm resembles a chain. Obviously, the common thread is weaker in the linked company.

Figure 17-3 fleshes out Carborundum's diversification and illustrates an additional point: US corporations have been moving from a constrained form of diversification to a linked type. Carborundum's strategic evolution has been similar to that of many US and European corporations (Rumelt, 1974).

Research by Chandler (1962), Channon (1973), Scott (1973), and Rumelt (1974) shows that big businesses worldwide have diversified and become more loosely diversified in their product market scope—in some cases adopting global strategies to operate across the world as one integrated and coordinated competitor, sometimes in many industries.[2]

Let us examine US practice. From *Table 17-1*, we can see just how extensive the trend towards product market diversity has been. *Table 17-1* catalogs the scope and type of diversification of the *Fortune* 500 over the period 1949 to 1974. Note in the top half of the table the shrinking proportion of those dominated by a single business. Similarly, note the growth of the related and unrelated categories. Within the dominant and related categories, linked diversification has become more common over time (Rumelt, 1982).

[2]Chandler (1966), Wrigley (1970), Channon (1973), Pavan (1972), Dyas (1972), Thanheiser (1972), Scott (1973).

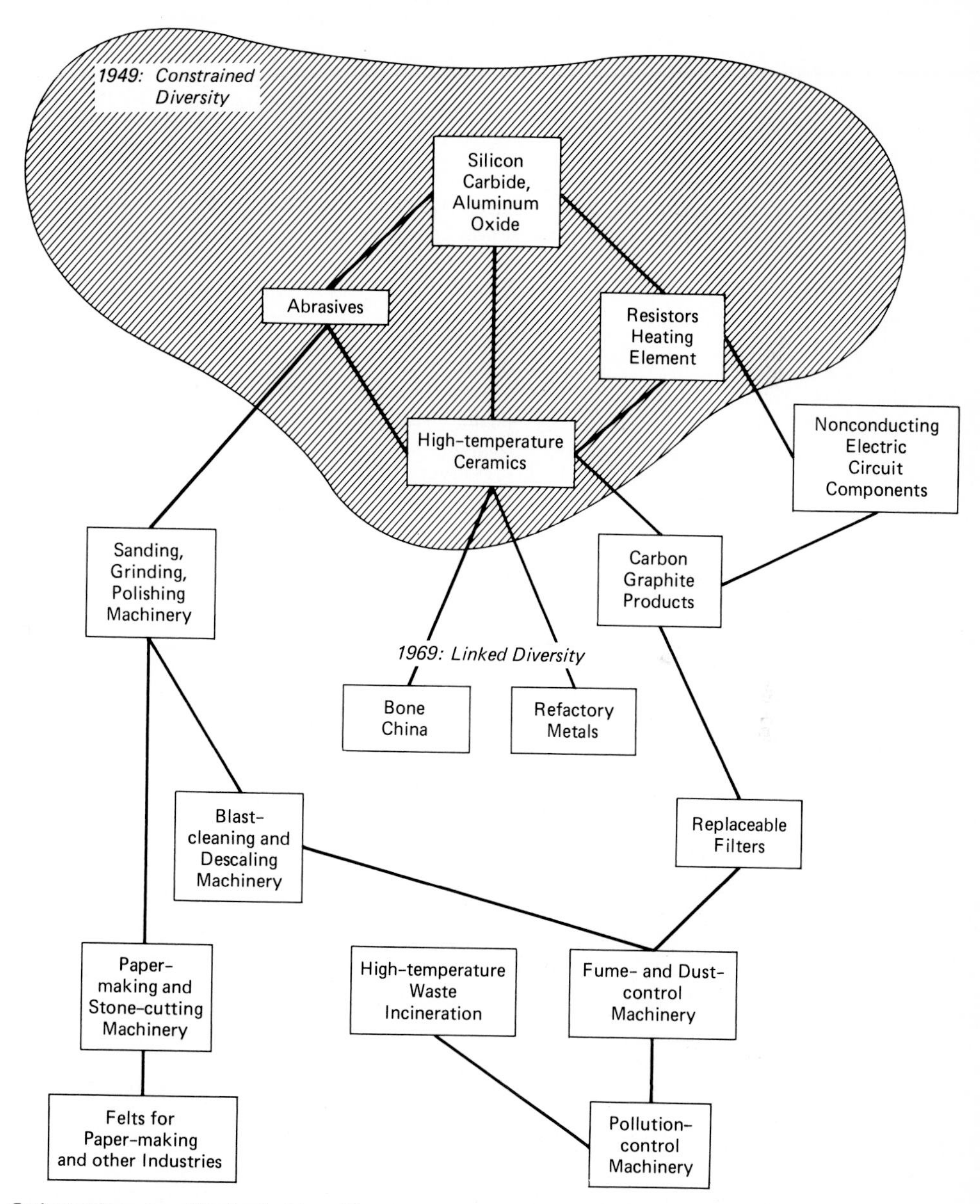

FIGURE 17-3 Carborundum, Inc., Strategic Diversification, 1949–1969, from Constrained to Linked

Source: Rumelt, *Strategy, Structural and Economic Performance*, Boston, MA: Division of Research, Harvard Business School, 1974.

TABLE 17-1
Diversification of the Fortune 500, 1949–1974

Major Category	Approx. % Revenue from Single Production-Distribution Chain*	Examples**	Estimated % of Fortune 500 Firms in Each Category					
			1949	1954	1959	1964	1969	1974
Single-Business	95	Maytag, Iowa Beef, Crown Cork & Seal, American Motors	42.1	34.1	22.8	21.5	14.8	14.4
Dominant	70–95	ARCO, Caterpillar, Hershey, Xerox, Deere, IBM	28.2	29.6	31.3	32.4	25.1	22.6
Related	45–70	GE, Merck, Dow 3M, Bristol Myers, Dupont	25.7	31.6	38.6	37.4	41.4	42.3
Unrelated	45	LTV, Rockwell Mfg., Litton, TRW	4.1	4.7	7.3	8.7	18.7	20.7
			100.0	100.0	100.0	100.0	100.0	100.0

**Strategic Management Journal* 81, Mimeo 1 (77; 2) undated mimeo
***Strategy, Structure and Economic Performance* 74
Source: Adapted from Rumelt, "Diversification Strategy and Profitability," *Strategic Management Journal*, 3, no. 4, Oct.-Dec. 1982, 359–70. © 1982 by John Wiley & Sons.

MULTIBUSINESS OBJECTIVES

Since the facts point strongly toward diversification as the strategy of choice, we can speculate about management's motives. In 1978, Wesley J. (Jack) Howe, by then President of Becton Dickinson for six years, was quoted in his company's annual report as follows: ''The purpose of this diversification is both to allow steady growth in earnings and to reduce business risks by limiting the company's overall reliance on any single product.'' Writing about Beckton Dickenson in the same annual report, Peter Vanderwicken, consultant to the company, noted:

> The single-business company has a relatively easy task: Its strategy must be to nurture and protect its business. But a diversified company—and Beckton Dickinson is the most diversified in its industry—risks diluting its resources, neglecting its best opportunities, and doing little right.

Howe explains this risk associated with diversification:

> Our [planning] process is a continual review of the portfolio of businesses we're in, examining their characteristics and making appropriate conclusions. We are continually challenging, questioning, testing, and correcting. It's a living process. Its virtue is that we can't try to hold onto a dying business too long, or overlook some embryonic gem, because it's overshadowed by something that's bigger right now.

Note that Howe says his company has diversified to allow *steady* growth and to reduce the risk of over-reliance on one product. However, Howe acknowledges the existence of a different risk—the risk of neglecting opportunities and of being dominated by the past—which he implies is exacerbated by diversification itself.

FINANCIAL MOTIVATION FOR DIVERSIFICATION

Passive investors can eliminate nonsystematic risk of investment in their personal affairs by diversifying. Rumelt linked personal investment and corporate diversification this way:

> Until fairly recently it was commonly assumed that the smaller the commitment made to any particular security (or business) the more perfect the diversification. The application of the modern Markowitz diversification theory [theory that diversified portfolios spread risk] to the securities market has shown that the best possible diversification is achieved by portfolios consisting of a few carefully selected securities (often less than ten). The key requirement for efficient diversification is that negatively correlated returns be sought—if one goes up the other goes down. This result suggests that "too much" diversification can increase the risk faced by a corporation and that optimal diversification, in the statistical sense, is *not* necessarily obtained by investing in completely unrelated areas. For example, the ultimate diversified company, participating in all sectors of the economy would, by definition, have an average return and still bear the risk associated with major economic cycles. A firm active in military, space, and consumer electronics might earn an equal or better return and obtain superior protection against economic cycles. (1974, p. 80)

Nevertheless, although prudent investors may reap some benefits from diversification, we believe that their fate is different from that of a diversified corporation which operates businesses. Investors accept the risks attached to one stock or another, subject to the high degree of liquidity offered by the market. Managers have a more complex task: they have to manage risk, eliminating it if they can, and many of their corporate commitments are illiquid.

The major difference between business and investment portfolio diversification is that management has to *work* to create value: Management has an active role, not a passive one like an investor. Furthermore, "Although a decrease in non-systematic risk is the rationale for portfolio diversification of marketable securities, there is no evidence that firms can create value through the simple ownership of diverse assets" (Rumelt, 1982, p. 364).

While the risk of commitment to one business may be avoided by diversifying, a price of that risk avoidance is "absorbing" inexperience. *Figure 17-4* illustrates this point. If a company puts all its eggs in one basket, it can watch it more carefully. As it diversifies into areas where it has less experience, management has more and more difficulty controlling its operations. It may be possible to become too diversified.

Of course, there are many risks in business. The acquisition of a countercyclical business may reduce the impact of a downcycle on a corporation's earnings, but reduce the benefits of the upswing. Indeed, other strategies more closely tuned to the cycle of the

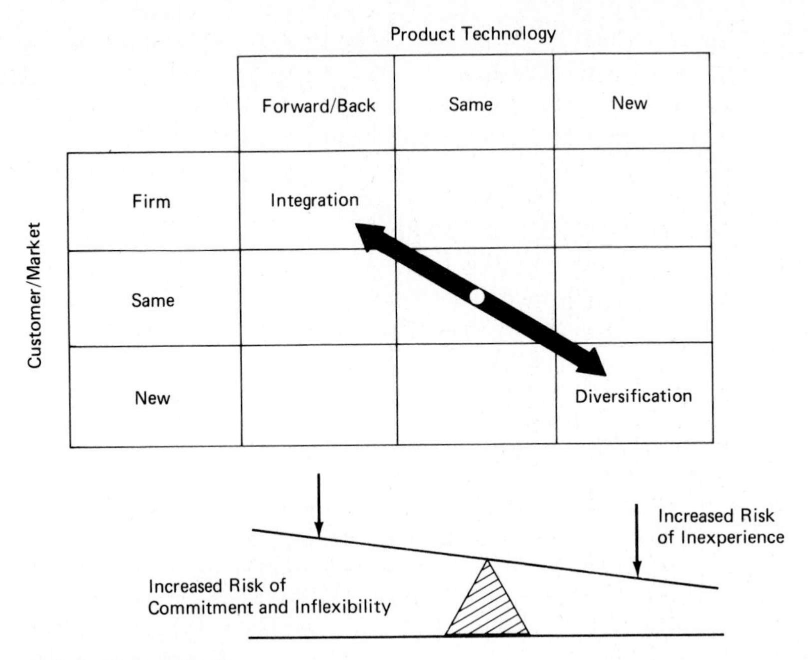

FIGURE 17-4 Risk and Diversification

corporation's dominant business—for example, using reduced financial leverage and just-in-time inventory, or lowering fixed costs and breakeven volume—may protect a corporation from the effects of a downswing in the economy without adding the risk of inexperience to the company through increased diversification.

This leaves management in a quandary. While management seeks stable growth and reduced risk, the evidence points to a need for considerable effort and self-discipline if the advantages of diversification are to be realized. Moreover, at the level of the firm, there must be some doubt that diversification per se can reduce risk—leaving us with growth as the more certain primary objective of diversification.

Such a position fits closely with the theories of the economists Baumol (1967) and Marris (1964), who argued that the fundamental motivation for growth is managerial compensation and prestige which seem to increase with growth rather than with simple profitability. Bass and his colleagues (1977), while admitting the validity of the growth objective, argued that companies diversified because their primary markets were saturated, leaving management short of opportunity close to home. He labeled many diversification programs "defensive." Others have seen diversification, particularly conglomerate diversification by acquisition, as seizing opportunity. Lewellen (1971), for example, saw many conglomerate mergers as opportunities to seize, leverage, and redeploy underutilized assets.

Although Ansoff is an early and much-quoted writer on diversification, his thinking is different from that of most others who have written on diversification. He did not mention risk reduction as an objective of diversification; moreover he seems to have omitted this deliberately because he recognized that *diversification is risky:*

> By its very definition diversification is the more drastic and risky of the two strategies [expansion is the other] since it involves a simultaneous departure from familiar products and familiar markets. (Ansoff, 1965, p. 113)[3]

Ansoff (1965) explained motivations for diversification as follows: corporations diversify if they can't meet their objectives within the scope of their current product markets; if their profitability is high and they have idle resources; if the opportunity for profit in another product-market promises to be larger than what they presently enjoy; and if management is unsure of what lies ahead. Ansoff also used the term "synergy" to describe opportunities attractive to the diversifying corporation's managers.

SYNERGY

Synergy promises a combined return on resources greater than the sum of the parts because of joint effects and shared costs; "2 + 2 = 5" is its popular form, although we know of a successfully diversified firm whose annual report refers to synergy as "2 + 2 = 7." Synergy may exist, for example, in sales via the use of common distribution channels or shared sales administration, in shared production experience, in transferred research and development, or, possibly, in management experience. Synergy should result from more intensive use of corporate resources. Hence, synergy promises added value at low cost.

Ansoff (1965) noted that synergistic potentials often exceeded actual performance in both start-ups and ongoing operations. Echoing President John F. Kennedy's "Ask not what your country can do for you but what you can do for your country," Drucker stated his primary rule of a successful acquisition:

> An acquisition will succeed only if the acquiring company thinks through what it can contribute to the business it is buying. Not what the acquired company will contribute to the acquirer, no matter how attractive the expected "synergy" may look. (1981, p. 31)

During the merger booms that sweep US industry periodically, few recall Ansoff's warnings or Drucker's rule. Indeed, "2 + 2 = 3"is negative synergy that can develop when mergers miscarry, as they often do (Kitching, 1967). In this regard, Ansoff wrote:

> In the absence of synergy, the performance of a conglomerate firm will in general be no better than it would have been if the divisions operated as independent firms . . . [with] no operating competitive advantage (e.g., lower costs). . . . There is evidence that under abnormal conditions, such as recession, conglomerate firms have less staying power than concentric ones and hence suffer sharper reversals. (1965, p. 119)

[3]Ansoff saw the strategy of expansion as the alternative to diversification, expansion being growth by market penetration or product development.

HOW CAN DIVERSIFICATION CREATE VALUE?

Whatever motivations are attributed to management, financial theorists and policy researchers alike essentially argue that the one motive that embraces all business activity is the drive to create value. This is the ultimate objective, the ultimate purpose of management and so of management action.

Classic finance and common sense point to price as the best measure of value. The price of a share of common stock represents the value of the cash flows expected by the buyer because of ownership—dividends and any receipts on sale. In the simplest of terms, value is the price paid to own the future earnings of a business, share by share if you like.

However, price is a fickle measure of value, real as it is, and price can vary substantially over time, doubtless as market expectations shift (Beaver and Morse, 1978); *Table 17-2* illustrates this. This result is relevant for diversified companies, since their purchases are generally illiquid and they are ''stuck'' with portfolios of businesses developed earlier. In *Table 17-3,* for example, we can see how stock price movements are explained by the performance of the economy, industry, and company. We can note that only the economy-related price changes can be regarded as systematic—indeed systemic might be a better word (Mullins, 1982). Moreover, of the rest, 49 percent of stock price changes are associated with industry, mostly with industry narrowly defined (at the four-digit Standard Industry Code (SIC) level).

These data, along with Ansoff's warnings, should give managers pause: The *big*

TABLE 17-2 Rank Correlations of Portfolios Formed by Price/Earnings Ratios in Subsequent Years

	Years Following Base Year													
Base Year	*1*	*2*	*3*	*4*	*5*	*6*	*7*	*8*	*9*	*10*	*11*	*12*	*13*	*14*
1956	0.96	0.87	0.88	0.65	0.78	0.70	0.82	0.85	0.69	0.74	0.62	0.36	0.41	0.59
1957	0.85	0.91	0.83	0.84	0.89	0.89	0.90	0.81	0.86	0.72	0.51	0.67	0.78	0.44
1958	0.95	0.73	0.64	0.52	0.43	0.55	0.49	0.30	0.60	0.22	0.24	0.49	0.41	0.18
1959	0.96	0.91	0.91	0.73	0.57	0.88	0.74	0.69	0.33	0.46	0.69	0.56	0.40	0.56
1960	0.94	0.94	0.93	0.89	0.88	0.79	0.70	0.63	0.80	0.73	0.61	0.61	0.50	0.24
1961	0.98	0.96	0.86	0.89	0.85	0.76	0.74	0.87	0.83	0.87	0.76	0.72	0.55	0.64
1962	0.92	0.89	0.93	0.94	0.87	0.69	0.86	0.73	0.78	0.76	0.87	0.78	0.77	
1963	0.99	0.98	0.95	0.89	0.71	0.77	0.75	0.61	0.79	0.93	0.77	0.76		
1964	0.95	0.96	0.94	0.72	0.88	0.89	0.72	0.88	0.90	0.81	0.82			
1965	0.99	0.93	0.83	0.83	0.77	0.86	0.93	0.91	0.80	0.71				
1966	0.96	0.89	0.95	0.96	0.84	0.95	0.89	0.80	0.79					
1967	0.98	0.98	0.94	0.89	0.85	0.58	0.57	0.69						
1968	0.98	0.95	0.88	0.84	0.63	0.53	0.35							
1969	0.89	0.92	0.95	0.74	0.80	0.82								
1970	0.95	0.79	0.63	0.72	0.73									
1971	0.96	0.80	0.70	0.67										
1972	0.96	0.96	0.96											
1973	0.99	0.97												
1974	0.97													
Median Correlation	0.96	0.92	0.91	0.83	0.80	0.78	0.74	0.76	0.79	0.73	0.69	0.64	0.50	0.44

Source: Beaver and Morse, "What Determines Price/Earnings Ratios?" *Financial Analysts Journal,* July/Aug. 1978, p. 66.

TABLE 17-3 Stock Price Effects

Economy (general market)	31%	
Industry (broad definition)	12%	49% total
Industry (narrow definition)	37%	
Company (sample of large, single-industry firms)	20%	

Source: Benjamin F. King, "The Latent Statistical Structure of Security Price Changes," unpublished Ph.D Dissertation, University of Chicago, 1964.

decision is what industry to be in. The critical action in a diversifying corporation is, therefore, the redeployment of its resources to a more attractive industry, exploiting its existing and continuing operations as resources to fund change.

AN ACID TEST FOR DIVERSIFICATION

Price is a function of current earnings, expected earnings growth, and the risks attached to that future earnings stream, that is:

$$\text{price} = f(\text{earnings, risk}).$$

We can state quite normatively that managers should diversify only if the diversification will add value to the firm by increasing income and decreasing risk and the vulnerability of the corporation to an earnings decline.

This is the acid test for diversification: Only if management can *realistically* expect to create value should it diversify. In terms of *Figure 17-5,* this will be accomplished if we lift our return above the ''fair'' rate by redeploying our resources:

1 to increase our return, our reward;
2 to reduce risk; or
3 to do both, increase rewards and cut risk.

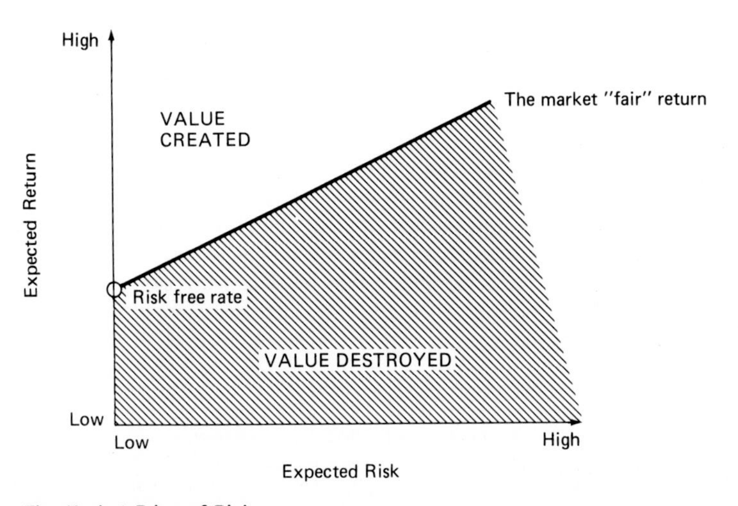

FIGURE 17-5 The Market Price of Risk

Note that any of these outcomes would lift performance into the top section of *Figure 17-5*.[4] Obviously, action should be taken only if expected rewards exceed expected costs, here measured by the market's ''fair'' return.

The test could be applied to both current or proposed new business activity. If an existing business neither adds earnings to the corporation nor cuts risk, the business adds no value and should be examined closely to determine how it might be improved or how it can be liquidated. If the test is applied to a proposed acquisition or new venture and the results are negative, there is prima facie evidence that the proposal is without merit, at least until it is reworked, repriced, or perhaps until demand or the competitive situation changes.

Furthermore, note the importance of resource allocation. Corporations operate through businesses by allocating resources to some and taking resources from others. Usually the trend of results earned by ourselves or our competitors in this or similar businesses points the way.

A straightforward rule is to take resources from the low-return businesses and allocate them to those earning a high return: Move out of businesses promising low ROA and invest in those promising a high ROA if they each allow a similar degree of financial leverage. If their leverage differs significantly, as it does for example in financial services, discriminate on a return on equity basis (ROE). Obviously, this is one of the simplest canons of finance, as simple as the ''buy low, sell high'' rule and as difficult to implement. Managers will increase value if they take money out of low return-on-asset ventures and redeploy it into higher-return businesses, *ceteris paribus*. Of course, all is rarely equal, especially in the expected future and with respect to risk. That is why managers are needed and why many companies engage specialist consultants to help them develop their corporate and business strategies.

The problem is that, although past and present earnings and returns point to the future, the future requires investment now. Thus, managers must give the likely future, about which they know little, the heaviest weight in their investment decisions. And when we analyze a set of competitors, it is their investments that we have to monitor, so that we can identify what they think the future will be.

Common sense suggests, as we have demonstrated, that there are some very simple rules to guide management investment activity. Violations of these rules carry a penalty, specifically wasted resources, lost opportunities, and the destruction of value. Let us state the rules explicitly:

1. *Invest* where returns promise to be high and reliable, that is, where you'll have a competitive advantage. Remember, no advantage, no profit.
2. *Divest* from businesses where earnings and growth are falling and risk is rising.
3. Try to *eliminate* those risks that you can; manage the rest.
4. Take as little risk as possible, but as much as necessary.
5. Diversify *only* if value will be created by increased earnings, reduced risk, or a redeployment of assets from a low ROA or ROE to a higher ROA or ROE business.

[4]*Figure 17-5* is based on the simple premise that investors demand a return for the use of their funds—even if the investment is free of ''risk''—and demand a higher return if risk increases. If net present value is positive, a diversifying action is expected to add value; if the internal rate of return equals the fair return, the net present value is zero; and, if the net present value is negative, value is destroyed. Note that this model suggests that managers can manipulate value upwards by increasing return or cutting risk (Harrington, 1983).

6 Don't diversify if current returns are high and future earnings growth is likely to be strong. In these circumstances, continued focused investment will probably pay off.

Remember that value-creating managers must develop relationships and opportunities to get the resources they need. Managers who act like conservators trying to preserve assets are likely to underachieve and earn inferior returns. If they follow the ''prudent man'' rule and seek a fair return, for example, they'll probably underachieve and lose value. Managers must strive for more than prudence in order to create value.

Now, given that we know that the largest corporations are diversified, and since we have a robust normative position to guide us, how has diversification served its devotees in practice?

DIVERSIFICATION RESULTS

Since so many large corporations have diversified, how have things turned out—especially for their shareholders? Has diversification led to enhanced earnings, reduced risk, and higher stock prices?

Diversifying Acquisitions

With respect to diversifying acquisitions, Salter and Weinhold (1978) presented evidence that the answer to the second question is, ''No.'' Between 1967 and 1977, acquisitive diversifiers earned 20 percent less on assets than the average *Fortune* 500 company—a relatively diverse set of companies, as we have seen. On December 31, 1977, the diversified acquisitors in Salter and Weinhold's sample had a price earnings ratio 30 percent less than that of the average New York Stock Exchange company. (The New York listed companies, about 2200 in 1984, are on average less diverse than the *Fortune* 500.) Although the diversified acquisitors enjoyed a return on equity 20 percent greater than the *Fortune* 500 average in 1967, Salter and Weinhold reported that in 1975, the acquisitors' return on equity was 18 percent below the 500's average. Ansoff's (1965) position seems vindicated. Commenting on the effects of diversification on risk, Salter and Weinhold wrote:

> Gulf and Western's systematic risk adjusted for financial leverage differs insignificantly from that of a comparable portfolio. . . . Whatever benefits Gulf and Western provides its shareholders, reduction of investment risk apparently is not one of them. (1978, p. 168)

Comparing such corporations to mutual funds, Salter and Weinhold point out that for the investor, widely diversified companies may actually be *less* attractive investments because of the illiquidity of their asset commitments.

Salter and Weinhold continue by prescribing a set of rules to create value: Acquire and diversify only if income is increased or its variability is expected to be reduced. As we might expect, they recommend the exploitation of joint effects of synergy, more intense exploitation of *shareable* resources, leveraging underutilized financial assets, internal redeployments of funds to higher return businesses, and sticking close to home—that is, to businesses you know and to those where you can reach competitive scale.

It seems that these recommendations are little different from what can be deduced from basic finance. Yet they were not made idly. Although management is surely aware of the rules, they are difficult to live by and difficult to implement. Besides, we should not be surprised by Salter and Weinhold's negative findings. Ansoff (1965) warned that diversification was risky; Kitching (1967; 1974) pointed out that many mergers miscarry. Diversifying by acquisition adds risk to risk and we should expect the results to reflect the costs of these risks.

Acquisitions promise an easy remedy: They may appear cheaper than a start-up venture (but recall the maxim, "You get what you pay for"). But it is easy for management to be caught up in deal fever, forgetting that the price of a business may be bid up by competition to such an extent that the opportunity for value creation is lost, or at best long delayed.

Diversification in Practice

Indeed, one of the less obvious but very important social issues in business is whether the management is fulfilling its fiduciary responsibilities to the corporation's shareholders and creating value by retaining earnings for investment in diversification. Is management creating more value than the shareholders could get by investing dividends at market rates? So it is appropriate to ask, how successful is diversification per se—that is, in its many forms besides acquisition?

For a few moments, let us look at the results of diversification in the US. Rumelt (1974) reported that corporate profitability varied with diversification, pointing to a correlation between scope and type of diversity and results earned. *Figure 17-6* illustrates some of his observations.

As *Figure 17-6* shows, performance differences seem related more to type of diversification than to scope or amount of diversity—that is, related more to the way in which a firm's businesses are related to each other than to the number of products or markets offered or served. Both *Figures 17-6* (*a*) and (*b*) show the "constrained" diversifiers doing better than the rest—they are companies that drew on or added to some central strength or competence. The unrelated diversifiers and the vertically integrated companies (the very diversified and the companies intensely committed to one business) were the apparent low performers. The acquisitive conglomerates used high leverage to multiply their returns on capital to greater returns on equity. Among dominant and related businesses, those firms whose diversification was further afield did worse over the 1949 to 1969 period than those Rumelt described as having "chosen or been able to limit their product market scopes."

Yet, when Rumelt examined price/earnings ratios, he found the market statistics contrary to other measures of corporate performance. The related business category, particularly the related linked group of firms, enjoyed unusually high price/earnings ratios, even when the effects of growth, earnings stability and retention were taken into account, as *Table 17-4* shows. Rumelt commented, "The only plausible explanation for the continued existence of this difference over twenty years is that investors believe the related linked firms to be more likely to maintain their performance over the long term,"

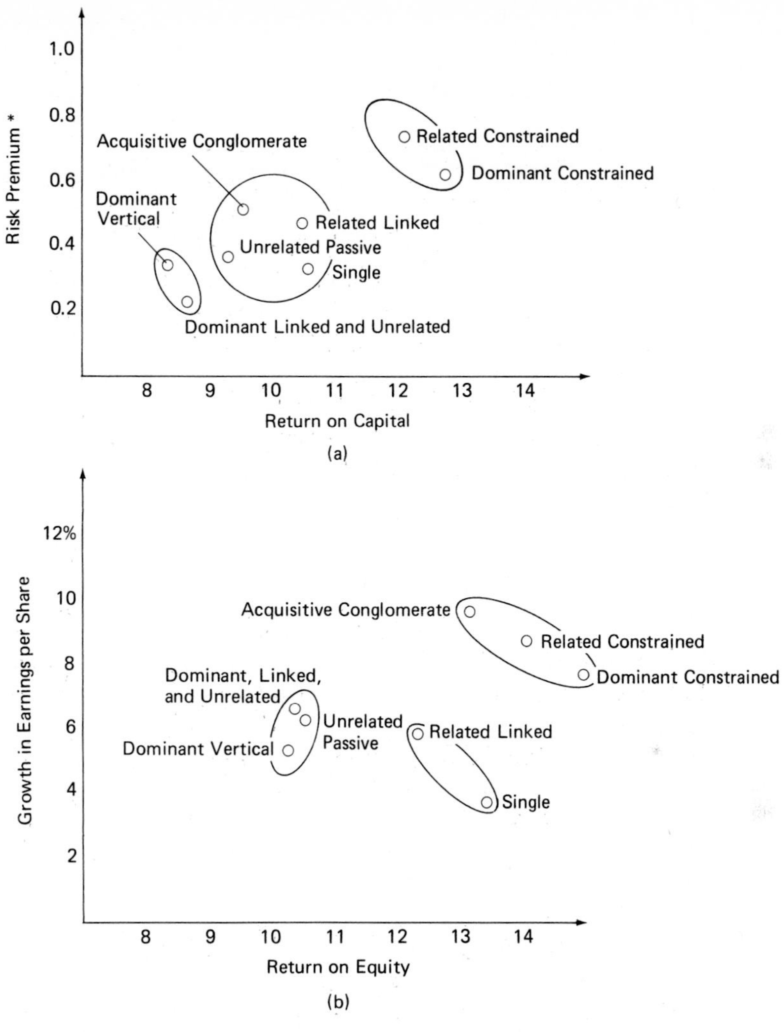

*Rumelt defined the Risk Premium as the ratio of (GEPS – 0.015)/SDEPS, i.e., as an adjusted ratio of EPS growth to the variability in the rate of EPS growth. 1.5% was his estimate of the after-tax risk-free rate.

FIGURE 17-6 **Risk and Return Category Means**

Source: Rumelt, *Strategy, Structure and Economic Performance,* Boston, MA: Division of Research, Harvard Business School, 1974.

perhaps because a single business is ultimately more transient than one growing from diversity.

The research results do not mean that vertically integrated companies should be transformed to related constrained or related linked companies (Rumelt, 1974, p. 101). Vertical integration implies commitment to one industry and may preclude rapid redeployment to other industries—although not precluding evolutionary redeployments of financial commitments within one industry chain (McLean & Haigh, 1954). The oil industry has had more success redeploying its assets among the different production and distribu-

TABLE 17-4
Price-Earnings Multiple Gap

	Single	*Dominant-Vertical*	*Dominant-Constrained*	*Dominant-Linked and Unrelated*	*Related-Constrained*	*Related-Linked*	*Unrelated-Passive*	*Acquisitive Conglomerate*	*All Firms*
Actual Price-Earnings Ratio	14.60	15.68	15.92	15.41	19.19	19.27	13.77	17.43	17.02
Calculated Price-Earnings Ratio*	17.02	16.64	16.84	17.19	17.50	16.94	16.55	16.89	17.02
Difference	−2.42	−.96	−.92	−1.78	+1.69	+2.33	−2.78	+.54	0.00
t-Ratio	−2.44	−1.15	−.81	−.81	+2.34	+2.11	−1.59	+.33	—
Level of Significance	.02	—	—	—	.01	.02	.06	—	—

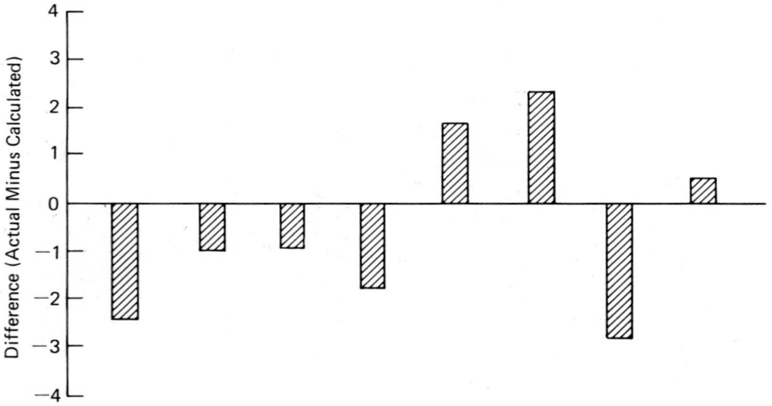

Difference (Actual Minus Calculated)

*PE = 10.97 + 4.8 Time + 0.127 GEPS −0.075 SDEPS + 3.72 RTN
R^2 = 0.48 F ratio = 24.9 (4,337).
Source: Rumelt, *Strategy, Structure and Economic Performance*, Boston, MA: Division of Research, Harvard Business School, 1974.

tion stages commercializing crude than it has in diversification—witness Mobil Oil's acquisition of Montgomery Ward and Exxon's acquisition of Reliance Electric, both apparently unsuccessful.

Advising us to interpret his research carefully, Rumelt warned that he had observed an association between performance and diversity, not causality: it may be that high performance eliminates the need for diversity rather than that diversity leads to high performance (Rumelt, 1974, p. 124). This observation is in line with Bass's hypothesis that the major motivation for diversification is defensive, as primary markets mature. Rumelt concluded:

> While it may be that these strategies tend to produce good results, it is more likely that firms already rapidly growing and profitable think it wise to restrict their scopes of activity to businesses that directly relate to their currently successful areas of competence. Nevertheless, the intensive cultivation of a single field has proven, on the average, financially more successful than bold moves into uncharted areas. (1974, p. 156)

Addressing his own questions about the fit of certain strategies to particular industries and whether the differences he observed were due more to "industry" than to "diversification," Rumelt's investigations were frustrated by the data available. Extreme observations and small numbers of observations within industry groups precluded meaningful statistical analysis. He wrote:

> Taking a broader point of view, it seems evident that more of the strategy-related performance differences are due to industry differences, but that the two effects are simply not separable. The higher performing industries tend to consist of mostly Related Business firms, and Related Business firms tend to belong to higher performing industries. Which came first? The answer seems to be that they came together; the same conditions that produce above average performance—science-based proprietary strengths, growth in markets served along with rapid product innovation—produce diversified firms. (p. 100)

Subsequent research by Christensen and Montgomery (1981), Bettis and Hall (1981), and Rumelt (1982) has accumulated evidence indicating that industry choice is probably the most important factor in determining the success of a diversified firm. Christensen and Montgomery extended a subset of Rumelt's data to 1977, exploiting "line of business data" in the Securities and Exchange Commission data in Corporate Form 10-K's. Working with data for the period 1972 to 1977, these researchers found "no statistical grounds for asserting that significant performance differences exist" between categories of diversified firms (p. 333).

However, when data on thirty-one vertically integrated firms were added to their sample, certain performance variables became significant. Since "the vertical integrated companies were distinctly low performers" in their own and Rumelt's sample data, Christensen and Montgomery suggested cautious inference-making—statistics can be sensitive to extremes, as *Figure 17-7* illustrates. Lines A and B may be reasonably representative of the two groups of firms, but Line C is likely to be a poor representative of each and lead to incorrect inferences, since it is probable that the data is heterogeneous

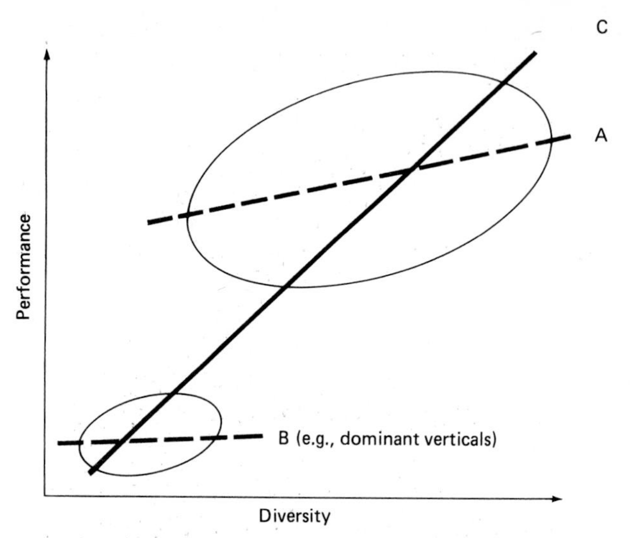

Consider the impact of including the data B in a regression with A. The true relationships A and B are masked by the aggregation, and C is the estimate.

FIGURE 17-7 Statistics and Extreme Values

rather than homogeneous (Rumelt, 1974; Hatten and Schendel, 1977; Hatten, Schendel and Cooper, 1978).

Continuing their analysis to separate out the effects of market structure—that is, industry profitability rates and company market shares—on the performance of diversified companies, Christensen and Montgomery found that the unrelated portfolio firms (Rumelt's unrelated passive and acquisitive conglomerates) had lower market shares, were positioned in less profitable and less concentrated markets, and were smaller than other firms in the sample. Related constrained firms, in contrast, were in more profitable, faster-growing, and more highly concentrated markets than other firms. They concluded:

> First, following a strategy of constrained diversification is not sufficient to assure high earnings. The constrained diversifiers appear to be more profitable in part because they operated in very profitable, highly concentrated markets, and were able to acquire large shares in those markets. These firms' above-average market shares also suggest that they possess a sufficient level of the skills and resources critical to success in these high opportunity markets—a condition which may have developed due to diversification close to the original business. Successful performance is the outcome of market opportunity combined with the capacity to take advantage of that opportunity. In diversification planning, it is unwise to fail to analyze either.
>
> Second, the rather uninspiring performance of unrelated-portfolio firms suggests the dangers of inattention to market structure in entry decisions or of knowingly entering highly fragmented, low profit markets. To the degree such markets are entered because businesses can be purchased for attractive prices, a longer-run point of view is needed. If these businesses are acquired because of unrealistic expectations of improving performance with new ownership, a hard look at market structure variables can lead to more realistic assessments of turnaround potential. (1981, pp. 339–40)

Like Christensen and Montgomery, Bettis and Hall (1981) focused on the related category, linked and constrained, again supplementing Rumelt's sample with later data but adding data on new firms as well. Observing that many of Rumelt's related constrained category were pharmaceutical companies, they asked the question whether Rumelt's findings were more representative of pharmaceutical companies (another extreme group) than related diversification. The results pointed to the influence of extremes, the pharmaceutical companies: With these included, significant differences were observed; without them, the differences were not significant. Bettis are Hall concluded that the differences Rumelt observed between the performance of the groups labelled related and unrelated diversified were due probably to the presence of the pharmaceutical firms in the related category rather than to differences in the efficacy of diversification strategies per se. They found no evidence of significant risk reduction with increased diversity.

Rumelt (1982) worked with 1970–1973 data and contrasted actual and expected return based on industry investment patterns using a straight-forward model:

$$R_j = \sum_i P_{ij} R_i$$

^{R}j, the expected return on the j-th firm, is the sum of the firm's returns in each of i industries. Those returns are simply the product of the proportion of firm capital invested in each industry, P_{ij}, and the average return on capital earned in that industry, R_i. By simply examining the return premium, the difference, P, between the actual return on capital, ROC, and the expected return based on industry participation, $\hat{R}$, that is,

$$P = ROC - \hat{R}$$

Rumelt could "test" the efficacy of alternate diversification strategies. The results are shown in *Table 17-5.*

TABLE 17-5 Return, Expected Return, and the Return Premium

Category	*Observations*	*ROC*	$\hat{R}$	P	$P\text{-}P_{UB}$
SB	23	10.4	9.30	1.64[b]	3.53[a]
DV	33	8.48[b]	8.80[a]	−0.32	1.57[b]
DC	12	11.78	9.83	1.96[b]	3.85[a]
DLU	9	10.97	9.96	1.02	2.91[b]
RC	41	11.63[a]	10.68[a]	0.95	2.85[a]
RL	38	9.33	9.77	−0.44	1.45
UB	31	7.55[a]	9.44	−1.89[a]	—
Total/average	187	9.82	9.70	0.12	
Estimated σ		4.34	2.15	3.88	
F-statistic	[6, 180]	3.98[a]	2.60[b]	3.17[a]	

Significance tests for ROC, R, and P test hypothesis that value displayed is equal to the population mean.
Significance tests for $P\text{-}P_{UB}$ test hypothesis that value displayed is zero.
[a]Level of significance = 99 per cent.
[b]Level of significance = 95 per cent.
Source: Rumelt, "Diversification Strategy and Profitability," *Strategic Management Journal*, 3, no. 4, Oct.-Dec. 1982, 367. © 1982 by John Wiley & Sons.

Rumelt commented:

> According to the F-statistic, the observed R's are not homogeneous across the categories ($p = 0.05$); the major contributors to this result are the low expected return, R, of the DV group and the high expected return, R, of the RC group. . . . These data show that the high ROC of the related constrained group was primarily an industry effect and that the RC firms perform as would be expected given the industries in which they participate. (1982, pp. 367–68)

He concluded, and we agree, "More remains to be understood about why firms diversify and the proper management of different patterns of diversification."

Summary on the Results of Diversification Research

The growing evidence is that for most corporations, diversification per se does little to reduce risk or increase returns. In fact, Rumelt's results under P, the return premium in *Table 17-5*, point to increased diversity's being associated with lower than expected performance once industry choice is taken into consideration.

It seems that in many corporations management has diversified, but it has not learned to make diversity pay. The high performance of the related and dominant constrained groups points to the advantage of staying close to home and building off a core technology. The dominant constrained and related constrained firms may be the beneficiaries of opportunity, or their skill may be to enter businesses where the renewal and extension of products is technologically possible. Rumelt writes that diversification succeeds "by replacing products that are stagnant or declining with close functional substitutes that are profitable and growing for reasons related to the decline of the original products" (1974, p. 157). This interpretation is substantially consistent with Bass and colleagues' (1977) position that diversification is a defensive strategy used by firms with stagnant products and markets.

Note, however, that most of the research available is based on averages which extend across large numbers of companies. Our own research within industries and the experiences cited above point to the dangers of pooling heterogeneous data. To understand more about diversity, we need to look at the exceptions, too—the high and low performers—to learn what makes them successful and unsuccessful (Hatten and Schendel, 1976; Hatten and Hatten, 1985).

One step in this direction was reported by Dundas and Richardson (1982). By contrasting high- and low-performing conglomerates, they were able to identify some of the characteristics apparently associated with successful conglomerates. These were a "narrow focus" on like industries, a limited commitment or dependence on any one business (not more than 30 percent of revenues or assets in one), and market leadership, full control, growth by friendly acquisition, and consistent administrative practices—including executive compensation to Return on Investment (ROI). They concluded, however, that the key administrative requirement was to allocate the firm's capital effectively.

NEEDED: CORPORATE STRATEGY

Corporate strategy is about being in the right businesses. Many have overlooked this message from the diversification research: Diversification has added little value per se, but it is a tool which allows corporate renewal. We should focus, therefore, on "the industries they're in" and the reasons and organizational structures and systems used to get there, as we analyze successful management techniques for diversification.

Research has shown that few companies outperform their industry choices, and that risk reduction and increased returns are elusive. Henderson commented:

> A multidivision company without an overall strategy is not even as good as the sum of its parts. It is merely a portfolio of non-liquid, non-tradable investments, with added overhead and constraints. Such closed-end investments properly sell at a discount from the sum of the parts. Intuition alone is an inadequate substitute for an integrated strategy. (Henderson, 1979, p. 28)

Henderson suggests that many corporations lack an *integrating* corporate strategy. Without integrating objectives and strategies, it is unlikely that managers can administer their corporations effectively or efficiently—they will neither be doing the right thing nor doing things right.

The question confronting management is how to judge what is right, how to create value more effectively. As noted in our discussion of single-business companies, it is difficult to modify a company's present strategy and do so responsibly until you know what you are doing and how well it is working. You have to identify your strategy before you fix it—before you know whether it needs fixing at all.

At this point, let us review what we know about diversification. First, it succeeds or fails principally because of industry choices. Second, it promises great advantages if the businesses can be related—if the skills and resources of one business can be used in concert with those of another to strengthen one or the other or both. Third, the simple rules of investment apply: increase returns and cut risk by skilled redeployment of resources from low-return businesses to those where you can earn high returns hereafter, thereby using the successes of the past to establish strength for the future. In Chapter 18, we focus our thinking on resource deployment, and on portfolio models, laying the foundation for Business Analysis, a tool for corporate strategy identification presented and demonstrated in Chapter 19.

chapter 18

Portfolio Analysis: Tracking the Deployment of Funds

INTRODUCTION

Resource deployment is the critical task of the corporate-level strategist. The principles of diversification are well-known, but the results are disappointing. Why?

In the first place is the problem and cost of entry and exit. Businesses are not liquid investments, and it is difficult to redeploy assets. Second, relatedness is difficult to realize quickly and at best takes time to develop. Third, the simple rule of investment—put your capital in higher-return businesses—is difficult to live by. All this adds up to what Henderson (1979) called a lack of an integrating corporate strategy. Few managers would disagree, yet most would point to the difficulties they have in conceiving such a strategy and living it.

Living the strategy and living by the rules that facilitate administration and that we have enumerated in Chapter 15 is difficult because it threatens the established power bases of the firm. Redeploying resources means reallocating power, and typically those who have power act to preserve it. Remember, they had to struggle to get it. We believe that any failure to appreciate the social consequences of power changes puts a strategy into jeopardy. Power and resources go hand in glove.

Diversification means change in resource deployments and priorities. It threatens power. Those who have power find it hard to let go—even if they themselves are the architects of change. We know of CEO's who have wisely initiated diversification programs committing to new product development and acquisitions, yet have not let go of their old power base in the business that made them a success. Instead of sharing power with the managers of their new venture, they have held it, losing valuable people, pouring disproportionate resources into the old businesses, and unconsciously restricting the new. It is a failure to let go of the past. Revealed by inappropriate resource deployments and a failure to delegate, it is an administrative failure which threatens the success of their diversification.

Successful change, and diversification is change, comes only when power is shifted to implement the strategy. Power has to shift ahead of the strategic change and be committed to the corporate future, not the past. Diversification programs often atrophy because this timely marriage of power and strategy is not consummated (Barnes and Hershon, 1976).

The fault lies at the top. Except when resources are committed not only to the act of diversification but to the diversified way of life, we believe diversification will be a failure. The evidence we have seen in corporation after corporation is that the successes of the past can consume the resources needed for the future. In fact, a failure to appreciate the consequences of an enacted strategy which probably unconsciously suits the old power structure but not the future vitality of the corporation is probably the reason why diversification per se has been associated with nonperformance.

PORTFOLIO ANALYSIS

Since the mid-1960s, such unconscious misallocations of capital and people have become less easy to explain, because of the simple analytical tools available to audit resource deployments—the portfolio models. Although they do little more than a straight sources-and-uses-of-funds statement could do, they provide most managers with data in a more readily digestible form.

Portfolio analysis is an analytical approach which asks managers to view corporations as portfolios of businesses to be managed for the best possible return. Linking industry characteristics, the company's competitive strengths, and resource deployment patterns, portfolio analysis gives managers an opportunity to see their companies from a different point of view and think about the future implications of their current resource commitments.

The value of the portfolio lies in its simplicity. The matrices or portfolio charts we will describe are superficially easy to understand; they confront management with particular views of their business anchored in fact. They thus facilitate discussion and thinking about the firm's competitive positions and provoke questions about the contribution of the firm's current resource allocations to its long-run vitality.

Most importantly, portfolio approaches help management relate its separable businesses to each other and so to the corporation *through* their respective objectives. Since portfolio analysis helps management see how its resources are being deployed and suggests achievable objectives for each business, it gives corporate management an opportunity to use its businesses as resources to achieve corporate objectives. We will explain portfolio analysis in this chapter, and you will see it used as one of the important elements in our approach to corporate strategy identification developed in Chapter 19.

ITS SUPPORTERS

Portfolio analysis has been held partly responsible for the improved profit performance of many companies. For example, General Electric during the 1970s substantially increased its return on equity and attributed its success to portfolio analysis, among other things. The Mead Corporation's and Armco Steel's managements also attributed their success in part to their use of portfolio concepts. William Verity, Armco's Chairman and CEO, wrote:

> We are now committed to the Product Portfolio concept of planning. If there were one single answer I could give to the question . . . Why a portfolio of businesses? . . . it would be that a balanced portfolio is necessary for the survival of the multiproduct company and essential for its profitable growth. Actually, we had always managed our business as one of many products serving many markets, but by grouping our products and markets into discrete business units, and identifying the position of each such unit vis à vis its competitors, we make better use of present investments and can make better plans for future investments. (1975, p. 50)

Armco is one of many corporations which have used portfolio concepts in their planning. Haspeslagh (1982) estimated that 36 percent of the *Fortune* 1000 and 45 percent of the *Fortune* 500 have employed the approach to some extent. Commenting, he wrote, "Most important, however, portfolio planning seems to have profoundly affected the way executives think about the management of their businesses" (p. 59).

TYPES OF PORTFOLIO ANALYSES

Portfolio analysis takes the view that a corporation is a portfolio of investments to be managed to produce the best *total* return. Most portfolio analysts recognize that each business has unique competitive problems and opportunities and is capable of making different contributions to corporate performance if it is allocated resources appropriate to its task, the objectives or mission given it by the corporation. Portfolio analysis helps management determine what those objectives should be—that is, what corporate objectives are most attainable for the portfolio of companies.

Many different portfolio analysis approaches are used across the world. The most commonly used form, shown in *Figure 18-1,* was developed by Boston Consulting Group and combines growth with market share. *Figure 18-2* compares the major portfolio models beginning with BCG's two-by-two product portfolio in 1. The McKinsey matrix, 2, a three-by-three matrix, is usually associated with General Electric and Shell and combines industry attractiveness and business strength. The Strategic Planning Institute, well-known as the proprietor of the PIMS (Profit Impact of Market Strategy) study, contrasts industry average profitability with the corporation's profitability within that industry in 3.

Marakon Associates' profitability matrix, 4, allows users to compare profitability and relative growth. Arthur D. Little & Company use business strength and life cycle stage in 5. Industry market/book ratios are contrasted with the internal deployment of funds in matrix 6, which links deployment directly to the stock market and so to value creation. Matrix 7 adapts the concept to the eleemosynary sector, contrasting social need and the revenue-generating potential of a portfolio of Young Men's Christian Association (YMCA) programs. Since a matrix is often associated with a strategy consultant, a skeptic could be excused if he saw the differences between matrices being due more to consultants' needs for market differentiations than to distinct theoretical positions.

These different portfolios all share a common parentage in the rules of successful diversification: Enter businesses where future returns are likely to be high; strive for synergies and the efficiencies promised by relating one business to another; deploy your assets in a disciplined way, withdrawing assets from low-return or low-value situations; and invest where returns are high and highly valued. All the matrices help management track its deployment of funds. They relate to market value, since most encompass the major correlates of value, earnings, growth, and risk, either directly or via some other variable or set of variables which correlate with one or more of these.

Each portfolio or matrix suggests generic strategies. For example, BCG's product portfolio in *Figure 18-1* with its dogs, cows, wildcats, and stars categorizes businesses in terms of their cash use or generation and implies a prescription to withdraw from dogs, milk cows, build wildcats, and sustain or maintain the growth and market shares of stars. If a business plots in a specific quadrant, say as a cow, then we can suggest it as a primary candidate for management as a cow to be milked of the cash flow it produces each operating cycle. Each grid is populated by bubble charts proportionately representing the corporation's separable business activities by sales or assets or some other measure of commitment.

McKinsey's (GE/Shell) matrix differs from the BCG matrix because industry attractiveness is a multidimensional characteristic, either simply judged or computed based on weighted judgments about such factors as cyclicality, regulation, vulnerability to inflation and technological obsolescence, capital intensity, and pricing flexibility. Business strength embraces supply, market share, distribution strengths, service capability, production cost position, capacity, product and process engineering, quality, and, indeed whatever characteristics give a business strength (Hussey, 1978). In principle, corporations should invest in attractive businesses where they have strengths or can develop them at reasonable cost.

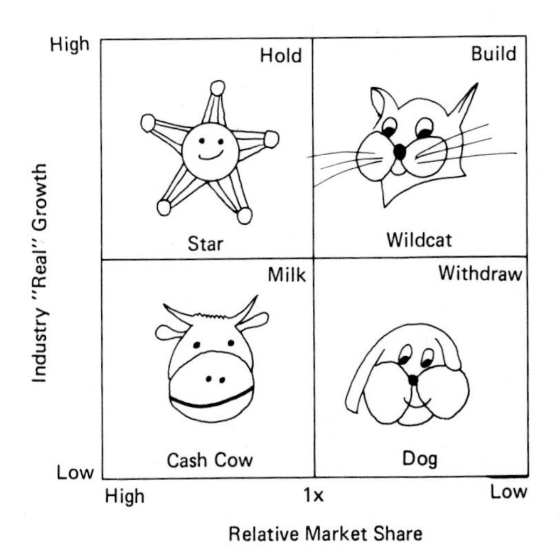

FIGURE 18-1 BCG's Product Portfolio
Source: Adopted from Bruce D. Henderson, *The Product Portfolio*. Boston: Boston Consulting Group, 1970

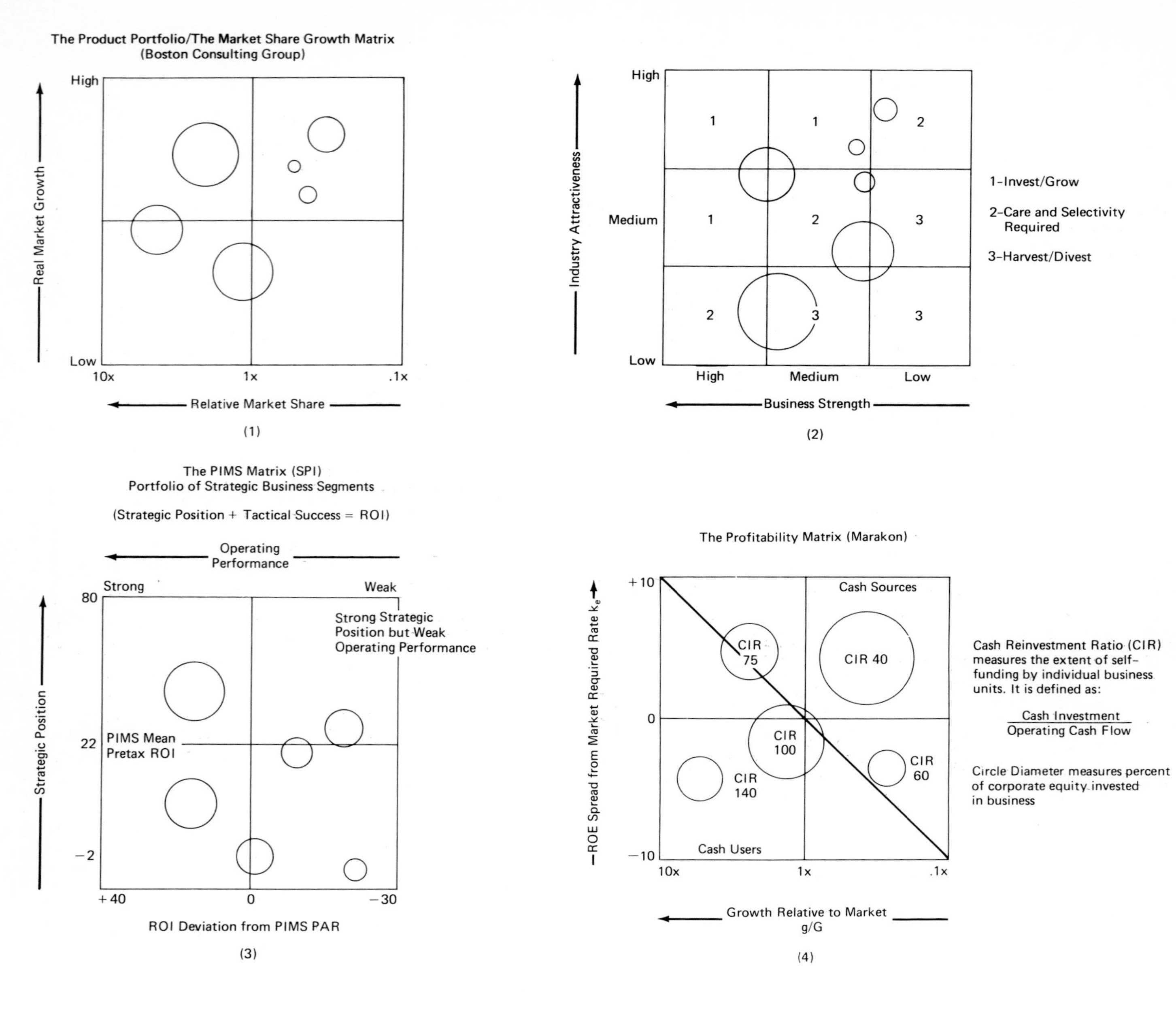

The Product Portfolio/The Market Share Growth Matrix
(Boston Consulting Group)
High
Low
Real Market Growth
10x
1x
.1x
Relative Market Share
(1)
High
Medium
Low
Industry Attractiveness
1
1
2
1
2
3
2
3
3
High
Medium
Low
Business Strength
(2)
1-Invest/Grow
2-Care and Selectivity Required
3-Harvest/Divest
The PIMS Matrix (SPI)
Portfolio of Strategic Business Segments
(Strategic Position + Tactical Success = ROI)
Operating Performance
Strong
Weak
80
22
−2
Strategic Position
Strong Strategic Position but Weak Operating Performance
PIMS Mean Pretax ROI
+40
0
−30
ROI Deviation from PIMS PAR
(3)
The Profitability Matrix (Marakon)
+10
0
−10
ROE Spread from Market Required Rate k
Cash Sources
CIR 75
CIR 40
CIR 100
CIR 140
CIR 60
Cash Users
10x
1x
.1x
Growth Relative to Market
g/G
(4)
Cash Reinvestment Ratio (CIR) measures the extent of self-funding by individual business units. It is defined as:
Cash Investment
Operating Cash Flow
Circle Diameter measures percent of corporate equity invested in business

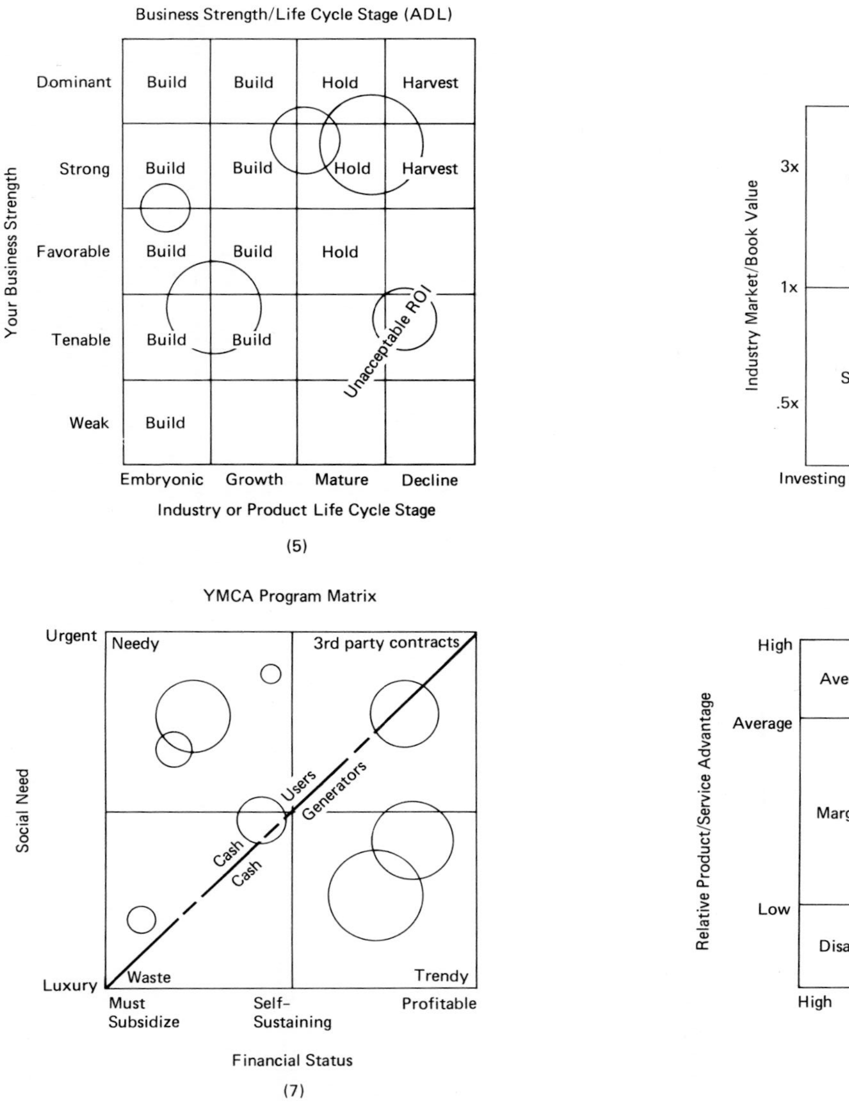

FIGURE 18-2 Portfolio Matrices

In contrast with the GE matrix, which is based on judged multidimensional characteristics, the Strategic Planning Institute's matrix under the PIMS (Profit Impact of Market Strategy) banner is based on cross-sectional, multidimensional regression studies of the profitability of more than 2000 businesses. It compares business average profitability, an "industry" characteristic, with performance in the business. Loomis (1980), then President of Dexter Corporation, implies that the choice of industries is a strategic issue and can be addressed in part on the basis of average (that is, PAR) ROI, while deviation from an industry PAR ROI is an operating outcome (he calls it tactical). Because it is regression-based, the PIMS model avoids judgmental weightings of the importance of the components of strength and attractiveness and substitutes statistical relationships estimated from past experience. Although statistically derived and scientifically inspired, the PIMS models have been criticized, primarily because the population used is heterogeneous—that is, contains many apparently dissimilar businesses—and the models largely neglect the impact of time since they are cross-sectional and do not distinguish one time period from another (Anderson and Paine, 1977; Hatten and Schendel, 1976).

Marakon, a San Francisco-based firm, has developed a different approach based on earnings above the cost of equity capital and growth relative to market. Attractive opportunities are those in the upper right-hand side and unattractive options are those in the lower left. Marakon (1981) also labels the businesses of the firm according to their cash reinvestment ratio (our internal redeployment ratio).

Arthur D. Little & Company's matrix links business strength and the product life cycle. The value management matrix contrasts market/book value with a company's internal deployment of funds. As drawn in 6, we have a company squandering value on A and B, apparently low-value businesses, while starving potentially value-creating businesses D and E. Ansoff and Leontiades (1976) offered another variation on these themes with an ROI/product life cycle portfolio.

Matrix 7, the YMCA matrix, shows a simple adaptation of the portfolio format to a not-for-profit charitable organization. By contrasting social need and financial character, the organization's management, here a YMCA executive team, could use the matrix to think about program and service mix and its ability to financially sustain the organization while serving the community. MITI, the Japanese central planning organization, is reputed to use a similar need/national resources approach in identifying those Japanese industries which deserve investment priority. Matrix 8 shows yet another variation on the theme: a simple mapping of two critical dimensions of competitive ability (Hall, 1980).

THE USEFULNESS OF PORTFOLIO ANALYSIS

Let us emphasize our view that, while differences in axis and category names appear important at first glance, a little thought shows that for the most part they are not highly differentiated, one from another. First, the dimensions on the axes of most portfolio approaches could normally be expected to be correlates of industry growth or profitability and market share, whether they encompass only one or many variables directly or through a regression model (as in the PIMS portfolio). This means we are considering *similar* types of situations, whatever portfolio we use.

Second, and more importantly, these matrices are not exact tools, despite their apparent graphic precision. They do not give answers but help us raise questions. We question the need for precision and the value of subtle distinction, since any portfolio model is really a tool to isolate crude patterns of funds deployments, misallocation of funds, and glaring gaps in the mix of businesses. Their virtue is simplicity, not precision. They point to the need for research, not to simple answers. The prescriptions of the matrices are catalysts for simple "what if" questions about the future investments of the firm.

Probably the most distinctive and usable portfolios are those which most closely relate to "estimated" market value, the matrices numbered 4 and 6 in *Figure 18-1*. Estimated market value is not stable, however, a point we made in Chapter 17 where we cited Beaver and Morse's (1978) work demonstrating the instability of price/earnings ratios over time. Businesses lose their stock market popularity—cosmetics and oil services were the darlings of the 1960s and the 1970s markets; bioengineering and computers enjoyed brief periods of market favor in the early 1980s. Note, we use estimated value because the business units of few diversified firms are publicly traded and their values, therefore, must be estimated based on "industry P/E ratios and risk levels" in the jargon of finance. This is a nontrivial task for any large corporation and one where, of necessity, apparent precision masks many assumptions, including substantial assumptions about the liquidity of business units and the stability of market value.

We can note here that portfolio models can be applied to both a corporation and its competitors, so that the cash commitments and resources of each can be quickly compared. Furthermore, they can be applied at the corporate group and business level and even at the level of the product line. In every situation, they can be used to bring facts to management's attention so that it can see its firms or businesses through different lenses. Portfolio models provide opportunities for managers to take fresh views anchored in reality. Mixing metaphors, they allow managers to "call a spade (in the matrix) a spade," as they identify in the BCG case, for example, the animals populating the matrix.

A CLOSE LOOK AT THE PRODUCT PORTFOLIO

Figure 18-3 presents BCG's product portfolio again. The two axes are real industry growth and relative market share, where relative share is simply defined as the ratio of your share to your leading competitor's share. Only the market leader has a relative share greater than one, since only the leader enjoys the second-rank company as its "leading" competitor (General Motors' lead competitor in the US auto industry is Ford; Ford, Chrysler, and AMC all have General Motors as their lead competitor).

The portfolio links an industry characteristic (growth) and an indicator of competitive strength (market share) setting the stage for a visual display of the firm's market commitments and, indirectly, of its current resource deployment (since sales-to-assets ratios are normally stable over moderate time periods across industries). The logic of this portfolio is that growing while maintaining or building market share requires investment, whereas the operations of a competitively strong business in a low-growth industry will throw off cash which corporate management can redeploy. Cash generated can be balanced with cash used, as *Figure 18-3* suggests; growth uses cash, while market strength and profitability are potential sources of cash. Notice the line drawn above the matrix in *Figure 18-3* indicating the increased expected cash-generating potential of businesses with

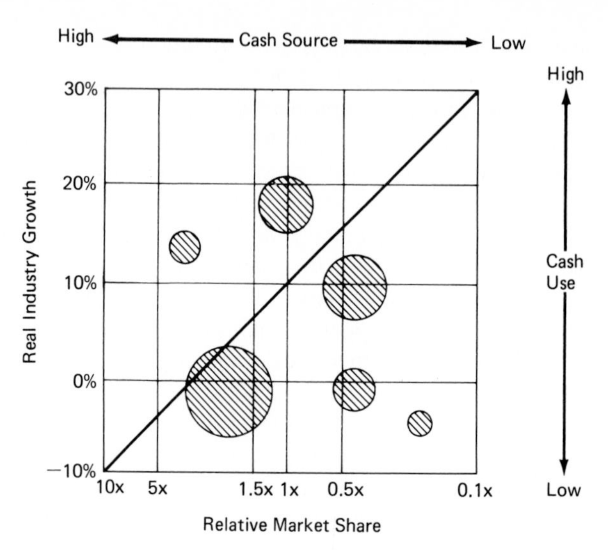

FIGURE 18-3 The Product Portfolio

increasing market share. To the right is the cash use characteristic of a typical cow, dog, wildcat, or star business, with cash use increasing as market growth accelerates. Here cash use and cash source are used deliberately to emphasize the explicit relationship of the product portfolio to the firm's funds statement. Note the net cash balance, category by category. More funds generated is indicated by plus (+), less by minus (−); more funds used is indicated by a minus, less funds used by plus:

BCG Category	*Source/Use*
Cow	+/+ Funds Available
Dog	−/+
Wildcat	−/− Funds Needed
Star	+/−

By positioning each of the corporation's businesses according to its industry's growth and its achieved market share, managers can see where their commitments are and judge their "quality." Relative market share (your share divided by your largest competitor's share) is the measure of relative competitive position used in the market share/growth matrix. It is plotted on a logarithmic scale. Hedley, then a BCG director, advised that this is necessary:

> . . . to be consistent with the experience curve effect which implies that profit margin or rate of cash generation differences between competitors will tend to be related to the ratio of their relative competitive positions (market shares). (1977, p. 12)

Hedley explains that 10 percent "volume" growth is a typical but arbitrary dividing line for high and low growth, adding that for high-growth and low-growth businesses, different ratios of "competitive positions" or market share divide cash users and cash generators. In high-growth industries, Hedley suggests a relative share of 1.5x, to distinguish stars from wildcats. Hedley advises us to use a relative share of 1x to separate cows and dogs in low-growth industries.

These divisions, it seems, "ensure a sufficiently dominant position that the business will have the characteristic of a star in practice" (p. 12). Hedley comments on cows that "acceptable cash-generation characteristics are occasionally, but not always, observable at relative strength as low as 1 times" (p. 13). He warns that these dividing lines are "only approximate guides," advice justified by the findings of MacMillan and his colleagues (1982), Hambrick and MacMillan (1982), and Christensen and colleagues (1982), whose collective research shows that dog businesses can outperform—or indeed underperform—their simple category expectation. Hambrick and MacMillan sensibly point out that in the simple structure of the matrix, most US businesses are dogs, yet many prosper and enjoy a positive cash flow. They conclude:

> Certain strategic factors are associated with high performance among dogs. The notable factors are low capital intensity, attention to efficiency, a narrow focus, high product quality, and low to moderate prices. (1982, p. 94)

Keep in mind that business classification is a crude tool. But it can help us uncover fundamental deployment patterns and glaring inconsistencies. And it can alert us to explore just how many opportunities for performance improvement and resource redeployment exist.

The significance of each business unit's position is its cash use or generative characteristics in practice—its growth, capital intensity, and profitability. An ability to manage a business as a cow or a star, or to avoid falling into the dog trap, depends on your ability to realistically appraise your business's relative competitive advantage. If it is sufficiently large and the competitive structure is stable, then it is probably safe to take cash out; if it is too low or erratic, then any effort to improve the situation is almost certainly unwarranted, given the firm's other opportunities.

By centering a "bubble" or "balloon" on each business's portfolio position so that the area of the bubble is proportionate to the percentage of corporate sales generated by each business, management can see not only where its businesses lie, but the likely cash balance of the firm, where cash is *probably* being generated and where it is *probably* being used. Biggadike (1978) advises those who wish to draw a product portfolio precisely that

> the radius, r, of a circle representing a product is equal to the square root of the product of the percentage, p, (expressed as a decimal) of total sales represented by that product and the square of the radius R of the large circle representing total company sales.
>
> $$r = \sqrt{pR^2}$$
>
> As a rule of thumb, the radius of the total sales circle should be about half of the distance from any axis to the interception of the index lines (the lines dividing high and low market share), along either one of the index lines. This rules ensures that a circle representing the total sales of the company will fit within one quadrant. Some trial and error may be necessary. (p. 4)[1]

[1]Within an industry where sales/asset ratios are stable and similar among companies, assets might be used as an alternate to sales.

Notice, too, that ''probably'' is a necessary qualifier, since portfolio position suggests a likely or expected funds balance for each business—reality could be different. When analysing diversified companies, always check the actual cash flow. For example, perhaps because of ''when we look,'' a business whose management has determined to increase market share may be increasing its share by cutting prices but still be reaching for a stable, profitable position; it could have relatively high market value, but not a positive cash flow. Unless volume allows a firm to garner market power over its customers and so receive higher prices, or unless volume allows experience to accumulate—experience that is associated with a sustainable cost advantage—efforts to expand market share may not pay.

SOME THOUGHTFUL CRITICISM

Portfolio models are not without their critics, of course, as these last remarks suggest. Again, the BCG model can serve as a bench mark for our discussion; the user must beware of the implicit assumptions underlying it.

The product portfolio suggests four archetypical sets of objectives and strategies for the business units (or products) of a corporation, depending upon their positions within the matrix, as noted earlier:

- Cow—milk and redeploy cash flow
- Dog—divest and redeploy proceeds
- Star—build competitive position and grow
- Wildcat—invest heavily and selectively to improve competitive position.

Market share is assumed to be valuable because it is profitable. BCG explains the profits as the fruit of an advantageous cost position due to the rapid accumulation of experience. It is also assumed that market growth ultimately slows to allow the market leader to take cash out of the cow business.

The product portfolio is a pictorial representation of a sources and uses of funds statement. The model assumes that market share gains are associated with profitability and that growth will be followed by a decline, giving the firm an opportunity to deploy its funds.

Yet:

1. Gaining market share is costly, and some never recover the investment,
2. Many products have short and even attenuated life cycles, e.g., electronics.
3. Some products have extremely long life cycles and require continued investment.

Hence, there is no guarantee that there will be an opportunity to redeploy funds in every case.

The assumptions underlying the model are not always applicable. *Figure 18-4* suggests sources of potential error. Growing market share, the horizontal axis of the product portfolio, is not always profitable. Some believe that market share has to pass a threshold to be profitable, others that there is a U-shaped function, similar to 'ACD' in

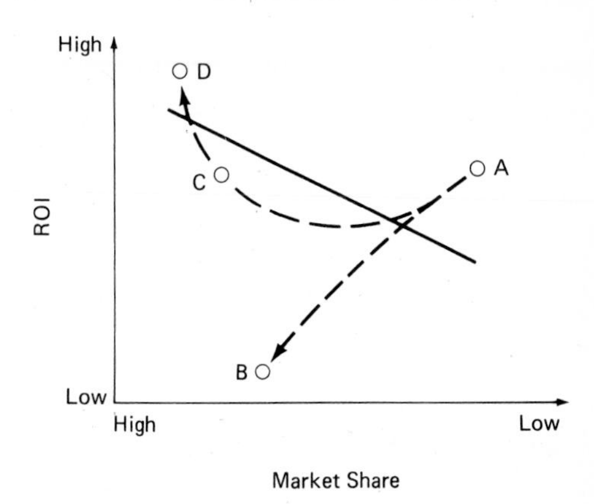

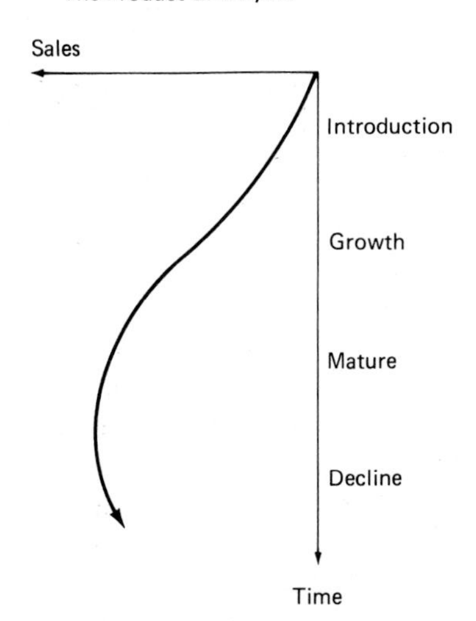

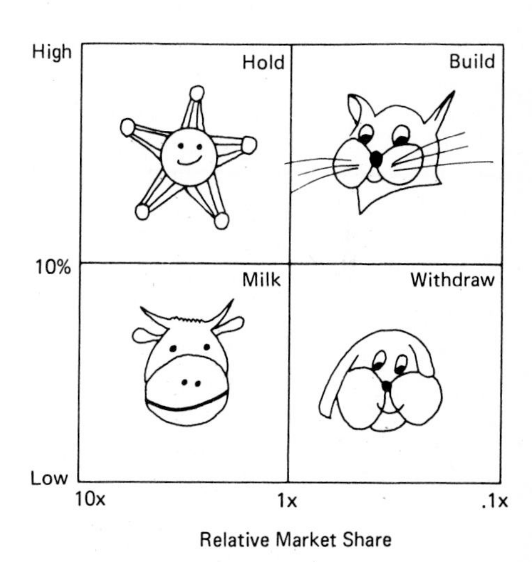

FIGURE 18-4 The Assumptions of the Product Portfolio

Figure 18-4(A), with untenable middle ground between high and low share positions (Porter, 1980). Fruhan (1974) and Chevalier (1974) documented the costs of building market share and the uncertain payoff associated with increased share, much like AB in Fig 18-4(A). Moreover, the model is a static representation of the firm. Attempting to change share is always risky. Attempts to increase share usually cut profits, at least in the short run, and so violate the implicit positive profit market share assumption of the model, the solid line in Fig 18-4(A).

With respect to the assumption as to growth and decline which underlies the vertical axis of the product portfolio, we can note again that the product life cycle (Figure 18-4B) is an unreliable descriptive model of business evolution. Some staples (bread, for example) are very long-lived while some electronic components and fashion goods are very short-lived. Bread is, of course, a very wide product category—particular bread types may come and go, although bread's "popularity" endures. Assumptions relating to the profit-market share relationships over time are relatively simple to expose, but the model also makes implicit assumptions about the timing a firm should use to capture its share of the value it creates by entering a particular market.

However, whenever the value of market share is threatened or the certainty of having time to get capital out of a business is low, the product portfolio is likely to be inapplicable. Abell and Hammond (1979) suggest that care is needed if value added is low; if competitors have low cost positions because of some resource or relationship that is not experienced-based; if technology is rapidly transferred among firms by equipment manufacturers or licensing, for example; or when the effects of scale are low. Patents, seasonality and cycles can also complicate the use of the portfolio concept.

Abell and Hammond (1979) and Day (1977) point out one important issue in the use of the product portfolio: market definition. Is it helicopters, heavy helicopters, or heavy military helicopters; is the geographic scope the US or the world? It's the same problem as with bread. The answer is important, of course, not simply to drawing the matrix and placing the business within it, but to helping the management of a particular firm or product line identify the relevant customers and competitors and focus effort accordingly.

Wensley (1981) makes another critical comment, applicable to most portfolio models, which relates to an implicit assumption about the firm's sources of funds. First, he points out that the portfolio approaches tend to view the corporation as an "independent cash recycling" entity. This is itself a useful model, but taken to an extreme, it may be unnecessarily constraining. If projects are sufficiently rewarding, debt or equity can be raised without earnings dilution.

Continuing, Wensley criticizes the implicit value of the "high growth business" in the BCG model. He argues that, because high growth markets generate demands for capital anyway, these businesses don't have to be highlighted. Moreover, Wensley maintains that, because the preference for high growth seems to depend upon the ease and value of gaining share, there is little evidence that share is valuable per se.

Finally, we suggest you take particular care in using product portfolio models whenever the capital intensiveness of mapped businesses differ greatly, for example, in the analysis of a multi-profit-centered company with manufacturing and service businesses such as many computer companies. Similarly be careful when the businesses you analyze enjoy the possibility of markedly different leverage: Financial service companies may have businesses leveraged 15:1 or 20:1 on an asset/equity basis, such as banks or near banks, and others whose leverage is as low as 5:1.

Remember, there is validity in the picture and in the numbers which describe the real cash flows. When dealing with diversified companies, always review the numbers on a business-by-business basis and explore any inconsistencies between numbers and pictures carefully.

To sum up, we suggest a relaxed but informed use of the models. The portfolio approaches really have stimulated managers to think about their businesses in new ways. They helped some companies purge themselves of wasteful relics of bygone ages and considerably improve their performance.

The managements of GE, Becton Dickenson, Dexter, Mead, Olin, and other companies all saw these models as valuable. In 1970, GE enjoyed a margin of 3.7 percent; by

1976 it had reached 5.9 percent and by 1984 increased to 8.2 percent. Bettis and Hall (1981) report on the performance of another portfolio user lifting its return on total capital from 6.0 to 12.9 over a period of ten years. Remember that most portfolio models were used first as marketing tools by strategy consultants. Although they contain really nothing new, they document resource deployment in a helpful way. They are the product of the creative insights of people who made fundamentals fresh and, for a time, contributed to the efficient use of internal capital. Their creators never intended that they be used alone, but as one of a set of analytical tools to help managers define better questions and talk about solutions.

SOME COMMENTS FROM USERS

William Verity, then Chairman and Chief Executive Officer of Armco Steel, described his company's application of BCG's product portfolio concept as follows:

> Obviously we want to distribute our cash . . . and assets, where they will provide the best possible return with the least possible risk exposure. The desired end result is the balanced portfolio.
>
> Portfolio management also means definition of our market position for each business as against those of our competitors . . . and delineation of cost advantage in those markets we choose to enter. Do our costs drop, as they should, as we gain experience? This is the experience curve effect, so important to portfolio management. We found that if we did not treat steel as a monolithic block but as one composed of discrete business units, which it is, we could manage it as a portfolio of business. By discrete business units we mean: "Those with clearly defined markets . . . that have their own marketing group, . . . their own manufacturing . . . and an identifiable investment in property, plant and equipment." (1975, pp. 57–58)

Loomis of Dexter commented on his use of the GE/Shell matrix:

> I was, at first, startled by the idea of forcing a distribution of one's business into the best, middle, and worst thirds and then looking upon the bottom third as a source of capital for the top two-thirds of one's portfolio. At the time that seemed like dropping the baby off the back end of the sled to prevent the wolves from running down the horses. However, as inflation takes bigger and bigger bites of capital, more firms are finding that they lack the resources to expand all of their businesses. Divestiture and liquidation are rational alternatives. (1980, p. 8)

Howe of Becton Dickinson, which employed the ADL model in the late 1970s, described the objectives as follows:

> The overall objective of the system is to maintain a strategic balance at the late growth stage. That means we must build or acquire enough new and early-growth businesses to offset the natural maturing of our existing portfolio. With its portfolio balanced at the late growth phase, the substantial cash flow from mature businesses should equal the cash needs of embryonic and early-growth ones, thus balancing the

company's overall investment requirements. In addition, profits increase most dramatically at the late growth stage. With the entire company poised at that point, it should be able to achieve its primary financial objective—a sustainable average of 15 percent annual growth in earnings per share.

With care, the product portfolio can be used to identify or design links between the operating units of a diversified corporation. Properly used in situations where its assumptions are met, it can provide good information to a manager, helping him or her add value while managing diversification. The product portfolio focuses management's attention on resource deployments and in this way is a major managerial aid in corporate strategy identification, as we will show in the next chapter.

chapter 19

Identifying Corporate Strategies

INTRODUCTION

Since corporate strategy is what corporations do to get what they want, we will focus on what they are doing and use that knowledge to identify the corporate strategy and infer its objectives, so that ultimately we can determine whether change is warranted. As we noted in our discussion of single-business companies, it is difficult to modify a company's present strategy and do so *responsibly* until you know what you are doing and how well it is working. Again, this means you have to identify your strategy before you fix it and, we suggest, in order to know whether it needs fixing. Identification is the starting point for any discussion of corporate strategy.

Let us define an approach for indentifying strategies at any level: To identify the strategy of any level, look down at its parts and seek the interrelationships between them; strategy will be revealed by these interrelationships. At the *business* level, we look down to the functions, infer their objectives, and seek interrelationships between them. At the *corporate* level, we look to the businesses of the firm, infer their objectives, and seek interrelations between them. At the *business* level, we exploit *functional analysis*. At the *corporate* level, we turn to *business analysis*. And, as we did when we identified a business's strategy from its functional actions and objectives, at the corporate level we will move from analysis to synthesis, from the separate actions of the businesses of the firm to the integrative objectives and relationships that bind them to the whole corporation.

BUSINESS ANALYSIS

As noted, the purpose of business analysis is to highlight the key relationships between the businesses of the corporation so that we can synthesize its strategy. What are these relationships?

Research on diversification suggests that industry choice is critical, that the growth strategy and relatedness are important, and that the administrative discipline which guides strategy implementation and the deployment of resources is a major determinant of success. *Figure 19-1* lists these four components and suggests some guidelines and caveats that are well-founded in research. We note that these four components encompass Ansoff's (1965) components of corporate strategy: Product-market scope, the growth factor, synergy, and competitive advantage. Ansoff suggested that these components plus the corporate objectives defined the concept of the firm's business. As noted in Chapter 17, research since 1965 has confirmed the wisdom of his choices. Competitive advantage is included here under the heading Industry Choice because we believe that it is foolish for a corporation to enter a business where it enjoys no advantage and is unlikely to attain it. Relatedness is the potential source of synergy, although experience suggests that synergy is elusive and difficult to attain. We add administrative discipline because it is the lynchpin between strategic design and implementation.

In business analysis, we examine all of the corporation's businesses—how it entered them, manages them, and deploys its assets between them. Analagous to functional analysis, business analysis structures data to highlight patterns of behavior and the relationships across businesses which reveal corporate strategy. Portfolio deployments of funds, using the idea of some business activities funding others, will guide our analysis.

Figure 19-2 provides a framework for business analysis which encompasses the components of corporate strategy, although it may require customized adaptation to suit particular needs. Note that the character of the corporation and its repeated actions suggest areas of emphasis within the business analysis framework. For an aggressively diversify-

FIGURE 19-1 Components of Corporate Strategy

Industry Choice (product-market scope)
- Keep it narrow.
- Focus.
- Enter where you have or can develop a competitive advantage.

Growth: Acquisition or Internal
- They're different.
- Acquisitions are risky.
- Diversification is risky.

Relatedness
- Synergy is elusive—and is a result of management.
- Stick close to what you know.
- Develop your distinctive competences.

Administrative Discipline
- Redeploy your assets from low-return to high-return opportunities.
- Manage risk: Limit to what you can absorb, or share it.
- Share power so that decisions can be made by those with the information to make them.

		Business	#1	#2	#3	#4	#5 ...
Entry/Growth							
Industry Characteristics							
Management	Marketing						
	Operations						
	Resource Deployment						
	Administrative Discipline						
Results							
Business Objectives							

FIGURE 19-2 Identifying the Corporate Strategy: Business Analysis

ing corporation, we might pay particular attention to the condition of the target company and the target industry at entry. For a company whose product-market mix has been stable for many years, we might emphasize operations more than entry and be careful to understand the degree and type of vertical integration the company employs. For a high-technology company, we might specify technology and research function more closely.

Note, too, that consistent patterns of resource deployments and results point to sound administrative strategies. If they are inconsistent, some closer examination of administrative practices is warranted.

In using *Figure 19-2,* we suggest that you track the diversification of the firm over time, that you seek patterns in entry strategy and the principal economic characteristics of the target industries. Under the heading Management, look for patterns which indicate marketing and operating relatedness and try to explain the firm's resource deployments in the light of the results earned and objectives sought. Many diversified firms' activities will be characterized by market relatedness or integrated operations or financial asset redeployment; only very large, mature, and successful firms, like General Electric, are likely to use the three types of managerial interrelatedness concurrently.

Figure 19-3 details the preceding framework and suggests the types of data required for a complete analysis. *Figure 19-4* lists a set of questions you might address once the basic descriptive data are collected. As in the case of the single-business firm, we should expect the objectives of the separable businesses to reveal much of the corporate strategy.

		Business	#1	#2	#3	#4	#5 ...
Entry/Growth		Entry Year Scale of Entry Acquisition/Internal Condition Terms					
Industry Characteristics		Average ROA Leader Share Sales Growth Profit Variance Key to Success Number of Competitors Key Competitor(s) Risk Sources					
Management	Marketing	Customers Product/Service Price Promotion Place-Channel					
	Operations	Sources Product Technology Process Technology Number of Plants Scale Value Added Productivity Integration					
	Resource Deployment	Percent of Assets Committed Internal Investment Personnel Quality					
	Administrative Discipline	Locus of Power Investment Criteria Performance Rewards Nature of Controls					
Results		ROA Relative Share Growth Profit Variance Technical Strength Competitive Strength					
Business Objectives		Stated Objectives					
		Unstated/Enacted Objectives					

FIGURE 19-3 Identifying Corporate Strategy: Business Analysis Detailed Information

FIGURE 19-4 Identifying the Corporate Strategy

1. What are the firm's businesses?
2. How has the firm entered those businesses? By acquisition or internal development?
3. What common characteristics are shared by the businesses? For example, along the industry chain, are there common suppliers, competitors, or customers; perhaps similar marketing or operations strategies? Are there shared resources, joint effects, or other managed synergies?
4. Are the businesses integrated in any way? By ownership, business relationships, or operations?
5. How are the firm's resources deployed? How are they being redeployed? How do the resource deployments trade off risk for reward?
6. Business by business, what are the results and how does the firm react to them?
7. Are the firm's resources being deployed in a manner consistent with the results earned and the potential earnings of each business?
8. What are the roles of headquarters and divisional management? How does power vary by business and function? How is control exercised?
9. What are the objectives of each business? How do the objectives of each business relate, one to the other?
10. What does the pattern of objectives mean? Looking down from the corporate level, what is the strategy they add up to?

THE HIERARCHY OF OBJECTIVES AND STRATEGIES

The corporation is partly, perhaps principally, coordinated by the hierarchy of strategy and objectives. In corporations, higher-level strategies define lower-level objectives in the same way that business strategy "defined" functional objectives and the synthesized "sum" of the functional objectives specified the strategy.

Remember, too, an important feature of strategic analysis: What looks like a strategy from above is likely to be seen as a set of objectives from below. Top management's strategy defines the objectives of those who report to them. Middle management's objectives are to implement the top management's strategy. Middle management's actions are means to ends, specified in turn by higher-level means and ends. Thus, the corporation's actions are coordinated by a hierarchical chain of means and ends which we call strategies and objectives.

BUSINESS ANALYSIS FOR A DIVERSIFIED CORPORATION: THE BIC CORPORATION

Let us examine one small, moderately diversified company, the Bic Corporation, to illustrate business analysis. Bic, well known for its ballpoint pens, disposable lighters, and razors, has for many years been an increasingly pressing and successful competitor of Gillette.

Put yourself in the position of the general manager of Gillette's razor division. Now for the first time you have a personal stake in the outcome of Gillette's competition with Bic. An important question for you is: What is Bic's strategy?

To answer this question, we will first outline Bic's history, describing its operations and its efforts to diversify. Then we will use the frameworks for functional and business analysis to identify Bic's corporate strategy so that we will be able to better understand its strategy in the razor business.

In 1958, Marcel Bich, a successful French businessman, acquired the Waterman Pen Company in Waterbury, Connecticut. Waterman was a troubled company whose product, fountain pens, had been declining for many years. Bich was the French manufacturer of low-priced, throwaway ballpoint pens, and he intended to produce ballpoints in the Waterbury plant.

Between 1958 and 1964, the Bic Pen Corporation (USA) lost money. But although it was losing money, Bic was building market share, a distribution channel, and a brand image. In 1961, Bic cut the price of its original crystal pen from 29¢ to 19¢ and began to promote its product more heavily. In essence, Bic had converted the Waterbury plant to ballpoint pens, developed its manufacturing capabilities as the crystal pen's sales increased, and invested some of the resulting cash flow in promotion. During this period, the French parent presumably subsidized its US offspring. By 1964, however, Bic broke even and then achieved an after-tax profit of 26.6 percent in 1975.

During the seven years between 1958 and 1965, Bic had matched its mass production capabilities with a mass marketing capability. It had developed a brand name and two distinct channels of distribution—the first through the ma and pa stores of America and the second through the then rapidly growing discount retail chains. In addition, the Bic Company had mastered the use of television mass advertising to complete its conquest of the American pen market.

Figure 19-5 is our functional analysis of Bic Corporation, circa 1972. At this point Bic was a ballpoint pen company. We have already outlined the marketing strategy of the company but it is important to note the sophisticated manufacturing strategy adopted by Bic. Its cost position was low and the company had in fact used almost every opportunity available to reduce its costs, including, you may note, the adoption of stable and secure employment conditions for its workers (in many ways, Bic has been managed like a Japanese company or perhaps as a Z-type organization). Under the heading Finance, we can note that Bic at this time was highly liquid, with about one year's operating cash flow on hand. It had no budgets, yet was tightly controlled. The explanation, of course, lies in its management practices. Bic's was an informally managed but tightly knit family of managers who enjoyed close personal supervision by their President, Robert Adler, and Marcel Bich.

Function by function, Bic's objectives can be readily inferred. Marketing strove for volume, manufacturing for a low cost position subject to meeting all product specifications. The financial objective appears to have been to ensure that funds were available for investment when needed, while the management objective was to maintain a low-cost, flexible, controlled corporation. Bic's strategy at this time was to be a ballpoint pen company operating at high volume, low cost, constantly reinvesting to improve both its volume and cost positions while managing itself as leanly as possible.

The reinvestment into promotion stimulated volume by "pulling" product into the market. Its constant reinvestment in manufacturing combined with its volume production

FIGURE 19-5 Functional Analysis: Bic Pen Corporation, 1973

Marketing	*Operations/Productions*	*Finance*	*Management*
Market: Retail Big commercial share in crystals **(not porous in '73)** *Product:* Quality ballpoint pens *Price:* Cut in 1961 Products low-priced 19¢ pen stable '61-'72 *Promotion:* Explosive introduction Emphasis on "Bic" name Heavy introduction use of TV Point of purchase advertising Jobbers and company salesforce Discounts, etc. *Distribution:* Two-channel -Direct to mass market -indirect to *old* base Ma and Pa stores (NB, 19¢ retail receipt 8.5¢ to manufacturer)	*Plant:* Single plant *Process:* Highly automated and integrated (brass bought from France) *Cost Position: Recipe for Low Cost:* -Integrated -Automated assembly -Invest to cut costs -Simple line -Standard parts -Simplified design -Relatively specialized -Intense quality control by workers (25%) -Smoothed production -Inventory buffer *Labor:* Unionized (rubber) Secure jobs: no layoffs Promotion within Retraining/Flexible use Wages high Family recruiting Experienced Workers	*Source:* Earned *Liquidity:* Very high *Dividend:* 25% payout EPS (Earnings per Share): Smooth growth No budgets No R&D	*Structure:* Informal Tightknit family Big bonuses Few rank differences Information widely shared Understaffed Personal control by Bich and Adley
Volume	+ Specified Quality at Low Cost	+ Funds Available	+ Control at Low Cost

Source: Data from Bic Annual reports

cut costs and gave the company an ability to keep its prices low and stable. This helped "push" product into the distribution channels and so to the market.

Bic had developed a consistent and tightly knit business strategy in the pen business. In 1973, however, it became apparent that the crystal pen's sales had begun to decline: Its market share had fallen from 36 percent in early 1972 to 31 percent by 1973. Bic's response was to introduce a series of new products in relatively quick succession. As *Figure 19-6* shows, the company added porous pens in late 1972, disposable lighters in 1973, pantyhose in 1974, and the disposable razor in 1976. It is significant to note that over this period of time, Bic's self-concept changed from ballpoint pens to writing instruments; then to the manufacturer and marketer of everyday, throwaway, mass pro-

FIGURE 19-6 Product & Concept Evolution—Bic Pen Corporation (USA)

Year	*Product Added*	*Corporate Concept*
1958	Crystal ballpoint pen	A ballpoint pen company
1968	Clic retractable ballpoint pen	
1972	Porous pen	A writing instrument company
1973	Disposable lighter	A company in the inexpensive, disposable, mass produced, high-quality goods business distributed through writing instrument channels.
1974	Pantyhose	A marketing company
1976	Disposable razor	

duced, high-quality, low-priced goods distributed through writing instrument channels; and finally, to a marketing company.

Let us look at Bic's performance, the results. *Figure 19-7* shows Bic's sales, profits, and profit margin between 1964 and 1973. Note the flat sales and earnings over the period 1969 to 1971. The subsequent results point to the reason for diversification: To stimulate the continuing growth of the company.

But note that in 1968, 1972, and 1973, the years when new product lines were introduced by the company, profit margins fell. The estimated pretax margins for each

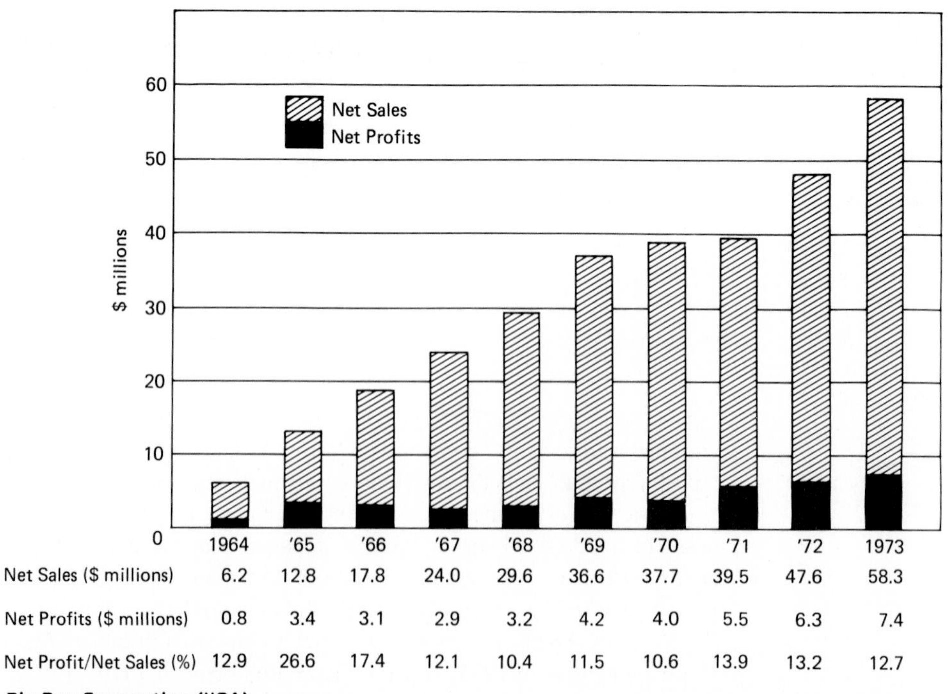

	1964	'65	'66	'67	'68	'69	'70	'71	'72	1973
Net Sales ($ millions)	6.2	12.8	17.8	24.0	29.6	36.6	37.7	39.5	47.6	58.3
Net Profits ($ millions)	0.8	3.4	3.1	2.9	3.2	4.2	4.0	5.5	6.3	7.4
Net Profit/Net Sales (%)	12.9	26.6	17.4	12.1	10.4	11.5	10.6	13.9	13.2	12.7

FIGURE 19-7 Bic Pen Corporation (USA)

Source: BIC Pen Corporation Annual Report, 1973

TABLE 19-1 Estimated Profit Margins: Bic Pen Corporation (USA) (c. 1974)

Product	*Profitability*
Crystal pen	>30%
Clic pen	≤10%
Porous pen	≃30%
Lighter	15-21%
Hose	15%

product line, circa 1974, are estimated in *Table 19-1*. These estimates suggest that each time the Bic company diversified, its profit margin declined.

One explanation of this profit decline is the presence of competition. In its later product introductions Bic confronted more established and more significant competition. Its crystal pen had been introduced into the market against no-name brands at a time when the Scripto Company withdrew from the low-priced pen market, allowing Bic a window to enter. Its porous pen, in contrast, confronted Gillette's Flair which then enjoyed a 45 percent share of the porous pen market. Its lighter again confronted Gillette. At the time of Bic's entry, Gillette's Cricket held one-third of all disposable lighter sales.

Are there other explanations for Bic's decline in profitability? *Figure 19-8* shows Bic's products on a generic life cycle curve. Referring to *Table 19-1*, we can see that Bic's early products are profitable and its late products appear to have been less successful. There appears to be some correlation between Bic's time of entry to the market and its long-run profitability, as shown at the top of *Figure 19-9*. Bic's profitability appears to be dependent upon its market share, as the lower part of *Figure 19-9* suggests. As *Table 19-2* shows, since 1972 Bic has become an increasingly alert and timely competitor, entering the market for razors virtually coincidentally with Gillette's introduction of disposable razors.

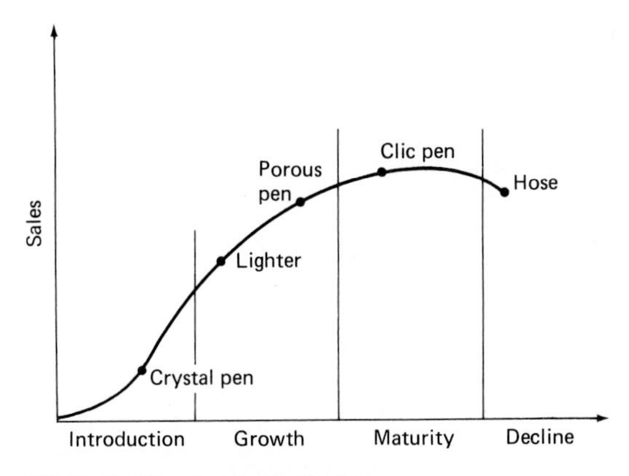

FIGURE 19-8 Life Cycle Stages, Bic Products

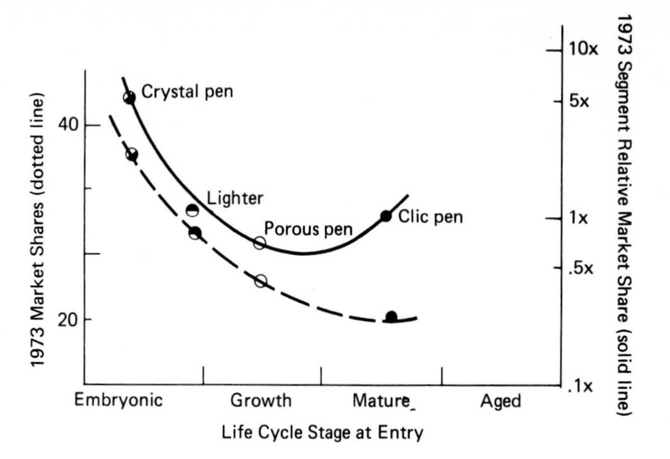

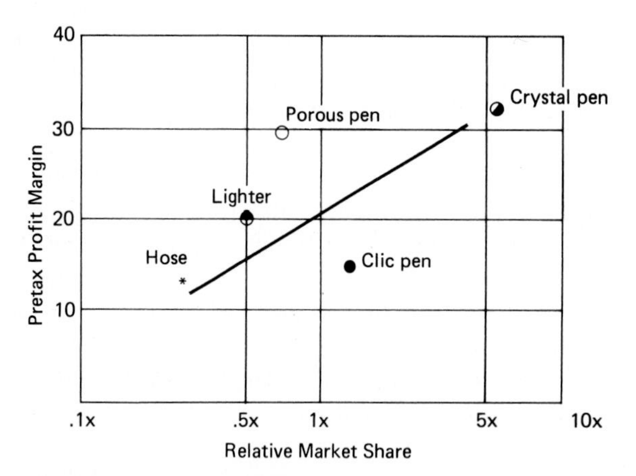

FIGURE 19-9 **Bic's Performance (c. 1973)**
Source: Data from Bic annual reports

TABLE 19-2 **Time of Bic Entry Compared with Leader**

Bic Products	*Bic Entry*	*Time after Competitor's Market Entry*
Porous pen	1972	6 years
Lighter	1973	2 years
Hose	1974	1 year
Razor	1976	6 weeks

TABLE 19-3 Financial Results: Bic (USA)

Year	*Sales*	*ROA*	*Leverage*	*ROE*	*EPS*
1972	47.6mil	18.8	1.14	21.5	1.00
1973	58.3	17.8	1.15	20.5	1.15
1974	74.5	11.6	1.30	15.1	.96
1975	93.0	11.2	1.46	16.4	1.16
1976	122.8	12.1	1.60	19.3	1.55
1977	134.8	6.9	1.72	11.9	1.06
1978	153.6	7.4	1.84	13.6	1.31
1979	179.0	6.8	1.91	13.0	1.36
1980	192.0	8.8	1.86	16.4	1.91
1981	217.7	5.4	1.83	9.9	1.27
1982	218.1	5.0	1.66	8.3	1.11

Source: Data from Bic annual reports

Table 19-3 shows some additional financial results for Bic. Note how Bic's return on assets is falling, although its return on equity was generally maintained until 1981. The company has continued to grow and, for many years, its shareholders have enjoyed higher earnings, in spite of the profit margin declines we have seen.

A Changing Strategy

Let us consider how Bic's corporate strategy changed. In *Figure 19-10* we take the Framework for Business Analysis and apply it to the Bic Pen Corporation. The first line shows how Bic entered each of its product lines in the US. The entry to the US market was by acquisition from France, the crystal and porous pens were developed from French products but inside the US market. However, the fourth, fifth, and sixth products—lighters, pantyhose, and razors—were all initially imported to the US from other Bich-owned companies.

Moving to the next line, Industry Characteristics, we can note, as we observed before, that Bic is entering the market against more established and significant competitors, and, in the case of the last three products, against competitors who view lighters, pantyhose, and razors as increasingly important parts of their respective business.

Under Marketing, we can see that Bic introduced its first three products to the market at low prices. With the second three, Bic's initial prices more closely matched those of its competitors. With the first three products, its relative advertising expenditure was high compared to the competition, while with the last three, Bic's relative advertising intensity was lower.

Under Operations, we note that Bic manufactured the first three products in the United States, while it purchased the latter three products from the French company or its subsidiaries. Under Resource Deployments, in the case of the first three products, Bic was essentially self-financing from 1964 on. In the case of lighters, pantyhose, and razors, however, the Bic Company increasingly relied on debt to fund its business development. Leverage increased from 1.15 times equity in 1973 to 1.6 times equity in 1976, the year

		Crystal pen	Clic pen	Porous pen	Lighter	Hose	Razor
Entry/ Growth	Year	1958	1968	1972	1973	1974	1975
	Scale	Large	Medium	Large	Small	Small	Small
	Method	Acquisition Turnaround	Internal	Internal	Import	Import	Import
Industry Characteristics		No-Name's Limited capitaliza-tion Scripto leaving low end	Established brands	Gillette has 50% market	3 majors, Gillette holds 30%	3 majors, largest holds 9% Shrinking industry	Gillette has 55% ROA and very dominant share (gives razors away)
Management	Marketing	Low price High relative advertising	Low price High relative advertising	Low price Equal Advertising	Equal price Small relative advertising	Equal price Small relative advertising	Equal price Small relative advertising
	Operations	Single, highly automated plant	Same plant	Same plant	Importing from French parent, later own plant	Importing from French parent	Importing from French parent, later own plant
	Resource Deployment	Initial subsidy from French parent	Self-financed	Self-financed	Marketing investments only until position established	Marketing only	Marketing only until market position established
	Administrative Discipline	Pace of diversification controlled by French parent					
Results		Sales rising, margin and ROA falling, market position well-established, a dominant or #2 competitor. Company has achieved low-cost position technically dependent on French parent.					
Business Objectives		Growth has been given priority over profitability, moving company into a negative leverage position on sub-stantial short-term loans. EPS growth sustained with leverage until 1981.					

FIGURE 19-10 Business Analysis—The BIC Corporation (USA)

Source: Data from Bic annual reports

FIGURE 19-11 Bic's Competitive Advantages Through 1974

	Crystal Pen	Clic Pen	Porous Pen	Lighter	Hose
Quality	+	=	−	=	?
Price	+	=/+	+/−	=	−/=
Cost	+	+	+	=/?	=/−
Promotion	+	+	+/=	+	−
Distribution	+	+	+/=	+/=	−
Number of Competitors	5	6	Gillette and others	Gillette and others	Burlington Kayser/Roth Hanes

Bic introduced its disposable razor to the US market, reaching a high point of 1.9 times equity in 1979.

In *Figure 19-11,* we show the pattern of competitive advantages which a group of executives believed held for Bic's product line in the marketplace. You may note that above the diagonal line the signs are predominantly negative (''disadvantage Bic'') while below the lines the signs are generally positive (''advantage Bic''). Although not a perfect pattern, this is evidence which we believe means that each time Bic has diversified, there has been a tendency for it to lose competitive advantages. And, we note that it was losing those advantages in a market of increasingly well-funded and increasingly aggressive competitors, such as the Hanes company in the hosiery market and Gillette in razors. The Bic company appears to have moved into an increasingly risky competitive situation while at the same time adopting an increasingly risky debt position.

Before we proceed, let us note two other factors. First, the Bic company has continued to grow and its earnings per share continued to increase until 1981. Second, we might wonder whether the company's asset commitments were as risky as they might appear to the casual observer. However, note in *Figure 19-10* that since 1973 Bic's entry to the market with new products has been as a distributor of imported products only. As one company executive said at the time, ''Bic USA has increasingly become a marketing company.''

Obviously, Bic is using its basic strategy but adapting it to a particular market. Its results are not clear. Without completing the section on Business Objectives in detail, we can note that the company gave growth priority over profits. We can suspect that the early products were being used to help fund the development of later products and that for some reason, the corporation decided that earnings per share growth warranted a risky financial profile, since returns on assets dropped from 12.1 percent in 1976 to 6.8 percent in 1979, and to 5 percent in 1982 as the company's use of debt expanded.

In 1982, the Bic Company had very little long-term debt, but carried $42.8 million of ''notes payable—bank'' on its balance sheet, an amount equivalent to approximately 28.4 percent of its total assets. By this time the company's short-term debt position had placed it in a position of negative leverage, with the company earning less on its debt-financed assets than it was paying to its banks. The company's average interest rate on its outstanding balance during 1982 was 14 percent, that is, nine percentage points greater than its ROA.

Summary

With this in mind, let us think carefully about summarizing Bic's strategy as a corporation, and, in particular, let us return to our imagined Gillette general manager and think about the advice we could offer him or her about Bic's activities in the razor business. Bic is a diversified company. As its old products decay in the market place, Bic has introduced new products to sustain the growth of the company. Its old products, in part, fund the development of the market of the new products, in the classical cow to wildcat cashflow. As *Figure 19-12* shows, the crystal pen division's success has funded in large measure the development of the porous pen, lighters, hose, and razor businesses, moving them one by one to the left side of the matrix in the late 1970s and 1980s.

However, the company has not done this alone. Underpinning the Bic Company's US activity is its relationships with its French parent. The Bic Company has entered the market as a distributor of European (Société Bic) manufactured products. Recall that when Bic USA's market position for a particular product reaches what we call efficient scale, the company has invested in US-based manufacturing plant and severed its trading

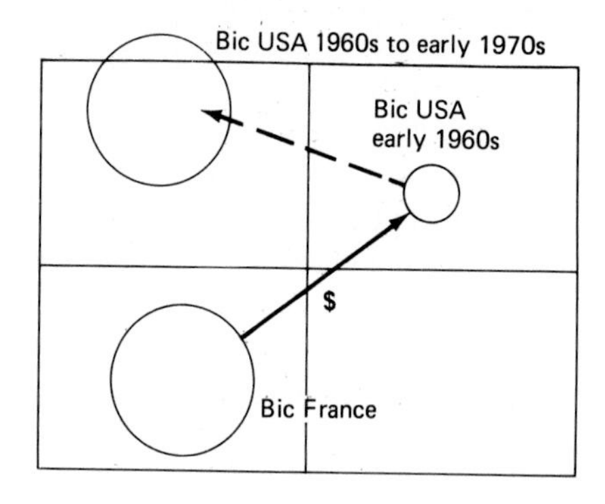

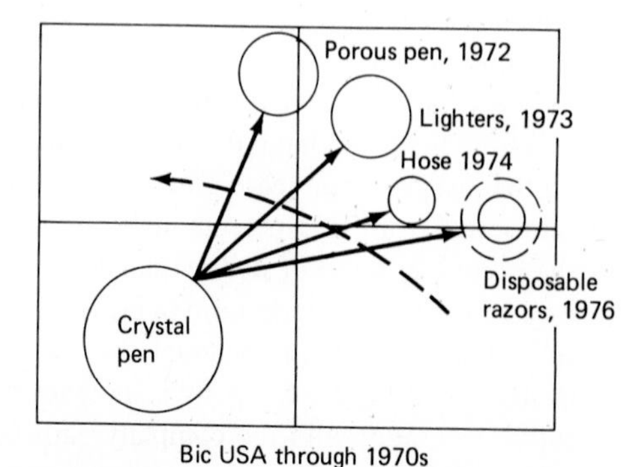

FIGURE 19-12 Portfolio Views of Bic

Source: Data from Bic annual reports

relationship with the French for that product. Essentially, Baron Bich reduces the risk of market entry by backloading capacity, that is, creating production capacity in the US *only after the market has been developed.* Bic USA is, in fact, part of a global corporation.

What do we tell the Gillette executive? He is competing with a company that is more than it seems. He is not competing with Bic USA but with the international resources of Société Bic. To properly hone his strategy, we could suggest that Gillette compete, not as a US-based company in the razor business, but as global merchandiser.

In Chapter 20, we will extend our examination to the global strategy of the Société Bic and consider its implications for Gillette's razor business.

chapter 20

International Competition and the Evolution of Global Businesses

INTRODUCTION

In Chapter 19, we completed our discussion of the diversification strategy of the Bic Corporation, the US member of Marcel Bich's international corporate empire. Indeed, the French presence is a significant part of Bic USA. The Bich family and Société Bic controlled 72 percent of the Bic Corporation as of March 1, 1983. The directors and officers of the Bic Corporation held an additional 7 percent of the corporation and the public the remainder. The Société Bic is a global business, and Bic Corporation is its US manufacturing arm and to a lesser extent one of its important distribution channels.

The Bic Corporation's existence in the United States, as *Figure 20-1* reminds us, stems from the early investments of its French parent. Recall that from 1958 to 1964 the then Bic Pen Corporation lost money, although it was growing. The French company has always controlled the R&D activity of Baron Bich's companies, presumably increasing the margin in the USA. The French company has always been a supplier to Bic USA, supplying the brass points of the crystal pen and later, as we have noted, lighters, hose, and razors—at least until the Bic Pen Corporation's US market position warranted fixed asset investments.

Global corporations play a different and broader competitive game than do purely national companies. We have already noted that Bic (USA) suffered a return on asset decline during the late 1970s and early 1980s, possibly exposing it to negative leverage, apparently as a cost of growth. However, we suggested that the risk associated with its growth was moderated by the relationships, both ownership and trading, between the French company and its US subsidiary. The ultimate challenge for our imaginary Gillette executive is to increase his understanding of Société Bic and to develop his own strategy for the Gillette razor business in light of that understanding. For a moment, then, let us

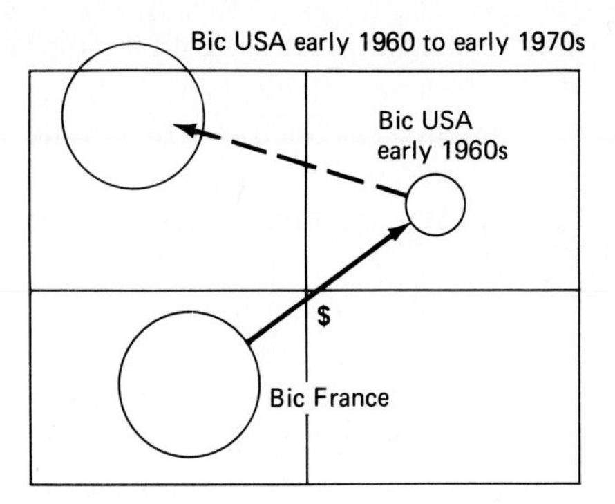

FIGURE 20-1 The Strategic Evolution of the Bic Group, Step 1
Source: Data from Bic annual reports

consider the implications of international competition and then turn to the evolution of Société Bic, S.A. as a global competitor.

THE GLOBAL CORPORATION

In his book, *My Years at General Motors,* Alfred Sloan wrote, ''Again let me say that companies compete in broad policies as well as in specific products'' (1964). The essence of a global competitor is that it views the world as one market, and positions itself to use all of its resources to become an effective competitor in that market. In Sloan's terms, it is competing with different policies than those of national firms. Such global strategies pose some particular problems for the managers of both the global company and its competitors, particularly those competitors who are essentially multinational, that is, companies who define competition in terms of discrete national markets.

A number of factors cause concern for managers engaged in global competition. First, global companies may be integrated by ownership, long-term sourcing contracts and trading relationships, R&D contracts, or board representation, for example (Williamson, 1975). Their perspective is necessarily broader and longer than simply national markets or single products in the short run.

Second, because of their global scope, these companies must address the concerns of wider constituent groups. Their stakeholder sets cross national boundaries and may include, to a greater extent than those of most U.S. companies, the governments of host countries. Indeed, state-owned enterprises may be suppliers, customers, and competitors simultaneously, and national competitors may be helped by product or employment regulations from their native governments, in addition to direct subsidization.

Third, the global nature of the enterprise complicates the task of business definition. In a global enterprise, the welfare of the whole must be given prominence over the welfare of the parts. Each business must be defined and managed in such a way as to make it as effective a competitor as possible, no matter who its competitors are and wherever they might be. Only in special circumstances, however, will the company's full competitive pressure be exerted simultaneously worldwide. It is more likely to be orchestrated market by market, and business by business, to maximize the value of the (parent) company as a whole. A worldwide competitive initiative at full strength is only practical when the resources available are enormous relative to the competition. In other circumstances, value is more likely to result from prudent and limited risk-taking across an interdependent set of markets, rather than across all.

Fourth, business definition and performance measurement go hand in hand. When interpreting the strategies and evaluating the competitive performance of the divisions or subsidiaries of a global enterprise, it is dangerous to place too much weight upon short-term results, for example, product level returns on assets (ROA). This caveat applies both to the firm's managers and to competitors. It is the performance of the enterprise as a whole and its long-run return on assets that counts more, and one of the best indicators of long-run performance is relative competitive strength. In a market where a globally oriented company is active and at low profit rates, the prudent competitor will pay particular attention to the development of local market strengths and international cost positions.

Fifth, global companies will for the most part work at efficient scale, that is, at efficient worldwide scale. In some markets, the scale of the enterprise will necessitate large domestic as well as export sales; in others exports will be used to lift local production to an efficient scale within a domestic or multicountry regional market. Market by market around the world, a global company will operate only world-scale efficient plants.

Let us note here that world scale applies to the current state of the art and to the technologies of production, not to worldwide demand. An alternative concept is a world standard cost advantage. Such a plant may, in fact, be capable of supplying only a region of a country, if that country is as large as the US; or it may be able to supply as much as half of Europe. World-scale production does not mean one plant but may involve many specialized and efficient-scale plants in a complex system of component production, transfer pricing, and assembly, taking advantage of technology and volume production while maintaining the political independence of the global enterprise.

Sixth, in a global enterprise, the ownership, administrative, and planning structures of a company are unlikely to be coincident across countries and businesses. This will complicate the administrative task of management at every level, particularly for those outside the strategy-formulating cadre of managers. Professional success for middle managers will likely depend on the ability to understand the reasons for the resource allocation and priorities given to their part of the whole corporation, yet it is unlikely that they will ever be privy to the true strategy of the enterprise. In essence, the middle managers of a company like Bic are in the same spot as the managers of Gillette: they have to determine for themselves what Bic's strategy is, and act accordingly.

Seventh, in a global enterprise, the company's regional and national investment strategies are likely to be conditioned by the status of the international currency markets. Exchange rates may affect the timing at which financial and competitive strength is built in certain markets. Repatriations of profits and redeployments of funds around the world are complicated by shifting exchange rates, although the need for profit repatriation can be modified by trading among corporate components and by shifting transfer prices in response to government action, tax policies, or internal interest rates. While these fiscal practices may mask the real competitive strategies of the enterprise, they demonstrate the impact of the widened stakeholder net on the pace of strategy implementation for the global corporation.

Société Bic: Global Operations

Let us now return to the Bic Corporation, broadening our analysis of a diversifying firm in Chapter 18 to that of a global competitor. In *Figure 20-1,* we showed the initial redeployment of funds from Société Bic, the French company, into the US market. In *Figure 20-2,* we show the relative status of the French company and its US subsidiary in the mid-1970s. Now let us return to the Framework for Business Analysis and consider how the Bic has evolved globally (*Figure 20-3*).

The French company was established in 1945 by Marcel Bich and his friend Edouard Bouffard in what was essentially a classical "garage type" entrepreneurial start-up, with capital of about $1000. The initial business was not ballpoint pens but ballpoint pen refills. It wasn't until Bich got the idea that a disposable pen would need no refills that the company began to look like the Bic Company of today.

In 1958, Bich acquired the Waterman Pen Company in Waterbury, Connecticut, a classic turnaround situation. The porous pen line appears to have been an internal development prompted in large measure by the management of Bic Pen US, suffering at the hands of Gillette's Flair. The decision concerning disposable lighters dates back to 1971 and Bich's purchase of Flaminaire, a French company. It is said that his objective was to market a substitute for matches, which were not freely available in Europe. The French business supplied the US for some years. In 1973, Bich took control of DIM S.A.—a $100-million company and the leading French hosiery maker—and, in 1974, began to supply the US market with pantyhose. Around 1975, Bich bought a Greek razor factory and again began to supply the US market.

In essence, we see a pattern which is production-driven. Acquisitions are followed by turnarounds founded upon volume built up both in a domestic market and interna-

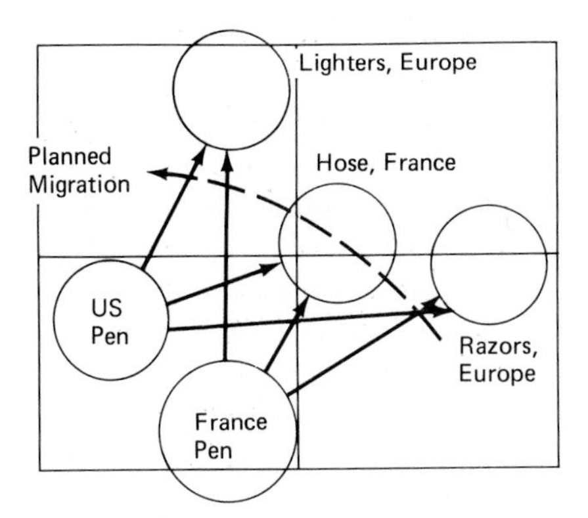

FIGURE 20-2 The Strategic Evolution of the Bic Group, Step 2
Source: Data from Bic annual reports

FIGURE 20-3 Business Analysis: Société Bic

	Pens		*Lighters*		*Hose*		*Razors*	
	France	*US*	*France*	*US*	*France*	*US*	*France*	*US*
Entry/Growth	1945 Garage start-up	1958 Acquisition turnaround subsidized by French parent	1971	1973 Acquisition turnaround French investments strengthened by US market distribution	1973	1974	1975	1976
Industry Characteristics	Weak competitors			Gillette	Largest in France		Gillette	
Management		Uses volume to achieve a low cost position and invests in cost improvements and promotion to strengthen market position, to build profitability. Initial profits sometimes take up to 7 years to achieve.						
Results		Worldwide sales and profit are rising. Company is achieving efficient scale production with a relative cost advantage, plant by plant.						
Business Objectives		Seizes opportunities to buy European manufacturers of low cost, disposable products. Uses US to build volume and gain manufacturing efficiencies in Europe. If US market position warrants world-scale plant, builds plant in US to exploit opportunity.						

Source: Data from Bic annual reports

tionally, particularly in the US. Where the US market has proven penetrable and of sufficient scale, Bich has later invested in manufacturing facilities to take full advantage of the business opportunity inherent to the market position created by his import distribution strategy.

Essentially, under Industry Characteristics *Figure 20-3,* we could suspect that Bich has always taken advantage of market trends. He has tended to enter markets when other companies leave them. He has been able to turn them around because he has been able to replicate his basic marketing and production strategies, business by business, country by country, around the world. In many ways, Baron Bich operates and manages his companies in a now-classical ''Japanese'' way: he has used his domestic market and export sales to reach efficient scale, to provide secure employment conditions, and to build brand recognition, in an integrated and consistent effort to turn competence to competitive advantage.

Bich's resource deployments, however, suggest his true business acumen. In *Figure 20-4,* we show a more complex series of portfolio charts which can help us track Bic's redeployment of its funds and, more importantly, its evolution as a global competitor.

Figure 20-4(a) shows Bic France and with it, the development of Bic (USA) through the early 1970s. Essentially, over time, the French investment converted a wildcat into a star. In *Figure 20-4(b)*, we show the Bic (USA) subsidiary alone, with its crystal pen in the apparent cash cow position for a sequence of new product introductions—porous pens, lighters, hose, and razors. The corporate objective appears to have been to convert these wildcats into stars.

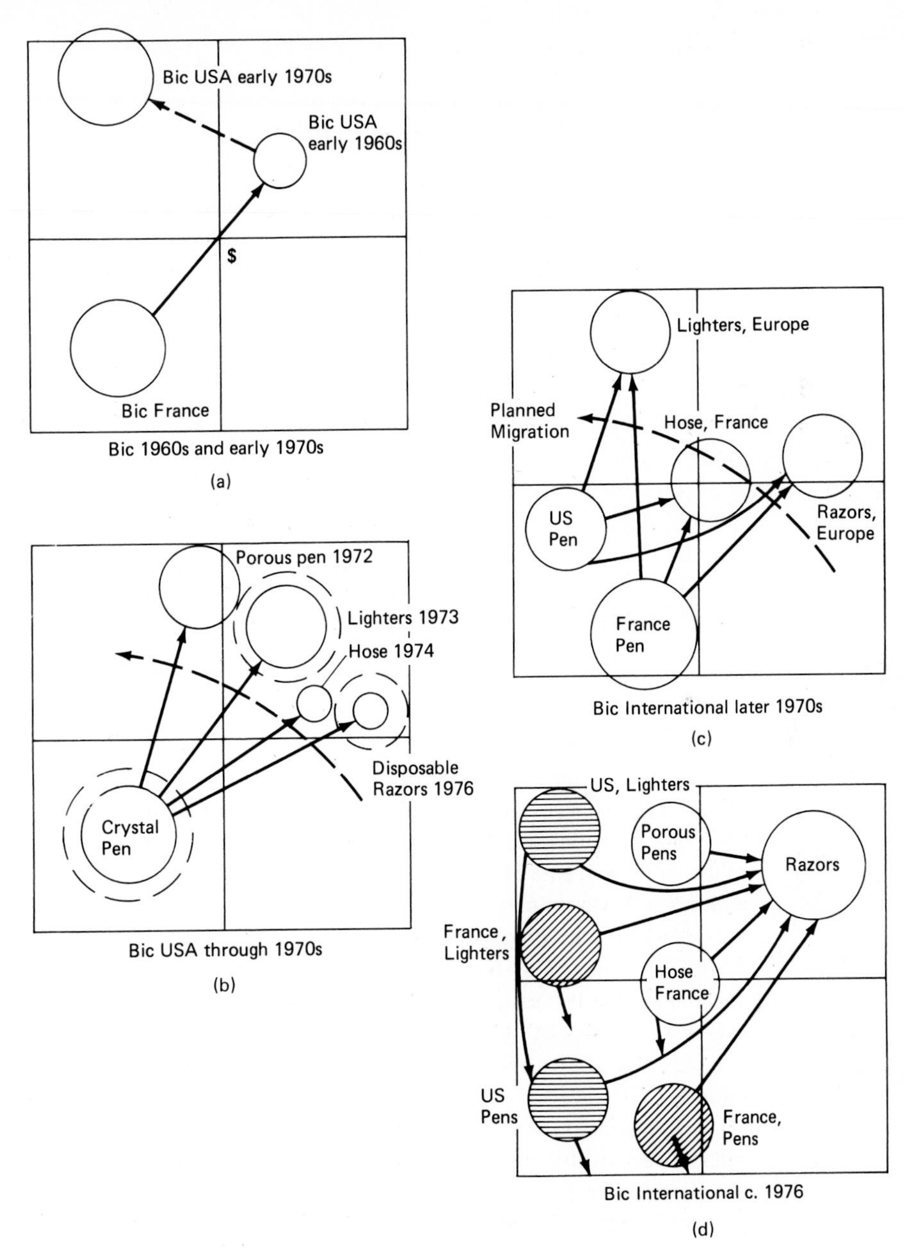

FIGURE 20-4 The Strategic Evolution of the Bic Group
Source: Data from Bic annual reports

Let us now take the perspective of the Société Bic in the mid-1970s. By this time, the US-based Bic Pen Corporation's initial products were declining in market share, in part due to new competitive entries by Gillette and other companies. From an international point of view, by the late 1970s, the Société Bic probably had two cows, the US crystal pen business and the French crystal pen business. Again from an international point of view, the major investments of the company were its newly acquired European corporations which manufactured lighters, hosiery, and razors.

We can suspect that, first, in either turning around or expanding the lighter and razor businesses, Baron Bich's objective was to convert them from wildcats to stars. Also, it is likely that the hosiery division, DIM, was essentially a dog which the Baron had to turn around before he could convert it to cow status.

We can note here that Baron Bich probably had the advantage of buying fixed assets in an industry that was essentially overcapacitied: hosiery in the 1970s. We would expect him, therefore, to have acquired his fixed assets at a discount so that, although a late entrant into the hosiery business, he may well have been one of the low fixed cost operators in Europe. We must also realize that the advent of low-cost supermarket hosiery distribution had taken place in the US in 1973 with Hanes's "L'Eggs" and Burlington's "No Nonsense," *only* a few months before his planned entry.

Over time, as *Figure 20-4(d)* shows, the Baron has been successful in converting not only his French and European operations into cash cows but in converting many of the US and French product lines into cash cows as well. With this herd of cows funding his entry to the disposable razor business, Baron Bich appears to have been willing to take on Gillette in its own pasture. He perceived that funding resources and his consistently successful global strategy outweighed his risk.

Bic and Gillette

For a moment, let us turn to Gillette. Gillette's razor-blade business is one of the most remarkable businesses in the world. In 1982, Gillette's profits from operations in its razor and blade divisions was $250 million on identifiable assets of $455 million—an operating return of 55 percent. This result must be viewed in the light of intense competition which the company was experiencing with Bic, and, in this context, it is worth noting 55 percent was the same rate of return which Gillette enjoyed in 1977. In 1976, however, shortly before Bic's entry to the razor market with its disposable razor, Gillette executives speculated that it was unlikely that the disposable razor would ever play any significant role in the US market. Only three years later, disposable razors made up over one-third of US razor sales, with Gillette and Bic holding roughly equivalent shares of this new market.

In a company like Gillette, with its razor and blade business earning such substantial rates of return, it would not be surprising to find the general managers of less profitable divisions under constant pressure for results. In this context, it is worth noting that the Gillette Company's commitment to the low-priced pen market waned at various times in the 1970s, with the result that Bic's share of the pen business jumped from about 60 percent to about 80 percent for a time. It is possible that by putting too high an ROA hurdle on its pen division, Gillette may have inadvertently created a larger and stronger cow in the Bic herd.

Later, as Gillette's lighter division suffered the onslaughts of competition from Bic, Gillette again seems to have wavered for a time, again inadvertently creating the window of opportunity which Bic needed. In a series of aggressive price cuts, Bic challenged Gillette for leadership of the lighter business and won. The results are shown in *Table*

TABLE 20-1 US Disposable Lighters—Bic Market Share

Year	Bic's Percentage	Number of Units Sold
1973	17	60 million
1974	25	110
1975	33	160
1976	41	225
1977	52	275
1978	50	320
1979	53	370
1980	52	400
1981	52	420
1982	52	430

Source: Bic Annual Reports, 1981 and 1982

20-1. Bic jumped to the leadership share position in the lighter business about 1977, a position it still held in 1984. More significant was the relative profit positions of Bic and Gillette in the 1980s: Bic's lighter division was profitable and probably a cash cow, while Gillette may have lost money in lighters and have had cash sink, possibly a dog. Bic reported a profit on lighters of $15.4 million in 1982. Gillette's ''other'' business segment, which included its Cricket disposable lighter (and other products), reported 1982 *loss* on operations of $11.5 million.

Figure 20-5 shows a different representation of the Bic empire, circa 1976, in a structural model. At this point in time, the heart of the Bic Company remained in France while its manufacturing operations were scattered about the world, in France, the US, and Greece. An example of global operations is the way in which these different manufacturing arms trade with the different distribution arms of Bic.

Consider the differences between the organizational forms and administrative practices of Bic and Gillette. To us it seems that Bic is further along in its evolution to a global enterprise than Gillette. Gillette, with its profit-centered management, product by product and region by region, is a classic American-managed multinational, a multibusiness enterprise which Hout, Porter and Rudden (1982) would call a multidomestic company. Power, for the most part, rests firmly within the United States and within the blade division.

Only in the last few years has the Gillette Company appeared to realize the benefits of competing with Bic on more fronts than one. By investing in its low-priced pen line, Write Brothers, and reintroducing it into the commercial market—ironically a market neglected by Bic because the distributors in that market demand large margins—Gillette has been able to make the pen business more competitive and less profitable for Bic. By competing in the pen business more aggressively, Gillette successfully cut the cash flow from Bic's pen business to its razor business. Bic reported a $2.1 million loss in its writing instrument business in 1982 on reduced sales of $73.9 million, down from $85.4 million in 1983.

Gillette may in fact have adopted Sloan's policy and begun to use all of its resources in the competition with Bic: Gillette suffered substantial losses in its ''other'' business segment (which encompasses lighters) in 1980, 1981, and 1982. However, we also noted

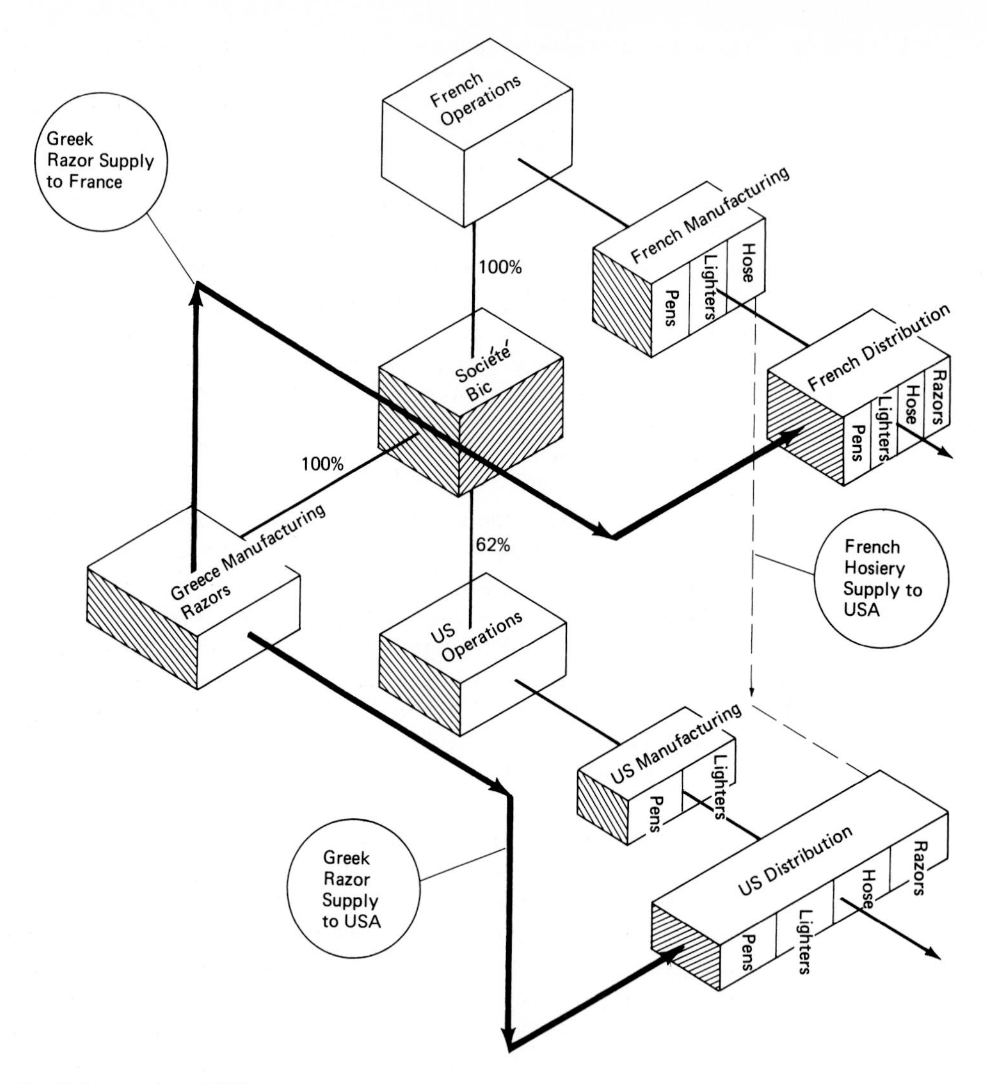

FIGURE 20-5 **Société Bic—circa 1976**
Source: Data from Bic annual reports

Gillette's stable 55 percent profit on operation in its blade and razor business across the full 1977 to 1982 period, some evidence that Gillette has protected its traditional cow successfully.

The Future for Gillette in Global Competition

Bic, we believe, is a global company. Thus, the challenge for Gillette was not to simply cut out the US-based cash cows in the Bic herd, but to compete on a global basis across all of the markets where the two companies operate. Indeed, the remainder of the world may provide the window of opportunity which Gillette needs. Bic, with its manufacturing competence, is a formidable competitor for its much larger rival, for a number of reasons.

Baron Bich's control of the Bic Companies rested in ownership, while Colman Moeckler's chairmanship of Gillette rested primarily on professional management skill and the results he earned. Moeckler's stakeholders were primarily those who believed in blue-chip investments—the institutions, widows, and orphans of America—all exerting tremendous pressure for steady and stable dividends. This demand for dividends represented a nontrivial constraint in the competition with an entrepreneur like Baron Bich.

Baron Bich's distinctive competence was manufacturing. Over time, in a number of countries, he built world-scale manufacturing capability in each of the industries in which he competed. Certainly Gillette is a world-scale competitor, but internationally it appears to operate at domestic rather than international scale. Gillette, moreover, seems accurately viewed by most people as a marketing company which is managed financially. Thus, when the competition is most intense and the margins low, it is more difficult for Gillette to invest in up-to-date manufacturing capability and capacity. By contrast, it is Baron Bich's advantage to have the most efficient production capability when margins are squeezed.

What does all this mean for the managers in Gillette's razor-blade division? In 1980, Bic lost $6.3 million in the disposable razor business. In 1981, the loss was only $2.2 million. Significantly, in 1982, Bic, by this time an integrated marketer and producer in the US, reported a profit of $2.2 million in its US operations. We would suggest that the prudent strategy for the Gillette Company is not going to be built upon simple rates of return in its US razor and blade business, but, rather, in a competition that encompasses all of its product lines and all of its resources in all of its markets, particularly those where it meets Bic.

GLOBAL CORPORATIONS AND THE FUTURE DIRECTION OF INTERNATIONAL BUSINESS

In a powerful critique of the misapplication of the marketing concept in the international business arena, Levitt (1983) suggests that it is unwise to assume that customers are kings who *know* what they want. Levitt makes the point that there is often a substantial difference between what is wanted and what would be preferred were it available. The experience of global businesses has shown that in one product market after another, low prices will shift preference structures from customized, national products to internationally standardized products.

The companies which produce customized products in the international markets are essentially those that Hout, Porter, and Rudden (1982) call *multidomestic,* that is, multinational companies functioning through independent market-based profit centers, each of which enjoys considerable autonomy to customize the product to local preferences. These companies typically compete with other companies on a market-by-market basis. Their multidomestic nature often locks them into a high cost position, with low scale economies, making them vulnerable to the price competition of a global firm which serves the world as one market.

The *global* firm is typically centrally managed and pits its worldwide resources against its competitors wherever they may be. It exploits interdependencies, sourcing, trading, and subsidizing its parts so that the competitive position of the corporation as a whole is enhanced across the world. Such corporations tend to adopt competitive measures of performance for their subsidiaries as opposed to simple financial measures such as ROA or ROI.

Bic is, as we have shown, an evolving global corporation. Gillette appears to us to be closer in kind to the multidomestic corporation. This is understandable because, for years, American companies like Gillette have enjoyed one of the world's largest standardized markets—the US. Companies that have evolved in Europe and Japan have had to export to survive and have had to find new ways to compete. The choice they have made of necessity is a movement towards globalization.

A CONFLICT WITH TRADITION

If the world is moving toward globalization, Levitt's counsel against customizing products must be heeded. Levitt has said that the twin forces of technological change and globalization will permanently change the character of the international marketplace. Technology is changing the preference structure of markets worldwide. And, technologies that provide value, that is, higher quality products and services at lower prices, have always prevailed (Burns and Stalker, 1959; Schon, 1967; Cooper and Schendel, 1976). Globalization is changing the economic realities of world competition, because global companies are seizing the opportunities presented by technological change and increasingly offering standardized goods worldwide at low competitive prices to increasingly homogenized markets.

The tradition of international business, however, is one of congenial adaptation to local conditions, accepting vestigial national differences without question, to paraphrase Levitt. Levitt describes this adaptation process as a respectful but thoughtless accommodation to what are believed to be fixed local preferences. The problem is that respectful sensitivity to local preferences, customs, and mores has led many otherwise capable firms into high-cost, many-featured product lines across the world. Each domestic market is managed idiosyncratically and economies of scale are lost in the quest to customize products.

Dealing with these markets one by one has made international business expensive and administratively complex. Worse, as noted earlier, cultural responsiveness has not made the market positions of these firms stronger. In fact, it has left them vulnerable to the aggressive price competition of global corporations.

The point is not to advocate insensitivity to local preferences, but to promote an awareness of the real value of using all the corporation's resources to their full competitive capability. Levitt points out that global corporations accept and adjust to local differences only after efforts to circumvent and reshape them. Even then, the global corporation will persist in its efforts to standardize its production across markets. For example, although Caterpillar could not fully standardize its earth-moving equipment, the components of the equipment are standardized, giving Caterpillar both production and service economies and quality.

It is perplexing that although competitive strength has come from exploiting the national market within the United States, the traditional international business approach, particularly of the American international business community, has been characterized by respectful responsiveness. Few American firms produce and serve America's regional markets with differentiated products and services, yet outside America totally differentiated products are common.

The differences between life in Boston and New York and the complexities of doing business between the two cities, as real as they may have been in 1690, are of only moderate importance to business in the twentieth century. Technology has removed the relevant differences. In like manner, the complexities of doing business between Boston and Paris in the 1980s are disappearing. Ultimately, technology will reduce the complexity of all of today's international business.

Technological advances in communication and greater ease of transportation are accelerating the trend towards worldwide markets. People everywhere want what people everywhere else have, from Coca-Cola to Hondas. Levitt writes:

> People understandably treat (money) with respect. . . . If the price is low enough, they will take highly standardized world products, even if these aren't exactly what mother said was suitable, what immemorial custom decreed was right, or what market-research fabulists asserted was preferred. (1983, p. 96)

Price sensitivity is the economic foundation of the global corporation.

Today's high-technology products are the commodities of tomorrow. Corporations which control their costs on such products are in a much better position to become global competitors, recognized for giving their customers value. As the Bic example has shown, the incremental market volume that multinational distribution can provide the units of the global corporation can quickly shift their production to world-scale efficiency. This is what Bic did in France when it used its US subsidiary as a distribution channel in the hose, lighter, and razor businesses.

GUIDELINES FOR INTERNATIONAL COMPETITION

As we noted earlier, some factors cause concern for the managements of global enterprises. Because of their integration and market scope, managing global enterprises is complicated by the complexity of business definition and the difficulty of performance measurement. Managing the global business requires, as Hout, Porter, and Rudden (1982) agree, apparently unconventional administrative practices.

The global corporation will normally choose volume over precise market matches. Its efforts will go to standardizing a product line and developing a relative cost advantage over its competitors. This means that in some markets the global corporation will offer overdesigned and underpriced products—that is, it will provide some consumers or users with exceptional value.

The appropriate point at which to measure return is at the higher level of the global corporation, not the business level. On a country-by-country basis, management is likely to approve of projects with varying degrees of profitability and quite different short-run financial performance characteristics. In making its investment decisions, the global corporation will distinguish between local projects which develop its competitive strength and the global businesses themselves. While the short-run return on investment characteristics of a narrowly defined project within a particular market may even be negative for a time, their value to the corporation is in the contributions they make to the competitive strength of the worldwide business. Global corporations do not invest without the promise of an economic profit at the higher level, over time. Their single-product, single-market decisions, however, may have apparently negative ROI's.

The Bic Corporation's history illustrates this point. In 1974, the Bic Pen Corporation (USA) was asked by its parent to introduce pantyhose into the US market. At the time, many observers wondered whether pantyhose fit well with Bic's concept of its business. They assumed that Bic's objectives in the US would be to dominate the hosiery market as it had dominated the pen business. At the time, Bic's competition was formidable indeed. Burlington, Hanes, and Kayser Roth, the three largest US competitors in an overcapacitied industry were many times larger than the Bic Company. In fact, their collective advertising budgets approximated the Bic Pen Corporation's total assets.

However, the mission that Société Bic (now) appears to have asked Bic USA to carry out was not market domination, but, rather, to gain additional volume for an underutilized French plant that Bich had recently acquired. Because the US market is over five times as large as the French market, even a small percentage of the US market would contribute a large incremental volume to the French company, and, presumably, was seen as being easier to get than a substantially larger share in France. This incremental volume helped move Bic's DIM subsidiary into a stronger competitive position in Europe and then to profitability. It is a classic example of apparent irrationality within a narrowly defined market being an opportunity for considerable market leverage and profitability when viewed from a higher and indeed broader perspective.

As this example suggests, *the management of global enterprises views national markets as interdependent entities rather than as single discrete businesses*. Moreover, in the more developed multibusiness global corporations, even businesses are managed interdependently. As we have shown in our description of the competition between Bic and Gillette, the battle for the worldwide razor business extends into the pen and lighter businesses, too, not only because Bic and Gillette compete for positions in the same distribution channels but because the cash flow earned in one business can be used to compete more aggressively in another.

Because of its own potential to compete across business and national borders, *the global corporation must consider what is a proper competitive practice in the countries in which it operates*. For the US-based global corporation, this poses something of a dilemma, for although the US Justice Department has attempted to apply the antitrust laws internationally, sovereignty is real and across the world there are different views about appropriate employment practices, the merits of industry consolidation, and predatory pricing, for example. In many countries, governments play a more active and explicit role in corporate affairs than in the US, and so are more critical stakeholders.

Country by country, a US global company is likely to confront competitors which are owned or subsidized by national governments, a situation which plagues the US-based international airlines as well as the international telecommunication industry. In fact, in telecommunications across the world, quite subtle forms of vertical integration exist between private and semi-public suppliers and the utilities which operate national telephone services. R&D subsidies, strong national preferences for locally-made products, safety, and reliability requirements characterize both explicit and implicit national industry policies.

In locating its plants behind national boundaries, the global company will have to consciously assess its own needs for power in negotiations with foreign governments, whose industry policies may favor domestic corporations. This may mean the creation of rationalized international manufacturing systems where critical components have multiple sources. Thus, the problems in any one location will not affect the business as a whole, while, at the same time, the global corporations will have bargaining chips in its inevitable dealings with sovereign governments.

By fostering interdependencies across its subsidiaries, the global corporation can increase the probabilities that the national government's interest in employment and international earnings are co-aligned with its own interests in smooth operations. Essentially, a global corporation enhances its monopoly power by operating as a single seller of products produced at coordinated multiple locations. Ultimately, the global corporation will tend toward cellular operating structures where the success of the whole is not dependent on the continuity or longevity of a particular cell, but rather on the network of communications and exchanges that produce, assemble, and distribute its products.

Over time, the global corporation's markets and productive strengths develop, enhancing its least-cost, high-volume position and usually giving it a long-lasting competitive advantage. Thus, for the global competitor confronting domestic or even multidomestic competition, time is an ally. The more time the competition allows the global company before responding to its initiatives, the stronger the global competitor will become over time.

Few competitive advantages last forever. Yet a strategy which is robust because of its delivery capabilities, service levels, and cost advantage can earn customer loyalty over time and so becomes difficult to beat whether times are good or bad. Indeed, the good times allow the firm to accumulate a "war chest" of profits which it can use to defend itself from future competitors.

In the pen industry, it would have been dangerous for companies like Gillette to assume that Bic's 1982 losses in its US writing instrument business were associated with operating difficulties across the world. The Bic Company is contending with a series of product innovations as well as direct competition. The Rolling Writer, erasible pens, ceramic-tipped pens, thin-point porous and calligraphic instruments are all recent entrants to the low-priced pen market. Bic's US losses may be associated with problems or with heavy investments of "expensible" funds into business renewal.

For a global business, success requires a top management patient enough to wait for the opportunities it needs to develop its competitive strength. It takes time to renew a business and it takes time to build a business. It takes even more time to build a global business, and taking time requires patience. Bich once said, "We just try to stick close to reality, like a surfer to his board. We don't lean forward or backward too far or too fast. We ride the wave at the right moment."[1]

THE ESSENCE OF GLOBAL COMPETITION

Some think the essence of competition is to beat the competition. The real principle of competing successfully in business, however, is simultaneously to avoid competition and strengthen oneself. Business confrontations cost a great deal of money and management

[1] "Going Bananas Over Bic," *Time*, December 18, 1972, p. 93.

time. In business as in war, winning battles is not the same as winning the war. In business, a competitive war holds no victory unless the peace is won, too. In business, this usually means the biggest piece of the market, a particularly important consideration for high-volume global firms.

Henderson (1967) pointed out that in most countries, governments will tolerate neither collaboration among competitors nor wholesale competition resulting in the annihilation of a competitor and the reduction of competition. Competing successfully on a global basis demands balance between moving too fast and too slowly vis à vis the competition and the broader environment. We believe this balance can be found if management constantly keeps in mind the need to strengthen its own corporation—rather than the havoc it can wreck on others.

The real essence of competition is to use all of your resources to achieve your objectives as efficiently as possible. Competition between companies ultimately comes down to competition between concepts of what their business is. At the top, no one defines the industry or the business. Management has to do it itself. Different concepts ensure competition without confrontation.

Creating such concepts requires vision. Garnering the resources needed to implement the concept requires patience, self-discipline, and leadership. Indeed the purpose of all management is entrepreneurial, that is, to create value. Businesses must create value by creating customers and keeping them. This is best done by giving the customers value, so they have no reason to shift their business to others.

Market niches will always exist, even in the globalized setting of tomorrow's international business community. As they are discovered by other corporations seeking volume, however, these niches are likely to be limited in growth potential and increasingly at risk. For the value-creating managers of the future, profitability, growth, and risk management are the keys to prosperity. And we believe, like Baron Bich, that prosperity is easier to gain if you ride the waves of the times.

Riding the waves of the industrial environment and determining their significance means you can commit your resources confidently to (your) future. Levitt (1983) wrote, "Data do not yield information except with the intervention of the mind. Information does not yield meaning except with the intervention of imagination" (p. 99). Change is unlikely to be well directed without considerable thought, imagination, and effort. However, for those who make the effort, the reward is the opportunity to lead their organizations into the future. We discuss leadership in Chapter 21.

chapter 21

Leadership, Values, and Objectives

INTRODUCTION: WHAT IS LEADERSHIP?

Is leadership a superior or mystical quality beyond the reach of ordinary men and women? "Leadership is the force that selects your dreams and sets your goals. It is the force that propels your endeavors to success." So wrote Robert Schuller, a Reformed Church minister, in his 1983 book, *Tough Times Never Last, But Tough People Do!* He was writing not for managers but for people everywhere. There is leadership potential in us all.

Schuller's buoyant definition and his implicit assumption that we all have some potential for being leaders are inspiring. And, it is inspired self-leadership that is needed in organizations confronting change.

Yet, at times, our potential for self-leadership is unrealized. We need a leader to set the direction, motivate us and mediate for us in the world or in the environment in which we work. Perversely, people often take leadership for granted while they enjoy its benefits. Nevertheless, they eventually become acutely aware of the absence or failure of leadership. Selznick explains:

> When institutional leadership fails, it is perhaps more often by default than by positive error or sin. Leadership is lacking when it is needed; and the institution drifts, exposed to vagrant pressures, readily influenced by short-run opportunistic trends. This default is partly a failure of nerve, partly a failure of understanding. It takes nerve to hold a course; it takes understanding to recognize and deal with the sources of institutional vulnerability. (1957, p. 25)

Leadership, in fact, like strategy, may be more noticeable when it is absent than when it is present. The drift and wandering to which Selznick refers will be revealed by a failure to maintain vital objectives, by poor results and a waning reputation, by failures to foresee impending crises, by capricious and inconsistent actions which waste resources which might otherwise be the basis for future prosperity, and by missed and wasted opportunities. In leaderless organizations, other symptoms often observed include an isolated top management, a second-tier management characterized by internecine conflict and high turnover, privileged cadres of low performers, devitalized junior positions, and a failure to plan for succession in the ongoing business.

Barnard wrote:

> Among those who cooperate the things that are seen are moved by things unseen. Out of the void comes the spirit that shapes the ends of men. (1966, p. 284)

This spirit, we say, is the spirit of leadership. It is this spirit that must be sparked. Barnard uses the word ''fulminator'' to describe the leader's role.

A ''fulminator'' provides the fire or lightning that sets things moving, that sparks creative, focused cooperation throughout the organization and infuses countless decisions with consistency even as the environment changes. Discussing this ''necessary'' leadership role, Barnard says that,

> Reflecting attitudes, ideals, hopes, derived largely from without themselves, [leaders] are compelled to bind the wills of men to the accomplishment of purpose beyond their immediate ends, beyond their times. (p. 283)

Leaders, indeed, change their times.

Leaders give organizations direction and drive; they represent the purpose of the organization inside and outside its boundaries. Direction comes from objectives which articulate what can be and make the leader's vision of the future tangible and realizable. Direction reduces uncertainty about what should be done and so promotes coordination and focus. Drive describes an organization where people want to achieve their objectives. Leaders promote drive with their vision of the future and by example.

Leaders motivate their followers by driving themselves to do more and by rewarding results, thereby reinforcing purposeful action. They symbolically represent the organization inside and outside by carefully and artfully explaining its mission, its purpose, its objectives and strategies, and by educating the organization so that its members can appreciate the significance of environmental change (Smith, 1975). After many years, their presence alone may contribute substantially to the organization's ability to stay the course.

The environment flows and change occurs; the trick for the leader is to move with the flow to accomplish purpose. To cite Sun Tzu: ''A skilled commander seeks victory from the situation and does not demand it of his subordinates'' (1963, p. 93). Chang Yu, a commentator, explained: ''One must take advantage of the situation exactly as if he were setting a ball in motion on a steep slope. The force applied is minute but the results are enormous.'' Leaders are a minute part of organizations, but they fulminate enormous releases of focused human energy so that their followers get results.

Successful leaders take such great advantage of the flow of events that often they themselves are considered lucky rather than smart; leadership may often be unrecognized. Sun Tzu writes, ''And therefore the victories won by a master of war gain him neither reputation for wisdom nor merit for valor'' (p. 87). And a commentator echoes, ''When you subdue your enemy without fighting who will pronounce you valorous?'' Indeed, both leadership and strategies are often best noticed by the chaos apparent when they are absent. They are generally identifiable backwards, through time, except by those few who can move men and women to the accomplishment of purpose and indeed strategize and lead.

Leaders inspire people to lead themselves, by articulating their personal vision of a better future and by changing the way people think about ideal performance (Zaleznick, 1977; Henderson, 1979). In the language of the strategist, leaders set new objectives and make new strategies realizable. They use objectives and strategies to give dreams substance.

THE LEADER OF THE ORGANIZATION

It is important to remember that in choosing objectives, leaders are not unfettered. Earlier, we cited Barnard: the leader is ''compelled'' and reflects ''ideals, hopes, derived largely from without.'' Yet leaders must be of the organization.

''Of the organization'' deserves emphasis because it encompasses one of the great contradictions of leadership: The leader leads the organization, yet is compelled by its members' desires and ideals and hopes to action.

How can this be? The answer is that leaders need followers as badly as followers need leaders; one without the other is only a potential source of energy. Something has to be done to get the two together. Followers are the resource that is critical to leadership.

Leadership can exist only in a social context and only if the leader has support. Such support will be forthcoming only if the leader is *of* the organization, not simply its highest ranking member, but its first follower. Without depreciating the importance of a ''concept of the organization,'' the limiting factor in organizational life and in the management of change is cooperation. And, as Barnard tells us, the limiting factor in cooperation is leadership.

The leader must be of the organization and hold its values with conviction. Although he or she can order action, the leader is not independent and may in fact be impelled to certain actions by the values he and the organization share. At once, the leader is constrained by the organization and able to unleash its resources (Salanacik et al., 1975; Lieberson and O'Conner, 1972).

How does the leader come to share the followers' values? Hegel writes:

> Leadership is possible not only on the condition that fellowship has been learned, but on the more radical condition that the leader has known subjection and thralldom. The mature leader not only must have known the travail of the follower; he must here and now incorporate within himself all that the follower is. (Litzinger and Schaefer, 1982)

The paradox is that the leader must be more follower than the followers, while acknowledging that there is leadership in the followers, too. ''People,'' folklore says, ''get the leaders they deserve.'' Leaders promote leadership so that an organization with a leader is an organization with many leaders. Barnard writes:

> Purposeful cooperation is possible only within certain limits of a structural character, and it arises from forces derived from *all* who contributed to it. The work of cooperation is not a work of leadership, but of organization as a whole. (p. 259)

Leadership is a complex endeavor. Nerve and understanding are needed in those who would take charge of an organization, control it and change it. It takes nerve to take charge and hold the course; it takes nerve and understanding to redefine the mission and set a new course.

But these alone are insufficient to the task: organizations only exist through cooperation—that is, when others pursue the objectives set. A leader with no followers is no leader at all. And, one test of mettle as a leader is whether followers can move from the present to the future in a timely way and at a rate acceptable inside the organization and adequate without. This means managing the tension between the need for continuity and the need for change, viewing resistance as a signal that something needs investigation (Lawrence, 1969), rather than as a phenomenon to be overcome. The Zen saying, "You can only dam a river if you allow it to flow" (Pascale, 1978), applies to the management of resistance. A leader must have not only highly-tuned abilities for analysis and synthesis to allow him or her to appreciate the total situation, but highly developed human skills to manage the rate of change productively (Katz, 1955).

THE CONTRADICTIONS OF LEADERSHIP

As we have suggested, leadership is an elusive quality. It is characterized, like life, by contradiction. Already we have mentioned that:

- it is easier to recognize the absence of leadership than its presence;
- organizations need leadership to define a vision in realizable terms, yet that personal vision must reflect the organization's ideals, hopes, and values;
- leaders lead, although they may be compelled to do so;
- leaders can only exist in a social context of followership.

From the social scientist's point of view, leadership is more easily understood looking backwards, although the important aspect of leadership is its forward-thrusting vision. The Danish philosopher Kierkegaard once wrote: "Life can only be understood backwards but must be lived forward." Research looks back to project forwards, but the very intangibility of leadership frustrates the researchers' methods.

The leader is at once directing and supporting the organization. People in the organization look to the leader for direction. Usually this is described as looking to the top, and so we have the image of the powerful leader issuing directives. Yet we are all aware of the burden of leadership. Looking up, the leader sees the organization needing support, and often the burden is great. The leader is at once on the top of and supporting the organization.

While the leader is on top, contrariwise the leader is also at the bottom and the helper of all. The Catholic Church uses the title, "The Servant of the Servants of God" for the Pope. Litzinger and Schaefer write,

> Where leader and follower alike are held in obedience to defined doctrine, neither may act on his own autonomous will alone. Leadership endures so long as it assumes a posture of humility, a spirit of followership. (1982, p. 79)

Moreover, just as leadership and followership fuse to create a leading organization, objectives and strategies fuse to create purposeful action. In what seems like another contradiction, however, just as it makes little difference whether we talk of a hierarchy of leaders or a hierarchy of followers, it makes little difference whether we talk about a hierarchy of objectives or a hierarchy of strategies. The statements that strategies are objectives and leaders are followers are both true because they model reality from different viewpoints or perspectives.

The leader must be a representative of the organization's members and indeed a member, too. Yet Zaleznick (1977) focuses on another contradiction of leadership by suggesting that the leader must be apart as well:

> Leaders tend to be twice born personalities, people who feel separate from their environment, including other people. They may work in organizations but never belong to them. Their sense of who they are does not depend upon membership, work roles, or other indicators of identity. (p. 74)

Zaleznick notes that managers, by comparison, are once born and their sense of self stems from harmony with the environment. Leaders, the twice born, have had less straightforward and peaceful lives, marked by a continual struggle to attain order. Zaleznick added that

> . . . for such people, self-esteem no longer depends solely upon positive attachment and real rewards. A form of self-reliance takes hold along with expectations of performance and achievement, and perhaps even the desire to do great works. (p. 75)

THE VALUES OF A LEADER

Values set leaders apart from other people, yet make them one with others. Values are the common bond with followers. The leader represents and is a custodian of the ideals and values of the organization. To the extent he or she can, the leader must live those values and not falter. This willingness to serve the values, even at a personal cost, promotes those values, distinguishes leader and follower, and concurrently unifies leader and follower through those shared values.

What leaders do that others cannot is to synthesize the old and new. They forge new values which encompass the old out of the organization's successes and failures. This ability allows leaders to choose a path while less able people have to wait until they can proceed (tentatively) or decide with confidence because they have information to be right. Hirschman's "Hiding Hand" (1967) should alert us to the fallacy of the words "right decision" in any really important matter, since the hiding hand implies that solutions beget problems and those problems new solutions.

In being apart and one with others simultaneously, the leader must reconcile belonging on one hand and separateness on the other. First, the leaders fit with the new orthodoxy rather than the old. Second, they fit the context, internal and external, and personally fulminate change by mentoring others, insisting on performance and demonstrating their personal integrity. Third, by controlling the rate of change so that time's passage allows experience to accumulate to satisfy their followers' needs for security, they give those people the opportunity to follow. Fourth, they maintain their separateness because for them reward, status, money, and even power are not personally valued per se but recognized as tools to help them implement their strategies and achieve their objectives.

The sage comment that a leader's self-esteem no longer depends on positive attachments and real rewards (Zaleznick, 1977), explains how leaders keep themselves free from the trapping of office that are characteristics of dysfunctional bureaucracies. This freedom allows a leader to use his or her person as a resource and to use rewards as tools to accomplish purpose.

THE MAKING OF A LEADER

Where do leaders come from? Vince Lombardi, at the time the head coach of the Green Bay Packers football team, explained it in a speech on leadership before the American Management Association. He believed leadership has a personal price that each of us has to determine for ourselves:

> No one person has all the qualities that grow up to make a leader. We've more or less developed a blend of them. No one has every particular quality. You develop your own blend . . . they are not born. They are made . . . only through one way . . . through work. That's the price we all pay. . . .
>
> If we would create something, we must be something. You can't dream yourself into character. You must hammer one out for yourself. You must forge one out for yourself. . . . The difference between a group and a leader is not so much in lack of strength, not so much in lack of knowledge, but rather in lack of will. (c. 1965)

It seems that the forge that makes leaders is nothing less than life's experiences of success and failure. Zaleznick's "born" and Lombardi's "made" are words used in a kindred spirit and are consistent with Hegel's view that the leader must have known the travail of the follower, both success and failure.

People who are sheltered from life's vicissitudes cannot lead. People who have never known failure cannot appreciate success. Only those who have known success and have experienced failure—and who have mastered themselves in both conditions, forging a set of values for themselves—have confidence founded in self-trust that is the ultimate source of cooperation. People who do not trust themselves cannot trust others or earn their trust. Without trust, cooperation is impossible and without cooperation, leadership and followship alike cannot develop.

The evidence is that each of us has to train ourselves for leadership. If you want to lead or share in the leadership of business corporations and other organizations, you have to develop a "will to lead," and prepare yourself by learning who you are and what you stand for.

RULES FOR PRESERVING LEADERSHIP*

Self-knowledge is important to a leader. So is the knowledge of how to preserve leadership. However, knowledge alone is insufficient. Discipline is necessary, too. A leader must follow certain rules.

The importance of the leader's relationship with the organization is stressed by the sociologist George C. Homans in *The Human Group* (1950), where he identifies eleven rules of leadership. First, he says, *the leader will maintain his position,* establish and maintain his rank and even delay any effort for change until his position is established.

Second, *the leader will live up to the norms of the group,* because any failure to do so undermines his rank and the presumption that his orders are to be obeyed. Homans makes the point that the relevant norms are the group's, not those the leader thinks ought to be. The leader, he warns, should look after his people in the matters they think are important.

The third rule is *the leader will lead.* If the decision is his, he must decide. Fourth, *the leader will not give orders that will not be obeyed.* Such orders would confuse his followers and raise questions about his competence.

Fifth, *the leader will use established channels in giving orders,* since in maintaining his subordinates' position he maintains his own. Sixth, *he will not thrust himself upon his followers on social occasions,* also to preserve the structure that supports him and facilitates action.

Seventh, *the leader will neither blame, nor in general, praise a member of his group before members.* Again, Homans explains, this is to preserve the rank of the followers on one hand and, on the other, to allow the organization to accept change in its own time.

Eighth, *the leader will take into consideration the whole situation.* Homans points out that "nothing succeeds like success." The leader has to foresee the consequences of social action and understand how interrelationships of technology and the internal and external social system will be affected. Homans made an impassioned plea that is as valid today as it was in 1950:

> Americans are taught adequate ways of thinking about technology and organization; they are not taught adequate ways of thinking about social systems. A leader cannot examine the whole situation inside and outside his group unless he has a method for taking up each element of the situation in order and in its relations to the other elements. It is not enough to have a mystic sense of the whole; nor is it enough to have intuitive "social skills" that, all too easily, lead up a dead-end street to the "big-time operator." What is needed is explicit, conscious, intellectual understanding. Even this is not enough, but, by all that is holy in the human spirit, without this the rest is dust and ashes. (p. 435)

Ninth, *in maintaining discipline, the leader will be less concerned with inflicting punishment than with creating the conditions in which the group will discipline itself.*

*George C. Homans, abridged excerpts from "The Behavior of the Leader," *The Human Group,* copyright 1950 by Harcourt Brace Jovanovich; renewed 1978 by George C. Homans. Reprinted by permission.

Essentially, unless we understand the reasons people disobey orders and resist change, the resistance is likely to persist and our haphazard efforts to overcome it could lead to resentment (Lawrence, 1969). The leader's job is to ensure that the mistake does not happen again and to encourage self-correction. Punishment may be necessary, but only if it serves the group (which includes preserving its leadership structure).

In the tenth rule, Homans advises that *the leader will listen,* adding that he or she must be informed about the whole situation inside and outside the group (and for us, the organization). Since authority and rank cut down interaction and break down free communications, the leader must show by action that he or she is friendly and interested and encourages interaction.

Homans also warns leaders to take no moral stand "while listening to someone else trying to say what is on his mind." Accept it and show you want to hear everything; any statement by the leader is carried with the weight of authority and may constrain further communication. He must "keep his mouth shut and listen."

Know yourself is Homans's eleventh and final rule. He writes:

> How often has the leader acted and later wished fervently he had not! He must be under great self-control in a situation where control is difficult. If, therefore, he must know his men well, he must know himself still better. He must know the passions in him that, unchecked, will destroy him as a leader, and he must know their sources in his personality. For how can we control a force, the source of whose energy we do not know? Self-knowledge is the first step in self-control. (p. 440)

Homans emphasizes the maintenance of the social order as critical in sustaining leadership, the importance of self-knowledge, and the leader's knowing and understanding organizational norms and the values underlying them. Especially when values are in conflict, the organization must come first.

VALUES AND THE PRESERVATION OF LEADERSHIP

We have put great stress on values, self-knowledge and self-control. Why? It is because the leader is, paradoxically, the greatest threat to the organization because he or she, more than any other, can put it into jeopardy.

Edward Boland Smith (1975) explained the pressure that hits the leader because of his role: ". . . a leadership role . . . complicates and intensifies his moral position. Additional moral codes [that is, sets of values besides his personal values] must now be answered to. Conflicts of codes now arise." Smith, drawing heavily on Barnard, notes that executives must not only be responsible but be capable of enduring complex moral conditions:

> Otherwise he will be "overloaded," and either ability, responsibility, or morality, or all three, will be destroyed . . . (with) fatal indecision or emotional and impulsive action with personal breakdown. . . . Leadership requires not only a sense of responsibility, but a high degree of morality and the ability to cope with the conflicting demands of those moralities (or values). (1975, p. 42)

The successful executive or leader must be able to resolve value conflict while personally supporting a highly sophisticated pattern of values and to act so that none are violated. Violations would undermine his or her leadership.

Barnard (1966) and Vickers (1965) tell us how successful leaders resolve value conflict. Barnard calls it the process of "determination." The first method is to analyze the environment to accurately determine the strategic or limiting factor, an analysis which may lead to the discovery of that "correct" action which violates no codes; examples of this include contractual, personal and organizational changes. The second is "to adopt a new detailed purpose consistent with general objectives," that is, to change the objective or strategy of the organizations or both. The third and most challenging approach is by changing culture, that is, the mutual expectations and self-expectations of (the organization's) members.

Smith explores what Barnard called the "distinguishing mark" of executive responsibility, the creating of (new) culture and values for others. Culture is established in two ways:

> The first constitutes the process of inculcating points of view, fundamental attitudes and loyalties to the organization; the second is a judicial function which implies the substitution of a new action to avoid conflict or providing a moral justification for exception or compromise (the exceptional case). (1975, p. 44)

Essentially, the leader facilitates change not so much by solving problems as by exploiting problems, especially those that are exceptions, and occasionally by creating turbulence. Indeed, exceptions are most important because they mark *the way things will be done* and signal the passing of the old ways, the old culture and old values. Exceptions are the opportunities for change and creativity and, as Barnard puts it, "leadership is the indispensible fulminator of its forces."

Smith extols the importance of this leadership function:

> Creating values becomes then "the highest exemplification of responsibility" for the executive. It demands conviction on the part of the leaders—"conviction that what they do for the good of organization they *personally* believe to be right." This creative function, according to Barnard, "is the essence of leadership." It is in fact "the highest test of executive responsibility, because it requires for successful accomplishment that element of 'conviction' that means identification of personal codes (values) and organization codes (values) in the view of the leader." (1975, p. 44)

Ultimately, these new values will be reflected in the organization's sense of an ideal state (of relating with its environment) and in new ideal standards of performance (Zaleznick, 1977; Henderson, 1979).

LEADERSHIP AND IDEALS

Indeed, ideals and leadership go hand in hand: The critical skill in maintaining a creative tension between continuity and change is social, and the ideal facilitates communication and is motivating.

Ideals are objectives set high. Leaders, to cite Machiavelli's *The Prince* (circa 1514),

> . . . behave like those archers who, if they are skillful, when the target seems too distant, know the capabilities of their bow and aim a good deal higher than their objective, not in order to shoot so high but so that by aiming high they can reach the target. (1961, p. 49)

Exceptions provide the opportunity to promote new ideals. There are objectives which we must reach quickly to survive and those we can defer. What is important and what is not is unclear to most people until a choice is needed and made. Thus, management by example is an important component of leadership, and exceptions focus the organization's attention on its new objectives.

Values are usually transmitted by leadership action, by example, by letting people see "this is the way we do it." By revising the ideals and exploiting exceptions, leaders use success to motivate the organization, examples to point the way, and failures as learning experience for all. The leader has to maintain a productive relationship with the organization, not overcoming resistance so much as using it to help him or her gauge the rate at which the organization's members can change their concept of the organization and performance.

LEADERSHIP AND RESISTANCE

Leaders develop an appreciation of these factors, especially resistance, because they have used their own lives as instruments of learning. They move with the times and their followers, the existing organization, adapting now for the future, preserving and creating what is needed for survival and success (Selznick, 1957). It is not an easy task and never has been. Machiavelli wrote,

> It should be borne in mind that there is nothing more difficult to arrange, more doubtful of success, and more dangerous to carry through than initiating changes in a state's constitution. The innovator makes enemies of all those who prospered under the old order, and only lukewarm support is forthcoming from those who would prosper under the new. Their support is lukewarm partly from fear of their adversaries, who have the existing laws on their side, and partly because men are generally incredulous never really trusting new things unless they have tested them by experience. (1961, p. 51)

This passage is a warning to any potential leader of powerful social forces against change. Resistance is natural, only overcome by the leader's ability to maintain and expand the base of organizational support for his or her program of change. Moreover, Machiavelli suggests one of the key differences between leaders and managers: leaders act on a vision of the future, managers on results or experience. Only in exceptional circumstances, when an organization is in crisis or its leader is very secure, or both, is rapid change possible.

LEADER AND MANAGERS

Giving us some additional insight into the leadership process, Zaleznick (1977) says leaders use themselves as instruments of learning, shaping ideas to influence the way people think about what is possible, desirable, and necessary. Exceptions provide one set of opportunities for shaping ideas. By using ideas and projecting those ideas into images that excite people, and by then developing choices, tangible objectives and strategies that give the projected images substance, the leader changes the focus of the organization and its sense of performance.

Managers, Zaleznick says, rely on trial and error and logical techniques and on constant analysis to accumulate experience and results which point the way to the future. They frame objectives passively and impersonally and focus on necessities rather than desires. Managers try to balance interests, judiciously eliminating choices as they go to maintain cooperative effort. Leaders synthesize the future from skeletal data and choose a way. Managers wait until they have enough information to decide, or at least to decide to proceed (Pascale, 1978).

A manager is a steward who conserves value and keeps things running. A leader, in contrast, is entrepreneurial and concerned with value creation and the future integrity and well-being of the organization.

CHANGE AND CONTINUITY

The critical role of leadership is to direct change. Leaders have to adapt their organizations to changing environments in a timely manner while maintaining the dynamic stability of their operating systems. This is nothing less than using the resources accumulated to create more value. Note, most unique integrated and synergistic strategies are ''associated with single powerful leaders'' (Mintzberg, 1978). Mintzberg explains,

> Perhaps the sophisticated integration called for in gestalt strategy requires innovative thinking rooted in synthesis rather than analysis, based on the "intuitive" or inexplicit processes that have been associated with the brain's right hemisphere. (p. 944)

Let us emphasize change and continuity and the mediating role of the leader. Failure can occur if the balance between inside and out is not developed and held in a productive and dynamic state of equilibrium. Mintzberg warns:

> A strategy is not a fixed plan, nor does it change systematically at prearranged times solely at the will of management. The dichotomy between strategy formulation and strategy implementation is a false one under certain common conditions, because it ignores the learning that must often follow the conception of an intended strategy. (p. 947)

Note, too, that Mintzberg said a strategy is not a fixed plan nor is will sufficient to affect change. Finally, note his warning that organizations have to learn and, remember, organizational learning consumes time.

Time is needed because for most people success depends upon the ability to operate productively in the context of an ongoing organization. Cataclysmic change occurs infrequently, and the need for major strategic change arises irregularly. Hence, to survive and prosper in the organization, people need first to understand the strategy and objectives of their organization at their own and other levels of responsibility; to interpret orders, directives, and requests; and to implement them successfully.

Yet, when continuity and incremental change are not enough to ensure the survival of the organization and leadership is needed, it is the managers on the spot who must share in that leadership as leading followers. Henry Mintzberg (1975) may have summed up managerial work when he wrote:

> The executives I was observing—all very competent by any standard—are fundamentally indistinguishable from their counterparts of a hundred years ago (or a thousand years ago, for that matter). (p. 54)

We agree wholeheartedly and have tried to support this point with quotations from the Bible, Sun Tzu, and classic as well as contemporary writers on management issues.

Strategic change demands leadership. And leadership demands informed understanding of the organization and its environment. Only if these are present can the conflicting demands of continuity and change be synthesized so that the organization is served and its members given an opportunity to prosper.

chapter 22

Epilogue

Herbert Simon (1964) emphasized the dual nature of objectives, noting that they can be used in two ways: as targets that we work from to develop strategies, or as bench marks or constraints against which we measure the potential or actual performance of a prospective strategy. Objectives can help us generate alternatives or test them. Simon warned that the strategies ultimately selected would likely depend on which objectives were used as constraints and which as targets, pointing out that the choice is inevitably personal and so a source of differences between the strategies of organizations with different management groups.

Although we, too, subscribe to the idea that there may not be only a single path for a corporation, we believe the choice is not unlimited. There is a feasible zone and several likely paths within it. Analysis helps us define the feasible zone. Personal experience and values influence us toward specific choices within that feasible zone.

Nevertheless, although there may be no one way to achieve many strategic and administrative objectives, and although a number of strategies may lead to satisfactory results, strategists have to choose. Once committed to their choice, strategists face a situation where no guarantees exist. Managers cannot guarantee a specific result. At best, they can underwrite specific performance with their jobs, act in the light of results, and change their subsequent actions to achieve their objectives.

In the context of a world where results count, what is the role of strategic analysis and planning? One executive responded this way: The basic issue of strategy is to get consistent, comprehensive, and longer-term thinking into current decision making. Strategy enables a manager to test results against plan and ask, "why?"

This book presents many different approaches to strategic analysis. Each one is a lens through which you can view an organization and its actions. Sometimes one lens will suffice. On other occasions, two or even more may be necessary before you see the path to the future to which you are prepared to commit.

In an optometrist's chair, the patient is asked to view the wall chart through a series of lenses. One is rarely enough. Some blur the chart, others clear it. The optometrist, however, uses the lenses and results in sequence to analyze the patient's vision problem. The analysis complete, an appropriate lens can be synthesized from all the lenses on the basis of the results achieved.

Analysis is followed by synthesis and then prescription. So, too, strategic analysis is a first step to strategy formulation and action. As your experience builds, you can choose the approach more skillfully and increase your efficiency by omitting some of the steps. Sometimes, however, you'll need to work slowly through the fundamentals, one by one.

Each method presented here relies on a model of purposeful action, but emphasizes different parts of the strategic problem. Simon pointed out that whether we use goal or constraint, we are taking different views of the same world. Similarly, "strategy," "operations," "resource," "structure," "industry," and "stakeholder" are all words which help us analyze and communicate ideas. They are themselves nothing more or less than convenient linguistic models of a reality.

Strategists need many models in their armory. Use those you find helpful. Try to develop your own ways to address the problems you'll confront en route to the future.

The essence of strategic management is analysis followed by action, and action by analysis of the results earned. Managers add value in many ways, but one of the most powerful is to conceive a vision of a better future, a concept of what can be and how it can be achieved, and to use it to focus and coordinate action. Experience and framework are combined to find the way to a prosperous future.

Action requires continuity, and the future often requires change. Balancing the two and monitoring the rate of change so that there is a controlled and dynamic equilibrium is the way most organizations move through the present to their future. Continuity is resource management; change is, too. Strategies are needed to exploit the environment, use and husband the corporation's resources, satisfy its stakeholders and so serve the best interests of all.

References

Chapter 1

ABELL, DEREK, F., ''Strategic Windows,'' *Journal of Marketing,* 42, no. 3 (July 1978), 21–26.

ANDREWS, KENNETH R., *The Concept of Corporate Strategy,* revised edition. Homewood, IL: Richard D. Irwin, 1980. First published, 1971.

ARGYRIS, CHRIS, ''Double Loop Learning in Organizations,'' *Harvard Business Review,* 55, no. 5 (September–October 1977), 115–125.

BARNARD, CHESTER L., *The Functions of the Executive.* Cambridge, MA: Harvard University Press, 1966. First printed, 1938.

DRUCKER, PETER F., *Management.* New York: Harper and Row, 1973.

FAYOL, HENRI, *General and Industrial Management,* trans. Constance Storrs. New York: Pitman Publishing 1972. First French edition, 1916.

OHMAE, KENICHI, *The Mind of the Strategist: The Art of Japanese Business.* New York: McGraw-Hill, 1982.

QUINN, JAMES BRIAN, *Strategies for Change, Logical Incrementalism.* Homewood, IL: Richard D. Irwin, 1980.

SALANCIK, GERALD R., and JEFFREY PFEFFER, ''Who Gets Power—And How They Hold on to It: A Strategic Contingency Model of Power,'' *Organizational Dynamics,* Winter 1977, 3–21.

SELZNICK, PHILIP, *Leadership in Administration,* New York: Harper & Row, 1957.

SUN TZU, *The Art of War,* trans. Samuel B. Griffith. New York: Oxford University Press, 1963.

Chapter 2

ANSOFF, H. I., *Corporate Strategy.* New York: McGraw-Hill, 1965.

ARGYRIS, CHRIS, ''Double Loop Learning in Organizations,'' *Harvard Business Review,* 55, no. 5 (September–October 1977), 115–125.

BRAYBROOKE, DAVID, and CHARLES E. LINDBLOOM, *A Strategy of Decision: Policy Evaluation as a Social Process.* New York: The Free Press, 1970.

BOURGEOIS, L. J. III, ''Performance and Consensus,'' *Strategic Management Journal,* 1 (1980), 227–248.

CYERT, R., and J. MARCH, *A Behavioral Theory of the Firm.* Englewood Cliffs, NJ: Prentice Hall, 1963.

EMSHOFF, JAMES R., IAN L. MITROFF, and RALPH H. KILMAN, ''The Role of Idealization in Long Range Planning: An Essay on the Logical and Socio Emotional Aspects of Planning,'' *Technological Forecasting and Social Change,* 11 (1978), 335–348.

FAYOL, HENRI, *General and Industrial Management,* trans. Constance Storrs. New York: Pitman Publishing, 1972. First French edition, 1916.

GILMORE, FRANK F., *Formulation & Advocacy of Business Policy,* revised edition. Ithaca, NY: Cornell University Press, 1970.

GILMORE, FRANK F., "Formulating a Strategy in Small Companies," *Harvard Business Review,* May–June 1971, 71–81.

HENDERSON, BRUCE D., *Henderson on Corporate Strategy.* Cambridge, MA: Abt Books, 1979.

LEVITT, T., "Marketing Myopia," *Harvard Business Review,* 53, no. 5 (September–October 1960), 26.

OHMAE, KENICHI, *The Mind of the Strategist: The Japanese Business.* New York: McGraw-Hill Book Company, 1982.

QUINN, JAMES BRIAN, *Strategies for Change: Logical Incrementalism,* Homewood, IL: Richard D. Irwin, 1980.

SCHOEN, DONALD R., "Managing Technological Innovation," *Harvard Business Review,* 47, no. 3 (May–June 1969), 156–165.

STEVENSON, HOWARD H., "Defining Corporate Strengths and Weaknesses," *Sloan Management Review,* Spring 1976, 51–68.

WOLF, WILLIAM B., *Management and Consulting, An Introduction to James O. McKinsey.* Ithaca, NY: Cornell University Press, 1978.

Chapter 3

ANDREWS, KENNETH R., *The Concept of Corporate Strategy,* revised edition. Homewood, IL: Richard D. Irwin, 1980. First published in 1971.

LEVITT, T., "Marketing Myopia," *Harvard Business Review,* 53, no. 5 (September–October 1975), 26.

MCCARTHY, E. JEROME, *Basic Marketing: A Managerial Approach.* Homewood, IL: Richard D. Irwin, 1960.

MINTZBERG, HENRY, "Patterns in Strategy Formulation," *Management Science,* 24, no. 9 (May 1978), 934–948.

RUMELT, R. P., *Strategy, Structure, and Economic Performance.* Boston, MA: Division of Research, Harvard Business School, 1974.

RUMELT, R. P., "Diversification Strategy and Profitability," *Strategic Management Journal,* 3, no. 4 (October–December 1982), 359–370.

SALTER, MALCOM S., *Diversification Through Acquisition: Strategies for Creating Economic Value.* New York: The Free Press, 1979.

SALTER, MALCOM S., and WOLF A. WEINHOLD, "Diversification via Acquisition: Creating Value," *Harvard Business Review,* 56, no. 4 (July–August 1978), 166–176.

Chapter 4

BARNARD, CHESTER L., *The Functions of the Executive.* Cambridge, MA: Harvard University Press, 1966. First printed in 1938.

VICKERS, SIR GEOFFREY, *The Art of Judgment, A Study of Policy Making.* New York: Basic Books, 1965.

Chapter 5

ACKOFF, RUSSELL L., and JAMES R. EMSHOFF, "Advertising Research at Anheuser-Busch, Inc. (1963–68)," *Sloan Management Review,* Winter 1975, 1–15.

ACKOFF, RUSSELL L., and JAMES R. EMSHOFF, "Advertising Research at Anheuser-Busch, Inc. (1968–74)," *Sloan Management Review,* Spring 1975, 1–15.

BARNARD, CHESTER L., *The Functions of the Executive*. Cambridge: Harvard University Press, 1966. First printed 1938.

CLEMENTS, W. W., quoted by Richard B. Schmitt, "Dr Pepper Co. Prods Peppers to Drink More," *Wall Street Journal*, Thursday, January 13, 1983.

HAYES, R. H., and S. C. WHEELWRIGHT, "Dynamics of Process-Product Life-Cycles," *Harvard Business Review*, 57, no. 2 (March–April 1979), 127–136.

HUSSEY, DAVID E., "The Corporate Appraisal, Assessing Company Strengths and Weaknesses," *Long Range Planning*, 1 (December 1968), 19–25.

JENNINGS, EUGENE E., "Managing Excellence, The Maze Bright Manager: Skills of Exceptional Executives." Presented at a *Business Week* Strategic Planning Conference on Business Unit Planning, New Orleans, LA, May 1–2, 1980.

MAJARO, SIMON, "Market Share: Deception or Diagnosis," *Marketing*, March 1977, 44–47.

OHMAE, KENICHI, *The Mind of the Strategist: The Art of Japanese Business*. New York: McGraw-Hill, 1982.

SKINNER, WICKHAM, "The Focused Factory," *Harvard Business Review*, 52, no. 3 (May–June 1974), 113.

STEVENSON, HOWARD H., "Defining Corporate Strengths and Weaknesses," *Sloan Management Review*, Spring 1976, 51–68.

SUN TZU, *The Art of War*, trans. Samuel B. Griffith. New York: Oxford University Press, 1963.

UTTERBACK, JAMES M., and WILLIAM J. ABERNATHY, "A Dynamic Model of Process and Product Innovation," *OMEGA, The International Journal of Management Science*, 3, no. 6 (1975), 639–656.

WEBSTER, FREDERICK E. JR., *Industrial Marketing Strategy*. New York: John Wiley & Sons, 1979.

Chapter 6

ABELL, DEREK F. and JOHN S. HAMMOND, *Strategic Market Planning: Problems and Analytical Approaches*. Englewood Cliffs, NJ: Prentice-Hall, 1979.

ABERNATHY, WILLIAM J., and KENNETH WAYNE, "Limits of the Learning Curve," *Harvard Business Review*, 52, no. 5 (September–October 1974), 109.

ALCHIAN, ARMEN, "Costs and Outputs," in M. Abramowitz, ed., *The Allocation of Economic Resources: Essays in Honor of B. F. Haley*. Stanford, CA: Stanford University Press, 1959.

ANDRESS, FRANK J., "The Learning Curve as a Production Tool," *Harvard Business Review*, 32, no. 1 (January–February 1954), 87–95.

BIGGADIKE, RALPH, "Scott-Air Corporation (B)." Working Paper, Colgate Darden School, University of Virginia, 1977.

BOSTON CONSULTING GROUP, *Perspectives on Experience*. Boston, MA: The Boston Consulting Group, 1972.

CHEVALIER, MICHEL, "The Strategy Spectre Behind Your Market Share," *European Business*, Summer 1972, 63–72.

CONWAY, R. W., and ANDREW SCHULTZ, JR., "The Manufacturing Progress Function," *Journal of Industrial Engineering*, 10, no. 1 (January–February 1959), 39–54.

DAY, GEORGE and DAVID B. MONTGOMERY, "Diagnosing the Experience Curve," *Journal of Marketing*, 47, no. 2 (Spring 1983), 44–85.

FRUHAN, WILLIAM E., JR., "Pyrrhic Victories in Fights for Market Share," *Harvard Business Review*, 50, no. 5 (September–October 1972), 100–107.

GHEMAWAT, PANKAJ, "Building Strategy on the Experience Curve," *Harvard Business Review*, 63, no. 2 (March–April 1985), 143–149.

HAX, ARNOLDO and NICOLAS S. MAJLEEF, *Strategic Management: An Integrated Perspective*, Englewood Cliffs, NJ: Prentice-Hall, 1984.

HIRSCHMANN, WINFRED B., "Profit from the Learning Curve," *Harvard Business Review,* 42, no. 1 (January–February 1964), 125.

HIRSCHLEIFER, JACK, "The Firm's Cost Function: A Successful Reconstruction," *Journal of Business,* 35, no. 3 (July 1962), 235–255.

KIECHEL, WALTER III, "The Decline of the Experience Curve," *Fortune,* October 5, 1981, 139–146.

LEVITT, T., "Marketing Myopia," *Harvard Business Review,* 53, no. 5 (September–October 1975), 26.

MCKINSEY, JAMES O., "Adjusting Policies to Meet Changing Conditions," General Management Series, no. 116, New York: American Management Association, 1932.

RAPPING, LEONARD, "Learning and World War II Production Functions," *Review of Economics and Statistics,* 47, no. 1 (1965), 81–86.

STOBAUGH, ROBERT B. and PHILLIP L. TOWNSEND, "Price Forecasting and Strategic Planning: The Case of Petrochemicals," *Journal of Marketing Research,* 12, February 1975, 19–29.

SULTAN, RALPH, *Pricing in the Electrical Oligopoly,* Volumes I and II. Boston, MA: Division of Research, Graduate School of Business Administration, Harvard University, 1975.

WRIGHT, T. P., "Factors Affecting the Cost of Airplanes," *Journal of Aeronautical Sciences,* 3, no. 4 (February 1936), 122–28.

Chapter 7

ABERCROMBIE, M. L. JOHNSON, *The Anatomy of Judgement* London: Hutchinson, 1967.

ABERNATHY, WILLIAM J., and JAMES M. UTTERBACK, "Patterns of Industrial Innovation," *Technology Review,* 80, no. 7 (June–July 1978), 1–9.

BASS, FRANK M., "A New Product Growth Model for Consumer Durables," *Management Science Theory,* 15, no. 5 (January 1969), 215–27.

BUZZELL, ROBERT D., BRADLEY GALE, and RALPH G. M. SULTAN, "Market Share—A Key to Profitability," *Harvard Business Review,* 53, no. 1 (January–February 1975), 97–106.

CHRISTENSEN, C. R., NORMAN BERG, and MALCOLM S. SALTER, *Policy Formulation and Administration,* 8th edition. Homewood, IL: Richard D. Irwin, 1980.

CHUDLEY, JOHN A., *LETRASET, A lesson in Growth.* London: Business Books Unlimited, 1974.

COX, WILLIAM E. JR., "Product Life Cycles as Marketing Models," *Journal of Business,* 40, no. 4 (October 1967), 375–384.

EMSHOFF, JAMES R., and R. EDWARD FREEMAN, "Who's Butting into Your Business?" *The Wharton Magazine,* Fall 1979, 44–59.

ENIS, BEN M., RAYMOND LAGARCE, and ARTHUR E. PRELL, "Extending the Product Life Cycle," *Business Horizons,* 20, no. 3 (June 1977), 46–56.

FAYOL, HENRI, *General and Industrial Management,* trans. Constance Storrs. New York: Pitman Publishing, 1972. First French edition, 1916.

FISHER, J. C., and R. H. PRY, "A Simple Model of Technological Change," *Technological Forecasting & Social Change,* 3 (1971), 75–88.

FREEMAN, EDWARD R., "Strategic Management: A Stakeholder Approach." Mimeograph for publication in *Latest Advances in Strategic Management,* November 1981, 1–47.

GALE, BRADLEY T., "Market Share and Rate of Return," *Review of Economics and Statistics,* 54, no. 4 (November 1972), 412–423.

GASTON, FRANK J., "Growth Patterns in Industry: A Reexamination." National Industrial Conference Board, Inc., New York, no. 75, 1961.

GOLD, BELA, "Industry Growth Patterns: Theory & Empirical Results," *Journal of Industrial Economics,* 13, no. 1 (1964), 53–73.

HATTEN, KENNETH J., and MARY LOUISE HATTEN, "Some Empirical Insights for Strategic Marketers: The Case of Beer,'' in H. Thomas and D. Gardner, eds., *Strategic Marketing and Management.* London: John Wiley and Sons, 1985.

HAYES, R. H., and S. C. WHEELWRIGHT, ''Dynamics of Process-Product Life-Cycles,'' *Harvard Business Review,* 57, no. 2 (March–April 1979), 127–136.

KROC, RAY, with ROBERT ANDERSON, *Grinding it Out: The Making of McDonalds.* New York: Berkley, 1977.

LENZ, RALPH C. JR., and H. W. LANFORD, ''The Substitution Phenomenon,'' *Business Horizons,* 15, no. 1 (February 1972), 63–68.

LEVITT, THEODORE, ''Exploit the Product Life Cycle,'' *Harvard Business Review,* November–December 1965, 81–94.

LEVITT, THEODORE, ''Marketing Myopia,'' *Harvard Business Review,* 53, no. 5 (September–October 1975), 26.

MCKINSEY, JAMES O., ''Adjusting Policies to Meet Changing Conditions,'' General Management Series, No. 116. New York: American Management Association, 1932.

MCLEAN, JOHN G., and ROBERT W. HAIGH, *The Growth of Integrated Oil Companies.* Boston, MA: Division of Research, Graduate School of Business Administration, Harvard University, 1954.

NEVERS, JOHN V., ''Further Applications of the Bass New Product Growth Model,'' Institute Paper No. 283. Institute for Research in the Behavioral, Economic, and Management Sciences, Purdue University, 1970.

PFEFFER, JEFFREY, and GERALD R. SALANCIK, *The External Control of Organizations, A Resource Dependence Perspective.* New York: Harper and Row, 1978.

POLLI, R., and V. J. COOK, ''Validity of the Product Life Cycle,'' *Journal of Business,* 42, no. 4 (October 1969), 385–400.

PORTER, MICHAEL E., *Competitive Strategy, Techniques for Analyzing Industries and Competitors.* New York: The Free Press, 1980.

RUMELT, R. P., and ROBIN WENSLEY, ''In Search of the Market Share Effect,'' *Proceedings of the Academy of Management,* 1981, 2–6.

SCHERER, F. M., *Industrial Market Structure and Economic Performance.* Chicago: Rand McNally, 1970.

SCHOEFFLER, SIDNEY, ROBERT D. BUZZELL, and DONALD F. HEANY, ''Impact of Strategic Planning on Profit Performance,'' *Harvard Business Review,* 52, no. 2 (March–April 1974), 137–145.

STIPP, DAVID and G. CHRISTIAN HILL, ''Texas Instruments' Problems Show Pitfalls of Home-Computer Market,'' *Wall Street Journal,* June 17, 1983, p. 29.

UTTERBACK, JAMES M., and WILLIAM J. ABERNATHY, ''A Dynamic Model of Process and Product Innovation,'' *OMEGA, The International Journal of Management Science,* 3, no. 6 (1975), 639–656.

UYTERHOEVEN, HUGO E. JR., ROBERT E. ACKERMAN, and JOHN W. ROSENBLUM, *Strategy and Organization.* Homewood, IL: Richard D. Irwin, 1977.

WILLIAMSON, OLIVER E., *Markets and Hierarchies: Analysis and Antitrust Implications.* New York: The Free Press, 1975.

WOO, CAROLYN Y., ''Evaluation of the Strategies and Performance of Low ROI Market Share Leaders,'' *Strategic Management Journal,* 4 (1983), 123–135.

YALE, JORDON P., *Modern Textiles Magazine,* February 1964, 33.

Chapter 8

ABELL, DEREK F., ''Strategic Windows,'' *Journal of Marketing,* 42, no. 3 (July 1978), 21–26.

BAIN, JOE S., *Barriers to New Competition,* Cambridge, MA: Harvard University Press, 1956.

BASS, FRANK M., PHILLIPPE J. CATTIN, and DICK R. WITTINK, ''Market Structure and Industry

Influence on Profitability,'' in Hans B. Thorelli, ed., *Strategy + Structure = Performance*. Bloomington, IN: Indiana University Press, 1977.

BAUMOL, WILLIAM J., ''Contestable Markets: An Uprising in the Theory of Industrial Structure,'' *American Economic Review,* 72, no. 1 (March 1982), 97–106.

BOSTON CONSULTING GROUP, *Perspectives on Experience*. Boston, MA: Boston Consulting Group, 1968 and 1972.

BUZZELL, ROBERT D., BRADLEY GALE, and RALPH G. M. SULTAN, ''Market Share—A Key to Profitability,'' *Harvard Business Review,* 53, no. 1 (January–February 1975), 97–106.

CAVES, RICHARD, *American Industry: Structure, Conduct, Performance*. Englewood Cliffs, NJ: Prentice-Hall, 1964.

COOKE, ERNEST F., ''Market Share Measures of Rivalry,'' unpublished Doctoral Dissertation, Case Western Reserve University, 1974.

COX, WILLIAM E., JR., ''Product Portfolio Strategy, Market Structure, and Performance,'' in Hans B. Thorelli, ed., *Strategy + Structure = Performance*. Bloomington, IN: Indiana University Press, 1977.

HATTEN, KENNETH J., and MARY LOUISE HATTEN, ''Some Empirical Insights for Strategic Marketers: The Case of Beer,'' in H. Thomas and D. Gardner, eds., *Strategic Marketing and Management*. London: John Wiley and Sons, 1985.

HATTEN, KENNETH J., DAN E. SCHENDEL, and ARNOLD C. COOPER, ''A Strategic Model of the US Brewing Industry: 1952–1971,'' *Academy of Management Journal,* 21, no. 2 (1978), 592–610.

HATTEN, KENNETH J., and DAN E. SCHENDEL, ''Heterogeneity Within An Industry,'' *Journal of Industrial Economics,* 26, no. 2 (December 1977), 97–113.

HENDERSON, BRUCE D., ''Brinkmanship in Business,'' *Harvard Business Review,* 45, no. 2 (March–April 1967), 49–55.

HENDERSON, BRUCE D., *Henderson on Corporate Strategy*. Cambridge, MA: Abt Books, 1979.

HIRSCHMANN, WINFRED B., ''Profit from the Learning Curve,'' *Harvard Business Review,* 42, no. 1 (January–February 1964), 125.

HUNT, MICHAEL S., ''Competition in the Major Home Appliance Industry,'' unpublished Doctoral Dissertation, Harvard University, 1973.

MCGEE, JOHN, ''Strategic Groups: Review and Prospects.'' Presented at Strategic Marketing Workshop, University of Illinois, May 10–11, 1982.

MILLER, JOSEPH C., ''Comments on the Essay by William E. Cox, Jr.,'' in Hans B. Thorelli, ed., *Strategy + Structure = Performance*. Bloomington, IN: Indiana University Press, 1977.

NEWMAN, HOWARD H., ''Strategic Groups and the Structure Performance Relationship,'' *The Review of Economics and Statistics,* 60, no. 3 (August 1978), 417–427.

PORTER, MICHAEL E., ''Consumer Behavior, Retailer Power, and Market Performance in Consumer Goods Industries,'' *The Review of Economics and Statistics,* 56, no. 4 (November 1974), 419–436.

PORTER, MICHAEL E., ''How Competitive Forces Shape Strategy,'' *Harvard Business Review,* 57, no. 2 (March–April 1979), 137–145.

SCHENDEL, DAN E. and G. RICHARD PATTON, ''A Simultaneous Equation Model of Corporate Strategy,'' *Management Science,* 24, no. 15 (November 1978), 1611–21.

SCHOEFFLER, SIDNEY, ROBERT D. BUZZELL, and DONALD F. HEANY, ''Impact of Strategic Planning on Profit Performance,'' *Harvard Business Review,* 52, no. 2 (March–April 1974), 137–45.

WENSLEY, ROBIN, ''Pims and BCG: New Horizons or False Dawn,'' *Strategic Management Journal,* 3 (1982), 147–58.

Chapter 9

ACKERMAN, ROBERT W., *The Social Challenge to Business.* Cambridge, MA: Harvard University Press, 1975.

ANDREWS, KENNETH R., *The Concept of Corporate Strategy,* revised edition. Homewood, IL: Richard D. Irwin, 1980.

ANSOFF, H. IGOR, *Corporate Strategy.* New York: McGraw-Hill, 1965.

BARNARD, CHESTER L., *The Functions of the Executive.* Cambridge, MA: Harvard University Press, 1966. First printed, 1938.

BOWER, MARVIN, *The Will to Manage.* New York: McGraw-Hill, 1966.

BOURGEOIS, L. J. III, "Performance and Consensus," *Strategic Management Journal,* 1 (1980), 227–248.

COHEN, HERB, *You Can Negotiate Anything.* New York: Bantam Books, 1982.

CYERT R., and J. MARCH, *A Behavioral Theory of a Firm.* Englewood Cliffs, NJ: Prentice Hall, 1963.

DALTON, DAN R., and RICHARD A. COSIER, "The Four Faces of Social Responsibility," *Business Horizons,* 25, no 3 (May–June 1982), 19–27.

DILL, W., "Strategic Management in a Kibitzer's World," in I. R. Ansoff, J. Declerk, and R. Hayes, eds., *Planning to Strategic Management.* New York: John Wiley and Sons, 1976.

EMSHOFF, JAMES R., and R. EDWARD FREEMAN, "Who's Butting into Your Business?" *The Wharton Magazine,* Fall 1979, 44–59.

FREEMAN, EDWARD R., "Strategic Management: A Stakeholder Approach." Mimeograph for publication in *Latest Advances in Strategic Management,* November 1981, 1–47.

FRIEDMAN, MILTON, *Capitalism & Freedom.* Chicago: The University of Chicago Press, 1962.

GREFE, EDWARD A., *Fighting to Win: Business Political Power.* New York: Law and Business Inc./Harcourt Brace Javonovich Publishers, 1982.

KAMI, MICHAEL J., "Gap Analysis: Key to Super Growth," *Long Range Planning,* 1, no. 4 (June 1969), 44–47.

MILLER, ARJAY, "Manager's Journal: A Director's Questions," *Wall Street Journal,* August 18, 1980.

MURRAY, EDWIN A. JR., "Strategic Choice as a Negotiated Outcome," *Management Science,* 24, no. 9 (May 1978), 960–972.

POST, JAMES E., *Corporate Behavior & Social Change.* Reston, VA: Reston Publishing Company, 1978.

POST, JAMES E., "The Internal Management of Social Responsiveness: The Role of the Public Affairs Department." Presented at "The Corporation and Society: Planning and Management of Corporate Responsibility," Seminar, University of Santa Clara, October 31–November 2, 1979.

POST, JAMES E., *Risk and Response: Management and Social Change in the American Insurance Industry.* Lexington, MA: D. C. Heath, 1976.

ROGERS, CARL R., *Carl Rogers on Personal Power.* New York: Delacorte Press, 1977.

SCHWARTZ, JULES J., *Corporate Policy.* Englewood Cliffs, NJ: Prentice Hall, 1978.

SELZNICK, PHILIP, *Leadership in Administration: A Sociological Interpretation.* New York: Harper and Row, 1957.

SELZNICK, PHILIP, "Private Government and Corporate Conscience." Mimeograph prepared for Symposium of Business Policy, April 8–11, 1963. Graduate School of Business Administration, Harvard University, 1964.

SIMON, HERBERT A., "On the Concept of Organizational Goal," *Administrative Science Quarterly,* 9, no. 1 (June 1964), 1–22.

SIMON, HERBERT A., *Administrative Behavior: A Study of Decision Making Processes in Administrative Organizations,* third edition. New York: The Free Press, 1976.

SUN TZU, *The Art of War,* trans. Samuel B. Griffith. New York: Oxford University Press, 1963.
VICKERS, SIR GEOFFREY, *The Art of Judgment, A Study of Policy Making.* New York: Basic Books, 1965.

Chapter 10

ANDREWS, KENNETH R., *The Concept of Corporate Strategy,* revised edition. Homewood, IL: Richard D. Irwin, 1980.

ANSOFF, H. I., *Corporate Strategy.* New York: McGraw-Hill, 1965.

CRAWFORD, C. MERLE, "The Trajectory Theory of Goal Setting for New Products," *Journal of Marketing Research,* 3, no. 2 (May 1966), 117–125.

HENDERSON, BRUCE D., *Henderson on Corporate Strategy.* Cambridge, MA: Abt Books, 1979.

KAMI, MICHAEL J., "Planning: Realities vs. Theory," *Management Thinking,* January 1968.

KAMI, MICHAEL J., "Gap Analysis: Key to Super Growth," *Long Range Planning,* 1, no. 4 (June 1969), 44–47.

LUCE, R. DUNCAN, and HOWARD RAIFFA, *Games & Decisions.* New York: John Wiley, 1957.

MINTZBERG, HENRY, *The Nature of Managerial Work.* New York: Harper and Row, 1973.

MUSASHI, MIYAMOTO, *A Book of Five Rings,* trans. Victor Harris. Woodstock, NY: The Overlook Press, 1974. First published, 1645.

PFEFFER, JEFFREY, and GERALD R. SALANCIK, *The External Control of Organizations, A Resource Dependence Perspective.* New York: Harper and Row, 1978.

SIMON, HERBERT A., *Administrative Behavior,* 3rd edition. New York: The Free Press, 1976.

SWALM, RALPH O., "Utility Theory—Insights into Risk Taking," *Harvard Business Review,* 44, no. 6 (November–December 1966), 123–130.

TILLES, SEYMOUR, "How to Evaluate Corporate Strategy," *Harvard Business Review,* 41, no. 3 (July–August 1963), 111–121.

WILLIAMSON, OLIVER E., *Markets and Hierarchies: Analysis and Antitrust Implications.* New York: The Free Press, 1975.

ZAMMUTO, RAYMOND F., *Assessing Organizational Effectiveness,* Albany, NY: State University of New York Press, 1982.

Chapter 11

ANDREWS, KENNETH R., *The Concept of Corporate Strategy,* revised edition. Homewood, IL: Richard D. Irwin, 1980.

ANSOFF, H. I., "Managerial Problem Solving," *Journal of Business Policy,* 2, no. 1 (Autumn 1971), 3–20.

ARGYRIS, CHRIS, "Double Loop Learning in Organizations," *Harvard Business Review,* 55, no. 5 (September–October 1977), 115–125.

BOWER, JOSEPH L., "Strategy as a Problem Solving Theory of Business Planning." Mimeograph, Harvard Graduate School of Business Administration, Presidents and Fellows of Harvard College, 1967.

BOWER, JOSEPH L., "Solving the Problems of Business Planning," *The Journal of Business Strategy,* 2, no. 3 (1982), 32–44.

BOWER, JOSEPH L., *Managing the Resource Allocation Process; A Study of Corporate Planning and Investment.* Boston: Harvard University Division of Research, Graduate School of Business Administration, 1970.

BRAYBROOKE, DAVID, and CHARLES E. LINDBLOOM, *A Strategy of Decision: Policy Evaluation as a Social Process.* New York: The Free Press, 1970.

Cooper, Arnold C., and Dan Schendel, "Strategic Responses to Technological Threats," *Business Horizons,* 19, no. 1 (February 1976), 61–69.

deBono, Edward, *New Think: The Use of Lateral Thinking in the Generation of New Ideas.* New York: Buni Books, 1968.

deBono, Edward. "Why Opportunities are Often Missed," *International Management,* 32, no. 9 (September 1977), 57–63.

Emshoff, James R., Ian I. Mitroff, and Ralph H. Kilman, "The Role of Idealization in Long Range Planning: An Essay on the Logical and Socio Emotional Aspects of Planning," *Technological Forecasting and Social Change,* 11, 1978, 335–348.

Galbraith, Craig, and Dan E. Schendel, "An Empirical Analysis of Strategic Types," *Strategic Management Journal,* 4 (1983), 153–173.

Henderson, Bruce D., *Henderson on Corporate Strategy.* Cambridge, MA: Abt Books, 1979.

Janis, Irving L., and Leon Mann, *Decision Making.* New York: The Free Press, 1977.

Levitt, T., "Marketing Myopia," *Harvard Business Review,* 53, no. 5 (September–October 1975), 26.

Levitt. T., "Innovative Imitation," *Harvard Business Review,* 44, no. 5 (September–October 1966), 63–70.

McLean, John G., and Robert Wm. Haigh, *The Growth of Integrated Oil Companies.* Boston: Division of Research, Graduate School of Business Administration, Harvard University, 1954.

Mitroff, Ian I., and James R. Emshoff, "On Strategic Assumption-Making: A Dialectic Approach to Policy and Planning," *Academy of Management Review,* 4, no. 1 (1979), 1–12.

Ohmae, Kenichi, *The Mind of the Strategist: The Art of Japanese Business.* New York: McGraw-Hill, 1982.

Porter, Michael E., *Competitive Strategy, Techniques for Analyzing Industries and Competitors.* New York: The Free Press, 1980.

Quinn, James Brian, *Strategies for Change, Logical Incrementalism.* Homewood, IL: Richard D. Irwin, 1980.

Utterback, James M., and William J. Abernathy, "A Dynamic Model of Process and Product Innovation, *OMEGA, The International Journal of Management Science,* 3, no. 6 (1975), 639–656.

Uyterhoeven, Hugo E. Jr., "General Managers in the Middle," *Harvard Business Review,* 50, no. 2 (March–April 1972), 72–85.

Uyterhoeven, Hugo E. Jr., Robert E. Ackerman, and John W. Rosenblum. *Strategy and Organization.* Homewood, IL: Richard D. Irwin, 1977.

Williamson, Oliver E., *Markets and Hierarchies: Analysis and Antitrust Implications.* New York: The Free Press, 1975.

Chapter 12

Bourgeois, L. J. III, "Performance and Consensus," *Strategic Management Journal,* 1 (1980), 227–248.

deBono, Edward, *New Think: The Use of Lateral Thinking in the Generation of New Ideas.* New York: Buni Books, 1968.

Henderson, Bruce D., *Henderson on Corporate Strategy,* Cambridge, MA: Abt Books, 1979.

Hirschman, Albert, *Development Projects Observed.* Washington, DC: Brookings Institute, 1967.

Janis, Irving L., and Leon Mann, *Decision Making.* New York: The Free Press, 1977.

Myerson, Adam, and Susan Carey, "Fletcher Byrom Doesn't Want to Hold Your Hand," *Wall Street Journal,* June 1, 1982, p. 26.

PRICE, ROBERT M., ''Uncertainty and Strategic Opportunity,'' *The Journal of Business Strategy,* 2, no. 3 (Winter 1982), 3–8.

SCHOEN, DONALD R., ''Managing Technological Innovation,'' *Harvard Business Review,* 47, no. 3 (May–June 1969), 156–163.

VICKERS, SIR GEOFFREY, *The Art of Judgment, A Study of Policy Making.* New York: Basic Books, 1965.

Chapter 13

BOWER, MARVIN, *The Will to Manage.* New York: McGraw-Hill, 1966.

DEAL, TERRENCE E., and ALLAN A. KENNEDY, *Corporate Cultures: The Rites and Rituals of Corporate Life.* Reading, MA: Addison-Wesley, 1982.

FORD, C. S., *Cross-Cultural Approaches: Readings in Comparative Research.* New Haven, CT: HRAF Press, 1967.

KLUCKHOLN, CLYDE, *Mirror For Man: The Relation of Anthropology to Modern Life.* New York: Whittlesey House, 1949.

PARSONS, TALCOTT, ''Suggestions for a Sociological Approach to the Theory of Organizations—I,'' *Administrative Science Quarterly,* 1, no. 1 (June 1956), 63–85.

SCHWARTZ, HOWARD, and STANLEY M. DAVIS, ''Matching Corporate Culture and Business Strategy,'' *Organizational Dynamics,* 10, no. 1 (Summer 1981), 30–48.

UYTERHOEVEN, HUGO E. JR., ''General Managers in the Middle,'' *Harvard Business Review,* 50, no. 3 (March–April 1972), 75–85.

WEST, MORRIS, *The Clowns of God,* New York: Bantam Books, 1981.

Chapter 14

ANDREWS, KENNETH R., *The Concept of Corporate Strategy,* revised edition. Homewood, IL: Richard D. Irwin, 1980.

BARNARD, CHESTER L., *The Functions of the Executive.* Cambridge: Harvard University Press, 1966. First printed, 1938.

BARNES, LOUIS B. and SIMON A. HERSHON, ''Trnasferring Power in the Family Business,'' *Harvard Business Review,* 54, no. 4 (July–August 1976), 105–114.

CHANDLER, ALFRED D. JR., *Strategy and Structure: Chapters in the History of the American Industrial Enterprise.* Cambridge, MA: MIT Press, 1962.

CHANDLER, ALFRED D. JR., *The Visible Hand, The Managerial Revolution in American Business.* Cambridge, MA: Harvard University Press, 1977.

CLIFFORD, DONALD K. JR., ''Growth Pains of the Threshold Company,'' *Harvard Business Review,* 51, no. 5 (September–October 1973), 143–154.

DAVIS, STANLEY M., and PAUL R. LAWRENCE, *Matrix.* Reading, MA: Addison-Wesley, 1977.

ERICKSON, ERIC, *Childhood & Society,* 2nd edition. New York: W. W. Norton, 1963.

FAYOL, HENRI, *General and Industrial Management,* trans. Constance Storrs. New York: Pitman Publishing 1972. First French edition, 1916.

GREINER, LARRY E., ''Evolution and Revolution as Organizations Grow,'' *Harvard Business Review,* 50, no. 4 (July–August 1972), 37–46.

HIRSCHMAN, ALBERT, *Development Projects Observed.* Washington, DC: Brookings Institute, 1967.

HUNT, J. W., *The Restless Organization.* Sydney: John Wiley and Sons, Australasia Pty. Ltd., 1972.

JENNINGS, EUGENE E., ''Managing The Maze Bright Manager: Skills of Exceptional Executives.''

Presented at a *Business Week* Startegic Planning Conference on Business Unit Planning, New Orleans, LA, May 1–2, 1980.

KOTTER, JOHN P., *Power in Management: How to Understand, Acquire, and Use It*. New York: Amacom, 1979.

KOTTER, JOHN P., *The General Managers*. New York: The Free Press, 1982.

LIPPITT, GORDON L., and WARREN H. SCHMIDT, "Crisis in a Developing Organization," *Harvard Business Review,* 45, no. 6 (November–December 1967), 102–112.

MCCASKEY, MICHAEL B., *The Executive Challenge: Managing Change and Ambiguity*. Boston: Pittman, 1982.

MCGREGOR, DOUGLAS, *The Human Side of Enterprise*. New York: McGraw-Hill Book Company, 1960.

MINTZBERG, HENRY, "Patterns in Strategy Formulation," *Management Science,* 24, no. 9 (May 1978), 934–948.

OUCHI, WILLIAM, *Theory Z. How American Business Should Meet the Japanese Challenge*. Reading, MA: Addison-Wesley, 1981.

OUCHI, WILLIAM and JERRY B. JOHNSON, "Types of Organizational Control and Their Relationship to Emotional Well-Being." *Administrative Science Quarterly,* 23 (1978), 293–317.

QUINN, JAMES BRIAN, *Strategies for Change: Logical Incrementalism*. Homewood, IL: Richard D. Irwin, 1980.

SALTER, MALCOLM S., "Stages of Corporate Development," *Journal of Business Policy,* 1, no. 1 (1970), 23–37.

SCOTT, BRUCE R., "Stages of Corporate Development, Part I." Cambridge, MA: President and Fellows of Harvard College, 1971 (ICCH Case # 9-371-294).

SUN TZU, *The Art of War,* trans. Samuel B. Griffith. New York: Oxford University Press, 1963.

THOMPSON, JAMES D., *Organizations in Action*. New York: McGraw-Hill, 1967.

WILLIAMSON, OLIVER E., *Markets and Hierarchies: Analysis and Antitrust Implications*. New York: The Free Press, 1975.

Chapter 15

BARNARD, CHESTER L., *The Functions of the Executive*. Cambridge: Harvard University Press, 1966. First printed, 1938.

BARNES, LOUIS B., "Managing the Paradox of Organizational Trust," *Harvard Business Review,* March–April 1981, 107–116.

BARNES, LOUIS B., and SIMON A. HERSHON, "Transferring Power in the Family Business," *Harvard Business Review,* 54, no. 4 (July–August 1976), 105–114.

BLANCHARD, KENNETH, and SPENCER JOHNSON, *The One Minute Manager*. New York: William Morrow, 1982.

BOWER, MARVIN, *The Will to Manage*. New York: McGraw-Hill, 1966.

DEUTSCH, CLAUDIA H., "Guidance Counselors: The Art and the Dangers of Having or Being a Mentor," *TWA Ambassador,* September 1983, 12–14.

GERSTEIN, MARC, and HEATHER REISMAN, "Strategic Selection: Matching Executives to Business Conditions," *Sloan Management Review,* 24, no. 2 (Winter 1983), 33–49.

GOVINDARGAN, V., and ANIL K. GUPTA, "Business Unit Strategy, Control Systems and Business Unit Performance." Research Paper funded by the Graduate School, Boston University and the Graduate School of Business, Harvard University, November 1981.

KOTTER, JOHN P., *The General Managers*. New York: The Free Press, 1982.

LIVINGSTON, J. STERLING, "Pygmalion in Management," *Harvard Business Review,* 47, no. 4 (July–August 1969), 81–89.

McGregor, Douglas, *The Human Side of Enterprise*. New York: McGraw-Hill, 1960.
Peters, Thomas J., and Robert H. Waterman, Jr., *In Search of Excellence, Lessons from America's Best-Run Companies*. New York: Harper and Row, 1982.
Salter, Malcolm, "What is Fair Pay for the Executive?" *Harvard Business Review*, 52, no. 3 (May–June, 1972), 5–13.
Selznick, Philip, *Leadership in Administration, A Sociological Interpretation*. New York: Harper and Row, 1957.
Sloan, Alfred P., *My Years with General Motors*. New York: Doubleday, 1963.
Stata, Ray, and Modesto A. Maidique, "Bonus System for Balanced Strategy," *Harvard Business Review*, 58, no. 6 (November–December, 1980), 156–163.
Stonich, Paul J., "Using Rewards in Implementing Strategy," *Strategic Management Journal*, 2 (1981), 345–352.
Stybel, Laurence J., "Linking Strategic Planning and Management Manpower Planning," *California Management Review*, 25, no. 1 (Fall 1982), 48–56.
Sun Tzu, *The Art of War*, trans. Samuel B. Griffith. New York: Oxford University Press, 1963. Circa 500 B.C.
Towl, A., "Patterns of Executive Compensation," *Harvard Business Review*, 29, no. 4 (July 1951), 25.
Vancil, Richard F., *Decentralization: Managerial Ambiguity by Design*. Homewood, IL: Dow Jones-Irwin, 1979.
Zaleznick, Abraham, "Managers and Leaders: Are They Different?" *Harvard Business Review*, 55, no. 3 (May-June 1977), 67–78.

Chapter 16

Ackoff, Russell L., *A Concept of Corporate Planning*. New York: Wiley-Interscience, 1970.
Ansoff, H. I., "Managerial Problem Solving," *Journal of Business Policy*, 2, no. 1 (Autumn 1971), 3–20.
Ansoff, H. Igor, Jay Avner, Richard G. Brandenburg, Fred E. Portner, and Raymond Radosevich, "Does Planning Pay? The Effect of Planning on Success of Acquisitions in American Firms? *Long Range Planning*, 3, no. 2 (December 1970), 2–7.
Argyris, Chris, "Double Loop Learning in Organizations," *Harvard Business Review*, 55, no. 5 (September-October 1977), 115–125.
Armstrong, J. Scott, "The Value of Formal Planning for Strategic Decisions: Review of Empirical Research," *Strategic Management Journal*, 3 (1982), 197–211.
Bales, Carter F., "Strategic Control: The President's Paradox," *Business Horizons*, 20, no. 4 (August 1977), 17–28.
Bourgeois, L. J. III, "Performance and Consensus," *Strategic Management Journal*, 1 (1980), 227–248.
Bower, Joseph L., *Managing the Resource Allocation Process: A Study of Corporate Planning and Investment*. Boston: Graduate School of Business Administration, Harvard University, 1970.
Bower, Joseph L., "Strategy as a Problem Solving Theory of Business Planning." Mimeograph, Harvard Graduate School of Business Administration, Presidents and Fellows of Harvard College, 1967.
Bower, Joseph L., "Solving the Problems of Business Planning," *The Journal of Business Strategy*, 2, no. 3 (1982), 32–44.
Bower, Marvin, *The Will to Manage*. New York: McGraw-Hill, 1966.
Cosier, Richard A., "Dialectical Inquiry in Strategic Planning: A Case of Premature Acceptance?" *Academy of Management Review*, 6, no. 4 (1981), 643–648.

Cosier, Richard A., "Further Thoughts on Dialectical Inquiry: A Rejoinder to Mitroff and Mason," *Academy of Management Review,* 6, no. 4 (1981a), 653–654.

Cosier, Richard A., and John C. Aplin, "A Critical View of Dialectical Inquiry as a Tool in Strategic Planning," *Strategic Management Journal,* 7 (1980), 343–356.

deBono, Edward, *New Think: The Use of Lateral Thinking in the Generation of New Ideas.* New York: Buni Books, 1968.

Dewey, John, *How We Think.* Boston: D. C. Heath, 1933.

Emshoff, James R., and Arthur Finnel, "Defining Corporate Strategy: A Case Study Using Strategic Assumptions Analysis," *Sloan Management Review,* Spring 1979, 41–52.

Emshoff, James R., Ian I. Mitroff, and Ralph H. Kilman, "The Role of Idealization in Long Range Planning: An Essay on the Logical and Socio Emotional Aspects of Planning," *Technological Forecasting and Social Change,* 11 (1978), 335–348.

Fayol, Henri., *General and Industrial Management,* trans. Constance Storrs. New York: Pitman Publishing, 1972. First French edition, 1916.

Henry, Harold W., "Formal Planning in Major U.S. Corporations," *Long Range Planning,* 10 (October 1977), 40–45.

Herold, David M., "Long-Range Planning and Organizational Performance: A Cross-Valuation Study," *Academy of Management Journal,* 15, no. 1 (March 1972), 92–102.

Hunsicker, J. Quincy, "The Malaise of Strategic Planning," *The Management Review,* 69, no. 3 (March 1980), 8–14.

Kami, Michael J., "Planning: Realities vs. Theory," *Management Thinking,* January 1968, 1–4.

Kidder, Tracy, *The Soul of a New Machine.* Boston, MA: Little Brown, 1981.

Lorange, Peter, and Richard F. Vancil, "How to Design a Strategic Planning System," *Harvard Business Review,* 54, no. 5 (September–October 1976), 75–81.

Lyles, Marjorie A., and R. T. Lenz, "Managing the Planning Process: A Field Study of the Human Side of Planning," *Strategic Planning Journal,* 3 (1982), 105–118.

Mason, Richard O., and Ian I. Mitroff, "Assumptions of Majestic Metals: Strategy Through Dialectics," *California Management Review,* 22, no. 2 (Winter 1979), 80–88.

McKinsey, James O., "Adjusting Policies to Meet Changing Conditions," General Management Series, No. 116. New York: American Management Association, 1932.

Mintzberg, Henry, "Planning on the Left Side and Managing on the Right," *Harvard Business Review,* 54, no. 4 (July–August 1976), 49–58.

Mitroff, Ian I., and James R. Emshoff, "On Strategic Assumption-Making: A Dialectic Approach to Polict and Planning," *Academy of Management Review,* 4, no. 1 (1979), 1–12.

Mitroff, Ian I., James R. Emshoff, and Ralph H. Kilmann, "Assumptional Analysis: A Methodology for Strategic Problem Solving," *Management Science,* 25, no. 6 (June 1979), 583–593.

Mitroff, Ian I., and Richard O. Mason, "Structuring Ill-Structured Policy Issues: Further Explorations in a Methodology for Messy Problems," *Strategic Management Journal,* 1 (1980), 331–342.

Mitroff, Ian I., and Richard O. Mason, "The Metaphysics of Policy and Planning: A Reply to Cosier," *The Academy of Management Review,* 6, no. 4 (1981), 649–651.

Naylor, Thomas H., and Horst Schauland, "A Survey of Users of Corporate Planning Models," *Management Science,* 22, no. 9 (May 1976), 927–937.

Pascale, Richard Tanner, and Anthony G. Athos, *The Art of Japanese Management, Applications for American Executives.* New York: Simon and Schuster, 1981.

Pennington, Malcolm W., "Why Has Planning Failed?" *Long Range Planning,* 5, no. 1 (March 1972), 2–9.

Peters, Thomas J., and Robert H. Waterman, Jr., *In Search of Excellence, Lessons from America's Best-Run Companies.* New York: Harper and Row, 1982.

REICHMAN, W., and M. LEVY, "Psychological Restraints on Effective Planning," *Management Review,* 64, no. 10 (1975), 37–42.

SHANK, JOHN K., EDWARD G. NIBLOCK, and WILLIAM T. SANDALLS, JR., "Balance, 'Creativity' and 'Practicality' in Formal Planning," *Harvard Business Review,* 51, no. 1 (January–February 1973), 87–94.

SLOAN, ALFRED P., JR., *My Years at General Motors,* New York: Doubleday, 1963.

STEINER, GEORGE A., "Top Management's Role in Planning" *Long Range Planning,* 2, June 1969, 2–8.

THOMPSON, JAMES D., *Organizations in Action.* New York: McGraw-Hill, 1967.

THUNE, STANLEY S., and ROBERT J. HOUSE, "Where Long Range Planning Pays Off: Findings of a Survey of Formal, Informal Plans," *Business Horizons,* 13, no. 4 (August 1970), 81–87.

WELCH, JOHN F., "Where Is Marketing Now That We Really Need It?" Presented to The Conference Board's Marketing Conference, 1981.

WOLF, WILLIAM B., *Management and Consulting, An Introduction to James O. McKinsey.* Ithaca, NY: Cornell University Press, 1978.

WRAPP, H. EDWARD, "Good Managers Don't Make Policy Decisions," *Harvard Business Review,* 45, no. 5 (September–October 1967), 91–99.

Chapter 17

ANSOFF, H. I., *Corporate Strategy,* New York: McGraw-Hill, 1965.

BASS, FRANK M., PHILLIPPE J. CATTIN, and DICK R. WITTINK, "Market Structure and Industry Influence on Profitability," in H. Thorelli (ed.), *Strategy + Structure = Performance.* Bloomington, IN: Indiana University Press 1977.

BAUMOL, WILLIAM J., *Business Behavior, Value, and Growth,* New York: Harcourt, Brace and World, 1967.

BEAVER, WILLIAM, and DALE MORSE, "What Determines Price-Earnings Ratios?" *Financial Analysts Journal,* 34, no. 4 (July–August 1978), 65–76.

BETTIS, RICHARD A., and WILLIAM K. HALL, "Risks and Industry Effects in Large Diversified Firms." Proceedings of the Academy of Management National Meeting, 1981.

CHANDLER, ALFRED D., *Strategy and Structure, Chapters in the History of the American Industrial Enterprise,* Cambridge, MA: MIT Press, 1962.

CHANNON, DEREK F., *The Strategy & Structure of British Enterprise,* Boston, MA: Division of Research, Harvard Business School, 1973.

CHRISTENSEN, H. KURT, and CYNTHIA A. MONTGOMERY, "Corporate Economic Performance: Diversification Strategy Versus Market Structure." *Strategic Management Journal,* 2 (1981) 327–343.

DRUCKER, PETER F., "The Five Rules of Successful Acquisition," *The Wall Street Journal,* 28, no. 3 (October 15, 1981), 31.

DUNDAS, K. M., and P. R. RICHARDSON, "Implementing the Unrelated Product Strategy," *Journal of Strategic Management,* 3 (1982), 287–301.

DYAS, GARETH POOLEY, "The Strategy & Structure of French Industrial Enterprise," unpublished Doctoral Dissertation, Harvard Business School, 1972.

HARRINGTON, DIANA R., "Stock Prices, Beta, and Strategic Planning, *Harvard Business Review,* 61, no. 3 (May–June 1983), 157–164.

HATTEN, KENNETH J., and DAN E. SCHENDEL, "Strategy's Role in Policy Research," *Journal of Economics and Business,* 28, no. 3 (Spring–Summer 1976), 195–202.

HATTEN, KENNETH J., and DAN E. SCHENDEL, "Heterogeneity Within an Industry: Firm Conduct in the U.S. Brewing Industry 1952–1971," *Journal of Industrial Economics,* 26, no. 2 (December 1977), 97–113.

HATTEN, KENNETH J., DAN E. SCHENDEL, and ARNOLD C. COOPER, "A Strategic Model of the U.S. Brewing Industry, 1952–1971," *Academy of Management Journal,* 21, no. 4 (December 1978), 592–610.

HATTEN, KENNETH J., and MARY LOUISE HATTEN, "Some Empirical Insights for Strategic Marketers: The Case of Beer," in H. Thomas and D. Gardner, eds., *Strategic Marketing and Management.* London: John Wiley and Sons, 1985.

HENDERSON, BRUCE, *Henderson on Corporate Strategy,* Cambridge, MA: Abt Books, 1979.

KING, BENJAMIN F. "The Latent Statistical Structure of Security Price Changes," unpublished Ph.D. Dissertation, University of Chicago, 1964.

KITCHING, JOHN, "Why do Mergers Miscarry?" *Harvard Business Review,* 45, no. 6 (November–December 1967), 84–101.

KITCHING, JOHN, "Winning and Losing with European Acquisitions," *Harvard Business Review,* 52, no. 2 (March–April 1974), 124–136.

LEWELLEN, WILBUR G., "A Pure Financial Rationale for the Conglomerate Merger," *The Journal of Finance,* 26, no. 2 (May 1971).

MADER, CHRIS, and ROBERT HAGIN, *Common Stocks,* Homewood, IL: Dow Jones-Irwin, 1976.

MARRIS, ROBIN, *The Economic Theory of "Managerial" Capitalism,* London: MacMillan, 1964.

MCLEAN, JOHN G., and ROBERT WM. HAIGH, *The Growth of Integrated Oil Companies.* Boston, MA: Division of Research, Graduate School of Business Administration, Harvard University, 1954.

MULLINS, DAVID W., JR., "Does the Capital Asset Pricing Model Work?" *Harvard Business Review,* 60, no. 1 (January–February 1982), 105–111.

PAVAN, ROBERT J., "The Strategy and Structure of Italian Enterprise," unpublished Doctoral Dissertation, Harvard Business School, 1972.

RUMELT, RICHARD P., *Strategy, Structure and Economic Performance,* Boston, MA: Division of Research, Harvard Business School, 1974.

RUMELT, RICHARD P., "Diversification Strategy and Profitability," *Strategic Management Journal,* 3, no. 4 (October–December 1982), 359–370.

SALTER, MALCOLM S., and WOLF A. WEINHOLD, "Diversification via Acquisition: Creating Value," *Harvard Business Review,* 56, no. 4 (July–August 1978), 166–176.

SCOTT, BRUCE R., "The Industrial State: Old Myths and New Realities," *Harvard Business Review,* 51, no. 2 (March–April 1973), 133–143.

THANHEISER, HEINZ T., "Strategy & Structure of German Industrial Enterprise," unpublished Doctoral Dissertation, Harvard Business School, 1972.

WRIGLEY, LEONARD, "Divisional Autonomy and Diversification," unpublished Doctoral Dissertation, Harvard Business School, 1970.

Chapter 18

ABELL, DEREK F., and JOHN S. HAMMOND, *Strategic Market Planning, Problems, and Analytical Approches.* Englewood Cliffs, NJ: Prentice Hall, 1979.

ANDERSON, CARL R., and FRANK T. PAINE, "PIMS: A Re-examination." Presentation to Academy of Management, Orlando FL, August 1977.

ANSOFF, H. I., and JAMES LEONTIADES, "Strategic Portfolio Management," *Journal of General Management,* 4, no. 1 (1976), 13–29.

BARNES, LOUIS B., and SIMON A. HERSHON, "Transferring Power in the Family Business," *Harvard Business Review,* 54, no. 4 (July–August 1976), 105–114.

BEAVER, WILLIAM AND DALE MORSE, "What Determines Price-Earnings Ratios?" *Financial Analysts Journal,* 34, no. 4 (July–August 1978), 65–76.

BETTIS, RICHARD A., and WILLIAM K. HALL, Strategic Portfolio Management in the Multibusiness Firm, *California Management Review,* 24, no. 1 (Fall 1981), 23–38.

BIGGADIKE, RALPH, "Drawing Portfolio Charts." Mimeograph UVA-M-187, Darden Graduate School of Business Administration, University of Virginia, May 1978.

CHEVALIER, MICHEL, "The Strategy Spectre Behind Your Market Share," *European Business,* Summer 1972, 63–72.

CHRISTENSEN, H. KURT, ARNOLD C. COOPER, and CORNELIS A. DEKLUYVER, "The Dog Business: A Re-Examination," *Business Horizons,* 25, no. 6 (November–December 1982), 12–18.

DAY, GEORGE S., "Diagnosing the Product Portfolio," *Journal of Marketing,* 41, no. 2 (April 1977), 29–38.

FRUHAN, WILLIAM E., JR., "Pyrrhic Victories in Fights for Market Share," *Harvard Business Review,* 50, no. 5 (September–October 1972), 100–110.

HALL, WILLIAM K., "Survival Strategies in a Hostile Environment," *Harvard Business Review,* 58, no. 5 (September–October 1980), 75–85.

HAMBRICK, DONALD C., and IAN C. MACMILLAN, "The Product Portfolio and Man's Best Friend," *California Management Review,* 25, no. 1 (Fall 1982), 84–95.

HASPESLAGH, PHILIPPE, "Portfolio Planning: Uses and Limits," *Harvard Business Review,* 60, no. 1 (January–February 1982), 58–67.

HATTEN, KENNETH J. and DAN E. SCHENDEL, "Strategy's Role in Policy Research," *Journal of Economics and Business,* 28, no. 3 (Spring–Summer 1976), 195–202.

HEDLEY, BARRY, "Strategy and the Business Portfolio," *Long Range Planning,* 10 (1977), 9–15.

HENDERSON, BRUCE D., *Henderson on Corporate Strategy,* Cambridge, MA: Abt Books, 1979.

HUSSEY, D. E., "Portfolio Analysis: Practical Experience with the Directional Policy Matrix," *Long Range Planning,* 11 (1978), 2–8.

LOOMIS, WORTH, "Strategic Planning in Uncertain Times," *Chief Executive,* 1980, 7–12.

MACMILLAN, IAN C., DONALD C. HAMBRICK, and DIANA L. DAY, "The Product Portfolio and Profitability—A PIMS-Based Analysis of Industrial-Product Businesses," *Academy of Management Journal,* 25, no. 4 (December 1982), 733–755.

MARAKON ASSOCIATES, *The Marakon Profitability Matrix.* San Francisco: Marakon Associates, 1981.

PORTER, MICHAEL E., *Competitive Strategy: Techniques for Analyzing Industries and Competitors,* New York: Free Press, 1980.

VERITY, C. WILLIAMS JR., "Why a Portfolio of Businesses?" *Chief Executive,* c. 1975, 54.

WENSLEY, ROBIN, "Strategic Marketing: Betas, Boxes or Basics?" *Journal of Marketing,* 45, no. 3 (1981), 173–182.

Chapter 19

ANSOFF, H. I., *Corporate Strategy,* New York: McGraw-Hill, 1965.

Chapter 20

BURNS, TOM, and D. M. STALKER, *The Management of Innovation.* London: Tavistock, 1959.

COOPER, ARNOLD C., and DAN E. SCHENDEL, "Strategic Responses to Technological Threats," *Business Horizons,* 19, no. 1 (February 1976), 61–69.

HENDERSON, BRUCE D., "Brinkmanship in Business," *Harvard Business Review,* 45, no. 2 (March–April 1967), 49–55.

HOUT, THOMAS, MICHAEL E. PORTER, and EILEEN RUDDEN, "How Global Companies Win Out," *Harvard Business Review,* 60, no. 5 (September–October 1982), 98–108.

LEVITT, THEODORE, "The Globalization of Markets," *Harvard Business Review,* 61, no. 3 (May–June 1983), 92–102.

SCHON, DONALD A., *Technology and Change,* New York: Delacorte Press, 1967.

SLOAN, ALFRED P., JR., *My Years at General Motors*. New York: Doubleday, 1964.
WILLIAMSON, OLIVER E., *Markets and Hierarchies: Analysis and Antitrust Implications*. New York: The Free Press, 1975.

Chapter 21

BARNARD, CHESTER L., *The Functions of the Executive*. Cambridge, MA: Harvard University Press, 1966. First printed, 1938.
HENDERSON, BRUCE D., *Henderson on Corporate Strategy*. Cambridge, MA: Abt Books, 1979.
HIRSCHMAN, ALBERT, *Development Projects Observed*. Washington, DC: Brookings Institute, 1967.
HOMANS, GEORGE C., *The Human Group*. New York: Harcourt, Brace & World, 1950.
KATZ, ROBERT L., "Skills of an Effective Administrator," *Harvard Business Review*, 52, no. 5 (September–October 1974), 90–99.
LAWRENCE, PAUL R., "How to Deal with Resistance to Change," *Harvard Business Review*, 47, no. 1 (January–February 1969), 4–13.
LIEBERSON, STANLEY, and JAMES F. O'CONNOR, "Leadership and Organizational Performance: A Study of Large Corporations," *American Sociological Review*, 37, no. 2 (1972), 117–130.
LITZINGER, WILLIAM and THOMAS SCHAEFER, "Leadership Through Followship," *Business Horizons*, 25, no. 5 (September–October 1982), 78–81.
LOMBARDI, VINCE, "Leadership and Teamwork in Management," AMA Personnel Conference, circa 1965.
MACHIAVELLI, NICCOLO, *The Prince*, trans. George Bull, Harmondsworth, England: Penguin Books, 1961.
MINTZBERG, HENRY, "The Manager's Job: Folklore and Fact," *Harvard Business Review*, 53, no. 3 (July–August 1975), 49–61.
MINTZBERG, HENRY, "Patterns in Strategy Formulation," *Management Science*, 24, no. 9 (1978), 934–948.
PASCALE, RICHARD TANNER, "Zen and the Art of Management," *Harvard Business Review*, 56, no. 2 (March–April 1978), 153–162.
SALANCIK, GERALD R., B. J. CALDER, K. M. ROWLAND, H. LEBLEBICI, and M. CONWAY, "Leadership is an Outcome of Social Structure and Process: A Multidimensional Analysis," in J. G. Hunt and L. L. Larson, eds., *Leadership Frontiers*. Kent, OH: Kent State University Press, 1975.
SCHULLER, ROBERT H., *Tough Times Never Last, But Tough People Do!*, Nashville, TN: Thomas Nelson, 1983.
SELZNICK, PHILIP, *Leadership in Administration: A Sociological Interpretation*, New York: Harper and Row, 1957.
SMITH, EDWARD BOLAND, "Chester Barnard's Concept of Leadership," *Education Administration Quarterly*, 11, no. 3 (Autumn 1975), 37–48.
SMITH, BRIAN P., "Leadership in Management: the Elusive Element," *Journal of Business Policy*, 2, no. 3 (Spring 1972), 3–14.
SUN TZU, *The Art of War*, trans, Samuel B. Griffith. New York: Oxford University Press, 1963.
VICKERS, SIR GEOFFREY, *The Art of Judgment, A Study of Policy Making*, New York: Basic Books, 1965.
ZALEZNICK, ABRAHAM, "Managers and Leaders: Are They Different?" *Harvard Business Review*, 55, no. 3 (May–June 1977), 67–78.

Chapter 22

SIMON, HERBERT A., "On the Concept of Organizational Goal," *Administrative Science Quarterly*, 9, no. 1 (June 1964), 1–22.

Index

A

B

C

D

E

F